Bernd Kortmann

English Linguistics

Essentials

2nd revised, updated and enlarged edition

J. B. Metzler Verlag

The author

Bernd Kortmann is Professor of English Language and Linguistics at the University of Freiburg, Germany, and, since 2013, Executive Director of FRIAS (Freiburg Institute for Advanced Studies). He has been long-time editor of the two international book series *Topics in English Linguistics* and *Dialects of English* as well as journal editor of *English Language and Linguistics*.

ISBN 978-3-476-05677-1
ISBN 978-3-476-05678-8 (eBook)
https://doi.org/10.1007/978-3-476-05678-8

Die Deutsche Nationalbibliothek verzeichnet diese Publikation in der Deutschen Nationalbibliografie; detaillierte bibliografische Daten sind im Internet über http://dnb.d-nb.de abrufbar.

J. B. Metzler
© Springer-Verlag GmbH Deutschland, ein Teil von Springer Nature, 2020

Umschlagabbildung: iStock

J. B. Metzler ist ein Imprint der eingetragenen Gesellschaft Springer-Verlag GmbH, DE und ist ein Teil von Springer Nature
Die Anschrift der Gesellschaft ist: Heidelberger Platz 3, 14197 Berlin, Germany

Contents

Preface

This is the completely revised, updated and enlarged second edition of *English Linguistics: Essentials*, first published in 2005 (by a different publisher) and reprinted many times since then. After 15 years, such a major overhaul was clearly called for. Major and minor changes have been made in all chapters, and yet anyone who has worked with the first version will recognize much that is familiar – simply better! New is Chapter 9 on turns and trends in 21st century (English) linguistics.

The nature and aims of this book have not changed. Its **primary aim** still is to introduce undergraduate and graduate students to **the central branches, core concepts, and current trends in the study of the English language and linguistics**, giving as much guidance as possible (also by visual devices). The individual chapters have been designed to serve a **dual purpose**: on the one hand, as an introduction to a given branch of linguistics and as a point of departure for more detailed studies on the basis of, for example, specialized textbooks or handbook articles and, on the other hand, as a point of reference to return to in order to check the wealth of knowledge acquired in the meantime against the information given in the book.

English Linguistics: Essentials has grown out of 35 years of teaching experience with students of English linguistics at all levels. It has done quite a number of student generations good service as **a companion all through their academic studies** – and I am more than grateful to all those student readers who got back to me over the years asking questions or pointing out things that are not sufficiently clear. I've enjoyed these mail exchanges, or conversations at my own institution, and learnt a lot from these questions and suggestions. In working on this new edition, I have made every effort to build on them, with the aim of leaving future generations of readers more enlightened when reading the relevant passages.

At many English departments in Germany, *English Linguistics: Essentials* serves as **a standard textbook** in introductory classes to linguistics. Advanced undergraduates, too, especially those approaching their exams in linguistics, and graduates enrolled in Masters programmes in linguistics as well as student tutors and teaching assistants have found (and, I promise, will continue to find) this book equally helpful.

Why this book has appealed to many readers: The book offers a reader-friendly layout with many mnemonic devices in the text, and a large number of survey figures and tables summarizing and putting in perspective the most important points. At the end of each chapter the reader will find checklists with key terms, exercises for revision and questions for further study, followed by a further reading section. In this new edition, we have tried to keep all these things and even improve on some of them. The **exercises and study questions**, which are extremely useful for self-study, have largely been replaced with new ones but, most importantly, exercises and answers for ALL of them (including the advanced exercises) are given on the **accompanying website**. This website also offers links to some of the most interesting online resources for anyone interested in exploring the rich world of the English language and (English) linguistics (corpora, databases, sound archives, electronic atlases, podcasts, apps, etc.).

Structure: Given the most encouraging feedback from many colleagues and student readers over the years, there was no reason to change anything substantial as regards the overall approach (largely theory-neutral, but functionalist in spirit), the selection of topics addressed in the book, its overall structure, the structure of the individual chapters, the style, or the layout. In six chapters, **the core branches of linguistics** are addressed: phonetics and phonology (chapter 2), morphology (chapter 3), grammar (chapter 4), semantics (chapter 6), pragmatics (chapter 7), and sociolinguistics (chapter 8). Chapter 5 is specifically concerned with the structure of **English from a contrastive (English-German) and typological perspective**. This chapter can be read profitably even by readers whose knowledge of German is rudimentary or non-existent since it places contrastive linguistics in the context of other branches of comparative linguistics and, adopting a specifically typological perspective, discusses bundles of distinctive structural properties of English not addressed elsewhere in the book. The only chapter that has undergone a major change in this second edition is the shortened chapter 1, which is now exclusively geared to introducing the reader to **the major dichotomies and research traditions of 20th century linguistics** (structuralism, formalism, functionalism). **New is chapter 9**, which simultaneously serves as an outlook and as an appetizer for the rich world of English linguistics beyond the essential core of the discipline. It puts the spotlight on **turns and major 21st century trends** in the development of novel theories, methodologies, research questions, and overall research paradigms.

How to read this book: In principle, the individual chapters can be read independently of each other. Also, it does not matter whether in a given introductory linguistics class a bottom-up approach is chosen (from sounds and sound structure to discourse and language variation) or a top-down approach. However, for the individual structural levels of English it will be most useful to follow the order of the chapters in the book, i.e. phonetics (2.1) preceding phonology (2.2), morphology (3) preceding grammar (4), English grammar (4) preceding English structure from a comparative and contrastive English-German perspective (5), semantics (6) preceding pragmatics (7), and the accounts given of the sound structure and grammar of English (2 and 4) preceding accounts of (especially non-standard) varieties of English in the chapters on sociolinguistics (8) and World Englishes research (9.3). This book is concerned with accounts of present-day English, only in chapter 9.4 will we take a look at modern historical (English) linguistics as developed over the past two or three decades.

Acknowledgements: The author would like to thank all those many colleagues, student readers and participants of his own classes for their feedback over the years on the individual formulations, exercises, and solutions in the first edition. Many thanks, too, to all those friends and former Freiburgers who gave highly useful input in the planning and writing stage of this edition (including Daniela, Lieselotte, Nuria, Marten, the two Christians and, with a word of special thanks, Ekkehard)! Most importantly, however, the present book would not have come about without the support of the members of my fabulous team. Every single paragraph in this book has been given a close read by several of the brightest people in English linguistics, and I have profited from every single one of their questions, critical comments and, generally, extremely helpful suggestions on every chapter in its various stages. Many an argument has been sharpened, many formulations have been polished several times over after intensive discussions with one or more of them. They have also worked hard on individual figures, tables, and the exercises and their solutions. A thousand heartfelt thanks go to Alice Blumenthal-Dramé, Beke Hansen, Verena Haser, Anna Rosen, Katharina Ehret, Yinchun Bai and, especially for the final stylistic editing, Kyla McConnell! Without the help of this dedicated and highly competent team, completed by Melitta Cocan, my next-door companion in the secretary's office for unbelievable 25 years, it would have been simply impossible to keep the deadline for the submission of the manuscript. It is immensely reassuring to have such knowledgeable, competent, critical, perceptive, inventive, efficient, supporting and, not least, always cheerful readers right next door! Every single one of them and the other people mentioned above has contributed to making this a better book. For any remaining shortcomings the author alone takes full responsibility. At the same time, all readers are encouraged and warmly invited to contact the author if they have questions, critical comments, or suggestions.

Dedication: Even 15 years after the first time I formulated this dedication, I see no reason to change a single word, just one number (guess which!). In the writing and production stage of this book (and others before), I have been extremely privileged to have had the support of a wonderful team consisting of assistant professors, postdoctoral, doctoral and graduate students – topped by the best secretary of all, Melitta Cocan! Looking back on a quarter century that I have now held a chair in English language and linguistics at the University of Freiburg, I can say that I have been truly blessed in this respect. It is to the current and former members of this marvellous team that I would like to dedicate this book – they are the real essentials in my professional life!

1 Linguistics: Major concepts and research traditions

1.1 | Setting the scene

Linguistics is the scientific discipline concerned with the study of language and languages, either by themselves or in comparison. *Language* (note: without an article preceding it) is to be understood as the vehicle for the expression or exchange of thoughts, concepts, information, feelings, attitudes, etc., while *a language* stands for entities like English, German, Russian, Spanish, Hindi, or Mandarin Chinese of which some 6,000 are currently said to be spoken around the globe. Note that, upon closer analysis, the notion of 'a language' itself is anything but self-explanatory and clear-cut: for instance, where is the boundary between a language and a dialect? However, in order not to complicate things too much too early, let us simply assume that all readers of this book share an intuitive understanding of what a language is.

defining language and linguistics

This book aims at offering a state-of-the-art account of linguistics as applied to the study of the English language. So let us also agree at this early point that we all have the same understanding of our key object of study: English. Only two points may be added by way of setting the scene for this book. Both are meant to stress the importance of what this book is about (English linguistics) and, above all, to serve as appetizers. Ever so briefly, the readers of this book should be made aware of the fascinating richness the English language offers and of the privilege of entering the world of linguistics via the study of this particular language.

English linguistics: appetizers

English as an international language: Let us first of all turn to English. With currently something like 1.3 billion speakers, English no doubt has become the most widely spoken language in the world and the most important one for international communication (especially communication among non-native speakers of English). It therefore comes closer than any other language in the history of humanity to the age-old dream of a universal traffic language (or: *lingua franca*) allowing communication across all languages and cultural boundaries. This, in turn, has made English the most important language in foreign language teaching worldwide, in the media (including social media), on the internet, in business, in advertisements, or in academic writing and publishing. Also there is a large, steadily increasing number of EMI (English as the medium of instruction) Bachelor, Master and doctoral programmes around the world.

The global spread and diversity of English: Largely due to the colonial past of the British Empire, the English language has enormously spread

J.B. Metzler © Springer-Verlag GmbH Deutschland, ein Teil von Springer Nature, 2020
B. Kortmann, *English Linguistics*, https://doi.org/10.1007/978-3-476-05678-8_1

across the globe in the course of the past 400 years. Currently close to 400 million people speak English as their native language, and there are close to 60 countries in the world with English as one of their official languages. In addition, English has been in contact with a vast array of other languages, so that there are also many varieties of English which may not have reached an official status in their respective countries, but which are nevertheless important tools, sometimes the most important ones, for (oral) communication. Add to this the diversity of English dialects especially in the British Isles and North America, and the result is a very rich research arena, consisting of more than 100 varieties of English around the globe. This offers ample research opportunities for any linguist – whether beginning, advanced, or experienced – who is fascinated by the English language, language variation and language contact.

The pioneering role of English linguistics: Ever since the 1940s and 1950s, English linguistics has been the most important laboratory and hothouse for linguistics in general. This applies both to the development of theories about and approaches to the study of (individual aspects of) language and languages, and to the development of novel methodology. The majority of what will be presented in this book goes back to ideas, concepts, theories, methods and research traditions established in the second half of the 20th century in Anglo-American linguistics, largely in the United States. Much of this theory development, not just in English linguistics but also in general linguistics, took place with English as the object of study. As a consequence, there is an enormous amount of research that has been published on English (and largely in English).

Given the importance of English in international communication and as a foreign language, there are also a very large number of linguists working on English at universities and research institutions outside native English-speaking countries (within Europe, notably in Germany, Switzerland, Belgium, the Netherlands, Sweden, Finland and Spain). Add to this the fact that there is so much reliable authentic English data available online and you can see why English is the best researched and arguably the most researchable language in the world.

Unique availability of data and research tools: For beginning students this may sound more like a threat than an opportunity, but really it is the latter. There is no language in the world for which such an astoundingly large and diversified amount of authentic data (ranging from the Middle Ages until today) is available, along with other research tools which make English uniquely easy, fascinating and rewarding as the subject of theoretically, empirically and methodologically highly advanced research (thus also consult the website accompanying this book and try to work on some of the advanced exercises in individual chapters). For many aspects of the English language, even beginning students will soon find that the answer to their research question is just a few clicks away.

advice to the reader Structure of chapter and book: Central aspects of how to go about the scientific study of language and languages can be made clear with the help of various pairs of oppositions (or: dichotomies). Anyone planning to investigate language or individual linguistic phenomena first needs to take a clear decision on which perspective to adopt, the ultimate goal(s) of the investigation, and the amount and nature of the data to be analysed for this purpose. These questions lead to some of the most important dichotomies (see section 1.2) and theoretical frameworks (or: research traditions) in the discipline (see section 1.3). More recent trends in the development of new theories, methodologies and research questions will be presented in chapter 9. Beginners in English linguistics are warmly advised to hold in check their curiosity and first work through chapters 1 to 8 before tackling the last chapter. They will be rewarded by a glimpse of the fascinating world of English linguistics lying beyond what will be presented as the essential core of the discipline in the bulk of this book.

1.2 | Central dichotomies

- synchronic – diachronic, synchrony – diachrony: Do we want to describe the state of a language at a particular point or period in time (i. e. take a snapshot of a language), or do we want to document linguistic change 'through time' (Greek *dia* = through, *chronos* = time) by comparing successive (synchronic) language states with one another and exploring the transitions from one language state to the next?
- descriptive – prescriptive: In a synchronic approach, do we want to give a neutral description of the actual language use, or do we want to adopt a normative approach and formulate rules for 'correct' language use?
- form – function, language system – language use: In a descriptive approach, do we want to investigate purely formal aspects, thus the structure (or: the system) of a language on its different levels (sound, word, sentence structure) in abstraction from language use, or do we want to investigate which functions linguistic structures fulfil and, dependent on the speaker and the speech situation, for which communicative purposes they can be used?
- language-specific – comparative: In a descriptive synchronic approach, do we want to investigate merely one language, contrast two languages with each other (e. g. for pedagogical reasons in foreign-language teaching; contrastive linguistics), or compare a multitude of languages with one another, with the aim of determining the patterns and limits of language variation and maybe even language universals (language typology)?
- applied – not applied: Do we want to apply the results of our study in, for example, foreign language teaching, translation, dictionary compilation (lexicography), or police work and law enforcement (forensic linguistics)? Or are our research results supposed to be of purely academic relevance? In the latter case, what we want to find out can be either of descriptive interest (i. e. we want to learn more about a particular language – either looked at in isolation or in comparison with other languages), or of theoretical or general interest. For example, we may want to learn more about language as the most important medium of communication among human beings, about general prin-

ciples of language structure, language use, language acquisition, language processing, language change, etc., and about the most appropriate theories or theoretical frameworks within which general (especially grammatical) properties of language can be modelled.

- empirical – introspective: What should form the basis of our linguistic analysis? Should it be based on authentic data, for example in large machine-readable corpora of the English language (the largest corpus available at present being the *Corpus of Global Web-based English* with 1.9 billion words)? Should linguistic research thus increasingly work quantitatively and with statistical methods (corpus linguistics, experimental designs)? Or should it be based on introspection, that is on the intuitions of linguists concerning what is and what is not possible in language or a language?

Different approaches: Depending on the answers to these questions, we are engaged in synchronic or diachronic linguistics, descriptive or prescriptive linguistics, formal or functional linguistics, contrastive linguistics or language typology, applied, theoretical or general linguistics. Whichever of these approaches (and others not mentioned here) is or are chosen, it is important to be aware of the fact that the different approaches often come with particular theories and models of language and linguistics and, as a consequence, with different viewpoints, methods and terminology. For this reason, it is frequently the case that different terms coexist for one and the same phenomenon, and that this phenomenon is judged and interpreted in different ways by different people.

synchronic, descriptive, empirical   Structure of this book: In accordance with the dominant orientation of modern linguistics in general and English linguistics in particular this book has a strictly synchronic, descriptive, and empirical orientation, focussing for the most part on the English language system (chapters 2–4 and 6: phonetics, phonology, morphology, grammar, semantics). This includes a comparison of the most important structures of English and German (chapter 5: contrastive linguistics). Language use, especially the use of English, as dependent on different speakers or groups of speakers and their communicative goals in varying communicative situations takes centre stage in chapters 7 (pragmatics) and 8 (sociolinguistics). Chapter 9 will cut across many of the branches of linguistics discussed in the previous chapters by highlighting some of the most important developments in English linguistics since the 1990s and early 2000s. Selected aspects of historical linguistics will be addressed in this chapter, too.

1.3 | Three major research traditions in 20th century linguistics

19th and 20th century in comparison: The two central dichotomies that capture best the fundamental changes of direction in the development of 20th century linguistics as opposed to linguistics in the 19th century are synchrony – diachrony and language system – language use.

The 19th century was the century of historical linguistics. Linguistic research was characterized by the search for regularities and laws in language change, the search for genetic links between languages (keywords: family trees, Indo-European), and the reconstruction of older language periods and languages in historical-comparative linguistics (or: comparative philology) by means of comparing with each other younger language periods and languages for which written data material was available. historical-comparative linguistics

The 20th century, on the other hand, is the century of synchrony. This is certainly the most important aspect of the paradigm shift which affected linguistics in the decade after 1900, a paradigm shift which is inseparably linked to the name of Ferdinand de Saussure, the famous Swiss linguist who taught at the University of Geneva a century ago. paradigm shift: focus on synchrony

1.3.1 | Structuralism

Ferdinand de Saussure is generally considered to be the founder of modern linguistics, more precisely the founder of structuralism, the 'Bible' of which is the *Cours de linguistique générale* (1916). The *Cours* offers an introduction to general linguistics based on Saussure's lecture materials and the lecture notes taken by his disciples and was not published until after his death (in 1913). In this book, the reader will find thorough discussions of numerous ideas concerning a new approach to the study of language only some of which are found in the works of linguists at the end of the 19th century (e. g. in the writings of the German Georg von der Gabelentz and, above all, those of William Dwight Whitney, the eminent American linguist of the late 19th century). *Cours de linguistique générale* (1916)

Primacy of synchrony and the system: Besides the call for a separation of synchrony and diachrony and for the primacy of synchrony, Saussure's structuralist approach to linguistics focusses on language as a closed system in which all elements are linked to one another, and in which the value (*valeur*) of every single element is defined by its place in the system alone. For example, the Simple Past in English (*she worked*) has a different status than its counterpart in German, the preterite (*Präteritum*), because it contrasts both with the Past Progressive (*she was working*) and the Present Perfect (*she has worked*). German grammar does not only lack a counterpart of the English progressive form; *Präteritum* (*sie arbeitete*) and *Perfekt* (*sie hat gearbeitet*) are in most contexts interchangeable without a difference in meaning. The different status of Simple Past and *Präteritum* within the grammars of English and German, respectively, thus partly results from the value of the Present Perfect in the English tense system in contrast to the value of the *Perfekt* in the German tense system. The view that every linguistic sign is part of the system and has no existence outside of it is an important reason for the structuralist position that every language system needs to be considered by itself. value / *valeur*

Langue-parole: According to Saussure, linguistics should solely be concerned with the systematic regularities of the abstract language system which is shared by all members of a speech community (*langue*), and not with its concrete use by the individual (*parole*). What stands at the centre of structuralist linguistics is the determination and description of the individual elements of this system (on all structural levels: sounds, words and their components, sentences and their constituents), and the relations holding between them on each of these levels.

choice vs. chain

Paradigmatic vs. syntagmatic relations: Within any system, there are two basic types of relations between linguistic units which have to be distinguished: relations of choice or interchangeability on the vertical axis (paradigmatic relations), and relations of 'chain' or combination on the horizontal axis (syntagmatic relations). A paradigmatic relation holds between the initial sounds of *ban, can, Dan, fan, tan* and *van*, whereas the relation between any of these sounds and the two following sounds is a syntagmatic one. (1) illustrates paradigmatic and syntagmatic relations on the sentence level:

(1)
$$\left\{\begin{array}{c} A \\ The \\ His \end{array}\right\} \left\{\begin{array}{c} man \\ girl \\ visitor \end{array}\right\} \left\{\begin{array}{c} saw \\ loved \\ hit \end{array}\right\} \left\{\begin{array}{c} my \\ your \\ our \end{array}\right\} \left\{\begin{array}{c} horse \\ cat \\ baby \end{array}\right\}$$

A choice (or paradigmatic) relation holds among the words within any of the braced brackets, a chain (or syntagmatic) relation between the words in the immediately neighbouring brackets. These relations are found on all structural levels of language (see figure 1.1):

branches of linguistics

object of study	form	function/meaning
sound	phonetics	phonology
word	morphology	(lexical) semantics
phrase, sentence	syntax	(sentence) semantics

Figure 1.1:
The structural
levels of language

Structural levels and interfaces: As far as these structural levels (sound, word and sentence structure) and the corresponding branches of linguistics are concerned, it is important to note that it is not always easy to determine the exact boundaries between them. Often we can observe interaction between the structural levels and, as a consequence, so-called *interfaces* between the relevant linguistic subdisciplines. When, for example, in the course of the derivation of the noun *pronunciation* from the verb *pronounce*, the sound shape of the root changes from /prə'naʊns/ to /prə,nʌns-/, we are not only dealing with a morphological (more precisely: word formation) process, but also with a phonological one. The same holds true in the case of the regular English plural formation, where the plural marker is pronounced /s/ (*kits*), /z/ (*kids*), or /ɪz/ (*kisses*) depending on the final sound of the singular form of the respective noun. The interface relevant for these two examples is called *morphophonology* or *morphophonemics* (see chapter 3.2). Other interfaces are, for instance, those between phonology and syntax, morphology and syntax, or syntax and semantics.

comparison with a sheet of paper

Model of the linguistic sign: Saussure's model of the linguistic sign, i. e. his model of what constitutes the nature of words (see figure 1.2), is another of his ground-breaking contributions to modern linguistics. The linguistic sign consists of two parts which are as inseparably linked to one another like the two sides of a sheet of paper: a sound or, typically, sound sequence (*signifier*; *significant*) on the level of expression and a concept (*signified*; *signifié*) on the level of meaning.

reciprocity, arbitrariness, conventionality

signifiant – signifié: Two kinds of relations hold between *signifié* and *signifiant*: on the one hand, a reciprocal relation, which means that the sound sequence automatically evokes the concept linked to it and vice versa (therefore the arrows in figure 1.2). Importantly, this relationship is arbitrary and conventional. Which *signifiant* ('signifier') is used for which *signifié* ('signified') is solely based on an 'agreement', a kind of 'contract' between the members of a speech community. Neither side of the linguistic sign has any special feature that would inevitably require the assignment of a particular signifier to a particular signified, or vice versa. That is why different languages have completely different expressions – all equally appropriate or inappropriate – for the same concept (for FLOWER just take /flaʊə(r)/ in English or /bluːmə/ in German), and why, conversely, the same sound image can refer to completely different concepts in different languages (consider /gɪft/, which denotes the concept PRESENT in English as opposed to TOXIC SUBSTANCE in German).

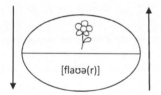 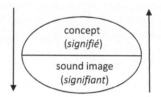

Figure 1.2: Saussure's model of the linguistic sign

Peirce's typology of signs

Linguistic sign = symbol: The crucial point about the linguistic sign is its arbitrariness, i. e. the lack of a motivated link between signified and signifier. According to the theory of signs by Charles Sanders Peirce (pronounced /pɜːs/), the linguistic sign therefore qualifies as a symbol, in contrast to the two other major types of signs he distinguishes, namely indices and icons.

Indices: The characteristic feature of indices is an existential or physical effect-cause or effect-reason relationship between the sign and what it stands for. Tears, for instance, are a sign of emotional turmoil (sorrow, disappointment, joy), smoke is a sign of fire, and slurred speech is a sign of drunkenness.

imagic iconicity

Icons and iconicity: The defining feature of icons is that there is a relationship of similarity between the sign and what it stands for. The nature of this similarity can be physical or imagic, i. e. consist in visual similarity (e. g. the pictogram of a telephone indicating a public telephone, or the pictogram of a running person indicating an emergency exit) or in phonetic similarity (e. g. *bow-wow* for barking, or *cuckoo* for the bird).

diagrammatic iconicity

However, icons can also display a rather abstract relationship of similarity. This kind of (so-called diagrammatic) iconicity holds, for example, between maps and the regions of the earth they represent, or between the order in which, on a list of topics for presentations and term papers, the topics are listed and the chronological sequence in which they are to be presented in the seminar. Iconicity thus is a special kind of motivation. Although in human language symbols are by far the most important and best researched type of signs, it should not be overlooked that there are definitely also words which, besides qualifying as symbols, are partly iconic (e. g. so-called *onomatopoetic expressions* like *bow-wow*, *moo*, *cuckoo*) or partly indexical (e. g. *here* and *today*, part of whose meaning refers to the here and now of the speaker; cf. chapter 7.2).

linguistics = part of semiotics

Semiotics is the science of linguistic and non-linguistic signalling systems and signing processes. From the perspective of the theory of signs, human language is a (rather complex) sign system and, as a consequence, linguistics a semiotic science. Traditionally, it considers its object of study from three angles: (a) the relation(s) between signs (syntax); (b) the relation(s) between signs and their meaning(s) (semantics); (c) the relation(s) between signs and their users (pragmatics). The subdisciplines exploring these three kinds of relations in the scientific study of signs therefore also belong to the central areas of linguistics.

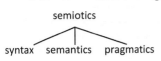

Figure 1.3:
Branches
of semiotics

Leonard Bloomfield, Prague School

Structuralism until the 1950s: The importance of structuralist thinking as we find it in Saussure's *Cours* and, in general, from the 1920s until the 1950s is largely undisputed in present-day linguistics. The two most important cases in point are American structuralism à la Leonard Bloomfield which was even more rigidly empirical and form-orientated than Saussure's vision of structuralism, and the Prague School of functionalism, which was primarily interested in the function(s) of language and linguistic elements (cf. also 1.3.3).

critical reflection of Saussurean dichotomies

Development of linguistics from the 1960s until today: The crucial difference, however, is that ever since the 1960s (starting, above all, in sociolinguistics) and especially since the 1970s (with the advent of pragmatics) and 1980s (especially due to cognitive linguistics; cf. chapters 6.4 and 9.2), linguistics has significantly gone beyond the description of a linguistic system and the search for purely system-inherent explanations for linguistic phenomena. Rather, as will be detailed in section 1.3.3, it has given priority to social, functional, and cognitive aspects, as well as aspects of language (use) grounded in communicative behaviour. Typically, these new approaches do not compete, but rather complement each other very well. What all these 'post-structuralist' approaches have in common is that the most important Saussurean dichotomies are increasingly critically reflected, and that linguists start to emancipate, or already have emancipated, themselves from these dichotomies.

4 directions of emancipation

Emancipation from Saussure: In the course of the renewed interest in processes of language change, for example, the strict separation between synchrony and diachrony has largely been abandoned (which makes sense especially if we consider, for example, the immediate link between language variation and language change; cf. chapters 8.6 and 9.4). It is furthermore no longer important to give priority to the system and to reduce linguistics to the study of the formal aspects, i. e. the structure, of language, which was typical of 20th century linguistics until the 1960s. Since then, research into language use (i. e. *parole* or *performance*) in the context of an individual speaker, their social and communicative situation, and their communicative goal(s) has gained significantly in importance. Therefore, at the latest since the 1980s, sociolinguistics and pragmatics also need to be counted among the disciplines constituting the core of linguistics. A third example of the emancipation from Saussure concerns his sign model, more precisely the central role he attributes to arbitrariness. Especially since the 1980s, it has increasingly been acknowledged that, both on the level of words and grammar, iconicity plays a bigger role than is traditionally assumed in Saussurean structuralism. Fourth, there is a general tendency in current linguistics that the idea of dichotomies (e. g. synchrony – diachrony, language system – language use, vocabulary – grammar, written – spoken language) and sharp category boundaries (e. g. main verb versus auxiliary) can be accepted only as idealizations which are pedagogically useful, but which, apart from that, should better be given up in favour of interfaces and fuzzy boundaries (thus the growing importance of so-called gradients, clines, or continua).

1.3.2 | Formalism / Generative linguistics

Noam Chomsky: Both the emancipation of linguistics from traditional structuralist ideas and the central status which especially pragmatics and sociolinguistics have developed since the 1960s and 1970s can also be seen as reactions to probably the most influential school of thought in the second half of the 20th century, namely generative linguistics. Noam Chomsky initiated this approach to the study of language at the end of the 1950s and has remained the key intellectual and major shaping force of generative linguistics during its various phases and its various guises until the present day.

Generative (Latin *generare* = generate) refers to the generation of language, more exactly to the full and precise description of syntactic structures by means of a limited (or: finite) inventory of rules. On the one hand, this inventory of rules allows linguists to make explicit statements concerning the grammatical well-formedness of a given phrase or sentence. On the other hand, it provides the theoretical and descriptive apparatus for predictions concerning the grammaticality (in the sense of grammatical well-formedness) of all possible grammatical sentences (and smaller syntactic units) in a language, or at least in its core grammar. definition

The beginnings of generative linguistics mark the second fundamental paradigm shift in 20th century linguistics. Within a few years, it came to be one of the most influential schools in linguistics; in the US (unlike in Europe) it is even the predominant approach, both in research and teaching. One of the crucial distinctive properties of this approach is a high standard of explicit and stringent theory-formation and argumentation. This and other essential features of the generativist (alternatively known 2nd paradigm shift in 20th century linguistics as *formalist*) paradigm as well as some of its major contributions to linguistic theorizing will be presented in this section.

The reader may note right away, though, that generativist positions will not play a role in any of the other chapters of this book. For example, semantic and pragmatic issues (especially the study of word and utterance meaning, and how the latter is negotiated in context) and, in particular, sociolinguistic and contrastive issues are for the most part ignored or represent no more than a sideline in mainstream generative linguistics because, given its overall aims, they are simply of little or no interest. Mainstream formalist research and theory development has always focussed on the study of syntax and phonology.

formalist main-
stream: focus
on syntax
& phonology

Mental grammar: Generative linguistics is probably still best-known as, and equated with, *Transformational Grammar*, the approach characteristic of Chomsky's 'classical' period in the 1960s, which has, however, been out of use for quite some time. It was and still is exclusively concerned with language as a mental phenomenon, more exactly with competence (as opposed to language use, performance). What is understood by competence is the entire (unconscious) mental knowledge an ideal native speaker (and hearer) has at his or her disposal. This knowledge allows him or her to be creative in their native language and to constantly (and successfully) produce and process new sentences according to the rules of that language. For Chomsky, a grammar of a given language thus is a theory of what constitutes the ideal native user's competence of that language.

competence vs.
performance

In Chomsky's view, this aim can be achieved without analysing large amounts of authentic linguistic data; indeed, given the often fragmented and/or ungrammatical structure of, for example, utterances in face-to-face interaction and spontaneous spoken language, the empirical analysis of natural language data is considered almost detrimental to the goals of generativist theory-formation. Therefore, generative linguistics still primarily relies on introspection, i. e. the linguist's intuition.

method: intro-
spection

Language acquisition device: The two central questions formalism is interested in are "How is this linguistic knowledge represented?" and, above all, "How is this linguistic knowledge acquired?". In other words, a primary interest for generative linguistics is (child, first) language acquisition. What matters here, however, is not so much the documentation and detailed empirical study of the concrete processes and phases of language acquisition. Key in Chomsky's paradigm is the question of how it is possible that, no matter which speech community a child is born into and which surroundings it grows up in, it develops enormous linguistic skills in an amazingly short amount of time. Chomsky's hypothesis is that humans are genetically predisposed to learn language, just as it is part of our genetic endowment to grow arms and legs. Indeed, Chomsky postulates the existence of a language acquisition device (LAD).

part of human's
genetic endow-
ment

Universal Grammar: This raises the all-important research question what kind of information is contained in this device, which is common to all human beings and thus universal. Or put differently: What constitutes Universal Grammar (UG)? Thus, when generative linguistics is said to search for universals, what is meant are not surface features common to all or at least a great number of languages, but the invariable, highly ab-

universals = highly
abstract innate
properties
& principles

stract innate properties and principles of the postulated language acquisition device. The reason why these properties and principles must be innate is that they are considered to be too abstract to be discovered, i. e. picked up or learnt, by the child in the process of language acquisition.

Universals: Two types of UG universals are typically distinguished: substantive universals and formal universals. Substantive universals are the grammatical categories which are universally available and necessary for analysing a language, e. g. the different word classes (nouns, verbs, etc.), their phrasal expansions (noun phrase, verb phrase, etc.), and the relevant grammatical categories which can be marked on them (for instance, case and number on nouns, tense on verbs). Formal universals concern the form the rules of a grammar can take. Take for example 'structure-dependency', which states that knowledge of language relies on structural relationships in the sentence rather than simply on the sequence of words. According to this universal, it is impossible for a language to turn a statement (e. g. *This is the good friend Alison met at the airport*) into a question by simply using the reverse word order (yielding an ungrammatical sentence like *airport the at met Alison friend good the is this?*). Consider, by contrast, a language like English in which, for this purpose, only the order of subject and predicate is changed, as in *Is this the good friend Alison met at the airport?*

substantive vs. formal universals

Other candidates for UG universals include the structural means for

- referring to real-world entities (reference) and saying something about them (predication),
- keeping track of referents and predications which are repeated in a certain stretch of discourse (reference tracking),
- quantifying (e. g. via numerals or elements like *all, some, few, every*, etc.; quantification), and
- allowing speaker and hearer to exchange roles easily and rapidly, e. g. in face-to-face interaction (speaker-hearer symmetry).

In sum: the ultimate goal of linguistic theory from a formalist point of view is to provide a precise formal (and, by necessity, highly abstract) characterization of these and other constitutive elements of Universal Grammar and thus to define 'a possible human language'.

defining a possible human language

1.3.3 | Functionalism

Whereas in formalist research the significance or impact of a linguistic study is ultimately determined by the extent to which it helps illuminate the nature of Universal Grammar, the corresponding all-important criterion in functionalist research is to what extent the relevant study is able to show

3 key questions

- why, in a particular domain of its structural system, language, a given language, or a set of languages is the way it is,
- what, in a particular context, motivates the choice of native users of a given language between two or more semantically equivalent alternative constructions, and/or
- how communicative functions may help shape language structure.

the key notion **Function:** The key notion in these questions is function, a concept which oscillates between what may be paraphrased as 'task, job', on the one hand, and 'meaning', on the other hand. This key notion will be detailed below, along with other pillars of functionalism, the second major theoretical framework, or research tradition, of late 20th century and current linguistics. The reader will soon notice that functionalism is incompatible, or at least in conflict, with most of the central assumptions as well as the ultimate goal of formalist linguistics. A summary of the relevant points will be provided at the end of the section.

External vs. internal functions: Two broad types of functions can be distinguished: the overall functions of language in communication (so-called *external functions*) and, language-internally, the varied set of communicative (so-called *internal*) functions served by different linguistic phenomena in individual, or partly even all, languages. Examples of internal functions include referring to people and entities in the real world, placing situations on a time line, expressing ongoing as opposed to completed events, coding known as opposed to new information, or directly observed information as opposed to information for which no or only indirect evidence exists.

typologies of external functions; Bühler (3) vs. Jakobson (6) **Organon model of language:** Famous typologies of external functions were suggested by Karl Bühler and Roman Jakobson. In his organon model of language (Greek *organon* = instrument, tool), Bühler distinguishes between three functions, or tasks, in the overall communication process: a referential (or: representational) function (that allows us to talk about the world), an expressive function (that allows the addresser, i. e. the speaker or writer, to express his or her beliefs, attitudes, and emotional state), and an appellative function (that allows us to make an appeal to the addressee, i. e. the hearer or reader, such as a request or command).

Jakobson's communication model: To these three tasks served by language, Roman Jakobson adds another three, one for each of the three new dimensions he adds to the model of communication: message, code, and contact. One function of language may lie in the way the message is formulated (poetic function, which is not to be understood as applying exclusively to use in literary texts), a second one in talking about language (metalingual function, which is the typical function of everything in this book or, for that matter, in any linguistics publication or discourse in a linguistics class). A third function relates to establishing contact between addresser and addressee, be it psychological contact (especially a social relation of some kind) or physical contact (as when talking on the phone in a tunnel or on a train, which regularly triggers questions such as *"Can you hear me?"* or *"Are you still there?"*).

Layers of external functions: It is crucial to note that language typically fulfils several of these tasks simultaneously, but that one of these external functions tends to predominate, depending on the central communicative goal in a given communicative situation or piece of discourse. For example, a statement like *"What lousy weather we've had for days now"* surely has a representational function, but in the context of a social get-together like a cheese and wine party, the primary function of this utterance is a

WORLD
(referential)

MESSAGE
(poetic)

ADDRESSER
(expressive)

CONTACT
(phatic)

ADDRESSEE
(appellative)

CODE
(metalingual)

Figure 1.4:
External functions
of language
(Jakobson 1960)

phatic one, i. e. it counts simply as an attempt at establishing social relations with another person by engaging in small talk (or: social noise). Similarly, an utterance like *"Quite a draft in here, I must say"* serves a representational as well as an expressive function, but its primary function may well be an appellative one, namely when intended as a request to do something against the draft, such as closing the door or window (for further details cf. chapter 7.3 on indirect speech acts).

Correspondingly, text types can be classified according to their predominant function, e. g. advertisements, cooking recipes or manuals as appellative texts, newspaper reports as representational texts, and private letters to close friends as expressive texts. More generally, this discussion of the external functions of language shows that, from a functional point of view, the entire communication process is relevant for linguistic analysis.

classification of text types

Focus on language use: Functionalists acknowledge that language is not something sterile, not something that takes place in a vacuum. Language can thus not be investigated independently from the primary function it serves, namely communication, from the participants involved in the act of communication, and from the general (e. g. social and cognitive) conditions in which communication takes place. In other words, the usage component (as opposed to an exclusively system-centred approach to the study of language as advocated by formalists and structuralists) is part and parcel of these models of the external functions of language and of functionalism, in general.

language in communication

Internal functions: Compared with the external functions of language, the range of internal functions is much wider and more varied. But, essentially, they all boil down to functions which individual linguistic units (down to the sound level), constructions or domains in grammar play in (spoken or written) discourse and the overall communicative process. The most important of these functions are those which enhance the ease and efficiency of what is called *online* production and processing, i. e. in oral communication the producing and processing of language while speaking and listening, for example by guaranteeing that a given utterance is organically embedded into a given piece of discourse.

enhancing spontaneous language production & processing

'Organic embedding': What is meant by 'organic embedding' here is that any sentence or utterance is typically part of a text or conversation. As a consequence, the way we formulate a sentence or utterance, the choice we make between structural options which English, for example, offers us is at least partially determined by the information which has been established earlier in the text/conversation and may also be determined by what we intend to write or say in its later parts. Relevant choices include the use of pronouns as opposed to common or proper nouns, the use of the indefinite article (*a*, *an*) as opposed to the definite article (*the*), active vs. passive, or the choice between *It was Alison who bought the book* and *What Alison did was buy the book*.

coherent discourse, information flow Pronouns as cohesive devices: A crucial function of pronouns, for example, is to help create a coherent text (which is why, from a functional point of view, they qualify as important cohesive devices): a pronoun indicates that it refers to the same person or entity as some noun phrase introduced in the prior discourse (*cross-reference*). Pronouns thus typically are an instruction to the reader or hearer to search for the referent in the previous discourse; at the same time, pronouns signal that the speaker/writer takes the information they provide for granted, that it qualifies as old, known, or given information. The same applies to definite articles. Besides creating a coherent discourse, smooth integration into the information flow of a given piece of discourse (in the sense of given and new information) is a second central aspect of what was loosely called 'organic embedding' above.

Contrasting the three research traditions: Examples (2) to (5) will make clear what the difference in outlook is between a functionalist, a formalist, and a structuralist when confronted with the following constructions in English grammar. The major contrast between the first two examples is one of active (2) vs. passive voice (3). The constructions in (4) and (5) are so-called *cleft constructions*. Those in (4) are called *it-clefts* and those in (5) *wh-clefts* or *pseudo-clefts* (cf. also chapter 5.2.2):

(2) John smashed the bottle with a hammer.
(3) a. The bottle was smashed by John with a hammer.
    b. The bottle was smashed.
(4) a. It was John who smashed the bottle with a hammer.
    b. It was the bottle which John smashed with a hammer.
    c. It was with a hammer that John smashed the bottle.
(5) a. What John did was smash the bottle with a hammer.
    b. What John did with the hammer was smash the bottle.
    c. What John smashed was the bottle (not the glass).

formulating rules vs. motivating choices Functionalism – appropriateness – communicative competence: Structuralists will largely content themselves with describing each of these constructions of English grammar. Formalists will concentrate on formulating the rules for the syntactic operations generating the constructions in (3) to (5) from an underlying structure which most likely closely resembles the active sentence in (2). Functionalists or, in this case, functional grammarians will go one step further and ask in which contexts the individual structural options would be used, thus trying to motivate their choice. They include the use(r) perspective and are not simply interested in making statements on the grammaticality or well-formedness of a given sentence. They are primarily interested in the appropriateness of the individual constructions in (2) to (5) given the communicative situation (participants, setting, topic, its predominant communicative purpose). Thus in functionalist accounts communicative competence, a notion developed by Dell Hymes (1966) in his ethnography of speaking as a counter-concept to Chomsky's definition of competence, clearly takes priority over the grammatical competence formalists are solely interested in.

Information flow/packaging: Relevant in this respect is, for example, information packaging, i. e. the distribution of information in terms of given and new information (or: information recoverable or non-recoverable from the prior discourse). Example (2) can be a neutral description of a situation (given a neutral intonation contour), but could also be used in a context where John was the topic of the previous discourse. (3a) would rather be preferred when the bottle was the topic, for example when answering the question *What happened to the bottle?*. An additional advantage the passive voice offers is that, as in (3b), we need not specify who was responsible for the relevant situation (i. e. the doer or agent). Compared with the neutral description in (2), the *it*-clefts in (4) all have in common that the highlighted, new information is given in the first part (*it was ...*), whereas the relative clause which follows contains the given information (e. g. (4a) could be an answer to the question *Who smashed the bottle with a hammer?*). In the pseudo-clefts in (5), on the other hand, it is the old information which comes first (*what John did/smashed*) and the new information which follows (e. g. (5a) could be an answer to the question *What did John do with the hammer?*). given vs. new

Motivation: In other words, it is a hallmark of functionalist thinking that, in a given context, the choice between competing, semantically equivalent constructions is not random. Rather, this choice can be functionally motivated and this knowledge also forms part of the native speaker's communicative competence. Motivation is indeed a key notion in functionalism since, ultimately, discourse functions cannot only be argued to determine the choice between alternative ways of coding a certain piece of information, but also the shape of language structure itself, i. e. of individual constructions. The assumption that the link between the form and meaning/function of grammatical constructions may be motivated goes against the basic structuralist (and also formalist) assumption of the arbitrariness of language (see section 1.2.1 above). another functionalist key notion

Iconicity: Functionalists do not shy away from operating with the notion of iconicity (i. e. some sort of, typically highly abstract, resemblance between form and meaning). They hypothesize, for example, iconic relationships between cognitive and structural complexity, or between cognitive relevance and structural distance. In the former case, iconicity lies in the fact that the more cognitively complex a given state-of-affairs is, the more structurally complex and often explicit (in the sense of more or more transparent coding material) the construction will be that is used to code it (the so-called *complexity principle*). Iconicity in the second case 2 iconic principles looks as follows: the more tightly two states-of-affairs are cognitively or semantically related to each other, the more tightly will the constructions coding these two states-of-affairs be interwoven (the so-called *iconic distance principle*). Let us look at these two principles in turn.

Complexity principle: The former type of iconic relationship, i. e. the complexity principle, can be illustrated with the help of adverbial (or: interclausal semantic) relations like simultaneity ('when', 'while'), anteriority ('after', 'since'), cause ('because'), condition ('if'), or concession ('although') and how they are explicitly signalled by adverbial subordinators (e. g. *when, after, if, because, although*) in English and many other languages. Adverbial relations can clearly be shown to differ according to the degree of world knowledge or context-substantiated evidence that is necessary before a given relation can plausibly be said to hold between two states of affairs (or: propositions). Establishing a causal link between two propositions, for example, requires more such knowledge or evidence than establishing an anterior link ('after', 'since'). A similar situation holds for concessive links ('although') compared with temporal links of simultaneity ('when', 'while'). Cause and, especially, concession thus have a considerably higher degree of cognitive complexity than temporal relations like anteriority or simultaneity.

cross-linguistic
evidence

It is thus interesting to see that there is a pronounced tendency across many different and unrelated languages for adverbial subordinators (and other types of connectives) marking concession to be morphologically considerably more complex (consisting of two or more morphemes or even words) and transparent than, say, temporal markers, which typically consist of a single morpheme. Transparency means that the morphological structure of these concessive markers can easily be identified and in many cases still reflects their origin (e. g. English *all-though*, *never-theless*, German *ob-wohl* 'whether/if-even', *ob-gleich* 'whether/if-even', Dutch *of-schoon* 'whether/if-already', Italian *sebbene* < *se-bene* 'if-well', or Spanish *aun cuando* 'even when').

Another, clearly related cross-linguistic tendency is that, of all major adverbial relations, concession is that relation which needs to be explicitly coded by some lexical marker, be it, in the case of English, by an adverbial subordinator like *although* or by a concessive marker in the main clause like *nevertheless*. Given its cognitive complexity, concession is hardest to infer and thus requires explicit lexical support.

Iconic distance principle: The examples in (6) illustrate the iconic distance principle, i. e. the iconic relationship between cognitive relevance and structural distance. In these examples, the cause-effect relation is most immediately or tightly coded in (6a), due to the use of the verb *sit* in a special, namely causative, meaning; the speaker (*I*) can almost be pictured as he or she physically puts a person in an armchair. In (6b) this relationship is less tightly, and in (6c) least tightly coded. Whereas the direct (in 6a even physical) responsibility for the caused action clearly lies with the speaker in both (6a) and (6b), this responsibility is less direct or loosened in (6c).

(6) a. I sat him in the armchair near the window.
    b. I made him sit in the armchair near the window.
    c. I caused him to sit in the armchair near the window.

Differences between functionalism and formalism: Two other major differences between functionalism and formalism concern the notion of autonomy and how to approach the study of (first, child) language acquisition. Within formalism, autonomy is broken down into three facets. There is, first of all, the autonomy of competence, as opposed to performance, which was mentioned already and which is rejected by functionalists. The other two types of autonomy concern the nature of linguistic knowledge as opposed to other domains of human cognition: the autonomy of syntax and the autonomy of grammar (or rather: language). autonomy in formalism: three facets

On a narrower scale, focussing just on the nature of syntactic knowledge, formalists postulate the autonomy of syntax as opposed to the meaning of language and language use in discourse. More exactly, the set of elements constituting the syntax component of human language (and thus UG) is held to be neither derived from nor to interact with the meaning component of language or with the use of language in communication. This claim does, of course, run counter to the functionalist position that function shapes form, i. e. that communicative needs may very well shape the language system. autonomy of syntax

On a more general scale, the third type of autonomy formalists postulate is the autonomy of grammar or, essentially, of language as an autonomous cognitive system. This part of the human cognition is thus taken to be independent from other cognitive systems of humans, such as the cognitive system of orientation in space or general principles of processing information (not just linguistic information, but also visual or auditory information, like the distinction and perception of foreground and background, i. e. so-called figure-ground constellations). Again, just as functionalists believe in the interaction between syntax and other structural levels of language, autonomy of grammar/language

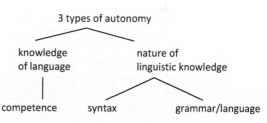

they also assume interaction between language and the other systems of human cognition, a point which is particularly forcefully made within cognitive linguistics (see, for example, chapter 6.4). Figure 1.5: Types of autonomy

First language acquisition: nature vs. nurture: Formalists and functionalists also entertain different views on how children acquire a language. As a consequence, they pursue different aims and research agendas when studying first language acquisition. At the centre of what is known as the 'nature vs. nurture debate' stands the question of how much weight should be attributed to genetic conditioning (i. e. preprogramming), on the one hand, and social conditioning (via communicative interaction with the child's social environment), on the other hand. More precisely, what is at the core of this debate is the following question: is it justified to make innate genetic structures (i. e., in formalist terms, the language genetic vs. social conditioning acquisition device or Universal Grammar) alone (!) responsible for the child's ability to acquire a(ny) first language with ease? This is the nature, or nativist, position. Or isn't it more realistic to assume, as functionalists do, that the child's ability to successfully acquire a language is to a large extent a result of the communicative interaction between the child and his/her family and wider social environment? This is the nurture position. Humans are, after all, social beings and the normal situation for children is to grow up in a social environment, with the family (including single parent and patchwork families) at its core.

nativist
(= formalist)
position

Social conditioning inevitably involves the child's exposure to performance data. Given the formalist assumption of the autonomy of competence, i. e. the ideal speaker's (unconscious) mental knowledge of his/her native language, social conditioning thus cannot explain how the child becomes a native speaker that knows how to produce and process all and only the grammatically well-formed sentences of its first language so efficiently and quickly. This is even more of a puzzle because it is assumed within the formalist paradigm that much of the linguistic input which children receive from their social environment is 'impoverished', i. e. often fragmented or even ungrammatical (the poverty of stimulus argument).

nurture
(= functionalist)
position

Unlike formalists, functionalists are primarily interested in the <u>process</u> of language acquisition and the way in which children's communicative interaction with the people around them, the linguistic input they receive, contributes to them acquiring a language. Recall that within the functionalist paradigm, language (use) primarily involves communicative competence, i. e. the ability of human beings to communicate with each other effectively and appropriately in changing situations and conditions, and not linguistic competence in the Chomskyan sense as a concept referring to tacit mental knowledge of a language.

Relevant cognitive abilities: domain-general, not language-specific: From this perspective, the nature and structure of the genetically preprogrammed blueprint for acquiring language is only of minor interest. This does not mean that such a genetic preprogramming is denied by functionalists (after all, language makes human beings unique among all species). In fact, functionalists have formulated a range of hypotheses on which basic cognitive, domain-general abilities (such as attention, pattern finding, generalization), which also feed into non-linguistic cognitive abilities such as object perception or motor processing, are responsible for, or significantly contribute to, the "language-making capacity" (Dabrowska 2015) characteristic of the human species (see also chapter 9.2). However, most functionalists differ from formalists in NOT considering the relevant candidates for language-making abilities as language-specific, i. e. as solely feeding into, let alone constituting, some human language faculty. At the very least they consider this an empirically open question. Moreover, functionalists will only take genetic factors into account when convincing 'nurture'-based facts, arguments or hypotheses can no longer be found or developed for explaining the language acquisition process. The main thrust of functionalist research in first language acquisition thus is on social conditioning (nurture), whereas the main thrust of the relevant formalist research is on genetic conditioning (nature).

Summary of major contrasts: The major contrasts between formalism and functionalism are summarized in table 1.1:

issues	formalism	functionalism
autonomy	(a) of grammar as a cognitive system	no separation of linguistic knowledge from general cognition; instead linguistic knowledge considered part of cognition
	(b) of syntax	syntax cannot be parcelled out from semantics and pragmatics
	(c) of competence	language is an instrument of interaction (communicative competence); language is a tool designed for a certain key purpose (communication), and this purpose continuously shapes the tool
language acquisition	'nature': genetically preprogrammed (innate language faculty; LAD)	'nurture': outcome of communicative interaction child – environment (but: genetic factors are not excluded)
universals	properties of Universal Grammar (formal vs. substantive universals)	functional typology: focus on search for universal tendencies rather than absolute universals and for correlations between properties of languages
explanations of universals	in terms of innateness (UG)	in terms of the usage-based factors determining their nature (e. g. online processing and production, communicative needs, external functions of language)
relationship between form and meaning/ function	arbitrary	motivated (e. g. iconicity, metaphor, metonymy)
synchrony – diachrony division	sharp	fuzzy or 'soft' (panchronic approach)
method	deductive	inductive
	introspection	strongly empirical (authentic data)
	reductionist, highly formal analyses	non-reductionist analyses

Table 1.1: The major contrasts between formalism and functionalism

Functionalist schools of linguistics: There is only a handful of truly functionalist schools of linguistics that explicitly call themselves *functional*. The first of these was founded in the late 1920s and is still highly respected for its work, which continued until the 1960s and 1970s: this is the Prague School (of Functionalism; famous members include Vilem Mathesius, Nikolaj Trubetzkoy, Roman Jakobson, Frantisek Danes). All the other relevant schools were founded in the late 1960s or 1970s: the Amsterdam School of Functional Grammar (founded by Simon Dik), (Systemic-)Functional Grammar (founded by Michael A. K. Halliday;

Prague School, Amsterdam School, Systemic-Functional Grammar, Functional Typology especially important for English linguistics), and Functional Typology (founded by Joseph Greenberg). Positively formulated, the functionalism which is subscribed to and practiced in these schools and elsewhere in linguistics is characterized by a high degree of heterogeneity and pluralism. Negatively formulated, it lacks the coherence and rigidity which characterizes the considerably larger family of formalist-driven schools. Nevertheless, the views functionalists entertain on the various points in table 1.1 represent more than just a loose bundle of assumptions and attitudes concerning the study of language. All or at least a substantial subset of them constitute what may alternatively be called the basic philosophy, set of beliefs and convictions, or declaration of professional faith of many linguists working in many different branches of linguistics these days. Especially linguists working in pragmatics (chapter 7), cognitive linguistics (chapter 6.4), corpus linguistics (see chapter 9.1 below) and most scholars working in sociolinguistics (chapter 8) are natural-born functionalists, as it were.

Another factor which, not surprisingly, unites the large and heterogeneous community of functionalists is that they disagree in many fundamental respects with the corresponding set of assumptions and views of the formalist paradigm. These two research traditions are not totally incompatible, but certainly anything but easy to reconcile.

common ground with both formalism & functionalism

Structuralism: The situation is different if we include in our discussion the third, but chronologically first, major research tradition of 20th century linguistics, namely structuralism (see figure 1.6). To a certain extent, structuralism can be said to mediate between functionalism and formalism. There are aspects of structuralism that functionalists subscribe to, and aspects of structuralism which formalists subscribe to, and these two sets of aspects partly overlap. As a consequence, someone can be a hardcore functionalist or a hard-core formalist and yet subscribe to certain basic structuralist ideas and positions. For example, the Prague School was at the same time a major structuralist school and the first functionalist-driven school of linguistics. But it is almost impossible that someone is at the same time a formalist and a functionalist. Too strongly do these two major research traditions (still) differ with regard to their aims and avenues of research. It remains to be seen whether formalism and functionalism will continue to diverge in the 2020s and thereafter, or whether at least for individual issues some of the findings and theories in one of these paradigms may also find their place in individual components of the other paradigm.

Figure 1.6:
The chronological order of structuralism, functionalism and formalism

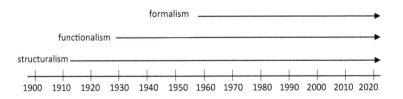

Checklist Linguistics – key terms and concepts

applied linguistics
appropriateness
arbitrariness
autonomy
communicative competence
competence ↔ performance
contrastive linguistics
conventionality
corpus linguistics
descriptive ↔ prescriptive
dichotomy
empirical ↔ introspective
form ↔ function
formalism ↔ functionalism
function (internal ↔ external)
general linguistics
generative linguistics
grammaticality
historical-comparative
   linguistics
icon
iconicity (types, principles)
index
information flow/packaging
interface
language acquisition
language acquisition device

langue ↔ *parole*
lingua franca
linguistics
mental grammar
models of communication
model of the linguistic sign
nature ↔ nurture
onomatopoetic expression
paradigm shift
paradigmatic ↔ syntagmatic
Prague School
reciprocity
research tradition
semiotics
sign
signifiant ↔ *signifié*
structuralism
symbol
synchronic ↔ diachronic
syntax
system ↔ use
transformational grammar
typology
Universal Grammar
universals (formal ↔ substantive)
well-formedness

Exercises

---

1. Which of the following research topics call for a synchronic approach
to the study of language?
a) the fixing of English word order before 1600
b) the topicalization of objects in Late Modern English
c) the division of tasks between Present Perfect and Simple Past in
   Early Modern English
d) the evolution of the pronoun system of English
e) the use of adverbial clauses in Early Middle English

---

2. Arrange the following terms in pairs. Note: some terms have no partner (see exercise 3):

signifier	symbol	nature	syntagmatic	prescriptive	arbitrary
parole	synchronic	expressive	conventional	formalism	empirical
competence	paradigmatic	introspective	appellative	nurture	icon

3.

    a) For those terms lacking a partner in the list in (2), add the partner yourself.

    b) Try to associate as many of the pairs or individual terms in (2) and (3) as possible with the name of the relevant linguist(s) mentioned in this chapter.

4.

    a) Find the matching communicative dimension or external function for each of the following six terms: addresser, appellative, code, message, phatic, referential

    b) What is the predominant external function in the following utterances, types of discourse or communicative situations?
   - weather forecast
   - speech by politician during election campaign
   - small talk with people you don't know during your best friend's wedding party
   - comment by another guest of the same wedding party: "I wouldn't say that they married. Rather SHE married HIM."
   - "Oh, damn!"
   - *Autumn* is clearly British English, while *fall* is preferred in American English.

5. Which of the following statements would be rejected by linguists working within a formalist framework?

    a) Human beings are genetically endowed with grammatical knowledge and the ability to learn any (first) language with maximum efficiency.

    b) Competence must be studied independently of performance.

    c) Large-scale language comparison is necessary for identifying language universals.

    d) The meaning of a message bears no influence on its form

    e) Language use as represented in corpora does not offer a key to Universal Grammar.

6. Which iconicity principle do the following sentences illustrate (Lakoff & Johnson 2003: 131)?

    a) Sam killed Harry.

    b) Sam caused Harry to die.

    c) Sam brought it about that Harry died.

7. In many varieties of English, prescriptively incorrect structures as in *This is the house which I painted it yesterday* are attested. How would formalists versus functionalists account for the existence of such structures?

8. Which of the following statements are true and which are false?

    a) Generative grammar is only interested in language production, not in language processing.

b) For icons there is a motivated link between signifier and signified.

c) Paradigmatic relations are relations of combination; syntagmatic relations are relations of choice.

d) Morphophonemics is a classic example of an interface in linguistics.

e) Formalists would agree with the statement "Linguistics is part of the social sciences."

f) Functionalists assume that language processing exclusively relies on domain-general abilities.

g) Concessivity is cognitively more complex than causality.

h) Structuralism has had no significant impact on American linguistics.

9. This is an exercise in functional grammar. Identify which sentence (left table, i–x) matches which construction (right table, a–j), based on the description of the form and function of each construction. For further guidance, you might want to consult a reference chapter on information packaging in English (e. g., Birner & Ward in Aarts & McMahon 2006). *Advanced*

i.	This one she forgot.	a.	**Left dislocation** makes it possible to introduce and highlight a new topic while avoiding having it placed in subject position (which is generally dispreferred for new information). A pronoun replaces the fronted constituent in its canonical (i. e., normal, typical) position.
ii.	Also starring in the show is John Smith.	b.	**It-clefts** highlight new information after *It is/was...* The highlighted constituent is followed by a relative clause, which contains old information.
iii.	On board were three linguists.	c.	In **subject extraposition**, 'dummy' *it* in canonical subject position allows the speaker to move 'heavy' (i. e., long, detailed) constituents to the end of the sentence (which is their preferred position).
iv.	There is a dog in the pool.	d.	**Right dislocation** is often used to specify an ambiguous referent.
v.	It is obvious that he's a liar.	e.	In **inversion**, two constituents occur in non-canonical position. This helps the speaker obey the general preference for presenting discourse-old before discourse-new information.
vi.	That job I gave you, it's the best one you've ever had.	f.	**Passives** are used to shift new information from the canonical subject position to the end of the clause.

vii. They're still here, the people from next door.	g. In **focus preposing**, the preposed part bears the main accent of the utterance. It provides hearer-new information on a topic which is salient from the prior discourse.
viii. It was the French student who knew the answer.	h. **Existential clauses** make it possible to shift new information from sentence-initial subject position to the end of the clause via *there*-insertion.
ix. The car was taken by Kim.	i. **Pseudo-clefts** (or: *wh*-clefts) give extra prominence to new information, which follows the verb.
x. What he did was crash the car.	j. **Topicalization**, a type of preposing, creates a connection to the prior discourse without highlighting the preposed constituent as hearer-new (it does not bear the main accent of the utterance).

10. This task is concerned with the conflicting positions in the formalism-functionalism debate from a structuralist point of view (see section 1.3.3). Try to determine in which respects structuralism is compatible (or clearly sides) with formalism, on the one hand, and/or with functionalism, on the other hand.

11. Find out more about the contribution of Leonard Bloomfield to the evolution of (especially American) linguistics in the mid-20th century. What, in particular, are major differences between American and European Structuralism (as represented by de Saussure and the Prague School)?

12. Based on Crystal's *Cambridge Encyclopedia of the English Language* (2018, 3rd edition), find out how many speakers of the following "Englishes" exist in the world:
a) English as a Native Language (ENL),
b) English as a Second Language (ESL), and
c) English as a Foreign Language (EFL).
What exactly do these labels refer to?

Sources and further reading

Amsterdamska, Olga. 1987. *Schools of thought: The development of linguistics from Bopp to Saussure.* Dordrecht: Reidel.

Auroux, Sylvain et al., eds. 2001. *History of the language sciences: An international handbook on the evolution of the study of language from the beginnings to the present.* [HSK]. 3 vols. Berlin/New York: de Gruyter.

Birner, Betty/Gregory Ward. 2006. "Information structure." In: Bas Aarts/April McMahon, eds. *The handbook of English linguistics.* Malden/Oxford: Blackwell Publishing. 291–317.

Boxell, Oliver. 2016. "The place of universal grammar in the study of language

and mind: A response to Dabrowska (2015)." *Open Linguistics* 2(1): 352–372.
https://doi.org/10.1515/opli-2016-0017.

Chomsky, Noam. 2004. *The generative enterprise revisited*. Berlin/New York:
Mouton de Gruyter.

Comrie, Bernard. 1989². *Language universals and linguistic typology*. Oxford:
Blackwell.

Croft, William. 1995. "Autonomy and functional linguistics." *Language* 71: 490–
532.

Croft, William. 2002². *Typology and universals*. Cambridge: Cambridge University
Press.

Crystal, David. 2018³. *The Cambridge encyclopedia of the English language*. Cambridge: Cambridge University Press.

Dąbrowska, E. 2015. "What exactly is Universal Grammar, and has anyone seen
it?" *Frontiers in Psychology* 6: 852. https://doi.org/10.3389/fpsyg.2015.00852.

D'Agostino, Fred. 1986. *Chomsky's system of ideas*. Oxford: Clarendon.

de Saussure, Ferdinand. 1983 [1916]. *Course of general linguistics*. edited by
Charles Bally and Albert Sechehaye. London: Duckworth.

Harris, Roy. 1987. *Reading Saussure*. London: Duckworth.

Helbig, Gerhard. 1989⁸. *Geschichte der neueren Sprachwissenschaft*. Opladen:
Westdeutscher Verlag.

Hymes, Dell. 1966. "Two types of linguistic relativity". In: William Bright, ed.
Sociolinguistics. The Hague: Mouton. 114–158.

Jäger, Ludwig. 2010. *Ferdinand de Saussure. Zur Einführung*. Hamburg: Junius.

Joseph, John Earl/Nigel Love/Talbot J. Taylor, eds. 2001. *Landmarks in linguistic
thought*. Vol. 2: *The Western tradition in the twentieth century*. London: Routledge.

Kortmann, Bernd. 1999. "Iconicity, typology and cognition." In: Max Nänny/Olga
Fischer, eds. *Form miming meaning. Iconicity in language and literature*.
Amsterdam/Philadelphia: Benjamins. 375–392.

Matthews, Peter. 1993. *Grammatical theory in the United States from Bloomfield
to Chomsky*. Cambridge: Cambridge University Press.

Newmeyer, Frederick J. 1986. *Linguistic theory in America*. New York: Academic
Press.

Newmeyer, Frederick J. 1996. *Generative linguistics. A historical perspective*. Lon-
don/New York: Routledge.

Newmeyer, Frederick J. 1998. *Language form and language function*. Cambridge,
Mass.: MIT Press.

Paul, Hermann. 1888. *Principles of the history of language*. translated from the
2nd edition of the original by H. A. Strong. London: Swan Sonnenschein.

Paul, Hermann. 1995¹⁰. *Prinzipien der Sprachgeschichte*. Tübingen: Niemeyer.

Pinker, Steven. 1995. *The language instinct. The new science of language and
mind*. London: Penguin.

Rohdenburg, Günter/Britta Mondorf, eds. 2003. *Determinants of grammatical variation in English*. Berlin: Mouton de Gruyter.

Sampson, Geoffrey. 1980. *Schools of linguistics: Competition and evolution*. London: Hutchinson.

Ward, Gregory/Betty Birner/Rodney Huddleston. 2002. "Information packaging."
In: Rodney Huddleston/George Pullum, eds. *The Cambridge grammar of the
English language*. Cambridge: Cambridge University Press. 1363–1447.

Wunderlich, Dieter. 2004. "Why assume UG?". In: Martina Penke/Anette Rosen-
bach, guest eds. *What counts as evidence in linguistics?* (*Studies in Language*).
Amsterdam/Philadelphia: Benjamins. 615–641.

2 Phonetics and phonology: On sounds and sound systems

Phonetics and phonology are the two branches of linguistics which deal with the properties and functions of sounds. Although they are tightly interrelated, they differ clearly from each other with regard to their re-search objects and the questions they ask.

Phonetics is concerned with sounds (or: phones; Greek *phon* = voice, sound) as such, particularly with the substance of those sounds used in human communication, no matter in which language they occur. Relevant questions asked in phonetics concerning human speech sounds include the following: How are these sounds produced? What are their articulatory features (that is, features determined by the speech organs)? What are their acoustic properties (in the sense of measurable oscillations)? How can sounds be described and classified using articulatory and acoustic informa-tion? How can sounds be transcribed, in other words be made visible in writing, with the help of a limited, manageable inventory of symbols?

sounds as such

Phonology: Unlike phoneticians, phonologists are solely interested in the function of sounds belonging to a given sound system: Does a certain sound have a meaning-distinguishing function within the system of a language or not?

function of sounds

Distinctive vs. redundant: In other words, is the difference between two sounds of the same language distinctive, like the difference between the initial sounds of *lip* and *rip*, or not? An example of a non-distinctive (or: redundant) sound difference is the one between the so-called 'clear l' in *lip* and the so-called 'dark l' in *pill*. In English, there is no pair of words where replacing one of these two sounds with the other in an otherwise identical string of sounds would lead to a meaning difference. Or just think of the difference between the 'trilled r' (*gerolltes Zungen-R*) and the 'uvular r' (*Zäpfchen-R*) in German. We are clearly dealing with two differ-ent sounds here, which are therefore also represented by different sym-bols in phonetics, but it is irrelevant, at least from the meaning perspec-tive, which one of the two we use, e. g. in German *rollen* or *Brot*. Phonol-ogy thus operates on a more abstract level than phonetics.

Phoneme / /: In the field of phonology, the research object is not the totality of all sounds actually uttered and processed in everyday life, but merely those units which constitute the sound system of a language, the so-called phonemes (Greek *phonema* = sound).

abstract level
(langue)

Allophone: Thus in some varieties of English, notably Received Pro-nunciation (RP), there is the phoneme /l/ with its phonetic variants (or: allophones) [l] in *lip* and [ɫ] in *pill*, and in German the phoneme /r/, which among others is realized by the allophones [r] and [ʁ].

concrete level
(parole)

J.B. Metzler © Springer-Verlag GmbH Deutschland, ein Teil von Springer Nature, 2020
B. Kortmann, *English Linguistics*, https://doi.org/10.1007/978-3-476-05678-8_2

The major differences between phonetics and phonology can be described with the help of the following pairs of contrast:

phonetics	phonology
sounds as such	sounds as parts of a sound system
language use (*parole*)	language system (*langue*)
not language-specific	language-specific
substance	function (meaning differentiation)
concrete	abstract
phone []	phoneme / /

Table 2.1:
Phonetics
vs. phonology

2.1 | Phonetics

2.1.1 | Transcription

high relevance
for English

Orthography ≠ pronunciation: A transcription system allows us to represent sounds in writing and thus to specify, for instance, the pronunciation of words in dictionaries. Phonetic transcriptions clearly show that spelling often does not tell us anything about pronunciation. Therefore, they are of utmost importance especially for those languages with a large discrepancy between pronunciation and orthography. A prime example of this is the English language, the spelling of which often tells us more about the origin of the words or their pronunciation towards the end of the Middle Ages than about their present pronunciation. Concerning the divergence of spelling (in angled brackets) and articulation (in square brackets), we can roughly distinguish four types:

(1) **different spellings for the same sound**
[i:]   < ae > Caesar < eo > people
      < ay > quay < ey > key
      < e > be, these < i > ski, police, fatigue
      < ea > sea, tea < ie > field, yield
      < ee > bee, sneeze < oe > amoeba, Phoenix
      < ei > seize, receive

(2) **the same spelling for different sounds**
< ea > [eə] bear, tear (verb) [ɑ:] heart
      [ɪə] beard, tear (noun), hear [e] head, dead
      [ɜ:] heard, learn [i:] heat, mead

(3) **silent letters**
know, honest, mnemonic, psychology, debt, listen, sword, column, bomb, sign, island; *optional in the case of* alright, often, sandwich

(4) **missing letters**
[j] in use, fuse, cute, futile, stew, new (BrE)

in this book:
Wells' model for RP

Transcription models: Especially for learners and teachers of English, phonetic transcriptions are indispensable. Table 2.2 gives an overview of the four currently most common transcription models for Received Pronunciation (RP), the standard accent of Southern – especially Southeastern – British English and the model used in all English language classrooms around the world targeting standard British English. The first three of these models were developed specifically for the transcription of RP, thus they do not pay attention to whether a particular symbol might represent a different sound in the transcription of a different language. This is not the case for the fourth model, the International Phonetic Alphabet (IPA), which was developed by the International Phonetic Association for the transcription of any linguistic sound. The phonetic symbols listed in table 2.2 thus form the relevant subset of the overall inventory of IPA symbols for the transcription of RP. The main difference between the models by Gimson, Wells, and Upton, on the one hand, and the IPA, on the other hand, is that the latter does not use the colon-like diacritic for the long vowels (as in [si:t] *seat* or [bu:t] *boot*).

Quantity – quality: All models have in common that long and short vowels are treated differently, not only concerning their quantity (length), but also their phonetic quality. Accordingly, long and short vowels are transcribed by different symbols (e. g. [si:t] *seat* in comparison to [sɪt] *sit*). In this respect they differ from the original model by the London phonetician Daniel Jones, from which all the current models have developed. In this book it is the Wellsian model which will be used. As a successor of Gimson's model, it is meanwhile the most widely used model for the teaching of English and English linguistics at schools and universities. Of no further importance, on the other hand, will be the transcription model that is frequently chosen in American publications on phonetics and phonology (see the last line in table 2.2). It differs strongly from all models introduced so far, apart from the fact that there are of course differences regarding the phoneme inventories and phoneme realizations between RP and General American (GA), the standard accent of American English (see chapter 8).

vowel length

Table 2.2: Transcription models*
* The asterisk indicates that for these vowels different symbols are used in the transcription models.

	Key word	seat*	sit	set*	sat*	star*	soft	sort*	stood	soon*	sum	sir*	suppose	say	so	sigh*	sow*	soil	steer	stare*	sure
	Upton	iː	ɪ	ɛ	a	ɑː	ɒ	ɔː	ʊ	uː	ʌ	əː	ə	eɪ	əʊ	ʌɪ	aʊ	ɔɪ	ɪə	ɛː	ʊə
RP	Wells	iː	ɪ	e	æ	ɑː	ɒ	ɔː	ʊ	uː	ʌ	ɜː	ə	eɪ	əʊ	aɪ	aʊ	ɔɪ	ɪə	eə	ʊə
	Gimson	iː	ɪ	e	æ	ɑː	ɒ	ɔː	ʊ	uː	ʌ	ɜː	ə	eɪ	əʊ	aɪ	ɑʊ	ɔɪ	ɪə	ɛə	ʊə
	IPA	i	ɪ	ɛ	æ	ɑ	ɒ	ɔ	ʊ	u	ʌ	ɜ	ə	eɪ	əʊ	aɪ	ɑʊ	ɔɪ	ɪə	ɛə	ʊə
GA	American textbooks	ij, iy, i	ɪ	ɛ	æ	ɑ, a	ɑ, a	ɔ	ʊ	uw, u	ʌ	ʌ(+r), ə	ə	ej, ey, e	ow, o	aj, ay	aw	ɔj, ɔy	(ɪ+r), (i+r)	(ɛ+r)	(ʊ+r)

There is a simple reason why only the phonetic symbols for the vowels are listed in Table 2.2. Concerning consonants there are no differences between the transcription models, again with the exception of the model widely used in North America, which uses the symbols [š, ž, č, ǰ, y] instead of [ʃ, ʒ, tʃ, dʒ, j].

consonants

narrow vs. broad
transcription
Phonetic vs. phonemic transcription: It is true that phonetic transcriptions are indispensable especially for languages like English. For the non-specialist, however, there are limits to the degree of precision that is still digestible. Most dictionaries and introductions to linguistics therefore refrain from using the fine-grained (so-called narrow) phonetic transcription which represents even the most subtle phonetic features with the help of diacritic signs. Examples of this are the tilda for marking the nasalisation of vowels, which takes place regularly before nasal consonants (e. g. in *run* [ɹʌ̃n] or *wrong* [ɹɒ̃ŋ] in British English), and the superscript 'h' indicating the strong aspiration of some voiceless consonants, meaning the strong burst of breath that accompanies especially their release, particularly word-initially, as in [pʰɪ̃n] or [tʰɪɫ]. Even the so-called broad phonetic transcription, which provides different symbols for dark and clear /l/ or the various roll sounds, is mostly avoided outside of publications on phonetics.

phonemic
transcription
Much preferred, on the other hand, is the simplest type of transcription, the so-called phonemic transcription. Not only does it dispense with diacritic signs (sometimes with the exception of the [ː] as a sign for length), but also with separate symbols for the various realizations of /l/ or /r/. In other words, this type of transcription takes into account only the phonemes of a language. For reasons of simplification, phonemic transcription will predominantly be used in the following parts of this chapter and book.

(5)   transcription

phonetic   phonemic

narrow   broad

ring [ɹɪ̃ŋ]   [ɹɪŋ]   /rɪŋ/
till [tʰɪɫ]   [tɪɫ]   /tɪl/

2.1.2 | Speech organs

Branches of phonetics: There are three branches of phonetics, each of which deals with one of the three phases of communication, namely
- sound production (articulatory phonetics),
- sound transmission (acoustic phonetics), and
- sound perception and processing (auditory phonetics).

Acoustic phonetics is concerned with the measurable physical properties of sounds. It falls primarily into the domain of physics and language processing by computers, e. g. automatic speech recognition. Auditory phonetics is of prime importance in medicine and psychology. Both branches will be of no further concern in this chapter.

Articulators: Articulatory phonetics is of central importance in linguistics, especially for (prospective) language teachers. It is located at the interface between linguistics, on the one hand, and anatomy and physiology, on the other. A large part of its terminology is taken from the latter two domains, e. g. terms for the speech organs and for the description and classification of speech sounds.

active vs. passive
articulators
The human speech organs (or: articulators) are shown below in figure 2.1 and identified and illustrated in table 2.3. It is easiest to feel the

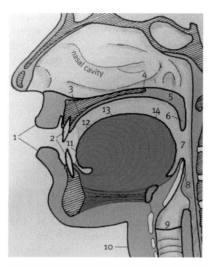

Speech organs

1. lips
2. teeth
3. alveolar ridge
4. hard palate
5. soft palate (velum)
6. uvula
7. pharynx
8. epiglottis
9. glottis – gap between vocal folds
10. larynx
11. tip/apex of the tongue
12. blade/lamina of the tongue
13. front of the tongue
14. back/dorsum of the tongue

Figure 2.1:
Speech organs

	place of articulation		adjective	examples of sounds []	examples
1	lips		labial	[p], [b], [m], [w]	puppy, Bob, mummy, word
2	teeth		dental labio-dental	[θ], [ð] [f], [v]	throne, the fan, van
3	alveolar ridge		alveolar	[t], [d], [s] [z], [n], [l]	turtle, dragon, sister zeal, nasty, lollipop
			post-alveolar	[ɹ]	rap
			palato-alveolar	[ʃ], [ʒ], [tʃ], [dʒ]	shanty, illusion, chips, gipsy
4	hard palate		palatal	[j]	yellow
5	soft palate / velum		velar	[k], [g], [ŋ]	ketchup, gorilla, song
6	uvula		uvular		
7	pharynx		pharyngeal		
8	epiglottis				
9	glottis		glottal	[h], [ʔ]	hat, *in many non-RP accents: bottle [bɒʔl]*
10	larynx		laryngeal	[ʔ]	*sometimes in RP before /p, t, k/: popcorn ['pɒʔp-kɔːn]*
11	tongue	tip/apex	apical	[θ], [ð], [ɹ], [l]	throne, the, rap, lollipop
12		blade/lamina	laminal	[t], [d], [n] [s], [z] [ʃ], [ʒ], [tʃ], [dʒ]	turtle, dragon, nasty sister, zeal shanty, illusion, chips, gipsy
13		front	(medio-)dorsal	[j], [ɪ], [iː], [e], [æ]	yellow, insect, leap, pet, pat
14		back/dorsum	(post-)dorsal	[k], [g], [ŋ] [ʊ], [uː], [ɒ], [ɔː]	ketchup, gorilla, song foot, food, ton, tall

Table 2.3:
Places of articulation and relevant English sounds (RP)*

*The examples in the right column refer to the initial sound (unless indicated otherwise). In Received Pronunciation there are no clear examples of the sounds in lines 6–8 and 10. An example of a uvular sound (line 6) is the *German Zäpfchen-R* ([ʁ], [ʀ]). Pharyngeal sounds (line 7) are a characteristic feature of Arabic, laryngeal sounds (line 10) are typical of Danish.

speech organs in the upper part of the oral cavity (alveolar ridge, hard and soft palate) when, starting out from the back of the front teeth, we let the tip of the tongue slowly glide back along the roof of the mouth. Most of the speech organs are movable, thus so-called active articulators; only the upper jaw, the hard palate, and the back of the throat (or: pharynx) are relatively immovable and therefore called passive articulators. It should be noted, however, that the so-called speech organs do of course primarily serve biological, not linguistic functions.

2.1.3 | Types of sounds

Vowels and consonants: The two main types of sounds in the languages of the world are vowels and consonants. This is one of the few cases in which we can speak of an absolute (i. e. exceptionless) universal. The main phonetic difference between these two sound types is that for vowels the air passes through the oral cavity relatively freely, whereas consonants are formed via a partial or complete obstruction of the airflow somewhere in the vocal tract. Moreover, vowels are generally voiced, that is the vocal folds (better known under the misleading term *vocal cords*) are vibrating, whereas consonants can be voiced or voiceless.

2.1.3.1 | Consonants

In general, three criteria (or: parameters) are used for the description and classification of consonants:
- vocal fold action: yes (voiced)/no (voiceless)
- place of articulation
- manner of articulation

Voiced consonants: The first criterion is about whether the vocal folds are approximating each other closely enough in order to be set vibrating by

the airflow coming up through the windpipe. If they vibrate (figure 2.2), the result is a voiced sound. These vibrations can easily be felt: simply put the tip of your index finger on the Adam's apple (often more prominent with members of the male sex) and produce in turns of three seconds [s] and [z] or, alternatively, [f] and [v]. Another indicator of voiced sounds is that only these may be hummed or sung.

Figure 2.2
a: voiced,
b: voiceless

vd/vl correlates
with fortis/lenis

Voiceless consonants, by contrast, result from the fact that the vocal folds are too far apart to be set vibrating (see the open glottis in figure 2.2b). Voiceless consonants further differ from voiced ones in that the intensity of muscle tension and emission of air is considerably larger for the former. That is why the distinction between voiceless and voiced consonants often – in English generally – correlates with the *fortis/lenis* (strong/soft) distinction, which refers to the degree of muscle tension and breath pressure when producing consonants.

Place of articulation: The second criterion (place of articulation) leads us back to the speech organs, in particular to figure 2.1 and table 2.3, and does not need any further explanation. Sounds which are produced at the same place are called homorganic sounds.

Manner of articulation: On the basis of their manner of articulation, the third relevant criterion, two major classes of consonants are distinguished: obstruents and sonorants.

Types of obstruents: With obstruents, the airflow is strongly, sometimes even completely, obstructed at some place in the articulation channel.

- If the air is pressed through a narrow articulation channel, friction is produced, which again generates a certain type of sound, the so-called fricatives (e. g. [v] or [s]).
- If the airflow is completely blocked due to two articulators touching each other, and this obstruction is suddenly released, then the result is an 'explosive' sound due to the escape of the blocked airstream (so-called plosives, e. g. [p] or [d]).
- A third type of obstruent are the affricates, as e. g. [tʃ] in *church* or [dʒ] in *judge*. For their production there is first – as for plosives – a complete obstruction of the airflow, which then, however, is not released abruptly, but rather slowly. Due to the narrow channel which opens between tongue blade and the area between alveolar ridge and hard palate, the accumulated air escapes slowly and, due to friction, produces a sound similar to fricatives.

homorganic sounds

fricatives

plosives

affricates

On the basis of the three criteria voicing, place of articulation, and manner of articulation, we are now in the position of describing, for example, [p] as a voiceless (bi)labial plosive sound, or [v] as a voiced labio-dental fricative. We can also formulate generalizations on individual groups of consonants, making for instance statements only about voiceless obstruents, voiced alveolar sounds, or all plosives, fricatives, or affricates. Together with their different places of articulation, these three types of obstruents are illustrated in the first three lines of table 2.4, which contains all 24 consonant phonemes of English.

Table 2.4: The English consonant inventory

place of articulation		bilabial	labio-dental	dental	alveolar	post-alveolar	palato-alveolar	palatal	velar	glottal
manner of articulation		vl. vd.	vl. vd.	vl. vd.	vl. vd.	vl. vd.	vl. vd.	vl. vd.	vl. vd.	vl. vd.

			bilabial	labio-dental	dental	alveolar	post-alveolar	palato-alveolar	palatal	velar	glottal
OBSTRUENTS		plosive	p b			t d				k g	
		fricative		f v	θ ð	s z		ʃ ʒ			h
		affricate						tʃ dʒ			
SONORANTS		nasal	m			n				ŋ	
	APPROXIMANTS LIQUIDS	lateral				l					
		roll				r RP [ɹ] GA [ɻ]					
		semi-vowel	w						j		

obstruents =
prototypical
consonants

Obstruents vs. sonorants: Not only do obstruents make up the majority of consonants, in comparison to sonorants they are also the more prototypical consonants. For example, almost all obstruents come in pairs (voiced/voiceless), whereas sonorants (at least in English) are usually voiced. As can be seen from table 2.4, there are different subsets of sonorants. Let us first turn to the nasals: similar to plosives, there is a complete obstruction of the airflow in the oral cavity for [m], [n], and [ŋ], but since the soft palate (or: velum) is lowered (see figure 2.3), the air can escape through the nasal cavity. Due to the similar manner of articulation, nasals and plosives are often also lumped together as stops, but then divided into nasal and non-nasal (or: oral) stops.

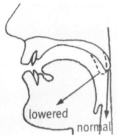

Liquids: On account of their combination of obstruction and simultaneous escape of the airstream, [l] and [r] are collectively referred to as liquids.

Figure 2.3:
Position of velum

- The term *laterals* for the various /l/-realizations stems from the fact that the air escapes along the sides of the tongue.
- *Rolls* (or: *trills*) is the term used for, among other things, particular phonetic realizations of /r/; these exist in the Celtic Englishes (Irish, Scottish, Welsh English), but not in the standard accents of British and American English.

Semi-vowels or glides: For liquids, although the air is escaping in a relatively unimpeded way, there is still contact between two articulators. This is different for the initial sounds of *we* [w] and *you* [j], which lead us right into the transitional zone between consonants and vowels and, at the same time, between phonetics and phonology. From the point of view of phonetics, these two sounds are rather vowels, more precisely gliding vowels, with the relevant articulators moving away from (for [w]) or towards (for [j]) the narrowing in the articulation channel.

distribution
in syllables

This is also mirrored in the terms that are commonly used for them, namely *semi-vowels* or *glides*. Only because of their distribution in syllables are they considered as consonants. They are exclusively located at the margins of a syllable, and thus, different from vowels, can never serve as the nucleus of a syllable, let alone constitute a syllable on their own. In other words, purely functional and thus phonological considerations ("Which function do these two sounds fulfil in the sound system of English?") are responsible for the classification of [w] and [j]. In principle, even if not to the same extent, a similarly 'inaccurate' manner of proceeding from a phonetic point of view applies to the classification of liquids. Here, too, the air can escape relatively freely from the oral cavity so that there is no audible friction of the escaping airflow.

Approximants: In phonetics, liquids and semi-vowels, in some accounts also [h], are therefore also grouped together as approximants (defining characteristic: two articulators approaching or touching each other without audible friction).

2.1.3.2 | Vowels

The biggest problem concerning the description and classification of vowels is that, in contrast to consonants, we cannot feel what is happening in the oral cavity during their articulation. It is true that we can observe differences in the lip position (e. g. spread lips for [iː] in *tree*, lip rounding for [uː] in *true*). But the lip position is only a secondary feature of vowels, especially in English where in contrast to German and most of the Germanic languages there are no rounded front vowels like [yː], as in German *Sühne* or [øː], as in German *Söhne* (see chapter 5). *Tongue* indeed is the key word: it is that speech organ on which everything in vowel production hinges. Both the quality and the quantity of vowels change depending on (a) which position (b) a particular part of the tongue remains in (c) for how long. On top of this, (d) the position of the tongue can even change in the course of the articulation of a vowel and thus produce a completely different vowel.

the tongue is key

Reference system: It is only with the help of detailed physiological studies in a phonetic laboratory that we can determine these four pieces of information, which are relevant for every single vowel sound. It was such a laboratory where the vowel diagram (or: vowel chart) was developed. It serves as an invariable reference system for the description and classification of any given vowel of a language.

cardinal vowel diagram by Daniel Jones

Cardinal vowels: The relevant reference vowels (see the nodes in figure 2.4) are called *cardinal vowels*. These idealized vowels are constructs and do not occur in any language, which is why they are generally placed outside of the vowel diagram (also known as the *cardinal vowel diagram*). They come in two sets, only the first of which is shown in figure 2.4:

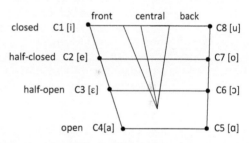

- The first set consists of the eight primary cardinal vowels (C1–C8).
- The second set consists of ten secondary cardinal vowels. The first eight of these (C9–C16) follow from the reversal of the lip position for the primary cardinal vowels. Thus, rounded lip position for the cardinal vowels C1–C5 yields the cardinal vowels C9–C13, and non-rounded lip position for the cardinal vowels C6–C8 yields the cardinal vowels C14–C16. Two closed central vowels (C17 and C18) complete the cardinal vowel system developed by Daniel Jones.

Figure 2.4:
The vowel chart

Figure 2.5: Area of tongue movement

The vowel diagram is an abstracted representation of that area of the oral cavity where the vowels are produced (figure 2.5). The two axes of the diagram relate to the tongue as the all-important speech organ in the production of vowels.

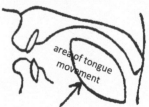

Front and back vowels: The horizontal axis indicates which part of the tongue (front, back, or central) is raised most during the production of a particular vowel; this is why we speak of front or back vowels. The vertical axis indicates the degree of tongue raising (high – mid – low). The vowel [ɪ] in *sit* is thus called an (unrounded) high front vowel, [ʊ] in *foot* a (rounded) high back vowel, and the schwa-sound [ə], which usually occurs in unstressed syllables only, is called a mid-central vowel. These three sounds have in common that the tongue remains in the respective position of articulation for a considerably shorter period of time than is the case for the vowels in *seat* [iː], *boot* [uː], and *sir* [ɜː].

Short vs. long vowels: Thus, how long the tongue remains in a particular position is a further relevant factor for the description and classification of vowels. Figures 2.6a and 2.6b show all short and long vowels of English; as we can see, and as is reflected in their transcriptions, short and long vowels do not only differ quantitatively, but also qualitatively, i. e. with regard to their tongue positions:

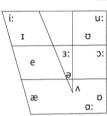

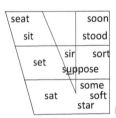

Monophthongs vs. diphthongs: The vowels in the two figures in 2.6 are called monophthongs (or: pure vowels) in contrast to the diphthongs (or: gliding vowels) in figures 2.7–2.9. The crucial criterion for the distinction of these two types of vowels is whether the tongue largely remains stable in its position during the production of the respective vowel, or whether it glides from one position towards another. The latter is true for diphthongs, but it is important to stress that at the end of this gliding process, the tongue never quite reaches the position in which it would normally be if the second element were articulated on its own. This is indicated by the arrows in figures 2.7 through 2.9. The eight diphthongs of the English sound system may be divided into two subgroups: those which end in [ɪ] or [ʊ] (so-called closing diphthongs), and those which end in the schwa-sound (so-called centring diphthongs).

Triphthongs: So-called triphthongs as in *fire, layer, royal, our* and *lower*, where we have two position changes of the tongue, are generally considered as combinations of the respective (closing) diphthongs and the schwa-sound, and not as part of the English vowel system, which comprises 20 phonemes altogether.

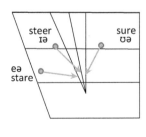

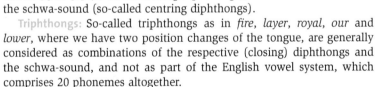

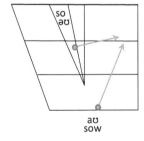

Figure 2.7: Closing diphthongs   Figure 2.8: Centring diphthongs   Figure 2.9: Closing diphthongs

In the classification of vowels, the main distinction is typically drawn between monophthongs and diphthongs, each with their respective sub-groups. It is just as well possible to give phonetic and phonological arguments for a different classification (see figure 2.10).

Tense vs. lax vowels: In analogy to the *fortis/lenis* distinction for consonants, there is a tense/lax distinction for vowels. Tense vowels require greater muscle tension and are produced more peripherally; this is the case during the production of long vowels and diphthongs. The short vowels, on the other hand, belong to the group of lax vowels. This grouping cannot only be motivated by a phonetic, more exactly articulatory, criterion (degree of muscle tension), but also by the phonological criterion of distribution. Only tense vowels can occur in stressed open syllables, i. e. stressed syllables which do not end in one or more consonants (e. g. *fee* [fiː], but not [fɪ]); on the other hand, only lax vowels can precede the velar nasal [ŋ], e. g. [sɪŋ], but not [siːŋ].

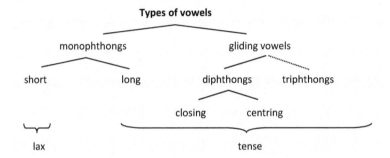

Figure 2.10:
Types of vowels

2.2 | Phonology

2.2.1 | On determining the phoneme inventory: Segmental phonology

Phonemes: Unlike phonetics, phonology is indisputably an integral part of linguistics. It abstracts from the multitude of different sounds used in a language and is only interested in those sound units which fulfil a meaning-distinguishing (distinctive or contrastive) function within the sound system (therefore also the term *functional phonetics*). These abstract, idealized sound units are called *phonemes,* and are defined as smallest meaning-distinguishing units of a language. They exist only in our minds, however, more exactly in our mental grammar; on the level of language use (*parole*), phonemes are always realized as phones.

Allophones: There is almost always more than one phone which realizes a given phoneme. The relevant phones are called the allophones of the respective phoneme. Clear and dark /l/, for example [l] in *lip* and [ɫ] in *pill,* are the two best-known allophones of the lateral consonant phoneme of English; a third one is, for instance, the voiceless [l̥], which occurs regularly after [p] as the initial sound of stressed syllables (e. g. in *place* or *please*). To be more precise, the phonetic transcription of this allophone would need to look like this [pʰ], since at the beginning of a syllable the voiceless bilabial plosive is aspirated, especially when vowels follow. However, this is not the case for all allophones of the phoneme /p/; in syllable-final position, there is normally no aspiration (*lap*, *rap*, *tap*). If an additional [t] follows, as in *apt* or *captain*, the closure is not even released, as is normally the case for plosives: the resulting sound is the non-released voiceless bilabial plosive [p̚].

Complementary distribution: In the vast majority of cases, it is predictable in which phonological environment which allophone of a phoneme will be used. This is known as complementary distribution of allophones, i. e. normally they never occur in the same environment; thus, a given allophone cannot simply be replaced by one of the other allophones.

Free variation: In contradistinction to these so-called contextual variants, there are also numerous free variants of phonemes. For instance, voiceless plosives may well be aspirated in the final position of a syllable or word, too, as in [læp] and [læpʰ] for *lap*, or [ʃʌt] and [ʃʌtʰ] for *shut*. We are dealing with free variation of aspirated and non-aspirated allophones here.

Minimal pairs: The all-important method for determining the phonemes (versus (allo-)phones) of a language is the so-called minimal pair test. Minimal pairs are pairs of meaning-carrying units which differ in exactly one sound, but apart from that have an identical sequence of sounds. More exactly, such pairs qualify as minimal pairs only if they additionally differ in their meaning. Since the meaning difference is only due to the sound difference, and the difference between the two relevant sounds therefore is distinctive, these two sounds must be ascribed phoneme status. For example, on the basis of the minimal pairs in (6a) and the series of minimal pairs (*minimal sets*) in (6b), the following phonemes of English can be determined: /t/, /p/, /r/, /f/, /e/, /æ/, /iː/, /ɪ/, and /aɪ/.

(6)   a.   ten-pen, time-rhyme, try-fry
      b.   set-sat-seat-sit-site

A minimal pair test thus consists of (a) substituting exactly one sound in a sequence of sounds by another, and (b) answering the question whether this substitution has resulted in a change of meaning of this sound sequence, that is, whether the result is a different word. If the answer is positive, we are dealing with a minimal pair, and a single minimal pair suffices for the identification of two phonemes. If, on the other hand, we look at phonetically contrasting pairs like [læp] and [læpʰ], or the postalveolar /r/ of Received Pronunciation and the retroflex /r/ of General American, we are inevitably led to the conclusion that in these cases we are merely concerned with different phonetic realizations of the same phoneme.

Distinctive features: In connection with the distinction between phonemes and allophones, a further central term of phonology becomes relevant, namely distinctive features. Similar to the way we proceeded in the phonetic description of the various types of sounds, phonemes can alternatively be defined as bundles of distinctive features.

- The phoneme /p/ could thus be described as a bundle of the features [+ CONSONANT, – VOICED, – NASAL, + LABIAL, + CLOSURE, + PLOSIVE], different from, for example,
- the nasal /n/ with its features [+ CONSONANT, + VOICED, + NASAL, – LABIAL, + CLOSURE, – PLOSIVE].

In these two examples, the important aspects from a phonological point of view are that for /p/ aspiration does not figure as a distinctive feature (precisely because it is not distinctive, i. e. not capable of bringing about a change in meaning), and that for /n/ the feature [+ VOICED] is superfluous (or: redundant) since all English nasals are voiced.

Phonological systems: It is important to note, however, that what applies to the English sound system does not necessarily apply to the sound systems of other languages. In Hindi, for example, an official language spoken by some 600 million speakers in India, aspirated and non-aspirated sounds like [pʰ] and [p] can carry minimal pairs and therefore need to be assigned two different phonemes (aspirated /pʰ/ and non-aspirated /p/). This shows that a (meaning-wise) redundant sound difference in one language can perfectly well be a distinctive sound difference in another language. As far as the English nasals are concerned, there is something else we can learn: a combination of certain distinctive features may be impossible in the sound system of one language (e. g. the feature [+ NASAL] in combination with [– VOICED]), but things may be totally different in another language. Thus, the phoneme system of Burmese, an official language of Myanmar spoken by some 30 million speakers, includes, besides the 'normal' inventory of voiced nasals, the corresponding set of voiceless nasals, namely /m̥, n̥, ŋ̊/. Or take Welsh with its voiceless lateral phoneme /ɬ/, which is furthermore a fricative (e. g. in *Llewellyn*). In English, on the other hand, the combination of [+ LATERAL] and [+ FRICATIVE] is impossible, even for an allophone of /l/. The sound systems (or: phonological systems) of languages thus differ with regard to the combinatory possibilities of certain features, which necessarily leads to differences in their phoneme inventories. English vs. Hindi, Burmese, Welsh

Phonotactics: Phonology does not only deal with those restrictions which concern the combination of distinctive features, but also with restrictions concerning the combination of phonemes in a language (so-called *phonotactic restrictions*). Relevant examples are < ps- > - /s/, as in *psychology*, or < kn- > - /n/, as in *knight*. Whereas /k/ can occur before vowels (*king, castle*) and liquids (*cry, clay*) at the beginning of words in English, it is not found before other consonants that belong to the same syllable. This branch of phonology is called *phonotactics* (Greek *phon* = sound, *taxis* = order). It essentially deals with the possible combinations of consonants (so-called *consonant clusters*) at the beginning or end of a syllable or word. consonant clusters

The most general definition of the English syllable from a phonotactic point of view is the following: (CCC) V (CCCC), i. e. a syllable consists of the English syllable a vowel as core or nucleus (/aɪ/ *I, eye*), which can be preceded by up to three consonants (/spraɪ/ *spry*, /stjuː/ *stew*), and followed by up to four consonants (/teksts/ *texts*, /glɪmpst/ *glimpsed*). Impossible at the beginning of a syllable (i. e. the onset) are, for example, /ŋ/ or combinations of a semi-vowel /w, j/ or a liquid /l, r/ in initial position with other consonants; the same is true for /h, w, j/ and the RP /r/ at the end of a syllable (i. e. the coda). In general, longer consonant clusters are possible in the coda of a syllable in English than in the onset. Two types of syllables are distinguished: open syllables end in a vowel, whereas closed syllables end in a consonant.

(7)

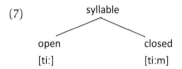

2.2.2 | Prosody: Supra-segmental phonology

Stress – rhythm – intonation: Phonology not only deals with the phoneme system of a language, and the properties and possibilities of combinations of phonemes. It also deals with phenomena like stress (or: accent), rhythm, and intonation, which all belong to the domain of prosody. Prosodic (or: supra-segmental) phonology is concerned with those phonetic features that extend over more than one phoneme (segment) and, from a functional point of view, can (and often do) make a significant contribution to meaning-making. With regard to stress, rhythm, and intonation, the most important relevant features are breath pressure (or from a perceptual point of view: loudness), length and pitch.

no general rule **Word stress:** In English, fixed word stress exists only in the sense that, apart from a few exceptions (e. g. *advertisement*), a given word is always stressed on the same syllable. There is, however, no general rule of word stress placement in English according to which, for example, the (main or primary) stress of words is generally placed on a particular syllable, e. g. the first (Finnish), the penultimate (Welsh), or the last syllable (French). Instead word stress in English varies, even though partly according to predictable principles. Here, the mixed vocabulary of English plays a major role (see chapter 3), that is the fact that, besides its inherited Germanic word stock, English also borrowed many words and word formation elements mainly from French, Latin, and Greek. Words of Germanic origin are frequently stressed on the first syllable of the root ('*father*, '*fatherly*), which is mostly not the case for polysyllabic words of French and Latin origin (*pa'ternal*). Words with particular (borrowed) endings are always stressed on the last syllable before the ending (*a'tomic, develop'mental, natio'nality*), or even on the last syllable (e. g. *-ee* in *trai'nee*).

distinctiveness
of stress **Stress shift:** Another, more important property of English on the word level is that, to varying degrees, stress alone can be distinctive. As a consequence, there are quite many minimal pairs which are based primarily

on a difference in stress placement, often in combination with changes in vowel quality in the syllables affected by this stress shift. Compare the noun/verb pairs in (8), the adjective/noun pairs or adjective/verb pairs in (9), as well as the examples in (10), where it is stress alone which distinguishes the compound nouns on the left from phrases in which an adjective precedes a noun (see also chapter 3.3.2).

(8) object N   /'ɒbdʒekt/   object V   /əb'dʒekt/
     subject N   /'sʌbdʒekt/   subject V   /səb'dʒekt/
     survey N   /'sɜ:veɪ/   survey V   /sɜ:'veɪ/
(9) content A   /kən'tent/   content N   /'kɒntənt/
     invalid A   /ɪn'vælɪd/   invalid N   /'ɪnvəlɪd/
     alternate A   /ɔ:l'tɜ:nət/ alternate V   /'ɔ:ltəneɪt/
(10) 'blackbird N   versus   'black 'bird (A + N)
     'blackboard N   versus   'black 'board (A + N)
     'English teacher N   versus   'English 'teacher (A + N)

As can be seen in the examples in (8) and (9), stress-shift typically goes hand in hand with a change of the vowel quality. In unstressed syllables, the vowel quality is reduced (or: weakened), mostly to a schwa /ə/, otherwise to /ɪ/, which is why these two are the most frequently occurring vowels in English. This phenomenon is also typical of stress in connected speech. Reduction, and in extreme cases, the total omission (elision) of vowels is found particularly frequently for function words (e. g. auxiliaries, prepositions, conjunctions, pronouns).

full vs. weakened vowel quality

Strong vs. weak forms: Especially for function words, we need to distinguish between strong and weak forms. When reading aloud *and, of* and *some* as isolated dictionary entries, they would come out as /ænd/, /ɒv/, and /sʌm/, respectively. If, however, we listen closely to how these function words are actually pronounced in spontaneous speech, the relevant transcriptions would look as follows: for *some* /səm, sm/, for *of* /əv, v/, and for *and* /ənd, ən, n/. From a phonetic perspective, function words often consist of only one syllable and are normally unstressed (in neutral, so-called unmarked, utterances). Of course, it is also possible to put heavy stress on these words, as in *Kate AND George went to the cinema*. Such cases of contrastive stress are rather the exception, though. The appropriate use of weak forms is important for natural-sounding spoken English, and has to be given special attention in the training of future teachers of English, particularly when it comes to transcriptions.

function words

Stress-timing: The reduction of unstressed syllables resulting in weak forms immediately leads to the perhaps most important property of English with regard to rhythm, namely stress-timing. This term describes the tendency of two stressed syllables in an English utterance to occur at fairly equal intervals of time, no matter how many unstressed syllables there are in between. Alternatively, this phenomenon of isochrony can be described with the help of the term *foot*.

rhythm

A foot is the basic rhythmic unit which exhibits various regular patterns of sequences of stressed and unstressed syllables. In languages dis-

isochrony & the notion of foot

playing isochrony, a foot starts out with a stressed syllable and comprises all (unstressed) syllables up to the next stressed syllable. Isochrony therefore means that in the relevant language, feet are approximately of the same length. The most important means for achieving isochrony are the lengthening of stressed syllables and, above all, the reduction of unstressed syllables. For the sentence *Kate and George went to the cinema*, uttered at normal speech speed and with an unmarked intonation contour, it would thus be claimed that the polysyllabic feet /ˈkeɪt (ə)n/, /ˈwɛnt tə ðə/, and /ˈsɪnəmə/ are about as long as the foot /ˈdʒɔːdʒ/ taken by itself:

(11)   //ˈKate and/ˈGeorge/ˈwent to the/ˈcinema//

typological
continuum **Stress-timed vs. syllable-timed languages:** What has been described concerning the intonation contour of (11) is the perceptual impression a hearer of English gets. In fact, there is a strong subjective element in this. Isochrony is not easily measurable, and even the measures which can be applied in a phonetic laboratory render only approximations, for example, when comparing different languages with each other. For this reason, the classification of languages based on this parameter into stress-timed (e. g. English, Russian, less distinctly also German), and syllable-timed languages (e. g. French, Spanish, Italian) should be taken with a pinch of salt, as a continuum rather than a clear-cut division. In syllable-timed languages, all syllables are said to occur at roughly the same intervals of time. However, all that is certain is that in such languages the syllable structure is simpler, that there is no tendency, for example, of condensing unstressed syllables (e. g. by means of reduction), and that word stress is not phonemic, thus not grammatically distinctive (i. e. there are no minimal pairs of the type 'abstract noun/adjective – ab'stract verb).

pitch movements **Intonation:** While rhythm has to do with the distribution of stressed syllables in normal speech flow, intonation (or: speech melody, pitch) relates to the distinctive use of pitch movements in an utterance and its organization into prosodic units (or: tone groups).

4 major functions **Grammatical functions:** The choice of a pitch movement fulfils a number of very important functions, especially grammatical, pragmatic, and attitudinal or emotional functions. The distinction between sentence types belongs to the grammatical functions, e. g. falling intonation in statements and exclamations (*She's a teacher*, *She's a teacher!*), and rising intonation in many interrogative sentences, notably in yes-no questions like *Is she a teacher?* or an echo question like *She's a teacher?*. The organization into prosodic units often marks syntactic units (phrases, clauses, sentences), like the difference between restrictive relative clauses (*The man who was sitting behind the driver looked out of the window*) and non-restrictive relative clauses (*The man, who was sitting behind the driver, looked out of the window*; see chapter 4.2.3). As far as grammar is concerned, intonation plays a similar role in spoken language as punctuation does in written language.

information
structuring **Pragmatic functions:** The central pragmatic function of intonation is information structuring, above all signalling the information status (new

information versus information which is old or which can reasonably be assumed to be part of the general background knowledge; see also chapter 5.2.2). This happens primarily in close interaction with the placement of the sentence stress, i.e. emphasis put on a particular syllable in an utterance. Compare *PEter lost* (as an answer to the question: *Who lost the match?*) with *Peter LOST* (as an answer to the question: *What about Peter? Did he win again?*).

Emotional and attitudinal functions: Perhaps the most important function of the various pitch movements, however, is the expression of attitudes, moods, and emotions (e.g. enthusiasm, surprise, interest, sarcasm, impatience, compassion, rage). In this respect, intonation is a much more reliable key to the speaker's true attitude to particular facts than the literal (word and sentence) meaning of what has been said. Just compare the clearly rising intonation contour in the honest praise in (12a) with the clearly falling one in the sarcastic praise in (12b). This book adopts a simplified version of transcribing intonation for didactic purposes but if you are interested in how intonation specialists transcribe aspects of intonation, you can check the references to the ToBI (Tone and Break Indices) and IViE (Intonational Variation in English) labelling guides in the further reading section at the end of this chapter. the key function of intonation

(12) a. *What a great* ^{idea}*!*   b. ^{WHAT} *a great* _{idea}*!*

Tone group: The unit of analysis in intonation research is the so-called intonation or tone group, which on the grammatical level most often corresponds to a clause or a phrase. It consists of a syllable which carries the main stress, known as the *nucleus*, and optionally of unstressed and less heavily stressed syllables preceding or following the nucleus. In (13a) the nucleus is framed exclusively by unstressed syllables, in (13b) three unstressed and two stressed syllables precede the nucleus: nucleus

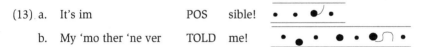

(13) a. It's im   POS   sible!

b. My 'mo ther 'ne ver   TOLD   me!

As these two examples show, the nucleus normally falls on the last stressed syllable of an intonation group, thus it is only followed by one or several unstressed syllables. An important means of signalling the boundaries of intonation groups are those pauses which coincide with syntactic units, in particular with the boundaries between clauses (*When she saw me / she left*) and between subject, predicate, and adverbial complements (*The Prime Minister of Great Britain / will soon meet the German Chancellor / at Downing Street No 10*).

Nuclear tones: We can roughly distinguish between five main nuclear tones (*nuclei*) in English (marked by means of bold type in (14)), which can again be further differentiated. The most important points in this respect are the direction of the pitch movement (fall, rise, or level), and the possibility of a further change of the pitch direction after the nucleus, which leads to complex nuclear tones (e.g. fall-rise, or rise-fall). For a 5 main nuclear tones more precise description, the onset (high, mid, or low) is specified relative to the pitch range. Each of these main nuclear tones and their variants can roughly be assigned certain properties and functions:

(14) **fall** `

high fall: contrastive sentence stress; strong emotional involvement

low fall: most neutral nucleus, e. g. in affirmative clauses; cold and distanced

full fall: emotionally involved (the higher the onset of the tone, the more involved the speaker is)

rise ´

high rise: non-emphatic *yes/no*-questions, often used in echoing what has just been said, emphatic *why*-questions; mild query or puzzlement; in spontaneous narratives, increasingly also in affirmative sentences. *So we stand there for a long time and then wander into class about five minutes late.*

low rise: enumerations, requests, incomplete utterances

full rise: emotionally involved (the lower the onset of the tone, the more involved is the speaker; 12a)

fall-rise ˇ   a strongly emotional tone; doubt, insecurity, hesitation, but also encouragement

rise-fall ^   strong emotional involvement; can express insecurity, enthusiasm, surprise, irony (12b)

level ‾   boredom, irony, sarcasm; similar to *low rise*

Intonation languages: These or similar types of nuclear tones should occur in all intonation languages (and thus essentially in all European languages). In general, the pitch contour in these languages is relevant only on the phrase and sentence level. It fulfils no distinctive function on the word level, i. e. it has no influence on the word meaning, or at least only in a relatively small number of cases (e. g. in Swedish).

Tone languages: This is different in so-called *tone languages*, which form the majority of languages in the world (e. g. in Chinese, in many South Asian and African languages) and where in many cases the pitch contour alone determines the word meaning. Thus, depending on the pitch contour, the phoneme sequence /ma/ in Mandarin Chinese can have as different meanings as, for example, 'mother' mā (high level tone) and 'horse' mǎ (falling rising tone).

2.2.3 | Phonological processes in connected speech

Spontaneous spoken language: At the end of this chapter, let us return to the weak forms of spoken English once more. They showed very clearly that it can make a big difference whether a word is pronounced by itself or as part of a phrase or whole utterance in a natural speech situation. As we have seen, vowel reduction and elision of sounds, in particular, are

typical of weak forms. There are several more such phenomena in so-
called *connected speech*, i. e. utterances which consist of more than one
word. The most important of these are assimilation, intrusion, and liaison.

Elision is the term used for the loss, or omission, of a vowel, consonant, or syllable. It is important to add that the regular omission of
post-vocalic /r/ at the end of a syllable in RP (the so-called /r/-dropping,
or absence of postvocalic /r/, in *car* or *card*) as well as the regular omission of /h/ at the beginning of a syllable in various regional accents (the
so-called /h/-dropping, e. g. in Cockney *'otel, 'is*) do not qualify as instances of elision. In both cases, the omission of the sound can already be
observed in isolated, context-free pronunciation of words, and thus does
not qualify as a phenomenon of connected speech but rather belongs to
the domain of phonotactics.

a note on elision

Assimilation: Things are completely different for assimilation. By assimilation, we understand the process by which, especially in (rapid)
spoken language, immediately neighbouring sounds become more alike
with regard to one or more articulatory features (partial assimilation in
(15a)), in extreme cases even identical (total assimilation in (15b)).

partial vs. total

(15) a.   width [wɪd̪θ], eighth [eɪt̪θ], tenth [ten̪θ], ten bikes /tem 'baɪks/
       b.   spaceship /'speɪʃʃɪp/, ten mice /tem 'maɪs/

In (15a) the first three are examples of dental allophones of the alveolar
plosives /d/, /t/ and /n/, i. e. the tongue in these examples touches the
back of the front teeth in anticipation, as it were, of the place of articulation of the following fricative. In *ten bikes* in (15a), the alveolar nasal in
ten becomes a bilabial nasal due to the following bilabial /b/ in *bikes*. In
(15b) the preceding sound even becomes completely identical to the following sound. All examples in (15) are characteristic of assimilation in
English, in so far as in the great majority of cases assimilation is regressive.

Anticipatory (or: regressive) assimilation: Alternatively, we also speak
of anticipatory assimilation, since during the articulation of the preceding
sound the speech organs already anticipate the articulation of the following sound. We are thus dealing with what is also known as *coarticulation*,
which is essentially responsible for allophony, and ultimately founded in
language economy (Least Effort Principle). On top of this, the examples
in (15a) are characteristic in the sense that in English assimilation usually
affects the place of articulation. In other words, there is a clear tendency
towards homorganic sounds.

coarticulation

Progressive and reciprocal assimilation: Besides regressive assimilation
as the prototype of assimilation, there are also the rather rare types of
progressive assimilation (/s/ to /ʃ/ in *lunch score* /'lʌntʃʃkɔː/) and reciprocal assimilation, where the two sounds concerned fuse and produce a
third one, as for example in /s/ and /j/ to /ʃ/ in *kiss you* /'kɪʃuː/, or /t/
and /j/ to /tʃ/ in *don't you* /'dəuntʃʊ/ or even *Tuesday* /'tʃuːzdeɪ/, increasingly heard in Southeast England.

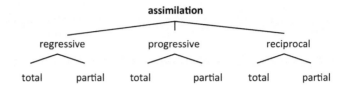

Figure 2.11:
Assimilation

Liaison and intrusion: While elision and assimilation are very wide-spread phenomena, only relatively few examples can be given for intrusion and liaison. The best-known cases of these two connected speech phenomena in English (above all in such accents as RP) are the so-called intrusive /r/ (cf. *law and order* /'lɔːᶉən(d)'ɔːdə/, *Asia and America* /'ɛɪʒəᶉən(d)'ə'mɛrɪkə/), and the so-called linking /r/ (in *My car is gone* / maɪ 'kaːᶉɪz'gɒn/). The two processes have in common that in connected speech a sound is added which is absent when the relevant word(s) is/ are pronounced in isolation. Moreover, both processes prevent the core vowels of two immediately neighbouring syllables from directly following each other. Instead, an /r/ is added to the second (normally unstressed) syllable, by means of which the utterance gains in 'fluidity'. The difference between intrusion and liaison is that in the case of intrusion, this addition is justified neither historically nor orthographically.

Checklist Phonetics and Phonology – key terms and concepts

approximant (semi-vowel / glide, liquid)
articulator (active ↔ passive)
aspiration
assimilation (regressive / anticipatory ↔ progressive ↔ reciprocal; total ↔ partial)
cardinal vowels
coarticulation
complementary distribution ↔ free variation
connected speech
consonant (obstruent ↔ sonorant; roll, lateral; fortis ↔ lenis; consonant cluster)
contrastive stress
distinctive ↔ redundant
distinctive feature
elision
foot
homorganic sound
International Phonetic Alphabet
intonation

isochrony
linking /r/ ↔ intrusive /r/
manner of articulation
minimal pair (minimal pair test)
obstruent (affricate, fricative, plosive)
phone, phoneme, allophone
phonetics (articulatory, acoustic, auditory)
phonological system
phonology (segmental ↔ supra-segmental)
phonotactics
prosody
Received Pronunciation ↔ General American
reduction
rhythm (stress-timing ↔ syllable-timing)
sonorant (liquids, nasal, roll, lateral)
stop (nasal ↔ plosive)
stress

stress-timing	velum
strong form ↔ weak form	vocal folds
syllable	vowel (short ↔ long; front ↔
tone group (nucleus)	back; monophthong, diph-
tones	thong, triphthong; tense ↔
transcription: phonetic (nar-	lax; schwa; quality ↔
row ↔ broad) ↔ phonemic	quantity)
universal	vowel chart

Exercises

1. Figures a–f illustrate six of the following places of articulation: alveolar, bilabial, dental, labio-dental, palatal, palato-alveolar, velar. You
can consult the following website for help: https://www.seeingspeech.
ac.uk. It features an interactive IPA chart with animations, MRI scans
and ultrasound.

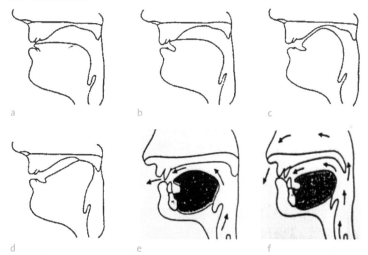

a) Identify the correct place of articulation for each of the six figures.
b) Provide for each place of articulation the phonetic symbol of two
sounds which are produced at this place.

2.

a) Provide a broad phonetic transcription of the noun *linguistics* and
describe the consonants in their order of occurrence using the following four parameters: vocal fold action, state of the soft palate,
place of articulation, manner of articulation.
b) Which of these consonants are homorganic?
c) Which of the sounds in *linguistics* are obstruents and which are
sonorants?

3.

a) Identify the vowel sound(s) in each of the following words using Wells' transcription model for RP:
fleece, kit, dress, trap, foot, lot, face, mouth

b) Classify each monophthong according to the parameters of length, lip rounding, tongue height and tongue position.

c) Classify each diphthong according to the movement of the jaw.

d) Identify which vowel is pronounced differently in RP and GA (see chapter 8, table 8.2 for help).

4.

a) Provide the phonemic symbols for those of the following descriptions that relate to sounds belonging to the sound system of RP:

a.	voiced bilabial plosive	e.	voiced velar nasal
b.	voiceless velar dental	f.	rounded high front vowel
c.	lax high back vowel	g.	voiced bilabial semi-vowel
d.	voiced dental fricative	h.	voiceless lateral fricative

b) Which description(s) is/are completely nonsensical?

5.

a) Correct the errors in the following RP transcriptions (one error per word):

leave /liːf/	flash /fleʃ/	start /stɑːrt/
bingo /ˈbɪngəʊ/	mail /mel/	other /ʌθə/
question /ˈkvestʃn/	emergency /ɪˈmɜːtʃənsɪ/	path /pæθ/

b) Which of these are errors most likely to be made by German learners of English? (More on this in chapter 5.)

6. Which of the following words would be treated as minimal pairs?
ten, live, bin, hippo, hen, tin, tale, leaf, pin, rose, lose, hippie, house, tail, tooth, smooth, love, thief

7. In each of the following groups the phonemes share one or more common properties, but in each group there is one phoneme which does not belong to the group. Identify the phoneme and specify in which respect(s) it is different from the rest of the group.
a) /f, p, m, θ, v, b/
b) /æ, uː, ɪ, e, ʊ, ə/
c) /z, v, s, ʒ, g/
d) /eɪ, aɪ, aʊ, ɔɪ, ɪə/
e) /m, n, g, d, p/
f) /l, r, w, ʒ/
g) /n, l, s, ʃ, z/
h) /ɔː, iː, ɪə, r, j, æ, l, ŋ, ɒ, aʊ/
i) /g, k, b, d, p, v, t/
j) /uː, iː, ɒ, ɔː, ɑː/

8. Which of the following statements are true, which are false?
   a) The hard palate and vocal folds are active articulators.
   b) [pʰẽn] represents a narrow phonetic transcription of *pen*.
   c) The majority of English sounds is produced with the velum raised.
   d) English lacks rounded back vowels.
   e) Liquids and semi-vowels belong to the same large class of sounds.
   f) Voiced plosives are generally aspirated in syllable-initial position.
   g) One minimal pair is sufficient for establishing two given sounds of a language as phonemes.
   h) Stress in English is phonemic.
   i) [s] and [ʃ] as realizations of the second consonant in *associate* are instances of free variation.
   j) In English stressed syllables tend to be compressed and reduced.

9. We can perceive a noticeable difference in vowel quantity in the following pairs:
   tag – tack, league – leak, rude – root, ridge – rich, ride – rite, plays – place, rib – rip, bud – but, love – laugh, use (V) - use (N)
   a) Describe this difference.
   b) Find a generalization concerning the environment which triggers this variation.

Advanced

10. We said that English has a certain rhythm.
   a) What exactly is this rhythm said to involve? Illustrate your answer with the help of the following example where stressed syllables are indicated by capitals.
   When my MOther came HOME, she WENT into the KITchen, Opened the FRIDGE and TOOK out a YOghurt.
   b) Identify the intonation units in the example above and show that in English the nucleus tends to fall on the last stressed syllable.
   c) Do you have any ideas as to the word class(es) which the word with this last stressed syllable tends to belong to? Can you make anything out of the so-called Last Lexical Item rule in English?

11. English is normally described as being a stress-timed language. However, does this apply on a global scale? Visit the *International Dialects of English Archive* (https://www.dialectsarchive.com) and listen to the sample "Italy 20". Pay special attention to how the speaker realises the vowel of *to* in *an escape point to go hiding* (03:46) in the free speech part. What do you notice?

12. Consider the realization of the negative prefix in the following words:
   inadequate /ɪn'ædɪkwət/, incomplete /ˌɪŋkəm'pliːt/, impossible /ɪm'pɒsɪb(ə)l/, immobile /ɪ'məʊbaɪl/, illegal /ɪ'liːɡəl/
   a) Which process is responsible for this variation in form?
   b) What exactly is responsible for the nasal and the following sound becoming more alike or even identical?
   c) What do the above examples have in common with the pronunciation of the vowels in *thin* [θĩn] and *thing* [θĩŋ]?

Sources and further reading

Beckman, Mary E./Gayle M. Ayers. 1994. "Guidelines for ToBI labelling." Version 2.0. URL: http://www.speech.cs.cmu.edu/tobi/ToBI.0.html.

Carr, Philip. 2013[2]. *English phonetics and phonology: An introduction*. Malden, Oxford, Chichester: Wiley-Blackwell.

Clark, John/Colin Yallop/Janet Fletcher. 2007[3]. *An introduction to phonetics and phonology*. Malden, Oxford, Carlton: Blackwell.

Collins, Beverly/Inger M. Mees/Paul Carley. 2019[4]. *Practical English phonetics and phonology: A resource book for students*. London: Routledge.

Cruttenden, Alan. 1997[2]. *Intonation*. Cambridge: Cambridge University Press.

Cruttenden, Alan. 2014[8]. *Gimson's Pronunciation of English*. London: Routledge.

Crystal, David. 2008[6]. *A dictionary of linguistics and phonetics*. Malden, Mass.: Blackwell.

Giegerich, Heinz J. 1992. *English phonology*. Cambridge: Cambridge University Press.

Gimson, Alfred C. 1996[5]. *An introduction to the pronunciation of English*. Rev. by Alan Cruttenden. London: Arnold.

Grabe, Esther. 2001. "The IViE labelling guide." Version 3. URL: http://www.phon.ox.ac.uk/files/apps/IViE/guide.html.

Gussenhoven, Carlos/Haike Jacobs. 2011[3]. *Understanding phonology*. Abingdon, UK: Routledge.

Hardcastle, William J./John Laver/Fiona Gibbon, eds. 2012[2]. *Handbook of phonetic sciences*. Oxford: Blackwell.

Ladd, Dwight Robert. 2012[2]. *Intonational phonology*. Cambridge: Cambridge University Press.

Ladefoged, Peter/Keith Johnson. 2014[7]. *A course in phonetics*. Stamford: Cengage Learning.

Lass, Roger. 1984. *Phonology: An introduction to basic concepts*. Cambridge: Cambridge University Press.

Laver, John. 1994. *Principles of phonetics*. Cambridge: Cambridge University Press.

McMahon, April. 2020[2]. *An introduction to English phonology*. Edinburgh: Edinburgh University Press.

O'Connor, Joseph D. 1988[2]. *Better English pronunciation*. Cambridge: Cambridge University Press.

Roach, Peter. 2009[4]. *English phonetics and phonology: A practical course*. Cambridge: Cambridge University Press.

Schmitt, Holger. 2011. *Phonetic transcription: From first steps to ear transcription*. Berlin: Erich Schmidt Verlag.

Scobbie, James M./Satsuki Nakai. 2018. Seeing speech: An articulatory web resource for the study of Phonetics. University of Glasgow. URL: https://www.seeingspeech.ac.uk.

Shockey, Linda. 2002. *Sound patterns of spoken English*. Oxford: Blackwell.

Upton, Clive/William A. Kretzschmar. 2017. *The Routledge dictionary of pronunciation for current English*. New York: Routledge.

Wells, John C. 1982 [1995]. *Accents of English, Vol. 1: An introduction*. Cambridge: Cambridge University Press.

Wells, John. C. 2008[3]. *Longman pronunciation dictionary*. Harlow: Longman.

Windsor Lewis, Jack. 1972. *Concise dictionary of British and American English*. London: Oxford University Press.

Zsiga, Elizabeth. 2013. *The sounds of language: An introduction to phonetics and phonology*. Chichester: John Wiley & Sons.

3 Morphology: On the structure and formation of words

Morphology is concerned with the internal structure of words and with the various processes which allow us to constantly expand the vocabulary of a language.

Morpheme: The basic morphological unit is not the word, but the morpheme (Greek *morphé* = shape, form), the smallest meaning-bearing unit of language. Thus, the word *singers* contains three morphemes: *sing*, *-er*, and *-s*. Each of these three morphemes adds to the overall meaning of *singers*: the verb *sing* makes the central contribution, while *-er* on its own means no more than 'someone who VERBs', and the *-s* merely gives grammatical information, namely plural. This simple example shows that we can distinguish between different types of morphemes. It is a widespread convention in linguistics to put morphemes in curly brackets, e. g. {SING}, {Plural}; however, most of the time this convention can be dispensed with without a loss of clarity. *(margin: definitions)*

Morphemes vs (allo-)morphs: On the level of morphology, morphemes are the exact counterpart to phonemes on the level of phonology. Just like phonemes, morphemes are abstract units which can be realized by more than one form. Just think of the plural morpheme in word forms like *kids*, *kits*, and *kisses*, where it is realized as /-z/, /-s/, and /-ız/ respectively. These concrete realizations of morphemes are called morphs, and in analogy to the allophones of a phoneme we speak of the allomorphs of a morpheme (more on this in section 3.2).

Word – word form – lexeme: The example *singers* also serves to show how important it is to deal with the term *word* in a more differentiated way. Is *singers* a different word from *singer*? No, *singers* is merely a different form, a so-called word form, of the noun *singer*. *Singer* itself, on the other hand, is not merely a word form of *sing*, but a different, new word, which has been formed by affixation of *-er* to the verb. In this case, we speak of a new lexeme with a new dictionary entry which has been created by a specific derivational process.

And what about *sing* itself: is it a word, a lexeme, or a morpheme? Three times yes: *sing* is a morpheme that can occur on its own (a so-called free morpheme); it denotes something in the extra-linguistic, i. e. real world, in this case a particular action or activity; it has an entry in the dictionary, and thus qualifies as a lexeme; and it is a word, if we adopt the prototypical use of *word* in everyday language. The example *sing* furthermore shows that words do not necessarily have an internal structure: it merely consists of one morpheme. The fact that *sing*, besides being *(margin: morphological structure ≠ syllable structure)*

J.B. Metzler © Springer-Verlag GmbH Deutschland, ein Teil von Springer Nature, 2020
B. Kortmann, *English Linguistics*, https://doi.org/10.1007/978-3-476-05678-8_3

monomorphemic, is also monosyllabic is irrelevant in this context: we need to keep syllable structure and morphological structure strictly apart. Just as monosyllabic words can consist of more than one morpheme (e. g. *sings*, *toys*, *loved*), polysyllabic words can perfectly well be monomorphemic (e. g. *finger*, *water*, *believe*). Morpheme boundaries are often not identical with syllable boundaries.

3.1 | Types of morphemes

Essentially, morphemes can be classified according to three criteria:

criteria of
classification
- autonomy
- function/meaning
- position

free vs. bound **Autonomy** relates to the question of whether a particular morpheme can occur on its own (*sing*), or whether it always needs to be attached to another morpheme (*-er*). According to this criterion we distinguish between free morphemes and bound morphemes (or: affixes).

bound
morphemes:
derivational
vs. inflectional **Function / meaning:** The all-important question in relation to the function or meaning of morphemes is whether they convey lexical or grammatical information (e. g. plural, case, tense). Depending on the answer, we distinguish between two kinds of bound morphemes: derivational and inflectional morphemes. The former create new lexemes (e. g. *-er* in *singer*, *painter*, *worker*), whereas the latter add purely grammatical information and merely produce different word forms (e. g. *-s* in *singers* or in *sings*; for more information on the English inflectional morphemes see chapter 4.1).

free morphemes:
content
vs. function words Among the free morphemes, we have to distinguish between two major groups (see also chapter 4.2): on the one hand, there are free morphemes which belong to one of the so-called lexical word classes (essentially nouns, verbs, and adjectives), and, on the other hand, there are those kinds of free morphemes which belong to one of the so-called grammatical or functional word classes (articles, pronouns, prepositions, conjunctions, auxiliaries, etc.). Lexical morphemes (or: content words) establish a relation between language and the world, among other things by denoting people and objects (nouns), actions and situations of all kinds (verbs), and properties of people and things (adjectives). Function words, on the other hand, have a mainly language-internal (grammatical) meaning.

open vs. closed
word classes **Autosemantic terms vs synsemantic terms:** The contrast between content and function words is often also described in terms of *autosemantic* vs. *synsemantic words* (Greek *autos* = 'self', *syn* = 'with, together', *semain* = 'mean'). Moreover, these two types of word classes differ with respect to two further properties. The functional (synsemantic) word classes are much smaller and largely closed, i. e. the spontaneous creation of neologisms in this area is practically impossible, and it takes considerably more time to enlarge the inventory of function words than to

coin new words in the lexical (autosemantic) word classes. Besides, function words are typically not stressed in connected speech, so that the distinction between strong and weak forms (e. g. *and* /ænd/ - /ən/, *have* /hæv/ - /həv, v/) is mainly relevant for this type of free morphemes (see chapter 2.2.2).

Within limits, all three of these differences between content and function words are also valid for derivational as opposed to inflectional affixes: the number of inflectional morphemes is very small (8), they form a closed set (adding a single new member would take many centuries) and are generally not stressed (whereas some derivational morphemes can be stressed).

Position: The third main criterion for the classification of morphemes can only be applied to bound morphemes. It refers to the position of the relevant bound morpheme relative to the modified part of the word (base, root, or stem; for definitions see below). bound morphemes: prefixes vs. suffixes

Prefix vs. suffix: If the affix precedes the base, it qualifies as a prefix (e. g. in *inadequate*, *enclose*), if it follows the base, we are dealing with a suffix (e. g. *soften*, *sings*). English prefixes are exclusively used for the derivation of new lexemes, whereas suffixes are used for both derivation and inflection.

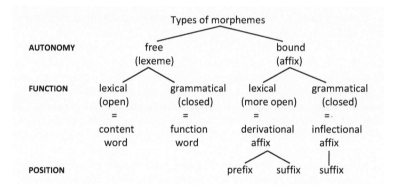

Figure 3.1: Types of morphemes

Special types of morphemes: With the help of the diagram in figure 3.1 we can capture the majority of morphemes. As always, there are a number of special cases. Among these are the following two: unique morphemes and so-called portmanteau morph(eme)s.

Portmanteau morphs: The term *portmanteau morph(eme)* goes back to Lewis Carroll, author of *Alice in Wonderland* (1865): It is used for the rather frequently occurring cases in which a particular morph instantiates more than one morpheme at the same time, i. e. has several different meanings (similar to the way in which we can put more than one piece of clothing into a *portmanteau* 'suitcase'). The /-s/ in *he sings*, for example, indicates third person, singular, present tense and indicative mood simultaneously. There are languages in which each of these four pieces of grammatical information is coded by a separate morph (see chapter 4.1). *His* is another example. Here, one morph provides three different pieces of information: possessive pronoun, masculine, and singular. The term multiple meanings mapped onto one form

non-existent in
isolation, unclear
meaning

bound roots

portmanteau morphs does not, however, apply to homonymous morphs (see chapter 6.3.3), like *-er*, which serves both as a derivational suffix deriving nouns from verbs (*sing* + *er*, *work* + *er*) and as an inflectional suffix forming the comparative of adjectives (*quick* + *er*, *fast* + *er*).

Unique morph(eme)s: Another type of morpheme, or more exactly morph, which the diagram in figure 3.1 does not capture are unique morphemes – a particular type of bound morphemes. The probably most famous examples in this context are the underlined morphemes in <u>cran</u>berry, <u>huckle</u>berry, and <u>boysen</u>berry. It is true that in all of these three cases, the second element *berry* makes clear that these nouns denote various kinds of berries. However, it remains completely unclear exactly which contribution the underlined morphemes make to the overall meaning of these three words. This is because *cran*, *huckle*, and *boysen* do not exist in isolation, that is as free morphemes; they only exist as morphemes which are attached to *berry*, and modify the latter. Their semantic contribution seems to lie merely in the distinction of these sorts of berries from others (e. g. *strawberry, gooseberry, blueberry, blackberry*).

However, although they only appear as bound morphemes, unique morphemes cannot be referred to as affixes, since the different *berry*-terms are, at least semantically, clearly compound words (see section 3.3.2). Therefore, the conclusion must be drawn that in the case of the bound morphemes in these so-called *cranberry-words* we are dealing with bound roots or bound bases.

Base – root – stem: This leads us to a last terminological question: How do we call the part of a word to which affixes are attached? Different terms are in use: *base – root – stem*. The safest, because most general term is *base* (here: $base_1$ as in 1d). For more fine-grained differentiations, the following guidelines, illustrated for the word form *removals* in (1), may serve as an orientation. What remains once all inflectional suffixes (here plural *-s*) are taken away is the stem (*removal* in 1a). What remains when taking away all affixes (*re-*, *-al* and *-s*) is the root (*move* in 1b), which is the minimal lexical unit and cannot be morphologically analysed any further. What remains if individual derivational affixes are taken away from the stem (here: *-al* from *removal*) is called the base in the narrower sense (here: $base_2$ *remov(e)* in 1c) - which is still larger than the root.

(1) a. stem: <u>removal</u>-s   b. root: re-<u>mov(e)</u>-al-s
     c. $base_2$: <u>remov(e)</u>-al   d. $base_1$: <u>removal</u>-s, <u>remov(e)</u>-al-s,
                                 re-<u>mov(e)</u>-al-s

     e. $base_1$
            stem $base_2$ root

Thus, *move* by itself can be $base_1$ (1d), root (1b), and stem (*move-s*). This applies to any inflecting monomorphemic word which also produces derived lexemes.

3.2 | Morphophonemics: Interface of morphology and phonology

Morpho(pho)nology/morphophonemics: In language, nothing happens in isolation. It is often difficult to draw neat distinctions because many things interact and move along a continuum. This is why the different levels of linguistic analysis (e. g. phonology, morphology, syntax) cannot be totally separated from one another. Rather, there are frequently areas of overlap, so-called interfaces. In this and the following chapter, we will get to know various such interfaces where two structural levels of language interact, for example the interface between morphology and syntax (chapter 4.1). At this point only the interface between morphology and phonology will be of interest, for which the following two terms are established: *morpho(pho)nology*, preferred in European linguistics, and *morphophonemics*, preferred in Anglo-American linguistics. This branch of linguistics is concerned with the systematic phonological realizations of morphemes and how they depend on their respective environments.

interfaces between structural levels of language

Conditioning of allomorphs: Just recall the distinction between morpheme and allomorph made at the beginning of this chapter. We noted that morphemes are abstract units, located on the level of the language system, or *langue*. However, on the level of language use, or *parole*, morphemes can perfectly well be instantiated by more than one morph. As an example, the plural morpheme was given with its three most frequent allomorphs /-z/, /-s/, and /-ɪz/ (*kids*, *kits*, and *kisses*). It is not by accident that precisely these three are the most frequent allomorphs of the plural morpheme – and likewise of the possessive marker (*Jill's*, *Jack's*, *Joyce's*) and the inflectional morpheme {3rd person singular present indicative} for verbs (*she runs*, *walks*, *blushes*): they are all predictable. We do not really need to learn when to use which of these three allomorphs, since the relevant allomorph arises rather naturally from the phonological environment, more exactly from the final sound of the word stem to which they attach.

Complementary distribution: The regularity underlying the complementary distribution of these three allomorphs can be described as in (2):

(2) /-ɪz/: after sibilants (or: hissing sounds), i. e. /s/, /z/, /ʃ/, /ʒ/, /tʃ/, /dʒ/
/-s/: after all other voiceless consonants, i. e. not for /s/, /ʃ/, /tʃ/
/-z/: after all other voiced consonants and all vowels (except for /z/, /ʒ/, /dʒ/)

Phonological, or regular, conditioning: All three allomorphs in (2) are phonologically conditioned. Fortunately enough, this type of regular, or rule-based, conditioning of allomorphs is the normal option for the vast majority of words. In most cases we do not have to learn the various realizations of a morpheme by heart; and even if we encounter a word that is completely new to us (e. g. invented nouns like *sloy*, *strack*, *spish*), we can fairly safely predict what its plural form will be (in our cases /slɔɪz/, /stræks/, and /spɪʃɪz/).

rule-based, predictable

unpredictable Lexical conditioning: Nevertheless there are quite a number of words in English whose plural, possessive or past tense allomorphs are not predictable, and thus have to be learnt and memorized along with the dictionary entry for the relevant lexeme. Among them are words in (partly highly) frequent use, such as nouns like *man, woman, foot* or verbs like *be, go, put, take*. This situation is referred to as *lexical conditioning*.

Two dimensions of irregularity: We can arrange the outcomes of lexical conditioning along two dimensions, or scales, which map two key aspects of morphological irregularity:

- the degree of formal dissimilarity when comparing the base to the outcome of the morphological process (essentially, the extent to which the base can still be recognized), and
- the degree, or scope, of non-productivity (the extent to which the irregularity is restricted to a small or very small group of lexemes, or even to a single lexeme).

Compare below: the plural forms *mice, wives, oxen* and *sheep*, and the past tense forms *was, went, brought, took,* and *put*.

(3)	base	plural form	not:
	mouse	mice	*mouse-s /s-ɪz/
	wife	wive-s /v-/ + /-z/	*wife-s /f-s/
	ox	ox-en /-ən/	*ox-es /-ɪz/
	sheep	sheep	*sheep-s /-s/
(4)	**base**	**past tense form**	**not:**
	be	was	*be-ed /-d/
	go	went	*go-ed /-d/
	bring	brought	*bring-ed /-d/
	take	took	*take-d /-t/
	put	put	*put(t)-ed /-ɪd/

base allomorphy vs. affix allomorphy Formal dissimilarity from base: Some of the inflected forms in (3) and (4) are still very similar to the relevant base (contrast *wives – wife, oxen – ox*) or even identical to it (*sheep – sheep, put – put*), while others are very different from it (contrast *mice – mouse, brought – bring, took – take*) or even completely unidentifiable as inflected forms of that particular base (*was – be, went – go*). So on the dimension of formal dissimilarity from the base we can arrange these inflected forms from low (in fact, zero) formal dissimilarity (*sheep, put*) to increasingly higher degrees (*oxen, wives, mice, took, brought*), placing cases like *was* or *went* at the top end, i. e. maximal formal dissimilarity from the base. In all cases of medium or high formal dissimilarity we speak of *base allomorphy*, whereas in the case of the plural allomorph /-ən/ in *oxen*, just as in all examples of regular, i. e. phonological, conditioning in (2), we speak of *suffix allomorphy* or, more generally, *affix allomorphy*.

Zero allomorphy: In principle, even cases in which a base undergoes a morphological process (e. g. plural formation) without any formal change (*one sheep – two sheep*) can be qualified as affix allomorphy due to lexical conditioning. In such cases, we also speak of a zero allomorph (Ø); as a linguistic construct, the zero allomorph belongs to the allomorphs of the plural morpheme, but with certain irregular verbs, for example, it also belongs to the allomorphs of the morphemes {Past} and {Past Participle}, e. g. in *He (had) put it there before*. As a type of irregular conditioning exhibiting absolutely no formal dissimilarity from the input base, zero allomorphy is placed at the bottom end of the dimension of formal dissimilarity from the base.

Suppletion: The situation is radically different for what is known as suppletion (Lat. *supplere* = 'substitute, fill up, make complete'). This applies to allomorphs bearing little (weak suppletion) or no resemblance (strong suppletion) to the root morpheme. Consider examples like *buy – bought, catch – caught* or *teach – taught* as instances of weak suppletion, and *good – better, bad – worse, go – went*, and *be – was* as instances of strong suppletion. On the dimension of formal dissimilarity, strong suppletion is thus on the opposite end of the spectrum as zero allomorphy.

Between the bottom end and the top end of the dimension of formal dissimilarity, the lexically conditioned allomorphs can roughly be arranged according to the following principles: instances of affix allomorphy (*sheep, oxen*) are placed at or near the bottom end, while instances of base allomorphy exhibit medium to high degrees of dissimilarity from the base. More exactly, one can say that those base allomorphs differ more strongly from their (singular, infinitival) base where the nucleus is affected (i. e. where a vowel change has taken place, as in *mice* vs. *mouse* or *took* vs. *take*) or both the nucleus and the coda (as in *brought* vs. *bring* or *taught* vs. *teach*).

Degree/scope of non-productivity: The second dimension of morphological irregularity is concerned with the question how restricted a given case of lexical conditioning is: is a certain irregular pattern truly restricted to a single lexeme, or rather to a (small) group of lexemes? For example, past tense forms like *went* or *was* are unique, no other verb in English has these past tense forms. Such cases of strong suppletion are thus at the top end of the scope of non-productivity (compare for adjectives similarly *good – better, bad – worse*). Other instances of lexical conditioning, as for example *mouse – mice*, are not unique, but there is only one more lexeme in English with a parallel way of forming the plural, namely *louse – lice*. (The historical process behind this, much more prominent in German, is known as *umlaut* or vowel mutation.) For yet other instances of lexical conditioning we may find a larger number of parallels, with group size varying nevertheless between small and very small, as illustrated for example in (5) for past tense formation:

(5)	a.	bring	/brɪŋ/	brought	/brɔːt/
		catch	/kætʃ/	caught	/kɔːt/
		teach	/tiːtʃ/	taught	/tɔːt/
	b.	take	/teɪk/	took	/tʊk/
		shake	/ʃeɪk/	shook	/ʃʊk/
		forsake	/fəˈseɪk/	forsook	/fɔˈsʊk/
	c.	weep	/wiːp/	wep-t	/wep-/ + /-t/
		sleep	/sliːp/	slep-t	/slep-/ + /-t/
		keep	/kiːp/	kep-t	/kep-/ + /-t/

strong vs. weak
verbs

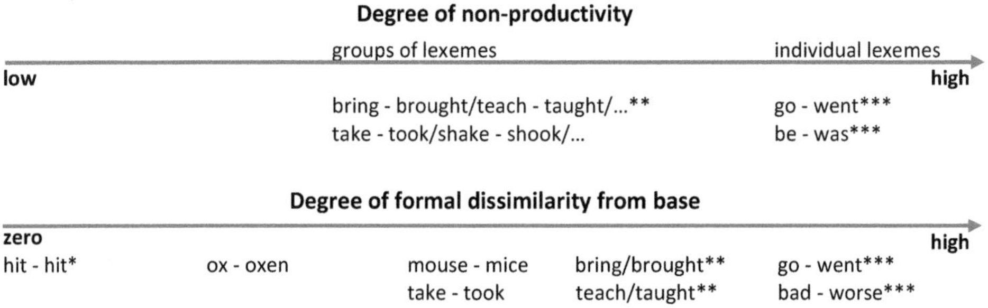

Figure 3.2:
Two dimensions of
morphological
irregularity
* zero allomorphy,
** weak supple-
tion, *** strong
suppletion

phonological
conditioning

suffix vs. prefix
allomorphy

One should not be misguided by such recurrent patterns of irregularity, though, to assume that verbs of similar phonological shape as those in (5a–c) follow the same patterns of past tense formation: just consider verbs like *reach – reached* (not: /rɔːt/), *fake – faked* (not: /fʊk/ or /fəʊk/) or *beep – beeped* (not: /bept/). Like the vast majority of verbs in English, *reach*, *beep* and *fake* are weak verbs, i. e. follow the regular pattern of forming past tense forms and past participles, whereas verbs as in (5) with irregular past tense and past participle formation are known as strong verbs. (In historical grammars of English and German, this type of morphophonemic alteration is known as *ablaut* or vowel gradation.) The group of verbs in (5c) illustrates furthermore that a given process of lexical conditioning may affect both the affix allomorph and the base.

Figure 3.2 represents the two dimensions of irregularity on which lexically conditioned allomorphs can be mapped:

Degree of non-productivity

groups of lexemes		individual lexemes
low		high
bring - brought/teach - taught/…** take - took/shake - shook/…		go - went*** be - was***

Degree of formal dissimilarity from base

zero				high
hit - hit*	ox - oxen	mouse - mice take - took	bring/brought** teach/taught**	go - went*** bad - worse***

Affix vs. base allomorphy: But let us return to phonological conditioning as the highly regular and predictable type of the conditioning of allomorphs. This kind of conditioning is of course not only found with inflectional suffixes. As was stated above, there are two types of allomorphy:

- affix allomorphy, where a particular free morpheme, i. e. base, demands the choice of a particular (form of a) bound morpheme, and
- base allomorphy, where, vice versa, a particular affix (be it derivational or inflectional) demands the choice of a particular form of the base.

The former type can be subdivided into suffix and prefix allomorphy. Exercise (12) in chapter 2, for example, dealt with a notorious case of prefix allomorphy, more exactly phonological conditioning involving the allomorphs of the derivational prefix {IN-}: /ɪn-/, /ɪŋ-/, and /ɪm-/ in *inadequate*, *incomplete*, and *impossible*. In chapter 2, we dealt with this well-known *homorganic nasal constraint* under the heading of 'assimilation'. For free morphemes, too, phonologically conditioned allomorphs may exist. This applies both to function words, like the indefinite article (unstressed *a* /ə/ or stressed *a* /eɪ/ before words that begin with a consonant, *an* /ən/ before words that begin with a vowel), and to lexical words, as in the examples in (6) and (7):

(6) electric   /ɪ'lektrɪk/   electric-ity   /ɪˌlek'trɪs-/ + /-ɪti/
    electric   /ɪ'lektrɪk/   electric-ian   /ɪˌlek'trɪʃ-/ + /-(ə)n/
    invade   /ɪn'veɪd/   invas-ive   /ɪn'veɪs-/ + /- ɪv/
    invade   /ɪn'veɪd/   invas-ion   /ɪn'veɪʒ-/ + /-(ə)n/
    part   /pɑːt/   part-ial   /pɑːʃ-/ + /-(ə)l/
    infuse   /ɪn'fjuːz/   infus-ion   /ɪn'fjuːʒ-/ + /-(ə)n/
    convulse   /kən'vʌls/   convuls-ion   /kən'vʌlʃ-/ + /-(ə)n/
(7) angel   /'eɪndʒəl/   angel-ic   /æn'dʒel-/ + /-ɪk/
    miracle   /'mɪrək(ə)l/   miracul-ous   /mɪ'ræk-/ + /-jʊləs/
    particle   /'pɑːtɪkəl/   partic-ular   /pə'tɪk-/ + /-jʊlə/
    photograph   /'fəʊtə,grɑːf/   photograph-ic   /ˌfəʊtə'græf-/ + /-ɪk/

Morphological conditioning: In all of these examples, the phonological shape of the base morpheme when used in isolation has changed with respect to one or two sounds in the course of a derivational process, i. e. the formation of a new lexeme by means of affixation (here more precisely: suffixation) of a derivational morpheme. As the forms of the base morphemes (e. g. /ɪˌlek'trɪs-/ and /ɪˌlek'trɪʃ-/ in comparison with /ɪ'lek-trɪk/) are triggered by suffixes, the relevant base allomorphs are said to be morphologically conditioned.

The reasons for these phonological changes in the base morphemes are diverse. In (6), coarticulation or progressive assimilation is responsible for the consonant change in the final sound of the base from /k, t, d, s, z/ to /s, ʃ, ʒ/ before /ɪ/ or /j/. Apart from the change /k/ to /s/, examples like those in (6) are processes of palatalization (/ʃ/ and /ʒ/ are palato-alveolar consonants). These palatalization processes are productive. Also productive are the changes affecting the base vowels in (7), which are merely a result of the stress-shift triggered by the derivational process: just recall what was said about full vowel quality in stressed syllables and vowel reduction in unstressed ones in chapter 2.2.2. While in (6) and (7) we are dealing with synchronically transparent consequences of phonetic and phonological processes, the examples in (8) go back to different historical developments of English and are no longer productive.

a variety of motivations

(8) pronounce /prə'naʊns/   pronunc-iation   /prə'nʌns-/ + /ɪ'eɪʃ(ə)n/
    profound   /prə'faʊnd/   profund-ity   /prə'fʌnd-/ + /-ɪti/
    divine   /dɪ'vaɪn/   divin-ity   /dɪ'vɪn-/ + /-ɪti/
    profane   /prə'feɪn/   profan-ity   /prə'fæn-/ + /-ɪti/
    appear   /ə'pɪə/   appar-ent   /ə'pær-/ + /-ənt/

Morphophonemic alternants: The examples in (6) to (8) once again draw our attention to a distinctive property of the English vocabulary: the frequently changing phonological form of base morphemes as a consequence of derivational or inflectional processes. For many base morphemes of English there exist so-called morphophonemic alternants, that is, formally similar allomorphs which differ from each other in at least one phoneme. The base morpheme {INVADE}, for example, has three morphophonemic alternants: /ɪn'veɪd/ in *invade*, /ɪn'veɪs/ in *invasive*, and /ɪn'veɪʒ/ in *invasion*.

3.3 | Word formation processes

Essentially, morphology comprises two branches: word formation and inflection(al morphology).

branches of morphology

- Word formation is concerned with the processes that expand the vocabulary of a language, i. e. create new lexemes, and will be our concern in the remainder of this chapter.
- Inflectional morphology, on the other hand, is concerned with the formation of word forms and with all those morphemes and processes that allow grammatical information to be coded directly on the stem, above all by means of affixation. This branch is already part of grammar and will therefore be dealt with in chapter 4.

major vs. minor word formation processes

Degrees of productivity: The word formation processes of English will be presented in two steps. Sections 3.3.1 to 3.3.3 will be concerned with the most productive word formation processes, that is with those that are responsible for the majority of neologisms. Essentially, these are derivation by prefixation (*ex-minister*) or suffixation (*friendship*), compounding (*foot + ball > football*), and conversion (*elbow > to elbow*). Among the less productive word formation processes, which are, however, constantly gaining in importance, are the various types of shortenings, like clippings (*ad < advertisement*), back-formations (*to babysit < babysitter*), blends (*brunch < breakfast + lunch*), and acronyms (*laser < lightwave amplification by stimulated emission of radiation*). These will briefly be presented in section 3.3.4.

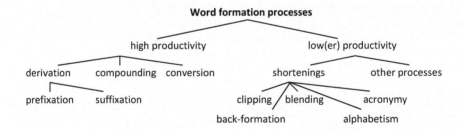

Figure 3.3: Word formation processes

Stages of a newly coined lexeme: In the remainder of this chapter we will work with examples that represent different stages of a newly coined lexeme with regard to its establishment in the vocabulary. Three such stages are widely distinguished:

- **nonce (or: ad hoc) formations**, e. g. *mega-multinationals, people-choked Tokyo, today's Warholized art world, the scientist-heroes emerging from the Coronavirus crisis*, or *the director has Gothicized the tale*, that is, formations which at least the word creator is convinced never to have heard or read before (although a model for such formations almost always exists). Due to the productive pattern, the meaning of a nonce-formation is typically largely transparent, i. e. its meaning can be deduced from the meanings of its component parts. Nonce-formations are particularly frequent in advertising and press language.
- **institutionalization**, that is, a neologism is also used by other mem-

bers of the language community. A gradual loss of transparency goes along with institutionalization, and an inclusion of the institutionalized word in one of the regularly published new editions of the dictionaries of a language.

- **lexicalization**, that is, the stage in which it is no longer possible for a lexeme to have been formed according to the productive rules of a language. Phonological lexicalization, for example, is present in (6), morphological lexicalization in *length* (< *long* + *th*) and *breadth* (< *broad* + *th*), and semantic lexicalization (and to a large extent a loss of transparency) in *understand* and *blackhead*.

3.3.1 | Derivation

We can distinguish between two major types of derivation – prefixation and suffixation – depending on whether the derivational affix is a prefix (*a-*, *auto-*, *co-*, *ex-*, *semi-*, *sub-*, *super-*, etc.) or a suffix (*-er*, *-ish*, *-ize*, *-ion*, *-ity*, *-ness*, etc.). In English, there are several interesting differences between these two derivational processes. They can be reduced to the following generalization: suffixation often involves more than just the formation of a new lexeme with a meaning different from that of the base.

Suffixation: The lexeme formed by suffixation frequently differs from the base both grammatically, that is with respect to its word-class membership, and phonologically. Just recall the examples in (6–8): in all these cases, suffixation (by, note, vowel-initial, never consonant-initial derivational suffixes) has led to a change of the phonological shape of the base, partly in combination with or as a consequence of a shift of the main stress, triggered by the derivational suffix. Moreover, there is a change of word class in examples (6–8). Together with some further examples, this is illustrated in Table 3.1:

two major types of derivation

	> noun	> adjective	> verb
noun		part-ial	woman-ize
		partic-ular	class-ify
		fashion-able	haste-n
		boy-ish	orchestr-ate
		clue-less	
adjective	electric-ity		modern-ize
	tough-ness		pur-ify
	free-dom		activ-ate
	social-ist		black-en
	warm-th		
verb	infus-ion	invas-ive	
	pronunc-iation	hope-ful	
	develop-ment	hope-less	
	employ-er	drink-able	
	employ-ee	frighten-ing	

Table 3.1:
Derivational suffixes changing word class

Word-class changing derivational suffixes: Among the word-class changing derivational suffixes, those forming nouns and adjectives constitute the two major groups. As for verb-forming suffixes, English possesses only a handful (*-ize, -ify, -en, -ate*). Of these, it is largely only the first two which are still productive. The best-known adverb-forming derivational suffix is of course *-ly*, which forms adverbs from adjectives (*quickly, strongly, hiply* 'in a hip manner'). Other adverb-forming suffixes include, for instance, *-wards* (*earthwards, northwards*) and the highly fashionable suffix *-wise*, which forms adverbs from nouns (*weatherwise, moneywise, taxwise, theatrewise, holidaywise*, etc.). Very similar to their German counterparts in *-mäßig* (*wettermäßig, gehaltsmäßig, sportmäßig, studienmäßig*, etc.), which also means 'with regard to X' or 'as far as X is concerned', the relevant adverbs often qualify as nonce-formations, whose productivity is nearly unlimited.

Word-class maintaining derivational suffixes: Not all derivational suffixes trigger a word-class change. As the examples in (9) show, nouns can frequently be formed from other nouns, and – even though only in relatively few cases – adjectives from other adjectives. There are, however, no derivational suffixes in English which form verbs from verbs:

(9) a. noun > noun: tutor-ial, music-ian, orphan-age, doctor-ate,
              host-ess, child-hood, king-dom, pig-let
     b. adj > adj: historic-al, green-ish, good-ly

Prefixation: What is exceptional for suffixes, namely examples like those in (9), is the rule for prefixes: they neither trigger a change of word-class membership, nor a phonological change of the base, be it in the form of a morphophonemic alternation or a shift of the main accent. There are only few exceptions to this generalization. A selection of prefixes that can bring about a change of word-class membership (more precisely: that can form verbs from nouns and, in some cases, also from adjectives) is given in (10) and (11):

(10) always change the word class:
      be-:   befriend, bedevil, bewitch, behead; belittle
      en-:   enjoy, enlist, enslave; enlarge, enrich
(11) sometimes change the word class:
      de-:   debone, defrost, dethrone
      dis-:   discourage, discolour, disillusion

most productive
affixes = non-
Germanic

Borrowed affixes: An important property of the English language in the domain of derivation is the fact that most productive affixes are not of Germanic origin, but of Romance (that is, Latin and French) or Greek origin. This property neatly fits the characterization of English as the prototype of a language with a 'mixed' vocabulary, that is, with an unusually high percentage of loan words and borrowed word-formation elements. But in this respect, too, prefixes and suffixes differ: While most prefixes of non-Germanic origin can be attached to any base, there is a much greater number of elements among the corresponding suffixes which can only be attached to bases of Latin or Greek origin (e. g. *-ity* or *-al*):

(12)   *mind – mental* (not: **mindal*), *nose – nasal* (not: **nosal*)

definition

Types of blocking: Derivation also serves to identify the limits of the seemingly unlimited possibilities of word formation. In particular, various types of blocking need to be mentioned at this point. By blocking we understand cases in which, due to the existence of another word, a new, mostly (more) complex word either is not formed at all or, as a consequence of low acceptance, is hardly used and in any event will not be institutionalized. Thus, in spite of the extremely high productivity of the nominal suffix *-er* in English (*singer*, *worker*, *writer*), we do not, for instance, find the lexeme **stealer*, because this slot is already taken by *thief*. There is also no reason to form the nouns **longness* or **warmness* by means of the nominal suffix *-ness* (*cleverness*, *thickness*, *thinness*), as the relevant meanings are already expressed by the lexicalized forms *length* and *warmth* (whereas there is no **thickth* or **thinth*). However, blocking can also be due to particular phonological, morphological, or semantic properties of an existing word.

Phonological blocking: The fact, for example, that there is no productive derivation of adverbs by means of *-ly* from adjectives like *friendly*, *stately*, or *miserly* (more exactly: that this process stopped being productive in the 18th century) is most probably due to their ending in *-ly*, which would lead to such tongue twisters as **friendlily* or **miserlily*. This is a case of phonological blocking.

Morphological blocking: Or let us consider the following situation: two of the suffixes for the formation of abstract nouns, *-ity* and *-dom*, are practically in complementary distribution, with *-ity* attaching almost exclusively to bases of Latin origin and *-dom* (nearly as consistently) attaching only to bases of Germanic origin. This is a case of morphological blocking.

Semantic blocking: Finally, why is it that words like *unhappy*, *unwell* or *unoptimistic* do exist, but **unsad*, **unill*, or **unpessimistic* do not? This results from the fact that the negation prefix *un-* only attaches to those adjectives of a pair of opposites (so-called antonyms; see chapter 6.3.2) which have, in the broadest sense, a positive meaning. In other words, this is an instance of semantic blocking.

3.3.2 | Compounding

definition

In terms of productivity, the only word-formation process playing in the same league as derivation is compounding, i. e. the stringing together of two or more free morphemes to one complex lexeme, the compound. The prototype of an English compound can be characterized with the help of the examples in (13):

(13)   daylight, fingertip, girlfriend, waterbed, deathbed, bedroom, legroom, cowboy, game show, wallpaper, term paper, computer nerd

N + N = proto-
typical English
compound

Endocentric compounds: The prototypical English compound is a noun consisting of two nouns, with the first modifying the second. From a semantic point of view, this modifier-head (or *determinans-determinatum*) structure of compounds results in the fact that they mostly refer to something which is a special case or a subset of what is denoted by the head (e. g. a waterbed is a particular type of bed). A compound of this semantic type is called *endocentric* (or: determinative). Another characteristic of the majority of compounds is that their meaning cannot be fully deduced from the meanings of their parts, which means that they are, to varying degrees, lexicalized (contrast, for example, *bedroom* and *leg-room*, or *wallpaper* and *term paper*).

rightmost free
morpheme = head

Syntactic types: Of course, there are also many compounds which do not correspond to this prototype. Table 3.2 gives some examples both of non-nominal compounds (i. e. those which are, for example, adjectives or, though a much rarer type, verbs) and of nominal compounds which are not made up of two nouns. In the case of the latter, as is generally the case with compounds consisting of free morphemes belonging to different word classes, it is usually the last free morpheme which determines the word class of the compound. Thus, the rightmost free morpheme qualifies as the head also from a grammatical point of view:

		noun	adjective	verb[*]
noun		(13)	waterproof	proofread
			knee-deep	gatecrash
		PROTOTYPE	sky-high	babysit
			airsick	tailor-fit
			scandal-weary	day-dream
adjective		small talk	deaf mute	fine-tune
		deadline	ready-made	double-book
		wild card	far-fetched	free associate
		greenhouse	short-sighted	short-list
verb		talk show	fail-safe	sleepwalk
		playboy	?	freeze-dry
		cry-baby		
		cutthroat		
		pickpocket		

Table 3.2:
Types of com-
pounds with
regard to word
classes and com-
binations of word
classes

[*] The vast majority of verbal compounds have not been formed by compounding, but by back-formation or conversion from nominal compounds (e. g. to *babysit* < *babysitter/babysitting* or to *short-list* < *shortlist*). Thus they should rather be called *pseudo-compounds* (for more details see below and section 3.3.4).

Semantic types: As far as the semantic classification of compounds is concerned, there are three other types besides endocentric compounds:

(14) a. **endocentric compounds** (A + B denotes a special kind of B): *darkroom, small talk*; for more examples see (13)
   b. **exocentric compounds** (A + B denotes a special kind of an unexpressed semantic head, e. g. 'person' in the case of *skin-head* or *paleface*; these compounds often have metonymic character, when one part stands for the whole, e. g. *paleface* for 'a person with a pale face', *egghead, blockhead, blackhead, birdbrain, redneck, greenback, paperback*
   c. **appositional compounds** (A and B provide different descriptions for the same referent): *actor-director, actor-manager, writer-director, singer-songwriter, poet-translator, maidservant*
   d. **copulative compounds** (A + B denotes 'the sum' of what A and B denote, i. e. the denotation of a copulative compound would be incomplete with one of the two elements A and B missing): *spacetime, tractor-trailer, Alsace-Lorraine, deaf mute, sleepwalk, freeze-dry*

Irrelevance of spelling for word status in English: From a contrastive perspective, endocentric compounds consisting of two nouns in English and German differ only in one respect, which leads us back to the discussion at the beginning of the chapter on how to define a word. Unlike in German, whether a string of free morphemes is written together or separately tells us relatively little about its word status in English. Consider the example of *word formation* with its alternative writings *word-formation* and *wordformation*. Whether written as separate words or not, whether with or without a hyphen, in all three cases we are dealing with the translation of the German compound *Wortbildung*. Likewise a string of words written together without a hyphen does not indicate a higher degree of lexicalization than if it were written with a hyphen, nor does the latter indicate a higher degree of lexicalization than a spelling as two separate words. So there it is again: our problem of how to define a word, which now, however, can be solved relatively easily. It is true that cases like *word formation, wallpaper*, or *small talk* consist of free morphemes, but each of them forms a lexeme.

> English vs. German compounds

Compound or phrase? What is more difficult to resolve is the problem of how, especially in spoken language, we should distinguish compounds as in (15a) from syntactic phrases in (15b):

(15) a. blackbird, darkroom, small talk, short story, no ball, yes-man
   b. black bird, dark room, small talk, short story, no ball, yes man

The examples in (15) show that this problem especially arises with nominal compounds which have an adjective as their first element. It is, however, not restricted to this kind of compound. Just consider *no ball*, a term taken from the world of cricket, and the opportunistic *yes-man* and his notorious *yes-man behaviour*. Nevertheless, the following guidelines should take care of most problems of this kind:

guidelines

- Compounds usually have only one main stress, namely on the first (or: left-hand) element (*a SHORT story* versus *a short STORY*).
- Compounds are not separable (cf. *a vivid SHORT story*, but not **a SHORT vivid story* as opposed to *a vivid short STORY* or *a short vivid STORY*).
- Compounds do not allow modification of their first element (**a very SHORT story*).
- Compounds are not fully compositional, that is, their meaning can not, or at least not completely, be deduced from the meanings of their component parts (see chapter 6.1); thus, they show different degrees of (semantic) lexicalization.

Hybrid formations and neoclassical compounds: A type of compound which is extremely frequent not only in English but also in other languages are so-called *hybrid formations*. These are compounds whose component elements stem from different languages, e. g. *bureaucracy* (*bureau-* French, *-cracy* Greek), or *spinmeister* (*spin-* English, *-meister* German). Since many of these elements (so-called combining forms) stem from Latin or Greek, the corresponding compounds are also called neo-classical compounds. The great frequency of formations like those in (16) fits the overall picture of English as a language with a mixed vocabulary:

(16) Anglophone, astronaut, barometer, biography, ecosystem, holograph, Francophile, psychoanalysis, technophobia, television, sociolinguistics

from free > bound
morpheme

Compounding ↔ derivation: Here we enter the transitional area of composition and derivation. Incidentally, these two major word-formation processes are also linked historically by the fact that there are cases in which a formerly free morpheme has developed from the element of a compound into a derivational affix. Well-known examples are *-hood* (< OE noun *had* 'state, quality'), *-dom* (< OE noun *dōm* 'verdict, jurisdiction'), *-ly* (< OE noun *līć* 'body'), and *-wise* (< noun 'manner'). Some people think that *man* is currently undergoing such a development, and that it develops an additional use as suffix-like word-formation element (semi-suffix or suffixoid). Take, for example, the nouns *walkman* or *discman*, two portable audio-devices for listening to cassette tapes and compact discs which were highly popular in the 1980s and 1990s: here the allomorph of *man* is not /mæn/, but /mən/; the plural is mostly formed according to the regular model for English nouns (*walkmans*, *discmans*); and, finally, the semantic features [+ ANIMATED], [+ HUMAN], [+ MALE], [+ ADULT] can no longer be attributed to *man* in *walkman* or *discman*.

very rare: bound
> free morpheme

Much more unusual is the reverse development, that is, from a bound to a free morpheme. This can perhaps be claimed for *burger*, which does not only appear in all kinds of variants in analogy to *hamburger* (*cheeseburger, fish burger, black bean burger, veggie burger, muesliburger, nut-*

burger, etc.), but meanwhile also as an independent lexeme (e. g. in *Do they sell burgers?*), and as the first element in such compounds as *burger restaurant* or *burger bar*.

3.3.3 | Conversion

While derivation and compounding have been the most productive word-formation processes since Old English, *conversion* has turned into a major word-formation process since Middle English (i. e. roughly since the 12th century) and particularly since Early Modern English (roughly since the 16th century).

By conversion, we understand the derivation of a new lexeme from an existing one without a specific morphological marker indicating the change of word class and meaning. (The term *zero-derivation* is sometimes used alternatively, reminding us of the theoretical construct of the zero-morph(eme), only that in the context of conversion it has the function of a derivational affix.) In other words: without any overt changes, a free morpheme develops an additional usage as a member of a different word class that can be used in entirely new syntactic contexts, meriting a new dictionary entry.

Productivity: In principle, there are hardly any limits to conversion in English (e. g. *no more ifs and buts, this is a must, to up the prices, to down a beer*); however, the three word-class changes in (17) to (19) are by far the most productive ones:

(17) **noun > verb:** bottle, butter, bicycle, carpet, father, knife, mother, mail, queue, ship, shoulder

(18) **adjective > verb:** better, calm, dirty, dry, empty, faint, idle, open, pale, right, total, wrong

(19) **verb > noun:** cough, cover, desire, doubt, guess, love, rise, smell, smile, spy, turn, want

Verbs are especially likely to be formed with the help of conversion. Verb > noun conversion is clearly rarer than conversion in the opposite direction. English thereby compensates for the fact that it can hardly form denominal verbs by derivation; the only productive derivational suffixes English has at its disposal for this purpose are *-ify* (*beautify, codify*) and *-ize* (*sympathize, containerize*).

Much less frequent among the productive conversion processes is conversion from an adjective to a noun. As many of the examples in (20) show, this is only possible in a particular syntactic environment. Many of these de-adjectival nouns are formed by omitting the head of a phrase consisting of article, adjective and noun (*a daily newspaper > a daily, a regular customer > a regular, the poor people > the poor*).

(20) **adjective > noun:** a (pint of) bitter, a crazy, a final, a gay, a natural, a red, a regular, a wet, a daily/weekly/monthly/etc., the poor, the rich

Margin notes:
productive since medieval times

definition

conversion to verbs

adjective > noun

interface with
syntax

Word-class internal conversion: Once again, this leads us to a transitional area of word formation and syntax. In fact, there are quite a number of further examples where conversion rather ought to be considered as the result of a syntactic process. This is particularly the case with word-class internal conversion, e. g. when non-count or mass nouns are used as count nouns (*beer* > *two beers, coffee* > *two coffees*), or non-gradable adjectives as gradable ones (*English* > *to look very English*). A type of conversion which is particularly interesting in this context is the one illustrated in (21). There are many cases in English where a verb which originally could not take a direct object (i. e. an intransitive verb) developed an additional transitive usage (21a), or vice versa, as in (21b), an originally transitive verb is used intransitively (see also various sections in chapters 4 and 5).

(21) a. **intransitive > transitive verbs:** march > to march the prisoners, run > run a horse in the Derby, stand > to stand the bank robbers against the wall

   b. **transitive > intransitive verbs:** read > the book reads well, scare > I don't scare easily

Partial conversion: There are also cases of so-called partial conversion, where the change of word class is not accompanied by a morphological, but by a phonological change. Thus, the word-final sounds change from voiceless to voiced fricatives in cases like those in (22a), or the main accent is shifted leftwards in cases as those in (22b) or (22c). The word-formation model in (22a) is no longer productive.

(22) a. the belief /f/ - to believe /v/, the use /s/ - to use /z/, the mouth /θ/ - to mouth /ð/

   b. to subJECT – the SUBject, to abSTRACT – the ABstract, to inSERT – the INsert

   c. to sit UP – SIT-ups, to take OFF – ready for TAKE-off, to show OFF – SHOW-off

The different types of conversion are summarized in (23):

(23)

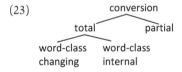

Direction of conversion: Especially in view of the prototypical examples of conversion, i. e. instances of total conversion as in (17) to (19), the question naturally arises as to how we know which direction the word-class change has taken. This question cannot be answered definitively in all cases. However, sometimes certain formal features indicate the direction, e. g. typical noun endings of verbs are a rather clear indication of noun > verb conversion:

(24) a. -eer: to pioneer, to mountaineer
    b. -or: to (co-)author, to doctor
    c. -ure: to lecture, to gesture
    d. -ion: to commission, to requisition, to vacation

Logical-semantic relationship: Where formal indications are missing, para-phrasing the word meanings often helps determine the direction of con-version. Thus, probably no one will question the nominal origin of any of the verbs in (17) or the following verbs: consider *to wolf* in *He wolfed his meal down*, the verb *to footnote*, or verbs derived from parts of the body like *head, face, eye, mouth, shoulder, elbow, hand, finger, foot (the bill)*. Similarly obvious is the direction of conversion for the verbs in (18) and, after a little more reflection, for the nouns in (19). Of primary importance for determining the direction of conversion is not a chronology of the 'conversion history' of a word, as we only find it for a minority of cases in a historical dictionary like the *Oxford English Dictionary* (OED). Most important in this respect is rather the logical-semantic relationship be-tween the original and the derived word, but frequency (derived forms are usually less frequent than base forms) and inflectional behaviour (de-rived forms usually follow the regular inflectional paradigm) are also rel-evant indicators.

English as a language type: The great productivity of conversion is one of the characteristic features of the English language. This is related to the morphological language type English represents. Unlike Latin, Russian, German or even Old English, contemporary English has very few inflec-tional endings and thus qualifies as a highly analytical or isolating lan-guage (see chapter 4.1). English has undergone a radical typological change during and after the Middle English period. This change and its consequences for the structure of modern English – especially in compar-ison with German – will be addressed on several occasions in this book.

highly analytical

3.3.4 | Shortenings

The majority of word-formation processes which are much less produc-tive (but constantly gaining ground) have one feature in common: their output is shorter than their input. Among these shortenings we can dis-tinguish five groups.

5 groups

Clippings (or: abbreviations): The first group is illustrated in (25):

(25) a. ad, bike, cig, deli (< delicatessen), exam, gas, gym, lab, log
       (< logbook), mike (< microphone), porn, prof, pub, typo
       (< typographic error); hi-fi (< high fidelity), sci-fi (< science
       fiction)
    b. bus (< omnibus), Net (< Internet), phone (< telephone),
       plane (< airplane)
    c. flu (< influenza), fridge (< refrigerator), jams (< pyjamas),
       tec (< detective)

These are all instances of clippings (or: abbreviations), where part of a word, usually the final part (25a), is omitted. Only rarely is a lexeme shortened at the beginning (25b), or at the beginning and the end (25c). Many of these clippings are of a rather colloquial nature.

Blends: In the three following types of shortenings, two or more words are affected. In the case of blends, two words are blended, typically the initial part of the first word and the final part of the second word (26a). There are also blends, however, where one (26b) or both of the underlying bases (26c) remain intact:

(26) a. brunch (< breakfast + lunch), chunnel (< channel + tunnel), fanzine (< fanatic + magazine), infotainment (< information + entertainment), motel (< motor + hotel), saunarium (< sauna + solarium), shoat (< sheep + goat), smog (< smoke + fog), vocktail (< virtual cocktail)
b. blog (< web + log), breathalyze (< breath + analyse), mor(pho)phonology, paratroops (< parachute + troops), rockumentary (< rock + documentary), vlog (< video + blog), webinar (< web + seminar)
c. slanguage (< slang + language), wargasm (< war + orgasm)

Acronyms and alphabetisms: Particularly popular in professional jargon (e. g. politics, military, economy, computer sciences) are so-called *initialisms*, which can be subdivided into the two classes of acronyms and alphabetisms. In both cases, a new term is formed from the initial letters of several words or, in the case of compounds, component parts of words. For acronyms, this term is also pronounced like a word (27), while alphabetisms are pronounced letter by letter (28):

(27) a. laser (Lightwave Amplification by Stimulated Emission of Radiation), radar (RAdio Detecting And Ranging), asap (As Soon As Possible), QANTAS (Queensland And Northern Territory Aerial Service)
b. UNESCO (United Nations Educational, Scientific, and Cultural Organization), UNICEF (United Nations International Children's Endowment Fund), OPEC (Oil Producing and Exporting Countries), NAFTA (North American Free Trade Association), GATT (General Agreement on Tariffs and Trade)
c. NATO (North Atlantic Treaty Organization), START (Strategic Arms Reduction Talks), SALT (Strategic Arms Limitations Talks)
d. BASIC (Beginners' All-purpose Symbolic Instruction Code), ASCII (American Standard Code for Information Interchange), DOS (Disk Operating System), RAM (Random Access Memory), ROM (Read Only Memory), WYSIWYG (What You See Is What You Get)

e. ERASMUS (EuRopean Action Scheme for the Mobility of University Students), TESOL (Teaching English to Speakers of Other Languages), TOEFL (Test of English as a Foreign Language), COBUILD (COllins Birmingham University International Language Database), DARE (Dictionary of American Regional English), eWAVE (electronic World Atlas of Varieties of English), WALS (World Atlas of Language Structures)

(28) a. TV, CD, LP, DJ, PC (Personal Computer, but also Political Correctness), VIP, USA, UK, LA (Los Angeles), UCLA (University of California at Los Angeles), ABC, BBC, CBS, CNN

b. OED (Oxford English Dictionary), BNC (British National Corpus), IPA (International Phonetic Association/Alphabet)

Small letters in acronyms often indicate that this term has made it into the general vocabulary, i. e. has reached a higher degree of institutionalization (*laser, radar, yuppy* (*Young Urban Professional*), or *dink(y)* (*Double Income No Kids*)). By far the greatest number of acronyms and alphabetisms, however, can be found in special dictionaries, often compiled for particular subject areas.

All shortening processes presented so far have three things in common. They involve neither a change of word class nor of meaning, and they can be motivated by language economy.

shared properties of shortenings

Back-formations: This is different for the fifth and last type of shortenings, so-called back-formations, as illustrated in (29):

(29) a. edit < editor, commentate < commentator, burgle < burglar, peddle < peddler, scavenge < scavenger, lase < laser, ush < usher

b. donate < donation, relate < relation, televize < television, intuit < intuition, attrit < attrition; enthuse < enthusiasm

c. contracept < contraception, self-destruct < self-destruction

d. babysit, window-shop, day-dream, sleepwalk, brainwash, headhunt, hangglide, stage-manage, chain-smoke, lip-read, sightsee, mindmelt

Back-formations result from taking away a real or putative derivational suffix. The output of this process, however, is a root or base morpheme which did not exist prior to the longer form. This runs counter to our expectations. After all, if there are derivational processes like *sing + er > singer, inspect + or > inspector*, or *inflate + ion > inflation, insert + ion > insertion*, why should *editor* not originate from *edit*, or *donation* from *donate*? Thus, back-formations demonstrate two things very nicely: first, that the members of a language community have internalized productive word-formation rules; and second, the power of analogy, which is one of the most important processes and driving forces of language change, leading to greater regularity in language.

power of analogy

Not all back-formations, however, result from the reversal of a derivational process. If this was the case, the 'back-formed' verbs in (29c) would have to read as follows: **contraceive* (model *deceive > deception*)

largest group: verbs

and *self-destroy (model *destroy* > *destruction*). As the examples in (29) clearly show, by far the largest group among back-formations are verbs which have developed out of nouns. This goes particularly for so-called 'pseudo compounds' as in (29d), which have been back-formed from nominal compounds (*babysit* < *babysitter*). But among back-formations there are also cases like those in (30):

(30) a. verb < adjective: laze < lazy, funk < funky, underdevelop < underdeveloped

b. adjective < noun: surreal < surrealism, autoimmune < autoimmunization

c. noun < adjective: paramedic < paramedical, paraphysics < paraphysical

d. noun < noun: bioengineer < bioengineering, aptitude < inaptitude

Figure 3.4:
Shortenings

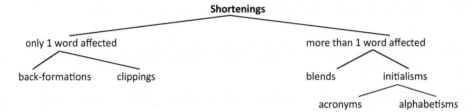

least productive of all **Coinage:** Finally, let us look at some examples of *coinage*, a word-formation process which does not belong to the group of shortenings, and is by far the least productive of all word-formation processes dealt with in this chapter:

(31) sandwich, Kleenex, watt, (to) hoover, (to) xerox, (to) boycott, (to) lynch

In all the examples in (31) a proper name has developed into a lexeme – thus the terms *words-from-names* or *coinage*. Either the name of a person (*sandwich, watt, lynch, boycott*) is used to denote an object, idea, activity, etc. which is linked to that person (cf. in German *röntgen, Röntgenstrahlen, Litfasssäule*), or a company or brand name is used to denote a particular product. German readers just need to think of everyday examples like *Tesa* instead of 'Klebestreifen', and *Tempo* instead of 'Papiertaschentuch' in questions of the type "Have you got a _____ ?". Such neologisms can quickly then be used as input for further word-formation processes, e. g. conversion (*sandwich* > *to sandwich, hoover* > *to hoover, xerox* > *to xerox, Google* > *to google*), compounding (*lynch law, sandwich board, sandwich course*), or clipping (*ampere* > *amp, wellington boots* > *wellies*).

Multiple word-formation processes involved: In general, we should not forget that there is often more than one word-formation process involved in the formation of many lexemes, e. g. compounding and conversion in *to kneecap*, or compounding, clipping, and derivation in *sitcomy* (e. g. in a phrase like *a sitcomy movie*). Thus, many neologisms are the result of different word-formation processes taking place one after the other.

Checklist Morphology – key terms and concepts

ablaut/vowel gradation
affix (prefix ↔ suffix;
    derivational morpheme ↔
inflectional morpheme)
allomorphy (affix ↔ base)
base ↔ root ↔ stem
blocking (phonological,
    morphological, semantic)
coinage
complementary distribution
compounding; compound
    (endocentric ↔ exocentric,
    appositional, copulative
    compound; hybrid forma-
    tion / neo-classical com-
    pound; combining forms;
    modifier-head-structure)
conditioning of allomorphs
    (phonological, lexical, mor-
    phological, dimensions)
conversion (total ↔ partial;
    word-class internal)
derivation (prefixation ↔
    suffixation)
free morpheme ↔ bound
    morpheme
head
institutionalization

irregularity (formal dissimi-
    larity, non-productivity)
lexeme ↔ word-form
lexicalization
lexical word-classes (autose-
    mantic terms) ↔ functional
    word-classes (synsemantic
    terms)
"mixed" vocabulary
morph, allomorph
morpheme (free ↔ bound,
    derivational ↔ inflectional)
morphophonemic alternant
morphophonology / morpho-
    phonemics
neologism
nonce formation
portmanteau morph(eme)
shortening (clipping, blend,
    initialism, acronym, alpha-
    betism, back-formation)
suppletion (strong ↔ weak)
transparency
umlaut/vowel mutation
unique morpheme
verbs (strong ↔ weak)
zero (allo)morph

Exercises

1. Fill in the blanks:
A morpheme is defined as the smallest ....-bearing unit of language. .... morphemes, for instance, add only grammatical
meaning to the stem they are attached to. They create a new word-
...... (or: token). Lexical information, on the other hand, is added by
.... morphemes. The result of this kind of ....ation is a new
lexeme (or: type). Analogous to phonemes, which may be realized by
a set of ...., called ...., there may be more than one ....
which instantiates a given morpheme. These are called the ....
of the relevant morpheme and are normally .... conditioned.

2.

a) Give a morphological analysis of *formalities* and *inconclusiveness*.
Make use of the terms *base, root* and *stem*.
b) Give all morphophonemic alternants of the following free morphemes:
{APPEAR} {LONG} {PHYSIC} {USE} {THIEF} {PHOTOGRAPH}

3. Give an account of the morphological status of *-en* on the basis of the
following lexemes: *earthen, wooden, widen, sweeten, deafen, oxen,
silken.*

4. By means of which word formation processes do we arrive at the
following lexemes? (When two or more word-formation processes are
involved specify their order.)

to enthuse	laptop	judgmental	to breathalyze
to netsurf	campaigner	modem	sitcomy
language lab	rockumentary	sexist	weatherwise
infotainment	neocolonialism	exec	

5. This question is concerned with the dominant types of English compounds in terms of (i) grammatical word-class of the compound, (ii)
grammatical word-classes of the elements of nominal compounds,
(iii) the logical-semantic relation between the elements of nominal
compounds, and (iv) the internal structure of compounds in terms of
head and modifier. Consider the groups of compounds in (a–d) below
with respect to (i–iv), respectively. In each group there is **only one**
compound which represents the dominant type. Identify this compound:
(a)   *classroom, overeducate, leadfree, whenever*
(b)   *pickpocket, doormat, breakfast, bluebell*
(c)   *paperback, actor-manager, flower-pot, Alsace-Lorraine*
(d)   *Secretary-General, motor-car, court martial, poet laureate*

6.

    a) Identify all lexemes with prefixes exhibiting atypical properties from a grammatical point of view (hint: think of word classes)
counterintuitive aloud bewitch international empower encode miniskirt rebuild debark discourage archbishop

    b) Give a morphological analysis of the following lexemes and identify the meanings of {-ISH}:
childish greenish feverish punish eightish foolish

7. Reconstruct the word-formation "stories" of the lexemes in bold print in (a–g) by identifying the corresponding sequence of word-formation processes from the set in (I–VII).

    a.   rap music > rap > to rap > **rapper**
    b.   rehabilitation > rehab > **to rehab**
    c.   vacuum cleaner > to vacuum-clean > **to vacuum**
    d.   campaign > to campaign > **campaigner**
    e.   tailor-fit > **to tailor-fit**
    f.   breathalyser > **to breathalyse**
    g.   brunch > **to brunch**

    I.   conversion – derivation
    II.   blend – conversion
    III.   compounding – clipping – conversion – derivation
    IV.   derivation – clipping – conversion
    V.   blend – back-formation
    VI.   compounding – back-formation – clipping
    VII.   compounding – conversion

8. Which of the following statements are true and which are false?

    a) English has more derivational than inflectional morphemes.
    b) Derivational morphemes produce word-forms of a single lexeme.
    c) *Enslave* and *enshrine,* on the one hand, and *empower* and *embitter,* on the other hand, illustrate the phenomenon of lexically conditioned prefix allomorphy.
    d) English has no inflectional prefixes.
    e) Any monomorphemic English word will also be monosyllabic.
    f) /ɪz/ in English /ɒksɪz/ is a phonologically conditioned allomorph of the genitive morpheme.
    g) Back-formation always involves a change of word-class.
    h) The majority of productive English affixes are non-Germanic.
    i) All derivational affixes of English change word-class.
    j) Two word-formation processes were involved in the formation of the verbs *to bus* and *to xerox.*

Advanced **9.** Discuss the extent to which the underlined elements in the following sets of words can be classified as unique morphemes, using the on-line version of the Oxford English Dictionary (https://www.oed.com) if you are unsure.

a) <u>Tues</u>day, <u>Wednes</u>day, <u>Thurs</u>day
b) re<u>ceive</u>, de<u>ceive</u>, per<u>ceive</u>
c) per<u>mit</u>, re<u>mit</u>, sub<u>mit</u>
d) <u>ident</u>ity, <u>ident</u>ify, <u>ident</u>ical
e) in<u>ept</u>, un<u>couth</u>, dis<u>gruntle</u>
f) <u>straw</u>berry, <u>goose</u>berry
g) <u>sn</u>ore, <u>sn</u>ort, <u>sn</u>iffle, <u>sn</u>eeze

10. Here are some more instances of so-called causative verbs like *widen*, *sweeten* or *deafen* in exercise (3): *madden, quicken, soften, whiten.* Now, if you contrast these verbs with those below, can you identify the phonological constraint on the derivation of causative verbs from adjectives with the help of the suffix *-en*?
*bluen, *concreten, *exacten, *greenen, *sanen, *slowen, *subtlen

11.

a) What is a basic difference between vowel-initial and consonant-initial (derivational) suffixes?
b) Find out about the difference between class I and class II affixes in a number of accounts of English derivation. Which arguments can be given against such accounts of English morphophonology?

12. Try to write a brief "story" of *tweet* from the point of view of the linguist. Use the following words (some of which are institutionalized, others nonce-formations), and try to reconstruct how everything started and which members of the *tweet*-family came into existence by means of which word-formation process(es). Can you think of more family members?

a) Twitter, to twitter frequently, to twitter a message
b) a tweet, to tweet frequently, to tweet a message
c) a retweet, to retweet, tweeter, tweetable, tweetworthy
d) tweetability, untweetable
e) Twittiot, tweetistics, tweetology, twitterverse, tweetbot
f) tweet eraser

Sources and further reading

Adams, Valerie. 2001. *Complex words in English*. Harlow: Longman.

Adams, Valerie. 2002 [1973]. *An introduction to modern English word-formation*. London: Longman.

Aronoff, Mark/Kirsten Fudeman. 2011². *What is morphology*? Malden, MA/ Oxford: John Wiley & Sons.

Baerman, Matthew, ed. 2015. *The Oxford handbook of inflection*. Oxford: Oxford University Press.

Bauer, Laurie. 2001. *Morphological productivity*. Cambridge: Cambridge University Press.

Bauer, Laurie. 2002 [1983]. *English word-formation*. Cambridge: Cambridge University Press.

Bauer, Laurie. 2019. *Rethinking morphology*. Edinburgh: Edinburgh University Press.

Bauer, Laurie/Rodney Huddleston. 2002. "Lexical word-formation." In: Rodney Huddleston/Geoffrey K. Pullum, eds. *The Cambridge Grammar of the English Language*. Cambridge: Cambridge University Press. 1621–1721.

Booij, Geert. 2012³. *The grammar of words: An introduction to linguistic morphology*. Oxford: Oxford University Press.

Carstairs-McCarthy, Andrew. 1992. *Current morphology*. London/New York: Routledge.

Carstairs-McCarthy, Andrew. 2017². *An introduction to English morphology: Words and their structure*. Edinburgh: Edinburgh University Press.

Don, Jan. 2014. *Morphological theory and the morphology of English*. Edinburgh: Edinburgh University Press.

Fábregas, Antonio/Sergio Scalise. 2012. *Morphology: From data to theories*. Edinburgh: Edinburgh University Press.

Fischer, Roswitha. 1997. *Sprachwandel im Lexikon des heutigen Englisch*. Frankfurt: Lang.

Giegerich, Heinz J. 1999. *Lexical strata in English: Morphological causes, phonological effects*. Cambridge: Cambridge University Press.

Haspelmath, Martin/Andrea D. Sims. 2010². *Understanding morphology*. London: Hodder Education.

Hippisley, Andrew/Gregory Stump, eds. 2016. *The Cambridge handbook of morphology*. Cambridge: Cambridge University Press.

Katamba, Francis. 1993. *Morphology*. London: Macmillan.

Leisi, Ernst/Christian Mair. 2008⁹. *Das heutige Englisch*. Heidelberg: Winter.

Lieber, Rochelle. 2016². *Introducing morphology*. Cambridge: Cambridge University Press.

Lieber, Rochelle/Pavol Štekauer, eds. 2011. *The Oxford handbook of compounding*. Oxford: Oxford University Press.

Lieber, Rochelle/Pavol Štekauer, eds. 2014. *The Oxford handbook of derivational morphology*. Oxford: Oxford University Press.

Marchand, Hans. 1969². *The categories and types of present-day English word formation*. München: Beck.

Matthews, Peter H. 1991². *Morphology*. Cambridge: Cambridge University Press.

Minkova, Donka/Robert Stockwell. 2009². *English words: History and structure*. Cambridge: Cambridge University Press.

Plag, Ingo. 1999. *Morphological productivity. Structural constraints in English derivation*. Berlin/New York: Mouton de Gruyter.

Plag, Ingo. 2018². *Word-formation in English*. Cambridge: Cambridge University Press.

Schmid, Hans-Jörg. 2016³. *English morphology and word-formation: An introduction*. Berlin: Schmidt.

Spencer, Andrew/Arnold M. Zwicky, eds. 2001. *The handbook of morphology*. Oxford: Wiley-Blackwell.

Welte, Werner. 1996². *Englische Morphologie und Wortbildung*. Frankfurt: Lang.

4 Grammar: The ground plan of English

Basic formal structure of English: What will take centre stage in this and the next chapter is the basic formal structure of English, or what could also be called the ground plan of the language. The most important structural characteristics of English will be presented from two different perspectives: in the current chapter by way of introducing the key concepts and terms in grammar, and in chapter 5 as part of a comparison of English and another West Germanic (and thus genetically closely related) language, namely German. In both chapters, we will adopt what may be called an "enlightened" traditional approach. This means that we will for the most part use the traditional, long established terminology (some of which is over two thousand years old), but in a critically reflected way, i. e. including the scientific insights and developments of recent research in the field of grammar. This approach is particularly suitable for teaching (foreign) languages at schools, colleges and universities; it is therefore the approach preferred for the linguistic training of future foreign-language teachers. A similar approach is used by Hurford (1994), Huddleston (1984), as well as by Quirk et al. (1985), Biber et al. (1999) and Huddleston/Pullum (2002), still the three most important English reference grammars.

an "enlightened" traditional approach

Grammar: Leaving aside grammar as language theory (as in *generative* or *transformational grammar*; see chapter 1), the term *grammar* can usually mean three different things:

definitions

- the study of the rule-based structure (or: the ground plan) of a language
- the object of study itself, i. e. the system of rules according to which a given language may combine words and the morphemes they consist of into larger units
- the book in which these rules are formulated and described

In the first sense, we can subdivide grammar into the grammatical structure of words (inflectional morphology, see section 4.1) and the grammatical structure of phrases, clauses and sentences (syntax, see sections 4.2 and 4.3). The linguistic units under investigation can be represented in the following hierarchy:

```
                    grammar
          _____/        _____
   inflectional                      syntax
   morphology
```

Figure 4.1: The major subdivisions of grammar

inflectional morphemes < words (including word forms) < phrases < clauses < sentences

Descriptive – prescriptive: Examining some central aspects of English grammar from an "enlightened" traditional perspective also means using

a descriptive approach

J.B. Metzler © Springer-Verlag GmbH Deutschland, ein Teil von Springer Nature, 2020
B. Kortmann, *English Linguistics*, https://doi.org/10.1007/978-3-476-05678-8_4

a descriptive approach rather than a prescriptive (or normative) one. Among the grammarians of the 18th and 19th centuries, it was common practice to lay down rules – which often appeared to be arbitrary – for the correct or "educated" use of English widely accepted among the higher social classes (*'how English should be spoken'*). This is not, however, the perspective taken in this book. We will instead be looking at English as it is actually spoken today. The reader will not find any criticism of such phenomena as the so-called *split infinitive* (e. g. *to quickly go*), the use of *I will* instead of *I shall* as future-tense marker, of sentence-final prepositions or the missing use of *whom*, as in *She's the woman who I'd like to talk to* instead of *She's the woman to whom I'd like to talk*. Note that this does not mean that descriptive grammars follow an *anything goes* principle. It simply means that each variety of a language has its rules, but that these rules are not necessarily the same for each variety.

focus on the structural core Standard varieties: Above all it must be noted that, from a linguistic perspective, no variety is inherently "better" than, or superior to, other varieties (which is why we especially disapprove of terms like *sub-standard*). The reason why standard varieties enjoy a privileged status (also compare chapter 8.1) is that they enable people from different dialect areas to communicate with each other. The standard therefore seems especially suitable for use in the mass media, in schools and universities and in foreign language teaching (think of *TESOL "Teaching English to Speakers of Other Languages"*). In this chapter, it is the structural core of the different standard varieties of English, notably British and American English, which will be examined in some detail.

4.1 | Inflectional morphology

only 8 in present-day English Inflectional morphemes are bound morphemes which are exclusively used to encode grammatical information. Only eight of the numerous inflectional morphemes found in Old English are still in use today. As mentioned in earlier chapters, English has developed into an analytic, more specifically (near-)isolating, language (for further explanation, see the paragraphs below on morphological language types). The few inflectional morphemes that have survived are used in the declension of nouns, the conjugation of verbs and the comparison of adjectives (see table 4.1).

English – a highly analytic language: As a result of the dramatic loss of inflectional morphemes in the course of the history of English, each of the three word classes mentioned above nowadays contains far fewer word forms in English than, for example, in German.

If we consider only those lexemes that follow the productive pattern (again compare table 4.1), we see that the English noun can occur in only two different forms (e. g. *boy, boys = boy's = boys'*), the English adjective in no more than three (*strong, stronger, strongest*) and the English verb in no more than four different forms (*walk, walks, walked, walking*). Even the irregular nouns and verbs – of which there are relatively few in English – have hardly more different forms. Irregular nouns can take on

word class	kind of inflection	inflectional morphemes	examples	number of word forms
noun	declension	{PLURAL}: {-s}	two boy-s	rule: 2
		{'GENITIVE'}: {-s}	the boy-'s toy	exception: 4
verb	conjugation	{3SG.IND.PRES}:{-s}	he work-s	rule: 4
		{PAST}:{-ed}	he work-ed	exception: 5 (8)
		{PRES.PART.}:{-ing}	he is work-ing	
		{PAST PART.}:{-ed}	he has work-ed	
adjective	comparison	{COMPARATIVE}:{-er}	strong-er	rule: 3
		{SUPERLATIVE}:{-est}	strong-est	

Table 4.1:
English inflectional
morphology

four – instead of two – word forms (e. g. *child, child's, children, children's*) and so-called strong verbs have five – instead of four – different forms (e. g. *sing, sings, sang, singing, sung*). Only the verb *to be* has eight forms (*be, am, are, is, was, were, being, been*).

Loss of inflectional morphemes: English has lost most of the inflectional morphemes it once possessed, resulting in a language in which each lexeme can appear in but a small number of word forms. It is therefore often characterized as a language of largely invariable words, i. e. as an analytic or isolating language (also see chapter 5.2.1). Another peculiarity resulting from this development is a phenomenon called conversion (already mentioned in chapter 3.3.3).

It becomes clear that English is indeed an analytic language when looking at the many grammatical categories which can be formed analytically as well as synthetically (i. e. by using inflectional morphemes), with the analytic patterns typically representing the historically 'younger' option. Take the comparison of English adjectives as an example. The decision whether the comparative and superlative of a certain adjective are formed by using *more* and *most* largely depends on the phonological complexity of the stem of the adjective (i. e. on how many syllables it has).

analytic patterns
younger

(1) Comparison of adjectives: synthetic or analytic?
a. 1 syllable: usually synthetic (*old-older-oldest*); but some adjectives may also take the analytic strategy (*mad, brave*)
b. 2 syllables: both strategies are possible (*polite*); inflection is preferred for adjectives with an unstressed final vowel, /l/ or /ə(r)/: *easy, narrow, noble, clever* (vs. *severe*)
c. > 2 syllables: exclusively analytic (*beautiful, interesting*); exception: adjectives with the prefix *un-* (*untidy*)

In a similar way, possessive relationships can be marked either synthetically by using the so-called genitive (more adequately called *possessive*) or analytically by using the *of*-construction (*my uncle's house* vs. *the house of my uncle*).

Progressive, Present Perfect Peripherastic constructions: The analytic nature of English becomes even more obvious when looking at grammatical categories which are always formed analytically, i. e. by using so-called periphrastic (or: "describing") constructions. Periphrastic constructions, such as *he is working* (Progressive) or *he has arrived* (Perfect, more precisely *Present Perfect*), consist of more than one word, at least one of which is a function word (e. g. an auxiliary or a preposition). It perfectly ties in with the overall picture that these two eminently important constructions (see section 4.3.2) became obligatory only during the periods of Middle English (about 1100 to 1500 A. D.) and Early Modern English (about 1500 to 1700), and that they have continuously conquered new territory, thus clearly qualifying as two strengthened grammatical categories of Late Modern English (about 1700 to 1920) and Present-Day English.

V up, N down Strengthened vs. weakened categories: Whereas the above two and other verbal categories have been strengthened in the history of English, all inflectional categories of the noun are weakened categories. From the relatively elaborate case system of Old English nouns, only two cases have survived: the unmarked *common case* and the possessive. English has completely lost its grammatical gender distinction (in German: *der* Baum, *die* Tasse, *das* Mädchen), nowadays distinguishing pronouns either by natural (e. g. *the boy – he, the girl – she, the tree – it*) or, marginally, metaphorical gender (e. g. *the sun – he, the moon – she, England – it/she, car – it/she*). Table 4.2 illustrates the marginal role inflectional morphology plays for the marking of grammatical categories in Present-Day English. We will take a closer look at the individual categories in sections 4.2, 4.3 and 5.

Interface morphology / syntax: Inflectional morphology is the connecting link, the interface, between morphology and syntax. This is shown most clearly by the fact that it is syntax which makes certain word forms necessary:

(2) a. Alice live_ in London, and ha_ live_ there all ___ life.
    b. Yesterday Alice walk__ past Fred_ uncle_ house, one of many house_ along the way.

Concord: The examples in (2) show that the most important function of inflectional morphemes is to establish *concord*, meaning the formal agreement between syntactically closely related units with regard to their grammatical categories. We have already observed two areas where inflectional morphology acts as the connecting link between morphology and syntax: the comparison of adjectives and the marking of the possessive case. Both can be marked synthetically as well as analytically, although in many cases only one strategy is possible (compare (1) above).

Group genitives: The close connection between inflectional morphology and syntax also becomes clear when considering the fact that English

categories	formal contrasts	kind of marking	marked on / relevant for
gender	masculine – feminine – neuter	no inflectional category neither synthetic nor analytic	only pronouns (*he-she-it, his-her-its*) natural gender (*the man-*he, *the girl-*she, *the table-*it) and metaphorical gender (*sun-*he/it, *moon-*she/it, *truck-*she/it)
case	common case – possessive	synthetic; possessive also analytic	nouns (possessive: *the kids' toys – the toys* of the kids); some pronouns additional object case: *he-his-*him, *who, whose, whom*
number	singular – plural	synthetic	nouns, pronouns, verbs (*he put-*s, plural only for *be:* are/were)
person	1/2/3 person	synthetic	verbs: only 3SG ind. pres. active (*he sing-*s, *is/has/does*); only for *be:* also 1st and 2nd person: *I* am, *you* are
tense	past – non-past	synthetic	verbs (*walk-ed* versus *walk*)
aspect	progressive – non-progressive (or: simple)	analytic	verbs (*be* + V-*ing*)
	perfect – non-perfect	analytic	verbs (*have* + V-*ed*)
mood	indicative – subjunctive	marginally synthetic, analytic	verbs: ind.; subj. only marginally (for *be: I wish I* were...; *I insist that he* go/should go)
voice	active – passive (– mediopassive)	analytic	verbs (*be* + V-*ed*)
comparison	absolute – comparative – superlative	synthetic, analytic	adjectives (*-er, -est, more, most*), adverbs (*more, most*)

Table 4.2:
Grammatical cate-
gories in English

has one inflectional suffix which may be attached not to the stem of the noun it actually modifies but to the whole phrase containing the noun as its head:

(3) a. the <u>Museum</u> of Modern Art's new director
     b. the <u>boy</u> next door's bicycle

This so-called *group genitive* is one of the rare cases where a suffix appears to have started to "emancipate itself" and develop into something like a preposition following its nominal complement (i. e. a postposition like English *ago* or German *halber*).

Free > bound morphemes: On the other hand, there is the opposite case (observed in many languages) of formerly free morphemes developing into bound morphemes. For example, it can be argued that the English negation suffix *-n't* is developing into a clitic which has started losing its independence and leans towards 'the left' to become the ninth inflec-

-n't = the 9th in-
flectional suffix?

tional suffix used with auxiliaries (as in *isn't, doesn't, don't, won't*). All of these examples illustrate that there are transition zones between (inflectional) morphology and syntax.

Latin (synthetic) vs. English (analytic)

Languages in comparison: This becomes even more evident when comparing different languages. There are instances where a grammatical category is marked by inflection in one language but can or must be coded syntactically in another language (i. e. by means of analytic or periphrastic constructions). In Latin, for example, the past and future tenses are synthetic (*amavit* 'he has loved', *amabit* 'he will love'), whereas English and German use analytic tenses (*he has loved, he will love*). Languages like Latin use inflection (more precisely, case marking) to indicate which argument of the verb is the subject and which is the direct object. The nominative case indicates subject function, while the accusative case marks the direct object (consider e. g. *puella videt puerum* 'the girl sees the boy'). In such languages, word order is relatively irrelevant or 'free'. The three sentences *puella videt puerum, puella puerum videt* and *puerum videt puella* have the same basic meaning. In analytic or isolating languages like English, this is totally different. Here, it is through word order that we recognize the subject and object of a sentence (compare *the girl sees the boy* and *the boy sees the girl*). By fixing the word order (subject-verb-object: SVO), syntax assumes the function fulfilled by inflection in such languages as Latin. For this reason, Latin represents a language type diametrically opposed to English, namely a synthetic or inflectional language.

morphological typology

Synthetic vs. analytic and inflectional vs isolating languages: We can therefore classify different language types according to their morphological characteristics. We call this morphological typology. Pairs of contrasting properties are synthetic – analytic and inflectional – isolating, keeping in mind that *synthetic* does not necessarily equal *inflectional*, and *analytic* does not necessarily equal *isolating*. Rather, inflectional languages are a special type of synthetic languages, and isolating languages can be seen as the most radical type of analytic languages.

From synthetic > analytic: In the past, European languages have undergone a change from synthetic to analytic (e. g. French as compared to Latin, or the modern Germanic languages as compared to the Germanic languages used over a thousand years ago). German, too, has lost part of its inflectional system and has become more analytic. Even so, it is still without any doubt a synthetic language – consider the case marking in sentences like *Der Mann gab dem Jungen den Schlüssel* (subject – nominative, indirect object – dative and direct object – accusative). English, on the other hand, underwent a much more radical typological change, losing a large part of its former inflectional system. Compared to Old English (about 500 to 1100 A. D.), it is now a strongly analytic – almost isolating – language where a single lexeme hardly ever exhibits more than one word form (see the "language of largely invariable words" mentioned above).

idealized & simplified

Morphological language types: The basic properties of the different morphological language types are summarized in (4); the relationships between the different language types can be seen in figure 4.2 (note that the language types are idealized types and the relationships between them are simplified). It goes without saying that there are fuzzy boundaries between the different language types, and that there are many languages which do not (or only to a certain extent) possess all properties of a given language type.

Agglutinating languages: In figure 4.2, one more synthetic language type relevant for the European languages is introduced: agglutinating languages, such as Turkish or Finnish. The basic difference between inflectional and agglutinating languages is that every grammatical morph carries exactly one piece of information in agglutinating languages (i. e. there is a 1:1 relationship between form and meaning), whereas in inflectional languages, one morph usually carries several pieces of information. The ending *-us* in Latin *dominus*, for example, signals not only nominative (case) but also masculine (gender) and singular (number). An agglutinating language would ideally use one inflectional morph for the encoding of each of these grammatical categories.

Turkish, Finnish

(4) a. synthetic: rich inflectional system; many word forms for each lexeme; subject-object marking by means of inflection; free word order

major morphological language types

    a₁. inflectional: mapping of different kinds of grammatical information on one morph; often morphophonemic alternations (e. g. Latin *pater-patres*, German *gib-gab*); therefore no clear segmentation into morphemes possible

    a₂. agglutinating: 1:1 relationship between form and meaning/function for grammatical morphs; transparent morphological structure (→ segmentation into morphemes easily possible)

    b. analytic: poor inflectional system; few word forms for each lexeme; periphrastic constructions; subject-object marking by means of word order (→ fixed word order)

    b₁. isolating: complete loss of inflectional endings; no word forms; usually monomorphemic words

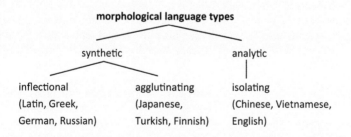

Figure 4.2: Morphological language types

morphological language types

synthetic		analytic
inflectional	agglutinating	isolating
(Latin, Greek, German, Russian)	(Japanese, Turkish, Finnish)	(Chinese, Vietnamese, English)

Inflection vs. derivation: Before concluding this section, let us return to the difference between inflectional and derivational morphemes. Chapters 3 and 4.1 have brought out a number of differences between these two types of morphemes and the corresponding morphological processes (see the summary in table 4.3). Most of them are also valid for languages other than English, but they are not universal. There are languages, for example, which have a much greater variety of inflectional than derivational morphemes.

inflection	derivation
part of the grammar	part of the lexicon
produces word forms (by means of suffixation)	produces lexemes (by means of prefixation or suffixation)
never changes word class	can change the word class
usually fully productive within one word class (e. g. possessive -s for all nouns)	only productive for subgroups of word-classes (e. g. -ity versus -dom)
very small inventory of inflectional morphemes with few very general meanings	large inventory with many relatively specific meanings
the meaning of the word form is predictable (e. g. boys, walked, higher)	the meaning of a new lexeme is not always predictable (singer = 'somebody who sings', but sweater = 'somebody who sweats'?)
closed class (two possible candidates for additional inflectional morphemes: negation and adverb-forming -ly)	more open class (e. g. -hood, -dom, -(a)holic in workaholic, chocaholic, shopaholic)
further away from the root (only after the derivational suffixes)	closer to the root
strongly syntactically determined	hardly syntactically determined

Table 4.3:
Differences
between inflection
and derivation

4.2 | Syntax: Building blocks and sentence patterns

definitions:
syntax, sentence,
constituent

Syntax (from Greek *syntaxis* = composition or combination) refers to both the study of the rules which make it possible to combine smaller linguistic units into well-formed (i. e. grammatically correct) sentences, and to the rule system itself. What is understood by *sentence* is the largest independent (!) syntactic unit of a language that is not embedded in any larger construction. The smaller building blocks that sentences are formed of, their so-called *constituents*, may vary in size and are hierarchically ordered:

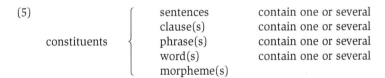

(5)

constituents

sentences   contain one or several
clause(s)   contain one or several
phrase(s)   contain one or several
word(s)   contain one or several
morpheme(s)

simple(x) vs. complex sentences

Sentences which consist of one clause only, i. e. sentences with no more than one simple subject-predicate structure (*The boy went to school*), are called *simple(x) sentences*. Sentences with more than one clause may contain either several main clauses (compound sentences like 6a) or one main clause and at least one subordinate clause (complex sentences, as in 6b). The two main clauses in (6) are double underlined, the subordinate clause in (6b) is underlined (also compare (9) below):

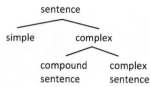

Figure 4.3:
Major types of
sentence structure

phrase vs. clause

(6) a. <u>The girl went to school</u> and/but <u>her brother stayed at home</u>.
   b. <u>The girl went to school</u> although <u>her brother stayed at home</u>.

The example in (7) illustrates a simplified syntactic analysis of a complex sentence. Each word is underlined, the phrases are put in square brackets, the clauses in angled brackets, and the sentence as a whole is indicated by braces. The basic difference between phrases and clauses is that phrases have no subject-predicate structure:

(7) { < [A [very old] man] [left] > < after [the bus] [had arrived] [at [the station]] > }
   a. clauses: *a very old man left* (main clause)
      after the bus had arrived at the station (subordinate clause)
   b. phrases: *very old* (adjective phrase)
      a very old man, the bus, the station (noun phrases)
      left, had arrived (verb phrases)
      at the station (prepositional phrase)

In what follows, we will present the most useful ways of classifying the syntactic units mentioned in (5). We will work our way up from smaller to larger units, starting with the classification of words. In section 4.3, we will then take a closer look at the most important phrase of the sentence, namely the verb phrase. In doing so, the focus will always be on the special properties of the English verb phrase. In chapter 5, these and further distinctive features of English syntax will be examined from a contrastive perspective by comparing them with German.

4.2.1 | Parts of speech

Ancient Greek tradition: The classification of words, or more precisely lexemes, into different syntactic categories (or: parts of speech) goes back to traditional grammars of classical antiquity, notably to the works by Aristotle and Dionysius Thrax. Their classifications and terminology are still widely used (*noun, verb, adjective, adverb, preposition,* etc.), but some of the basic assumptions underlying their classifications are no longer shared. In particular, the mixing of purely formal (i. e. morphological and syntactic) and semantic criteria is generally rejected nowadays. If a noun is defined as 'name of a person, place or thing', there is, for example, a problem for all abstract expressions (*freedom, permission*).

By contrast, it is completely legitimate to classify a lexeme as a noun if it can be morphologically marked for possessive and plural, if it can appear as a head in phrases like *many/much* or *in the/a*, and if it can function as the subject or object of a verb (as in [*Many tourists*]$_S$ *like* [*a drink*]$_O$ *in the garden*). Similar arguments based on morphological and syntactic behaviour, especially inflectional properties and syntactic distribution, can be found for the classification of lexemes as verbs, adjectives, adverbs, articles, prepositions, conjunctions, etc. Several problems need to be taken care of, however.

Problems with determining word classes: First of all – and this is especially important for English – a word form can belong to more than one word class (*round*, for example, can be a noun, verb, adjective, adverb or preposition; see chapter 3.3 on conversion). This means that multiple classifications are possible. Secondly, alternative classifications are also possible, which means that a certain lexeme or even a whole class of lexemes can be classified as belonging to either one word class or another. As will be shown later on, there are indeed reasons for relating function words like *after* or *before* not to three different parts of speech (*after school* – preposition, *after he left* – (subordinating) conjunction, *the day after* – adverb), but to one part of speech only, namely prepositions, which is subdivided into several groups. The third point to remember is that some parts of speech are more heterogeneous than others. This is especially true for adverbs, a part of speech which, due to its various modifying functions (notably as modifiers of verbs (*run quickly*), adjectives (*very quick*) and adverbs (*very quickly*)), has often been the "waste bin" for those lexemes which could not be clearly attributed to any other part of speech. Just think of a group of adverbs as heterogeneous as *quickly, yesterday, here, very, rather, only* and *however*.

Prototypicality: But what is even more important to understand is that basically all parts of speech are heterogeneous in themselves, which means that not all members of a certain word class exhibit all characteristics usually ascribed to that word class to the same degree (especially not the semantic ones; more on prototypes in chapter 6.4.1 below). If you compare, for example, the adjectives *quick, tired, top* and *asleep*, you will notice that only *quick* behaves like a prototypical adjective. It has a synthetic comparative (*quicker*) and superlative (*quickest*), it can be used attributively (*a quick man*) as well as predicatively (*the man was quick*), and it can serve as the root for an adverb formed by adding the suffix {-ly} (*quickly*). As shown in table 4.4, the adverbs *tired, top* and *asleep* behave differently. Compared to these three, *quick* can therefore be considered the "best" (meaning the prototypical, most representative) adjective, while *asleep* is least prototypical:

Table 4.4:
The internal heterogeneity of the word class ADJECTIVE

	Morphology			Syntax		
	comparative	superlative	adverb in {-ly}	attributive	predicative	*very*-intensifier
quick	x	x	x	x	x	x
old	x	x		x	x	x
top				x	x	x
asleep					x	

Gradients: Table 4.4 and the remarks preceding it point to a phenomenon that can be found on all levels of language and linguistics: there are transitions and fuzzy boundaries between different categories, and there are gradations (from most to least representative) within categories. It is thus useful to represent the internal heterogeneity of categories with the help of continua or gradients (also termed *clines*; compare chapters 1 and 6).

Open vs. closed word classes: Table 4.5 summarizes what has been said so far in this book on the various parts of speech and their most important properties. The most important criterion for the classification in this table has repeatedly been mentioned above: the distinction between lexical (open) and grammatical (closed) word classes. Interjections (like *Hey!*, *Ouch!*, *Golly!*, *Gosh!*, *Yuk!*, *Blast!*, etc.) have not been included here. Although they are traditionally treated as an independent word class, the status of interjections is often disputed due to their extremely idiosyncratic character.

	lexical	grammatical (or: functional)
parts of speech	noun, verb, adjective, adverb; in more recent syntactic theories also prepositions (incl. conjunctions)	articles, pronouns, numerals, auxiliaries; in traditional grammars also prepositions and conjunctions
phonologically	at least one stressed syllable; nucleus of intonation unit	normally neither stressed nor nucleus of intonation unit; in connected speech: weak forms
morphologically	open for neologisms; can be inflected (N, V, A); see table 4.2	for the most part closed; no inflection
syntactically	function as heads of phrases (NP, VP, AP, AdvP; see table 4.2); depending on the theory: also prepositions (PP)	cannot function as heads of phrases; exceptions: some types of pronouns (NP); depending on the theory: also determiners (DPs)
semantically	language-external, referential meaning (autosemantic terms)	exclusively or at least dominantly language-internal, functional meaning (synsemantic terms)

Table 4.5: Lexical vs. grammatical word classes

4.2.2 | Phrases and clauses

Phrases with and without a head: The syntactic criterion mentioned in table 4.5 leads us on to phrases. These may consist of either a single word (as in [*John*]$_{NP}$, [*saw*]$_{VP}$, [*me*]$_{NP}$) or of several words. In most phrases, one central, obligatory element (the head) is extended by adding one or several modifying elements (modifiers). The whole phrase is classified according to the syntactic category of its head. The head of a phrase also determines its position in the sentence. A noun phrase, for example, has the distributional properties of a noun (compare *The man* was reading *a book* with *John* was reading *Shakespeare*) while a verb phrase has the distributional properties of a (lexical, main) verb. Most phrases exhibit

endocentric vs. exocentric phrases

the same distribution as their heads when the latter are used on their own; they are called *endocentric phrases*. Those phrases which, by contrast, have neither the same syntactic distribution as their head nor that of any other of their constituents are called *exocentric phrases*. The best example are probably prepositional phrases (*in London, at the station, on the roof*), where the phrase as a whole can take neither the position of the preposition nor that of the noun phrase it is in connection with:

(8) a.   John sat in the garden.
     b.   * John sat in.
     c.   * John sat the garden.

	head	term	examples
ENDOCENTRIC	noun	noun phrase (NP)	Mary, she, the boy, a green apple, the man with the beard, the girl who stood at the corner
	verb	verb phrase (VP)	(has/was) asked, may ask, is asking, may have been being asked
	adjective	adjective phrase (AP)	(really) old, young and ambitious
	adverb	adverbial phrase (AdvP)	(very) quickly, right here
EXO-CENTRIC	preposition	prepositional phrase (PP)	at work, in the garden, on the roof, after the match, after the match had finished

Table 4.6: Types of phrases

Complexity of phrases: The examples in table 4.6 show that the complexity of phrases can vary a lot. At one end of the complexity scale, there are phrases consisting of a single word, such as *Mary* (NP) or *asked* (VP), while at the other end we find phrases containing a whole clause. Relative clauses – as in *the girl who stood at the corner* – are always part of a noun phrase. Some prepositions can take not only arguments consisting of a single noun phrase but also arguments consisting of a whole clause (e. g. *after the match*, *after the match had finished*). This is one reason why, especially in more recent syntactic theories, conjunctions introducing a subordinate clause (*subordinating conjunctions*) are classified as a subgroup of prepositions.

Finite vs. non-finite clauses: Unlike phrases, clauses have a subject-predicate structure, with the predicate being either finite (tensed) or non-finite (non-tensed). Finite verbs are inflected and marked for agreement with the subject, as in (9a, b). The infinitive ((*to*) V), the present participle (V-*ing*) as well as the past participle (V-*ed*), on the other hand, are non-finite verb forms (see the verb forms in bold print in 9c–e). A finite verb can serve as the only predicate in a simple sentence, whereas non-finite predicates by themselves are possible only in subordinate clauses:

(9) a. <u>John leaves</u> and <u>Mary stays</u>.
     b. <u>If John leaves</u>, <u>I'll leave too</u>.
     c. <u>Someone wants</u> <u>John **to leave**</u>.
     d. <u>**Leaving**, <u>I waved goodbye</u>.
     e. <u>**Left** by John</u>, <u>Mary was sad</u>.

As in (6), main clauses are double underlined, subordinate clauses underlined. In other words, (9a) is a compound sentence whereas (9b–e) are complex sentences (for details on the different types of subordinate clauses, see below and section 4.4).

4.2.3 | Grammatical relations

In the preceding sections, we primarily focused on formal aspects when classifying the constituents of a sentence. What will stand at the centre of interest in the present section are the syntactic functions of individual phrases and clauses in a sentence, i. e. the grammatical relations they express in a sentence. Many of the relevant terms are familiar from school grammars: *subject*, *object* (*direct* or *indirect*), *complement*, *predicate* and *adverbial*.

Complement: The latter three terms require a few words of comment, especially the term *complement*, for which varying definitions can be found. Note that here this term will be used in the narrowest possible sense, namely as referring to predicative complements of either the subject (*subject complements*, as in (10a)) or the direct object (*object complements*, as in (10b)) without which the relevant sentence would otherwise be incomplete. subject vs. object complements

(10) a. My father is <u>a teacher/very old/as happy as a lark</u>.
      b. I consider him <u>a hero/really witty</u>.

Predicate: The term *predicate* will also be used more narrowly here than in traditional grammar. Typically, a predicate is considered one of the two indispensable core constituents of a sentence, containing all obligatory constituents except for the subject (i. e. the verbal nucleus, object(s), complement(s) and those adverbials that are syntactically required). The assumption underlying this view is that every sentence consists of two parts: one part about which something is said (the subject) and the thing that is actually said (the predicate). The same view is adopted in more recent syntactic theories which favour a broader definition of the verb phrase, treating every sentence as a binary construction which can be divided (or: parsed) into a noun phrase (functioning as the subject) and a – sometimes very complex – verb phrase (the rest of the sentence).

(11) in traditional and
more recent approaches

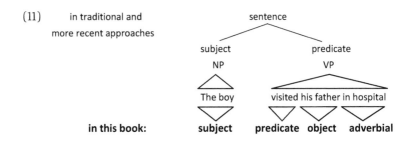

in this book: subject   predicate object adverbial

Verbal nucleus: Below, the terms *predicate* and *verb phrase* will exclusively be used as referring to the verbal nucleus of the sentence. This nucleus (core) can consist of up to five verb forms (see section 4.3): up to four auxiliaries followed by one main verb (*he might have been being inter-viewed*$_v$), or one finite verb form followed by up to four non-finite verb forms (*he might*$_{fin}$ *have been being interviewed*). It can also consist of non-finite forms only (*Having arrived at the station, I bought a city map.*)

the sentence periphery

Adverbial ≠ adverb: The function of adverbials can be fulfilled by adverbs (i. e. members of the word class ADVERB, as in *We left early*), but very often it is the case that phrases and clauses function as adverbials. Such phrases are usually prepositional phrases, as in *We left in the morning*, but noun phrases, as in *We left the same morning*, are also possible. An example of an adverbial clause is underlined in *We left as soon as we had finished breakfast*. Moreover, different from other grammatical functions, adverbials are often optional (as in *He (always) runs (quickly) (along the river)*) – although certain verbs do of course require a special adverbial (e. g. a subject adverbial as in *She lives in Manchester*, or an object adverbial as in *He put the watch on the shelf*). Adverbials are usually considered part of the sentence periphery. This is also reflected by the fact that they predominantly occur at either margin, i. e. at the beginning or the end, of sentences.

7 basic sentence patterns: Having established this inventory of grammatical functions or relations, we are now in the position to describe the seven basic sentence patterns of English. In table 4.7, the abbreviation 'V' stands for *predicate* or *verb phrase*, as defined above. The extent to which these sentence patterns are determined by different types of main verbs will be discussed in section 4.3.1.

Table 4.7:
The seven basic sentence patterns

pattern	subject	predicate/verb	object(s)	complement	adverbial
SV	The girl	was sleeping			
SVO	Her mother	was dressing	the baby (O$_d$)		
SVC	Little James	seemed		very happy (C$_S$)	
SVA	He	was sitting			on the table
SVOO	Mrs Bates	gave	her children (O$_i$) all her love (O$_d$)		
SVOC	Most people	considered	her (O$_d$)	a perfect mother (C$_O$)	
SVOA	She	had spent	all her life (O$_d$)		in the village

A simple sentence consists of at least one subject and one predicate. In double-object English, this "minimal sentence" can be followed by a maximum of two constructions obligatory constituents. If it is followed by only one obligatory constituent, this constituent can be either a direct object, a subject complement or an adverbial; if it is followed by two obligatory constituents, the first is an object and the second is either another object, an object complement or an adverbial. In so-called *double-object constructions* (as *He gave the boy the book*) the indirect object always precedes the direct object. In English, there is thus a syntagmatic differentiation of the two objects, whereas inflectional languages use a paradigmatic strategy, i. e. different case-marking, to distinguish between direct and indirect objects (e. g. in German, the accusative marks the direct object and the dative the indirect object). Word order plays no role in these languages (compare German *Er gab dem Jungen* $_{\text{Oi}}$ *das Buch* $_{\text{Od}}$ with *Er gab das Buch* $_{\text{Od}}$ *dem Jungen* $_{\text{Oi}}$). The basic ground plan of the English sentence can thus be reduced to the following formula:

(12) fixed word order SV(O)

$$\text{SV} \left[(O) \left\{ \begin{array}{c} O \\ C \\ A \end{array} \right\} \right]$$

Declarative vs. interrogative sentences: This formula captures the word English vs. German order (or more precisely the constituent order) in normal declarative sentences in English. In initial position (i. e. at the beginning of a sentence or as the first of the five constituents mentioned above), we find the subject, followed by the predicate which may or may not require further constituents (i. e. argument slots to be filled). If there are two constituents following the predicate, the first will always be an object. This is how we can typologically classify the English language as a language with a fixed word order, more precisely with an SV(O) pattern. This pattern may only be reversed in interrogative sentences and in a few other contexts which underlie very special and rigid restrictions. In such contexts, the subject follows the finite verb (*Did you know?*, *Never have I laughed like this*) – a phenomenon called *inversion*. Except for imperative sentences, the subject slot in English sentences always needs to be filled, even if only by a so-called *dummy* element like *it* or *there*. As opposed to German (e. g. *Mir ist kalt* or *Jetzt wird aber geschlafen!*), English has no sentences without subjects. The SV(O) order in English does not only apply to main clauses but also to subordinate clauses. This is another remarkable difference compared with German (*Er ging nach Hause* vs. *Ich weinte, weil er nach Hause ging*; for more details see chapter 5.2.2).

Adding complexity to the basic ground plan: One reason why the basic sentence pattern in (12) is also valid for sentences that are more complex than those represented in table 4.7 is that a clause or sentence can have several adverbials (as in [*Frankly,*]$_A$ [*as a child*]$_A$ he [*always*]$_A$ ran [*quickly*]$_A$ [*along the river*]$_A$ [*looking for dead fish*]$_A$). Each of these constituents can be much more complex. As already mentioned (see, for instance, the examples in table 4.6), they can be extended by additional modifying elements (e. g. [*Most of the almost two thousand people in her* *village]$_S$ [considered]$_P$ [her]$_{Od}$ [an absolutely perfect mother loved and admired by her family]$_{CO}$).*

Types of subordinate clauses: Besides individual words or phrases, whole clauses (subordinate clauses) can function as the subject, object, complement or adverbial of a sentence. Depending on which grammatical function they express, they can be classified as either subject, object or complement clauses, on the one hand, or adverbial clauses, on the other hand. Because the first three have a grammatical function similar to that of noun phrases (13), they are subsumed under the heading of *nominal clauses*. Relative clauses are excluded from our discussion here because they are always part of a noun phrase.

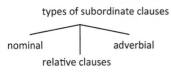

types of subordinate clauses

nominal adverbial

relative clauses

Adverbial clauses specify the circumstances under which the situation described in the main clause takes place. Among others, we distinguish adverbials of time, place, manner, cause, condition, concession, result and purpose (14). The vast majority of adverbial clauses are finite and introduced by a subordinating conjunction (more precisely an *adverbial subordinator*, e.g. *while, if, because, although*). English is special among the Germanic languages in that it makes relatively frequently use of adverbial clauses in which the predicate is a participle, most frequently a present participle (so-called *adverbial participles* as in (14h); also compare (9d, e)).

(13) a. subject clause: <u>That you are here</u> is a miracle.
   b. object clause: We knew <u>(that) he was a lousy driver</u>.
   c. complement clause: The problem is <u>how to stay away from trouble</u>.

(14) a. adverbial of time: We left <u>as soon as we had finished breakfast</u>.
   b. adverbial of place: He waited <u>where I had left him</u>.
   c. adverbial of manner: She behaves <u>as if she has problems</u>.
   d. adverbial of condition: <u>If you leave now</u>, you'll still reach the train.
   e. adverbial of cause: I was angry <u>because he came late</u>.
   f. adverbial of concession: <u>Although I love good food</u>, I eat very little.
   g. adverbial of purpose: He came <u>(in order) to help me</u>.
   h. adverbial participle: <u>Walking along the river</u>, he watched the fishermen.

Syntactic vs. semantic roles: So far in this section, the building blocks or constituents of a sentence have been classified according to formal aspects (complexity, syntactic categories) and functional aspects (grammatical relations). In conclusion, it needs to be mentioned that different grammatical relations (sometimes also termed *syntactic roles*) are linked to different semantic (or: thematic) roles:

(15)   The man   stroked   the dog.

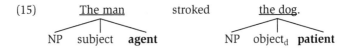

NP subject **agent**   NP object$_d$ **patient**

Agent vs. patient: In a prototypical active sentence, the subject is the element that carries out an action (the agent), the direct object is typically the element affected by the action (the patient), and the indirect object is the goal of the action and frequently also the element which profits from it (the recipient or benefactive).

Further semantic roles: Adverbials often assume one of the semantic roles of *time*, *place*, *source*, *goal* or *instrument*. A comparison with a play may help illuminate the notion of semantic roles. One could say that they define the participants involved in a certain situation, the actors of a play, as it were. The number of actors and the parts they play are determined by the verb. A verb like *think* requires only one actor, namely a subject with the semantic role of an experiencer (speaking of an agent would be inappropriate in this case). The verb *give* requires three actors: a subject serving as agent, a direct object serving as patient and an indirect object assuming the semantic role of recipient or benefactive. Once again, therefore, as pointed out in our discussion of the major sentence patterns of English, the verb turns out to be the dominating element, the anchor of any clause or sentence; in terms of the play analogy, we can say that it is the verb that gives the play its name or title.

comparison with actors in a play

Note that concerning semantic roles, English has a special property. Frequently (at least much more often than in German), the subject is not an agent and the direct object not a patient. Just consider the examples in (16) and (17) (for more details compare chapter 5).

(16) a. The car burst a tyre. (possessor)
     b. The bucket was leaking water. (source)
     c. This tent sleeps ten people. (place)
(17) a. They fled the capital. (source)
     b. The seagull was riding the wind. (place)

Table 4.8 provides an overview of the various grammatical relations, including for each of them the prototypical syntactic category/-ies and the prototypical semantic role(s) mapped onto them.

grammatical relation	prototypical syntactic category	prototypical semantic role
subject	NP	agent
predicate	VP	
object (dir.)	NP	patient
object (indir.)	NP	recipient, benefactive
complement	NP, AP	
adverbial	AdvP, PP	time, place, instrument

Table 4.8: Grammatical relations and semantic roles

4.3 | The English verb phrase

English VP: hub of
innovations

Verb = anchor of the sentence: There are two reasons why the verb phrase deserves a section of its own. The first is of a general nature and valid for all languages: the verb phrase, more precisely its head, i. e. the main verb, is the central element on which the entire sentence hinges. It is the main verb that determines how many obligatory constituents there are in a sentence, that is, whether only a subject is necessary or if one or two objects, a complement, or an adverbial are additionally required. In other words, for any given English sentence, the main verb is responsible for selecting the appropriate basic sentence pattern from those given in (12). The second reason specifically relates to English: both from a synchronic and from a diachronic point of view, the verb phrase simply is the most interesting phrase. In no other phrase has more happened in the course of the history of English and is currently happening in terms of interesting innovations – from an English-specific as well as from a cross-linguistic point of view.

Strengthened categories in the verb phrase: Although the English verb, like other parts of speech, has experienced a loss of inflectional markers for certain grammatical categories (person, number, subjunctive), it is especially in the verb phrase that Present-Day English has developed the greatest number of so-called *strengthened categories* (especially the progressive and the perfect). It is here, too, where we can observe the development of new and the strengthening of old verb types and syntactic options which in part compensate for the dramatic loss of inflectional morphemes and the fixing of word order. The development of English into a strongly analytic language with a fixed word order is best illustrated with examples taken from the verb phrase. Not surprisingly, this is also where some of the most important grammatical differences between English and German as well as between the different standard varieties of English can be observed (compare chapters 5 and 8).

highly transparent
& modular

Structure of the verb phrase: The English verb phrase has a highly transparent modular structure. It consists of a maximum of five verb forms (typically fewer), the last of which is always the main verb, i. e. the head of the phrase, and the first of which is always a finite verb. The order of the auxiliaries preceding the main verb is strictly determined: the grammatical categories modality, perfect, progressive and passive are always marked in this order. Additionally, every auxiliary determines the form of the verb following it, which means that a modal verb (*may, must, can, could, would*, etc.) needs to be followed by an infinitive, a form of *have* by a past participle, and a form of *be* either by a present participle (when marking the progressive) or a past participle (when marking the passive). All examples in (18) follow this pattern:

(18)	modal aux	perfect aux (HAVE + past. part.)	progressive aux (BE + pres. part.)	passive aux (BE + past. part.)	main verb
			is	being	interviewed
		has		been	interviewed
	may	have			interviewed
	may	have	been		interviewing
	may	have	been	being	interviewed

In what follows, starting out from the distinction between main verbs and auxiliaries and the central role of the (main) verb in determining the basic sentence pattern, we will first present different types of verbs (4.3.1) before giving an account of the most important grammatical categories of the English verb phrase (4.3.2).

4.3.1 | Verb types

Main verbs vs. auxiliaries: A fundamental distinction within the word class of verbs is the one between lexical and grammatical verbs, i. e. between main verbs and auxiliaries. It is one of the distinctive characteristics of English that, in the course of its history, it has developed an increasingly strict division between these two types of verbs. As a result, English auxiliaries nowadays form a separate group which – morphologically as well as syntactically – is very different from that of main verbs. The basic differences are summarized in table 4.9:

<small>strict division</small>

		auxiliary verbs		main verbs
the only verb in the sentence	no	(*He has), except in answers to questions of the type *Has/Is/Does he …?*	yes	(*He comes every day*)
inversion (V_{fin} S)	yes	(*Has he come?*)	no	(ˇ*Comes he?*)
negative contraction	yes	(*isn't, hasn't, can't, mustn't*)	no	(ˇ*comen't,* ˇ*walkn't*)
do-support				
in negations	no	(*He hasn't come;* not: **He doesn't have come*)	yes	(*He doesn't come;* not: ˇ*He walks not*)
in questions	no	(*Has he come?;* not: ˇ*Does he have come?*)	yes	(*Does he come?;* not: ˇ*Comes he?*)
emphatic	no	(*He HAS come,* not: ˇ*He DOES have come*)	yes	(*He DOES come*)
ellipsis of main verb after first occurrence	no	(*John will come and so will ___ Mary*)	yes	(*John came and so did Mary*)
additionally:		modal verbs		main verbs
bare infinitive	yes	(*He can come,* not: **He can to come*)	no	(ˇ*He comes see me;* but: *He comes to see me*)
non-finite forms	no	(ˇ*to can,* ˇ*canning,* ˇ*canned*)	yes	(*walk, walking, walked*)
3rd sg.ind.pres. -s	no	(ˇ*he cans,* ˇ*she musts*)	yes	(*he walks, she comes*)
past tense in simple declarative sentences always has past meaning	no	(*He could/might come tomorrow*)	yes	(**He came tomorrow*)

<small>Table 4.9: A comparison of auxiliaries and main verbs</small>

opposite ends of
a continuum
In some respects, the distinction between these two verb types is not clear-cut. Thus it makes sense to place main verbs like *see*, *walk* or *jump* and modal verbs like *can*, *may* or *must* at the two opposite ends of a continuum, putting (modal) verbs such as *dare*, *need* and *used to* or so-called semi-auxiliaries like *have to* and *be going to* at the centre of this continuum. Clearly, the massive strengthening of English auxiliaries as a grammatical word class is closely linked to the development of English into an analytic language; it even needs to be seen as an important out-come of this development.

Modal vs. primary verbs: The term *auxiliary* goes back to the tradi-tional grammar of verbs which have the same function as inflectional endings. This can be seen, for example, when considering the English perfect, progressive, passive, the analytic future formed with *will/shall* or English modal verbs, some of which have prac-tically taken over the functions of the subjunctive formerly marked on the verb stem (for details see 4.3.2). Both with regard to semantics and, especially, morphology and syntax (see table 4.9), modal verbs differ from the second major group of auxiliaries: the so-called primary verbs *be*, *have* and *do*.

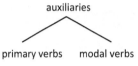

primary verbs   modal verbs

Figure 4.5:
Auxiliaries

The use of primary verbs is compulsory for the marking of different grammatical categories (*be*, *have*), but also when forming questions and negating main verbs (cf. the so-called *do-support*). A further basic differ-ence between modal verbs, on the one hand, and *be/have/do*, on the other hand, is the fact that only primary verbs may also be used as main verbs:

(19)   a.   Mary has a new car.
        b.   Mary did nothing to help me.
        c.   Mary is ill/a teacher/in the garden.

Copula verb: In (19c), *be* is a so-called linking or copula verb (or simply *copula*), i. e. a verb which establishes a link between the subject of a sentence and a certain property or attribute. That *be* in (19c) is not an auxiliary but has the formal properties of a main verb is easily shown by the fact that it can be combined with auxiliary verbs, and even with the progressive form of *be* (*Mary has been ill for quite some time*, *Mary will soon be ill*, *Mary is being a teacher*). Copula verbs form but a small group; they include verbs or certain uses of verbs like *seem*, *look*, *appear*, *be-come*, *remain*, *turn* or *grow* (*Yesterday she ... ill*).

Verb types and sentence patterns: Copula verbs lead us straight back to our discussion of basic sentence patterns in section 4.2. It was repeat-edly stated that sentences are formed around main verbs, and that main verbs therefore determine sentence patterns. Verbs determine both the number and the nature of their arguments by specifying their syntactic function in the sentence (i. e. their grammatical relation) as well as their semantic role. Copulas, for example, are responsible for the sentence pat-tern subject-predicate-complement because they require two obligatory arguments – a subject and a complement that attributes a certain prop-erty to the subject. In its spatial sense ('to be somewhere') *be*, together with other spatial verbs such as *live, stay* or *lurk*, is also responsible for the sentence pattern subject-predicate-adverbial, the adverbial in these cases being one of place (*John is/lived/stayed in London, John lurked behind a tree*). The same sentence pattern (but with an adverbial of time) is required by another type of verb, namely verbs which indicate duration (e. g. *It'll last/take five minutes*).

Valency: The other five basic sentence patterns found in English can all be explained by classifying verbs according to their valency. This term (borrowed from chemistry) is used in linguistics to describe the ability, especially of verbs, to open up slots around themselves which must or can be filled. The two terms related to this property which are well-known from school grammar are *transitive* and *intransitive*.

Transitive vs. intransitive verbs: Intransitive verbs require only one argument, namely a subject (e. g. *John slept/snored/smiled*); they are therefore monovalent. Transitive verbs, on the other hand, require not only a subject but at least one more argument, namely a direct object (e. g. *John wrote/read/forgot the message*), and can therefore be passivized (*The message was written by John*; for more details on the passive see the end of section 4.3.2). Transitive verbs which, apart from the direct object, require no further argument are monotransitive or divalent. But there are also trivalent verbs or uses of verbs; these require either an additional indirect object (ditransitive verbs as in *John gave/passed Mary the message*), an object complement (*Mary considered/called John a fool*) or an object adverbial (*Mary put/hid the message in her pocket*). Verbs like *consider* or *put* are sometimes described as *complex-transitive verbs*.

Avalent verbs: We have now derived all seven basic sentence patterns found in English from different types of main verbs (compare table 4.10). For the sake of completeness, it needs to be mentioned that the minimal sentence pattern consisting of one subject and one predicate is not only required by intransitive verbs but also by so-called avalent verbs, i. e. verbs with zero valency. Given their semantics, they do not even require a subject. In English, it is only due to the fixed word order that the subject slot of weather verbs such as *rain, snow, sleet, hail, drizzle* and *freeze* is filled by the so-called *dummy it* (e. g. *it rains, it snows*).

required arguments	valency type	transitivity type	examples	sentence pattern
0	avalent	–	rain, snow, freeze	SV
1	monovalent	intransitive	sleep, sit, walk	SV
2	divalent	– (copula)	be, become	SVC
2	divalent	–	live, stay, last	SVA
2	divalent	monotransitive	read, take, build	SVO
3	trivalent	ditransitive	give, offer, pass	SVOO
3	trivalent	complex-trans.	consider, call	SVOC
3	trivalent	complex-trans.	put, hide, spend	SVOA

Table 4.10:
Verb types and
sentence patterns

Transitive/intransitive use of verbs: Many English verbs can be grouped with more than one class concerning their valency or transitivity since they can be used either transitively or intransitively. Transitive verbs, for example, can be used intransitively simply by leaving the second required argument implicit (as in *Mary was eating* or *John writes/drinks/plays*). This is usually the case with verbs of personal hygiene, so-called verbs of grooming such as *wash, comb, dress, shave,* etc., which are used reflexively, i. e. where the referent of the subject takes care of him-/herself (*Mary dresses, John shaves*). On the other hand, basically intransitive verbs can develop transitive uses, as in (20b) and (20d):

(20) a. The policemen stood, the bank robbers lay on the ground.
       b. The policemen stood the bank robbers against the wall.
       c. She ran.
       d. She ran a horse in the derby.

Causative verbs: The meanings of the verbs in (20b) and (20d) can roughly be paraphrased as 'make someone or something VERB'. Such verbs are called *causative verbs. Stand* and *run* in the examples in (20) are instances of word-class internal conversion, a word-formation process which can be observed quite frequently in English (compare also chapters 3.3.3 above and 5.2.2).

Phrasal verbs: The distinction between transitive and intransitive verbs is also valid for another English verb type, which has become more and more important over the last 200 years: so-called *phrasal verbs,* such as *look after, look up, take off, take in, give in, give up, give away.*

(21) a. intransitive: John gave in. John looked up.
       b. transitive: Mary gave the secret away. Mary looked the word up.

At first glance, phrasal verbs are very similar to *prepositional verbs* (e. g. *believe in, invest in, thank for, wait for, pull down*), but they differ from the latter in various respects (see table 4.11):

Table 4.11:
A comparison of phrasal and prepositional verbs

	phrasal verbs		prepositional verbs
status of the particle following the verb	adverb and/or preposition		preposition only
position of the particle	(a)	preceding or following the NP which follows the verb (*look the word up, look up the word*)	only preceding the NP (*wait for the rain, *wait the rain for*)
	(b)	if NP is a pronoun, only following the pronoun (*look it up, *look up it*)	only preceding the NP, even if the NP is a pronoun
	(c)	not at the beginning of relative clauses (*the word up which he looked*)	possible at the beginning of a clause (*the rain for which I waited*)
	(d)	not at the beginning of questions (*Up what did he look?*)	possible at the beginning of questions (*For what did I wait?*)
stress on the particle	usually yes (frequently nucleus of the intonation unit: *It was the word he had looked UP*)		usually no (*Here at last was the rain I had been waiting FOR*)

Phrasal-prepositional verbs: There is a subgroup of prepositional verbs (rather found in colloquial language use) which combine a phrasal verb with a prepositional phrase. Examples of such *phrasal-prepositional verbs* are *put up with, get away with, do away with, look in on, face up to* and *let* someone *in on*. Note that in traditional grammar, the term *prepositional object* usually refers to entire prepositional phrases (*Fiona believes in me*), but it may also be used to refer exclusively to the noun phrase following the prepositional verb (*Fiona believes in me*).

4.3.2 | Tense

Tense and aspect: The central grammatical categories of the English verb phrase are tense and aspect. Simple sentences or main clauses obligatorily require a finite verb, and finiteness is primarily defined by tense marking (which is why the term *tensed verb/predicate* is sometimes used instead of *finite verb/predicate*).

How many tenses?: By way of introduction, we may consider the seemingly simple question: "How many tenses are there in English?" There is more than one answer to this question, depending on how wide or narrow our definition of the term *tense* is. The lowest possible number of tenses is 2, the highest possible number 16. But in the relevant literature we also find arguments in favour of 3, 6, 8, or 12 tenses and yet other values between 2 and 16 (compare table 4.13 below).

Let us take a closer look at some of the possible values. If we regard as tenses only what can be marked inflectionally directly on the verb stem, English has no more than two tenses. In fact, English has only one inflectional suffix with an exclusively tense-marking function, namely the past-tense marker {-ed}, as in *walk-ed*. This word form stands in contrast to the unmarked form (*walk*), which is more adequately called *non-past* (instead of *present*) because it can also be used to refer to both past (22a) and future events (22b): two tenses

(22) a. Listen what happened to me yesterday. This bloke walk<u>s</u> up to me and say<u>s</u>: ...
         (*historical present*)
      b. The train leaves at six am tomorrow.

If tense is not defined as a purely inflectional category, it makes sense to postulate three tenses for English, one tense each for placing a situation in the three time spheres past, present and future. In that case, the third tense is the future tense, coded by the analytic *will/shall* + infinitive construction. The *will/shall*-construction is the most neutral of the different constructions which are used to refer to events in the future. It is the one which is least restricted to a certain context, and therefore the most grammaticalized construction. All other constructions in (23) express slightly different meanings. three tenses

(23) a. The parcel will arrive tomorrow. (neutral prediction)
 b. The parcel is going to arrive tomorrow. (result in future of an action or intention in present)
 c. The parcel is arriving tomorrow. (result in future of an action that has already begun or is already completed)
 d. The parcel will be arriving tomorrow. (event is naturally going to happen in future)
 e. The parcel arrives tomorrow. (future event is a fact, follows from a fixed schedule)

tense = a deictic category

Absolute tenses: Since they take as an anchor point the here and now of the speaker, present, past and future tense are also called *absolute tenses*. Tense thus qualifies as a deictic category (from Greek *deíknymi* = to show; see also chapter 7.2), i. e. as a grammatical category which locates a situation on the timeline, always judging from the moment of utterance.

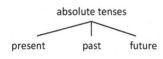

Figure 4.6: Absolute tenses

six tenses

Relative tenses: We take a different view when assuming that English has more than these three tenses, for example six (adding the three perfect tenses *Past Perfect*, *Present Perfect* and *Future Perfect*). These perfect tenses are often called *relative tenses* or *absolute-relative tenses*, because they express anteriority to some reference point in the past (Past Perfect), in the present (i. e. the moment of utterance; Present Perfect) or in the future (Future Perfect; for more details see below).

(24) a. When my parents arrived we <u>had left</u> already.
 b. Sorry, Mum. We<u>'ve left</u> already. (speaking from a mobile phone)
 c. Mum, we're about to leave. When you arrive, we<u>'ll have left</u> already.

Arguing in favour of English having six tenses therefore implies that tense is no longer considered a strictly deictic category, because the moment of utterance is no longer the direct point of reference for all tenses.

12–16 tenses

Combinatorial options: When combining these six constructions with the English progressive (*be* + present participle), we end up with twelve different "tenses". But if we decide to adopt this perspective, tense no longer exclusively defines the position of a situation as a whole on the timeline, but also applies to the internal make-up of the situation, e. g. whether it is in progress at a given point in time or not. The meaning of the term *tense* would be watered down even more if we additionally included *would/should* + infinitive constructions and their corresponding perfect and progressive forms. At least in direct speech, these constructions are no longer primarily responsible for situating events on the timeline, but rather express different kinds of modality or speaker attitude (assumption, obligation, possibility, probability, necessity, etc.). If we included these constructions, too, English would end up being a language with 16 tenses; indeed, English is represented as such in many school grammars.

Modular structure of the English verb phrase: We should not, however, confuse the picture by lumping everything together, but rather try to

bring out the modular structure of the English verb phrase and the possibilities of combining the different grammatical categories. An alternative
way of arranging and classifying the 16 verb constructions discussed
above is the following (also compare (18) above). The first step is to treat
constructions with *would* and *should* (sometimes called *conditional
tenses*) as combinations of a modal verb and a grammatically marked
(full) verb construction: *would have said* would thus be analysed the
same way as *must have said* or *may have said*. The second step is to
classify the contrast between progressive and simple form (*he is singing*
vs. *he sings*) not as a contrast in tense but as an aspectual contrast.

4.3.3 | Aspect

Aspect: (from Latin *aspectus* = viewpoint or perspective) is a grammatical
category that allows us to comment on the internal temporal make-up of a
situation, where *situation* is used as generic term for conditions or
states and different types of actions, events, etc. In English, the
progressive form (also known as *expanded form*) provides a grammatical means which allows, and sometimes even compels, the
speaker to explicitly indicate whether he or she regards a certain
action as completed or still in progress. Therefore, aspect – as opposed to tense – has a strongly subjective component. In many cases, however, marking aspect is not optional but obligatory, as can be seen in (25a):

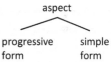

Figure 4.7:
Aspect

(25) a.   John is walking to work. (now, at the time of utterance)
      b.   John walks to work.   (usually, as a habit; not necessarily
                                      now)

Progressive: It is not easy to identify a core meaning of the progressive. It
is true to say, though, that the progressive describes a situation surrounding a certain point of reference (the so-called *temporal frame*), highlighting a certain phase of this situation, as if observing it through a magnifying glass or as if activating the freeze function of a recording device. The
progressive therefore describes only part of the situation while the simple
form covers the situation as a whole. The reference point that is indispensable for the progressive is generally introduced in the context, either by
a time adverbial (26a, b) or simply a tense marker (such as *looked* in
(26c) or the present tense in (25a)). Since the progressive always needs a
temporal reference (or: anchor) point, i. e. a point on the timeline where
we can place our magnifying glass, it can by itself never advance an action or, e. g. in a novel, the plot on the timeline, and thus not be used for
describing sequences of actions like the one in (26d):

(26) a.   I was having a nap at three.
      b.   When she arrived, he was cooking dinner.
      c.   Jack turned and looked at his sister. She was laughing.
      d.   He opened the fridge, took out a pie and went back to his room.
           (not: *was opening, taking out... and going back...)

Interaction with types of predicates: The progressive has conquered a lot of new territory in the course of the history of English, and continues to do so, especially in spontaneous spoken (including all non-standard) varieties of English (see chapter 8.3.1 below). As a result, it can nowadays be used in a much wider variety of contexts and for the expression of subtle differences in meaning (e. g. as future marker in (23c)). Not all of these uses can be attributed solely to the progressive interacting with different types of predicates (situation types, or so-called *aktionsarten*), neither do all of these interactions have predictable effects. However, some effects resulting from the interaction between progressive aspect and the *aktionsart* of a verb do occur regularly. Take, for example the effect of rapid repetition when the progressive is used with momentary verbs (27a), or the effect of incompletion (27c) or not reaching the endpoint of an action (27e) when using the progressive with so-called *telic verbs* (from Greek *télos* = aim or goal), i. e. verbs with an inbuilt endpoint.

(27) a. John was knocking on the door.   (several times)
b. John knocked on the door.   (only once)
c. John was writing a letter.   (letter not finished yet)
d. John wrote a letter.   (letter is finished)
e. John was drowning.   (danger of drowning)
f. John drowned.   (drowned)

Perfect vs. non-perfect forms: Excluding both the *would/should* and the progressive constructions, we are left with only six of the original sixteen candidates for English tenses. From these, we can subtract another three, namely the perfect forms. The contrast between perfect (as a cover term for *Present Perfect, Past Perfect* and *Future Perfect*) and non-perfect forms is often treated as a second aspectual contrast besides the progressive/non-progressive one.

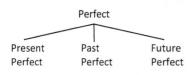

Present Perfect vs. Simple Past: This is primarily due to the contrast between Present Perfect and Simple Past. In contexts where the Present Perfect is neither obligatory (28a) nor impossible (28b), it depends solely on the view of the speaker which form is used to describe a situation in the past. Is the situation still relevant at the moment of utterance ("current relevance", as in (29a)), or is it considered completed (in the speaker's mind as well as in actual fact, as in (29b))?

(28) a. adverbials of time which include the moment of utterance (these can never combine with the Simple Past): *at present, so far, as yet, lately, before now, to this hour, for some time now, since Monday,* etc.
b. adverbials of time which refer to a specific moment or period in the past preceding the moment of utterance (these can never combine with the Present Perfect): *long ago, yesterday, the other day, last night, at that time, then, on Tuesday,* etc.

(29) a. A. Will you come to the party?
          B. Sorry, I've broken my leg and have to stay in bed.
      b. A. How was the weekend?
          B. Great! I broke my leg, my car was stolen and my girl-
              friend left.

Perfect as an independent category: Yet, there are also good reasons for adopting a different view of the category 'perfect', namely as a third category, independent of both tense and aspect. The main function of this category is to establish a relationship of anteriority between a certain situation and a point of reference on the timeline in the way described above. Similar to the category of tense, the perfect localizes an entire situation on the timeline, but it does *not* use the moment of utterance as an immediate point of reference, and it *always* involves a relationship of anteriority. Similar to aspect, the perfect is a non-deictic category which may depend on the speaker's perspective, but it does *not* give us any information about the internal structure of a situation. The differences and similarities of these three categories can be represented as in table 4.12:

aspect and perfect = non-deictic

	tense	perfect	aspect
localizes a situation on the timeline	yes	yes	no
deictic	yes	no	no
fixed sequence of situation and reference time	no	yes (anteriority)	no
focus on the internal make-up of a situation	no	no	yes (prog.)

Table 4.12:
The categories
tense, perfect and
aspect

Table 4.13 is an attempt at representing the complex tense and aspect system of English in its entirety. First, however, consider the three main uses of the *Present Perfect* in (30):

(30) a. (Would you shut the window, please?) I've (just) had a bath. (*resultative perfect*)
     b. Have you seen the Dali exhibition (yet)? (*experiential perfect, indefinite past*)
     c. I've known him for years. (*continuative/universal perfect*)

Compositionality: All the grammatical categories discussed in this section so far (mood, tense, perfect and aspect) can be combined with each other without any problems. However, the complete meaning of the resulting complex constructions cannot always be derived from the categories involved. It is therefore not always easy to prove that the meanings of the complex constructions are fully compositional (also compare chapter 6). Sometimes the meaning of the whole may well be more than a mere sum of the meanings of its parts.

Voice – the passive: What is still missing in this system of combinable verb categories is the so-called *genus verbi* or *voice*, which largely concerns the distinction between active and passive. Only transitive verbs

No of tenses?	form	term	The 16 verb forms resulting from the combination of different categories:			
			tense (referential)	perfect (have + V-ed)	aspect (be + V-ing)	modal constr.
2	walk	present	x			
	walked	past	x			
3	will/shall walk	future	x			
6	have walked	present perfect	x	x		
	had walked	past perfect	x	x		
	will have walked	future perfect	x	x		
8	would/should walk	conditional I	x			x
	would/should have walked	conditional II	x	x		x
12	6 + 6 x be walking	... progressive	x	x	x	
16	8 + 8 x be walking	... progressive	x	(x)	x	x

Table 4.13:
Tense and aspect
system

have a passive voice (not all, but most of them). In English, this takes the form of an analytic construction with either a form of the auxiliary *be* and a past participle (*Jerry was chased by Tom*) or *get* and a past participle (*He got (himself) arrested*). The *get*-construction is not quite as formal and is used to indicate that the speaker is emotionally involved in the situation he or she describes and/or that, especially when using a reflexive pronoun, the speaker considers the subject of the passive sentence as partly responsible for what has happened to him or her.

Figure 4.9:
Voice

The prototypical subject of a passive sentence has the semantic role of a patient (31a) or a benefactive (31b). Compared to other languages, English is special in that it cannot only convert the direct object (31a) and the indirect object (31b) of an active sentence into the subject of the corresponding passive sentence, but that it can do the same with the "objects" of prepositions (31c, d). In English, it is even possible to passivize an intransitive verb if the verb is followed by a prepositional phrase functioning as an adverbial of place (31d):

(31) a. The award was given to the actor.
      b. The actor was given the award.
      c. This problem must be disposed of.
      d. This bed has been slept in.

Mediopassive: Also possible in many cases is the intransitive use of transitive verbs. In such mediopassive (or: *middle voice*) constructions, the noun phrase functioning as the subject of the seemingly active sentence with an intransitively used verb is, from a semantic point of view, rather the direct object of a transitive verb, fulfilling the semantic role of a patient. In example (32a), it is not Kafka who translates something, but it is his work which cannot be (easily) translated. Bill in (32b) is not unable to scare other people but is not easily scared himself. In other words: in mediopassive constructions the supposed agent is affected himself. In English, this reflexive relationship between the actual grammatical subject and the "logical" direct object is not indicated by the use of a reflexive pronoun (as opposed to other Germanic languages; compare German *Kafka übersetzt sich nicht gut, Kafka lässt sich nicht (gut) übersetzen*).

(32) a. Kafka doesn't translate well.
     b. Bill doesn't scare easily.

Dynamic vs. statal passive: This opposition corresponds to the opposition between the *werden* and the *sein passive* in German. It is usually marked by the formal contrast between progressive and simple form:

(33) a. Dinner is being prepared. (still in preparation; dynamic passive)
     b. Dinner is prepared. (dinner is ready; statal passive)

Further contrasts between the grammatical structures of English and German will be discussed in chapter 5.

Checklist Grammar – key terms and concepts

adjective
adverb
adverbial
adverbial clause
agreement
aktionsart
argument
aspect
attributive ↔ predicative
case
clause (main, subordinate,
  declarative, interrogative,
  imperative)
clitic
comparison
complement (subject, object)
compositionality
concord
conjugation
constituents
declension
deictic category
descriptive ↔ prescriptive /
  normative
distribution

endocentric ↔ exocentric
  phrase
finite ↔ non-finite
gender
gradient
grammatical categories
  (strengthened ↔ weak-
  ened)
grammatical relation/func-
  tion (subject, object$_{d/i}$,
  complement$_{s/o}$, predicate,
  adverbial)
group genitive
head
imperative
inflectional ↔ isolating
inflectional morphology
inversion
modality
morphological typology (synthetic ↔ analytic, isolat-
  ing↔ agglutinating ↔ inflectional)
nominal clause (subject,
  complement, object)

noun
number
object (direct ↔ indirect)
passive (medio-)
perfect (present, past, future)
periphrastic construction
phrase (noun phrase, verb
   phrase, prepositional
   phrase)
predicate
preposition
progressive (form)
reference grammar
reflexivity
relative clause
sentence (compound sen-
   tence ↔ complex sentence)
semantic role (agent, patient,
   goal, benefactive, ...)
situation

subject
subjunctive
subordinating conjunction
   (adverbial subordinator)
syntagmatic differentiation
syntax
tense: absolute (present,
   past, future) ↔ relative
valency
verb (auxiliary ↔ semi-auxil-
   iary ↔ main/full verb; copula; modal; primary; transitive ↔ intransitive; causative; particle; prepositional;
   telic verb)
voice (active ↔ passive ↔
   mediopassive-)
word class
word form

Exercises

1. Which grammatical categories are marked on English nouns and verbs?

2.

   a) Identify, in traditional terms, all parts of speech in the following sentence:
   Then the boy rubbed the magic lamp and suddenly a genie appeared beside him.
   b) *Round* belongs to as many as five different word classes. Give one example for each of them.

3.

   a) Provide the appropriate labels for the following phrases and state which of them do not have a head: *below the window, rather slowly, Tom and Jerry, has been saying, fast and expensive car*
   b) Where else in this book did we talk about heads and modifiers? Can you make any generalizations about the preferred order of heads and modifiers in English?

4. Identify all phrases and their grammatical functions in the following sentences:
a) He spends all his money on horses.
b) John called me an idiot.
c) Mary left the next day.
d) They may be staying until next June.
e) His face turned pale when he saw me.

5.
a) Identify the adverbs and adverbials in the following sentence:
   Honestly, I did see him briefly in the park yesterday when he was feeding the ducks.
b) Give typical properties of adverbials, and then specify what is unusual about the adverbial in the following sentence:
   The whole thing lasted a mere thirty seconds.

6. Underline and identify the different types of subordinate clauses in the sentences below:
a) That cities will attract more and more criminals is a safe prediction.
b) This shows how difficult the question must have been.
c) Being a farmer, he is suspicious of all governmental interference.
d) We knew that he was a lousy driver.
e) I am very eager to meet her.
f) The problem is who will water my plants when I am away.
g) No further discussion arising, the meeting was brought to a close.
h) I'll show you what you can open the bottle with.

7. There are two main types of relative clauses. *Restrictive* (or: *defining*) *relative clauses* provide necessary information about the head noun whereas *non-restrictive* (or: *non-defining*) *relative clauses* provide additional, but non-essential information. Identify these two types in the examples below and determine the structural differences between them.
a) My daughter, who studies medicine, will come and visit me today.
b) My daughter who studies medicine will come and...
c) My daughter studying medicine will come and...
d) The car she'll be using is our old Austin Mini.
e) *The car, she'll be using, is our old Austin Mini.
f) The car that she'll be using is our old Austin Mini.
g) *The car, that she'll be using, is our old Austin Mini.

8. Which of the following statements are true and which are false?
a) English is a language with grammatical gender.
b) Normally, only transitive verbs can be passivized.
c) Modal verbs lack participles.
d) All copulas have the valency zero.
e) English has no inflectional future.

f) Languages with little or no inflectional morphology need a fixed SVO order.

g) All verbs demanding an object complement also demand an object, but not vice versa.

h) The subjects of active and passive sentences differ with regard to their prototypical semantic roles.

i) English is relatively rich in mediopassive constructions and adverbial participles.

j) There is an inflectional subjunctive in the sentence *We insist that the director resign*.

Advanced

9.

a) Which of the following verbs are phrasal verbs and which are prepositional verbs?
rely on, believe in, take in, take away, fill up, dispose of, blow up

b) There are two possible syntactic analyses of prepositional verbs and the NP following them: either as an intransitive verb followed by a PP (see A) or as a transitive verb followed by a direct object (see B):
A. [They] [trusted] [in a friend]
B. [They] [trusted in] [a friend]
If you consider the following sentences, which is the preferred analysis? However, note that there are also arguments for the alternative analysis: Try to find some of them.
a)   A friend in whom they trusted.
b)   In whom did they trust?
c)   They trusted steadfastly in a friend.
d) * They trusted in steadfastly a friend.

10. The progressive has constantly extended its territory in the course of the history of English. Consult a linguistic corpus, e. g. the *British National Corpus* or the *Corpus of Contemporary American English*, and look up the construction '*I'm being* + adjective.' Describe this construction and specify its meaning. Can all types of adjectives be used with the progressive? Give examples and specify the meaning of the relevant construction.

11. Draw up a list of arguments taken from different domains of grammar which illustrate that English is a strongly analytic language.

12. The following text should make you say goodbye to English grammar with a big smile. But there is also a task connected with it. Try to spot all grammatical and otherwise language-related terms, and ask yourself what exactly it is that creates the humorous effect in the individual cases. So off we go with a stirring courtroom-drama:

"The murder of the English language" – sometimes known as "The accusative case"

Prosecution: Are you Very Quickly, adverbial phrase?

Accused: I am.

P: Very Quickly, you are accused of splitting an infinitive! Say, how do you plead: Guilty or not guilty?

A: Not guilty, not guilty.

P: A double negative. How then would you explain your past imperfect?

A: I was going through an awkward phrase. There's no substantive proof! Now and then I just colon friends for a quick imperative before lunch.

P: And is that all?

A: Well no, there is rather a pretty feminine gender in the case, a Miss Pronunciation, who lives in suffix with her grammar and grandpa.

P: When was your first dative?

A: I met her at a participle! There she was supine and in a passive mood. She was superlative, absolutely pluperfect!

P: Mr. Quickly, would I be correct in this preposition: that you were aiming for an unlawful conjugation with this feminine gender? Answer the interrogative: How far did you get?

A: I made a parse at her, but she declined. She said her parentheses would object. And anyway she's about to become a noun.

P: Was this news neuter you?

A: Affirmative.

P: Thank you. What nationality is she?

A: Italic.

P: Mr. Quickly, you are in quite a predicate I can tell you. Officer, put him in brackets! You are also accused of immoral earnings from prose – and even verse, evasion of syntax.

Judge: And now the sentence: Off with his prefix!

Sources and further reading

Aarts, Bas. 2017[5]. *English syntax and argumentation*. London: Red Globe Press.

Aarts, Bas/Jill Bowie/Gergana Popova, eds. 2019. *The Oxford handbook of English grammar*. Oxford: Oxford University Press.

Biber, Douglas/Stig Johansson/Geoffrey Leech/Susan Conrad/Edward Finegan. 1999. *The Longman grammar of spoken and written English*. London: Longman.

Givón, Talmy. 1993. *English grammar: A function-based introduction*. 2 vols. Amsterdam/Philadelphia: Benjamins.

Greenbaum, Sidney/Randolph Quirk. 1990. *A student's grammar of the English language*. Harlow: Longman.

Halliday, Michael A. K. 2014[3]. *An introduction to functional grammar*. revised by Christian M. I. M. Matthiessen. London: Routledge.

Huddleston, Rodney. 1984. *Introduction to the grammar of English*. Cambridge: Cambridge University Press.

Huddleston, Rodney/Geoffrey K. Pullum. 2002. *The Cambridge grammar of the English language*. Cambridge: Cambridge University Press.

Hurford, James R. 1994. *Grammar: A student's guide*. Cambridge: Cambridge University Press.

König, Ekkehard. 1994. "English." In: Ekkehard König/Johan van der Auwera, eds. *The Germanic languages*. London/New York: Routledge. 532–565.

Leech, Geoffrey/Christian Mair/Marianne Hundt/Nicholas Smith. 2012. *Change in contemporary English: A grammatical study*. Cambridge: Cambridge University Press.

Leisi, Ernst/Christian Mair. 2008[9]. *Das heutige Englisch: Wesenszüge und Probleme*. Heidelberg: Winter.

McCawley, James D. 1998[2]. *The syntactic phenomena of English*. Chicago/London: The University of Chicago Press.

Miller, Jim. 2011. *A critical introduction to syntax*. London: Continuum.

Miller, Jim/Regina Weinert. 1998. *Spontaneous spoken language: Syntax and discourse*. Oxford: Clarendon Press.

Quirk, Randolph/Sidney Greenbaum/Jan Svartvik/Geoffry Leech. 1985. *A comprehensive grammar of the English language*. London: Longman.

Tallerman, Maggie. 2015[4]. *Understanding syntax*. New York: Routledge.

Thomson, Audrey J./Agnes V. Martinet. 2012[4]. *A practical English grammar*. Oxford: Oxford University Press.

Trask, Robert L. 1993. *A dictionary of grammatical terms in linguistics*. London/New York: Routledge.

5 Contrastive Linguistics: English and German

The present chapter aims to give an overview of the most important structural differences between English and German. It will reconsider some issues discussed earlier in this book, albeit from a decidedly different point of view, and explore how the basic structural differences between English and German are related to each other.

Bundles of contrasts: The focus of this chapter will be on clusters or bundles of contrasts, each of which can be derived from a fundamental structural difference between the two languages. The overarching objective will be to show how it is possible to bring order to the large variety of superficially unrelated contrasts between English and German which, after all, are two otherwise closely related languages. Thus, we will increasingly take a bird's-eye view of the two languages: the task will be to work out their essential characteristics and compare these to general tendencies among the world's languages. One crucial insight will be that many of the differences between English and German are not restricted to these two languages but represent more general contrasts between languages which – like English and German – represent different language types. Along these lines, we will have to restrict ourselves to a few select grammatical structures (section 5.2). Nevertheless, towards the end of the chapter the most important phonetic and phonological differences will be outlined, too (section 5.3).

But let us first find out more about the field of contrastive linguistics, in general, by focussing on the following three questions: What are its basic assumptions and premises? How did it develop? And how is it relevant to foreign-language teaching?

5.1 | Contrastive Linguistics

Contrastive Linguistics (CL) traditionally refers to the synchronic comparison of two languages with respect to a large number of linguistic structures (or parameters). Its objective is to work out not only what the two language systems have in common but especially in which respects they differ.

definition

Pedagogical bias of early contrastive linguistics: The motivation for focussing on the differences between two languages lies in the basic as-

early days purely educational

J.B. Metzler © Springer-Verlag GmbH Deutschland, ein Teil von Springer Nature, 2020
B. Kortmann, *English Linguistics*, https://doi.org/10.1007/978-3-476-05678-8_5

sumption of early CL (1940s to 1960s) that, when learning a foreign language, a speaker will find the structures that are different to his or her native language particularly difficult to acquire. The aim of early CL was purely educational. The systematic comparison of two languages was expected to help improve foreign-language learning and teaching by predicting potential sources of error and incorporating contrastive findings into more effective learning and teaching materials. The educational approach of CL is based on the following premises:

3 premises
of early CL

- First, foreign language acquisition is different from first language acquisition.
- Second, a foreign language is always acquired against the background of a speaker's native language.
- Third, foreign-language learners usually find certain features of a foreign language easy to learn and have difficulties with others.

transfer

Contrastive (Analysis) Hypothesis: According to this hypothesis, which was established by Robert Lado in 1957, speakers find those structures of a foreign language (L2) easy to learn that resemble equivalent structures in their own native language (L1). Differences between the two languages, on the other hand, may result in learning difficulties and are a major source of mistakes made by foreign-language learners. The contrastive hypothesis is therefore based on the idea of transfer, i. e. the tendency of foreign-language learners to transfer characteristic features of their mother tongue to the foreign language they are learning. Depending on whether this transfer supports or hampers the acquisition of a foreign language, we speak of positive or negative transfer.

negative transfer

Types of interference: Due to its focus on education, CL has always focused on *negative transfer*, so-called interference. From a contrastive perspective, the most important types of interference are substitution (1a), over- or underdifferentiation (1b) and over- or underrepresentation (1c). Only the former two can actually lead to mistakes. Over- or underrepresentation, i. e. speakers using a certain native-language construction either too often or too rarely in a foreign language, may only result in unidiomatic language use and give the impression that a native speaker would have expressed the same content or issue differently. Unlike normal interference, which leads to errors, underrepresentation or the complete avoidance of certain structures of the target language is especially frequent among beginners and advanced learners.

(1) a. **substitution:**
e.g. German /s/, /z/, /v/ for English /θ/, /ð/, /w/;
ich bekomme ein Bier > *ʼI become a beer*;
wenn ich ihn fragen würde, würde er ablehnen > *ʼif I would ask him, he would refuse* (not possible in Standard British English)

b$_1$. **overdifferentiation:**
differentiation of L1 does not exist in L2 (e. g. German *Frucht/ Obst* vs. *fruit*)

b_2. **underdifferentiation:**
differentiation in L2 does not exist in L1 (e. g. *shade/shadow* vs. *Schatten, snail/slug* vs. *Schnecke; Past Tense/Present Perfect* vs. *Perfekt* as narrow tense, *simple/progressive form* in English vs. "simple form" in German

c_1. **overrepresentation:**
speakers use structures of their mother tongue more often than native speakers would do, e. g. finite subordinate clauses with introductory relative pronouns or adverbial subordinators. It can also be observed that advanced learners overuse foreign-language structures in L2.

c_2. **underrepresentation:**
speakers use foreign-language structures more rarely than native speakers would do, e. g. shortened relative clauses (*The man sitting on the bench watched her all the time*), adverbial participles (*Sitting on the bench, the man watched her all the time*) or mediopassive constructions (*This book won't sell*).

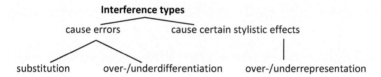

Figure 5.1:
Interference types

A critical look at "pedagogical" contrastive linguistics: From what is known today, some of the basic assumptions of CL – and hence its objectives – must be taken with extreme caution. Learning difficulties and mistakes, for example, need not always result from differences between a learner's native language and the target language. On the contrary, learner problems can also be due to similarities between the two languages. Consider the perfect in German and English. Both languages have very similar constructions (although Standard English has no equivalent of the German *sein* 'be'-perfect any longer: *Ich bin gekommen* but **I am come*). Nevertheless, the correct use of the English Present Perfect presents a major difficulty for many German learners. In German, especially in spontaneous speech, the perfect is almost exclusively used as an (absolute) past tense. It can easily replace the Simple Past (*Präteritum*) and is generally used as a narrative tense (see (2a)), whereas in English a story cannot be told in the Present Perfect (2b). There is a strict division of tasks between Present Perfect and Simple Past, and there are many adverbials of time which can only be used with one of the two tenses (see chapter 4.3.2).

L1-L2 similarities matter, too

(2) a. Gestern Abend sind wir erst im Kino gewesen. Dann sind wir zu Luigi gegangen und haben noch ein Eis gegessen. Dann ist es auch schon ziemlich spät gewesen, und Tina hat uns nach Hause gefahren.

   b. *Last night we've been to the cinema. *Then we've gone to Luigi's and have eaten ice cream. *Then it's been rather late already, and Tina has driven us home.

error analysis We should also be careful concerning the predictive power of contrastive analyses. Extensive empirical studies of errors made by foreign-language learners have shown that some errors predicted by CL were very rare or did not occur at all, whereas some frequently made mistakes had not been predicted. This can frequently be observed with regard to grammar, whereas predictions made by CL are more reliable in phonetics and phonology. Most importantly, however, the proportion of errors resulting from differences or similarities between two language systems, i. e. errors due to transfer, must not be overestimated. Although transfer is indeed responsible for a large number of errors (on average about 50 %), there are many additional factors which need to be taken into consideration.

strong CH: little prognostic value **Role of CL: prognosis → diagnosis:** To cut a long story short: the Contrastive Hypothesis and its basic assumptions about foreign-language acquisition have turned out to be far too strong. Following the peak of CL in the 1950s and 1960s, empirical studies in the 1970s showed that only some of the errors that occur during foreign language learning are due to structural differences between the two languages. CL must therefore be seen as having relatively limited prognostic potential. Its strength rather lies in its use as a diagnostic tool which, by considering different language systems, can explain a considerable amount of errors. Similarly disappointing has been CL's role in improving learning materials. Among the teaching materials of the last few decades, very few have incorporated CL findings. Moreover, there is no empirical evidence that learning and teaching materials based on CL findings are superior to traditional materials.

Shift to non-pedagogical CL: By the 1970s, after realizing that its applicability must not be overestimated, linguists ceased to view CL primarily as a branch of applied linguistics, regarding it instead as a branch of theoretical and descriptive linguistics. Even though they are not directly relevant to teaching practice, the insights obtained from non-pedagogical CL are valuable in themselves, especially for advanced foreign-language students and (future) foreign-language teachers. CL can therefore be considered to be one out of several branches of comparative linguistics (compare figure 5.2).

Figure 5.2: Comparative linguistics

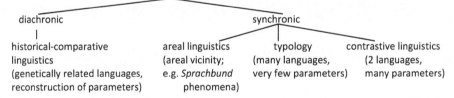

Comparative linguistics

diachronic	synchronic		
historical-comparative linguistics (genetically related languages, reconstruction of parameters)	areal linguistics (areal vicinity; e.g. *Sprachbund* phenomena)	typology (many languages, very few parameters)	contrastive linguistics (2 languages, many parameters)

language family trees **Historical-comparative linguistics:** The oldest branch of comparative linguistics is historical-comparative linguistics (or: comparative philology), the dominant linguistic approach of the 18th and especially 19th century. Its goal is to establish family relationships by comparing different languages (e. g. English and German as West Germanic languages, or Danish and Icelandic as North Germanic languages) and to reconstruct older stages of given languages or even the proto-languages from which different language families developed (e. g. Proto-Germanic as the "mother" of all Germanic languages, where *proto* means 'reconstructed, without written records'). The probably best-known fruit of historical-comparative research are language family trees.

Historical-comparative linguistics often shows how one of two genetically related languages develops in the same direction as, but lags behind the other, so that the former may be more similar to earlier stages of the latter. This exactly applies to the historical developments of and the current relationship between English and German. German is the language lagging behind, so that Present-Day German is more like English spoken a thousand years ago (in the periods of Old and Early Middle English) than like Present-Day English (for details, see 5.2). German: lagging behind English

Areal linguistics (or: areal typology) uses a synchronic approach in investigating languages which, over the course of time, have become more and more alike due to their geographical proximity, even though they are not related genetically. One famous example of such a linguistic convergence area is the Balkan *Sprachbund*. The languages forming the core of this group (Modern Greek, Albanian, Romanian, Bulgarian and Macedonian) have a number of linguistic features in common (e. g. postposed definite articles, loss of the infinitive) which, for example, Romanian does not share with any other Romance language, or Bulgarian and Macedonian do not share with any other Slavonic language. Balkan Sprachbund

Language typology: Of all comparative approaches, typology is the only one which matters in present-day CL. Its goal is to identify patterns and limits of variation among the languages of the world and to distinguish different language types via empirical analysis of a multitude of languages which are neither historically, genetically nor geographically related. To this purpose, typologists study representative samples of the more than 6,000 languages spoken worldwide, focusing on only a few parameters, or even just one. Well-known examples of such variation parameters are the type and complexity of inflectional morphology (which yields the morphological language types described in chapter 4.1) or the basic word order of subject, verb and object in simple declarative sentences. identifying patterns and limits of variation

One hallmark of typology is its constant effort to establish correlations between properties of different languages. For example, in most languages where the verb precedes the object (so-called VO-languages like English or French), prepositions and relative clauses follow their nominal heads. Conversely, most OV-languages (like Turkish and Japanese) have postpositions and relative clauses which precede their nominal heads. Such generalizations are preferably formulated as so-called implicational universals, e. g. 'A language which has SOV as its canonical word order is very likely to have postpositions.' implicational universals

New orientation: CL ↔ typology: Since the 1980s, CL has been increasingly inspired by typology, employing new methods, asking different questions, offering new explanations, and adopting a whole new framework for classifying the contrasts and similarities observed between the languages under investigation. Above all, typologically oriented CL tries identifying sets of contrasts to establish correlations between structural differences which appear to be completely unrelated at first sight. It then bundles these differences into sets of contrasts, and does not attempt to explain them solely by invoking properties of the structural systems of the relevant languages. Rather, it also sets out to predict to what extent we may expect these differences (but also the similarities) to occur among other languages of the same types. Section 5.2 will illustrate what such an approach looks like.

Markedness Differential Hypothesis **Typology and foreign language acquisition:** There are also links between typology and foreign-language acquisition. For example, the greater the difference is between the overall language types that two languages represent, i. e. the greater the typological distance between two languages, the longer it will take a native speaker of one of these languages to learn the other language, or to achieve a high degree of proficiency. A more specific type of typology-based prediction regarding potential difficulties in foreign-language acquisition zooms in on those domains in which a learner's native language differs from the foreign language to be acquired. It has been shown that foreign-language learners experience special difficulties in those cases where the target language is (more) marked as compared to their mother tongue, i. e. instances where the target language is typologically unusual and does not follow a universal tendency (*Markedness Differential Hypothesis*; see section 5.3 for a phonetic example). Thus, the modified Contrastive Hypothesis regains its relevance.

5.2 | The most striking grammatical differences between English and German

Before investigating some of the most important grammatical differences between English and German, it should be added that there are also quite a number of structural features they have in common. Since German and English are two closely related languages, this does not come as a surprise. Together with Dutch, Frisian, Afrikaans and Yiddish, they form the branch of West Germanic languages. With these, as well as with the slightly more remote North Germanic (or: Scandinavian) languages, English and German share a number of morphological and syntactic properties, for example:

shared properties
- the distinction between strong verbs (e. g. *sing-sang-sung, gehen-ging-gegangen*) and weak verbs (e. g. *work-worked-worked, lieben-liebte-geliebt*)
- only two tenses which are marked by inflection of the verb stem, namely past (or preterite, marked) and non-past (or present, unmarked)
- in simple declarative sentences, the predicate containing the finite verb usually comes second ($V_{fin}/2$)
- use of word order to distinguish between the basic sentence types ($V_{fin}/2$ in declarative sentences and $V_{fin}/1$ in questions)

- historically: increasing analyticity due to the loss of various inflectional morphemes

Typological differences as source of contrasts: In what follows, only the most central grammatical contrasts between English and German will be considered. They will not be discussed independently of each other or of the overall ground plan of English, as far as possible. Rather, they will be related to English and the language type it represents with regard to the following parameters: morphology (5.2.1), word order (5.2.2) and the mapping between form and function (5.2.3). One set of contrasts will be presented in each of these three sections, always starting out from a fundamental typological difference between the ground plans of English and German, which will then open the door to a variety of other (contrasting) properties. Note that there are, of course, causal links between these sets, and that some of them overlap. In English, the loss of inflectional morphology (5.2.1) has resulted in a more rigid word order (5.2.2), which, in turn, causes a loosening of the mapping between semantic structure and grammatical form (at least in a number of central areas of grammar (5.2.3)). In other words: the structural differences between English and German will be considered from three different perspectives, which will help us see the wood for the trees. Finally, section 5.2.4 offers an account of the most important structural contrasts which cannot be easily subsumed under one of the three sets of contrasts.

3 sets of contrasts in grammar

5.2.1 | Morphology

One important set of contrasts between English and German is related to the fact that English has travelled a long way from a strongly inflectional language towards an isolating language (see also chapter 4.1) while German has stayed rather conservative, also compared to the other Germanic languages. This fundamental typological contrast between a near-isolating language (English) and a still strongly inflectional language (German) manifests itself, for example, in the following morphological and syntactic differences.

German: more conservative

Contrasts within the NP: English has an eroded case system. Nouns can only occur in two different forms, either not marked for case (common case) or marked for the possessive. Pronouns can have an additional object form (e. g. *he – his – him, who – whose – whom*), but the object form of the relative and interrogative pronouns is used more and more rarely (at least in informal English), and most speakers prefer the unmarked form (*who*) or the zero pronoun in sentences like the following:

(3) a. The woman whom/who/Ø I met yesterday is a professor of linguistics.
    b. Whom/Who did you give the money to?

Concord/agreement – government: English articles and adjectives are not marked for case at all. So there is no concord in English noun phrases,

no case marking in English

that is, no formal agreement between the nominal head and the constituents which modify it. Also, prepositions and verbs in English do not require that the nominal argument they precede is marked for a certain case. German, on the other hand, has both of these properties, marking not only gender by means of inflectional morphemes (masculine/feminine/neuter) but also marking nouns, pronouns, articles and adjectives for nominative, genitive, dative and accusative case (as well as gender):

(4) a. concord: ein-Ø alt-er Mann-Ø (nominative masc. sg.)
ein-es alt-en Mann-es (genitive masc. sg.)
ein-em alt-en Mann-Ø (dative masc. sg.)
ein-en alt-en Mann-Ø (accusative masc. sg.)
b. government: *gedenken* + genitive, *bezichtigen* + genitive
wegen + genitive/dative, *durch* + accusative
in + dative (place/location: *er wanderte in dem Wald*)
in + accusative (direction: *er ging in den Wald*)

If the adjective is attributive, i. e. if it serves as a premodifier, German additionally distinguishes between 'strong' and 'weak' inflection (*ein toll-es Buch/ein-e toll-e Woche/ein toll-er Tag* vs. *das toll-e Buch/die toll-e Woche/der toll-e Tag*). English has completely lost this distinction.

again: German
extremely con-
servative

Grammatical functions: Another reason why case marking is so important in German is that it is the only means for indicating grammatical functions (or: relations) of verb arguments: the subject is nominative, the direct object is accusative, and the indirect object is dative. In this respect, German is the most conservative among the modern Germanic languages (together with Icelandic). In English, on the other hand, grammatical functions are determined by word order, which is relatively fixed: the canonical word order is subject – verb – (indirect – direct) object, in main as well as subordinate clauses (for further details see 5.2.2).

Contrasts within the VP: German has retained its numerous inflectional endings in the verb phrase to mark mood (indicative – *sie komm-t*, "Konjunktiv I" – *sie komm-e*, "Konjunktiv II" – *sie käme*), number and person, all of which have either been lost completely in English or are retained in no more than a rudimentary form. In English, the distinction between indicative and subjunctive, singular and plural, as well as first, second and third person is hardly ever made, except in the present tense where it is all expressed by one morpheme: the third person singular indicative {-s} (*she sing-s*). The verb *to be* is the only one with a separate subjunctive form (e. g. *if I were you*), which is, however, on the way out (e. g. *if I was you*). In all other cases, English uses other forms to indicate subjunctive mood (compare (5)):

(5) a. We demand that he <u>leave</u>. (infinitive without *to*)
b. If he <u>left</u>, we would all be happy. (Simple Past)

Higher degree of analyticity in English: In addition, there is a preference for constructions with modal *would* or *should* (e. g. *We demand that he* _should leave_), i. e. periphrastic constructions where inflectional languages would use, or at least may use, verb inflection (e. g. _sie sagte, er käme morgen_ vs. _sie sagte, er würde morgen kommen_). This behaviour reflects a basic property of the English verb phrase, namely its high degree of analyticity and stronger grammaticalization of periphrastic constructions as compared to German. This holds true for all auxiliaries (a group of verbs clearly distinguished from main verbs both morphologically and syntactically, see 4.3.1) as well as for the tense and aspect system. Consider, for example, the Progressive, of which (at least written Standard) German has no equivalent. Or take the use of the Present Perfect, which is much more restricted than the German _Perfekt_. (In English, it is only used to mark anteriority, never as a narrative tense.) Another case in point is the strongly grammaticalized _will/shall_-construction for the marking of future tense (for more details see 5.2.4).

5.2.2 | Word order

From relatively free to relatively fixed word order: As a result of its almost complete loss of inflectional morphology, English has experienced a dramatic typological change from a language with a relatively free word order to a language with a relatively fixed word order. German has not changed in this respect: its word order is still as free as it used to be a thousand years ago, which means that the order of subject, object and verb can vary considerably (within certain limits, of course). All the German sentences in (6) are grammatically correct, whereas English only allows the word order used in (6a):

again: German conservative

(6) a. Der Mann versprach dem Kind eine Überraschung. (SVO$_i$O$_d$)
     b. Dem Kind versprach der Mann eine Überraschung. (O$_i$VSO$_d$)
     c. Eine Überraschung versprach der Mann dem Kind. (O$_d$VSO$_i$)

Word order contrasts in main and subordinate clauses: Word order in English has changed dramatically in two additional respects:

For one thing, it has developed a fixed word order of subject-verb-object, the first two constituents of which are obligatory. This means that, besides a predicate, every English sentence has to have a subject, which is why we often need elements like _it_ and _there_ to take over this grammatical function. Consider the so-called _dummy subjects_ in (7):

dummy subjects

(7) a. It's late/raining/a long way to Tipperary.
     b. There are many different kinds of butterflies.
     c. There's two girls waiting outside.

Secondly, English underwent the change from a verb-final language (SOV) in medieval times to an SVO language both in main and subordinate clauses. German, by contrast, has again remained much more conservative: It is still considered a language with a basic verb-final (SOV) word order, a property which is most evident in subordinate clauses:

English: SOV > SVO

contrast ..., *weil er das Haus sah* with *er sah das Haus*, or ..., *weil sie das Fahrrad gefunden hat* with *sie hat das Fahrrad gefunden*).

German:
a finite-second
language **Position of finite verb in German:** In main clauses the verb in German is placed in second position, provided it is finite (or tensed; like *sah* and *hat* in the examples above), which is why "finite-second" is the most appropriate way of characterizing the word order of main clauses and simple sentences in German. The finite verb serves as the key anchoring point here, with much greater freedom in arranging the other (notably the nominal) constituents around it compared to English, as can be seen from the examples in (8) and (9). Neither does the subject in German obligatorily precede or the object obligatorily follow the verb (compare (8b–g)) nor does every sentence in German necessarily have a subject (9). The only element of the sentence which does not change its position in (8) and is also fixed in (9) is the finite verb, namely in second position (*brachte* in (8); *wird, fröstelt, wurde* in (9a–c) respectively).

(8) a. Mein Freund brachte mich gestern Abend nach Hause.
     b. Gestern Abend brachte mich mein Freund nach Hause.
     c. Gestern Abend brachte mein Freund mich nach Hause.
     d. Nach Hause brachte mich gestern Abend mein Freund.
     e. Nach Hause brachte mein Freund mich gestern Abend.
     f. Mich brachte gestern Abend mein Freund nach Hause.
     g. Mich brachte mein Freund gestern Abend nach Hause.
(9) a. Jetzt wird aber endlich geschlafen!
     b. Mich fröstelt.
     c. Ihm wurde geholfen.

Discourse pragmatics / information structure: theme/old – rheme/new: In German, as in all inflectional languages, the property of having a relatively free word order can be exploited for discourse-pragmatic purposes. The order of the constituents of a sentence is not subject to any grammatical requirements and can therefore be manipulated to fit the communicative needs of the speaker. In simple words: speakers of German can basically begin, continue and end a sentence as they please. If somebody asks *Wer brachte dich gestern Abend nach Hause?* (*Who brought you home last night?*), the answer may be (8'a) or, though less natural, (8'f).

(8') a. Mein Freund (brachte mich nach Hause).
      f. Mich brachte mein Freund nach Hause.

theme-rheme or
topic-comment The sentence in (8'a) starts with the new information whereas (8'f) starts with the information already known (i. e. established in the question), revealing the new information at the end of the sentence. In a neutral context, the way the information is distributed in (8'f) is usually considered to be the unmarked, in the sense of most frequently chosen, option in declarative sentences, progressing from old (or: given) information which is already known (e. g. as general world knowledge or shared knowledge of speaker and hearer) or can be deduced from the previous context to new information which cannot be deduced from the context.

This information structure is also known as theme-rheme or topic-comment structure.

In a German sentence like (8'f), a topic-comment structure can be easily accomplished by changing the position of the subject and direct object, whereas this is not possible in English – or in any other predominantly isolating language. English uses a fixed basic word order for marking grammatical functions, which is why the information structure in English sentences is subject to the restrictions of word order. To achieve the same effect as in (8'f), English has to use a passive construction (*I was brought home by my friend*). This is why inflectional languages are said to have a "pragmatic word order", while strongly analytical or isolating languages are said to have a highly fixed, grammaticalized word order.

German: a pragmatic word order language

English	German
relatively fixed	relatively free
strongly grammaticalized	pragmatic
SVO (in main and subordinate clauses)	$V_{fin}/2$ in main clauses; V-final in subordinate clauses

Table 5.1: Word order in English and German

In English, the relatively fixed order of syntactic elements also shows in other domains. As can be seen from the sentences above (8a, d, f, g), German permits other positions and sequences of adverbials of time and place than English. In English, both of these adverbials can only occur at the periphery of a sentence (with the adverbial of time always first or last):

position of adverbials of time and place

(10) a. Last year in Britain we met her for the first time. (not: In Britain last year...)
b. We met her for the first time in Britain last year. (not: ... last year in Britain.)

Consequences of the word order differences: What are the consequences of the fundamental word order differences between English and German? More precisely, what are the consequences of the strong restrictions on word order in English? There are, basically, three major effects:

- English has developed a number of means to compensate for its fixed word order, thereby permitting a reconciliation of discourse-pragmatic needs with structural requirements (i. e. SVO order).
- English sentence constituents may have lost their mobility within clause boundaries, but they have gained greater mobility across clauses. This results in what has been labelled *fused constructions* (*Konstruktionsverschmelzungen*) or *argument trespassing*, which often makes it difficult to identify clause boundaries.
- Considering the two consequences above from a different perspective, one will notice a loosening of the relationship between form and meaning (or function) in several central domains of English grammar. The meanings and functions of constructions, constituents and words often vary more in English than they do in German and can only be derived from the immediate context.

3 effects

Compensation strategies in English: We will now outline the first two of these developments. More detail about the third one will be added in section 5.2.3. The examples in (11) to (17) illustrate different strategies and information-structuring devices which English has developed in order to allow speakers to meet the word order requirements, but still be able to structure the information in their utterances (the distribution of "old" and "new" information) according to their communicative goals.

Clefts and pseudo-clefts: The first few sentences are examples of focusing constructions: cleft sentences (11a, b) and pseudo-cleft-sentences (11c, d), the use of which English has expanded considerably. These constructions make it possible to highlight (or focus on) single constituents of sentences like *John crashed my car*. In cleft sentences, the focus (and with it, often the new information) is found in the superordinate clause, whereas in pseudo-cleft sentences the focus is on the complement of the *be*-form in the second part of the sentence. In each of the following sentences the focused constituent is underlined:

(11) a. It was <u>John</u> who crashed my car.   (question: Who crashed your car?)

b. It was <u>my car</u> which John crashed.   (questions: What/Whose car did John crash?)

c. What John crashed was <u>my car</u>.   (question: What did John crash?)

d. What John did was <u>crash my car</u>.   (question: What did John do?)

English: more clefting options   Compared to German, English does not only use such constructions more frequently, but also has more clefting possibilities. The adverbial of an embedded clause, for example, can be the focus of a cleft sentence (12a, b). Besides, there is a variant of pseudo-cleft-sentences with an inverted information structure (12c):

(12) a. It was <u>yesterday</u> she said she would be coming ......

b. It's <u>because he had stolen</u> that he was sacked ......

c. Crash my car was what John did. (contrast with 11d)

Passive: Two further domains of grammar which are especially interesting from a contrastive point of view are the passive and the coding of grammatical functions. We have already mentioned the expansion of English passive constructions in this and previous chapters (also 4.3.2). Among other things, English uses the passive where German simply puts the object at the beginning of the sentence (compare 13a, b). In English, we can additionally use the indirect object of an active sentence (14a) and the object of a preposition (15a) as subjects, both of which are impossible in German.

(13) a. I was taken home by my friend.

b. Mich brachte mein Freund nach Hause.

(14) a. He was offered a large amount of money.
      b. Ihm/*Er wurde ein großer Geldbetrag angeboten.
(15) a. This car has been meddled with.
      b. An diesem Auto/*Dieses Auto ist an herumgefummelt worden.

In all of the above cases, the use of the passive allows the subject of the sentence to be the topic, and thus to align the 'topic/old before comment/new' information structure with the obligatory word order.

Semantic roles of subjects: Exactly as in example (14a), and especially in (15a), there is a wide variety of unusual subjects in English. They are unusual because they are not prototypical subjects, i. e. subjects of active sentences which have the semantic role of an agent, or subjects of passive sentences which have the semantic (or: thematic) role of a patient (see chapter 4.2.3). Two things are crucial about the unusual subjects in (16): first, these constructions allow for a greater number of topicalization strategies in English. And second: from a contrastive point of view, German has fewer possibilities in this respect, and also uses them less often.

unusual subjects in English

(16) a. The fifth day saw our departure. (time)
      b. The room seats 500 people. (place)
      c. The stove has blown a fuse. (place, possessor)
      d. The bucket was leaking water. (source)
      e. A pound once bought two pints of beer. (instrument)
      f. This ad will sell us a lot. (instrument)
      g. John wounded his leg in the war. (experiencer/patient)
      h. The latest edition of the book has added a chapter. (?)

Semantic roles of objects: In a similar vein, English has many unusual objects, especially direct objects which do not fulfil the semantic role of a patient. Of the examples shown in (17), only (17a and b) are relevant for the topic-comment structure. Both illustrate the emergence of a new rhematization device for objects. In each of these two sentences, the unusual object compensates for the loss of a construction consisting of a prepositional phrase with instrumental meaning (*with* + NP) which is immediately followed by a prepositional phrase with locative meaning (contrast (17a) with German *Sie strich mit ihren langen Fingern über den neuen Mantel*).

unusual objects in English

(17) a. She stroked her long fingers over the new coat. (instrument)
      b. He wiped the wet cloth over the dishes. (instrument)
      c. He swam the Channel in one day. (place)
      d. They fled the capital. (source)
      e. The albatross was riding the wind. (trajectory)
      f. He threatened violence. (instrument)
      g. The book sold two million copies. (quantifier?)
      h. The march protested the invasion of Harikutu. (?)

The examples in (16) and (17) illustrate a general development in English: the functional expansion of subjects and objects.

many more op-
tions in English

Transitivity: In more general terms, the functional range of transitive constructions has broadened considerably in English. This includes a development which was already mentioned as an example of word-class internal conversion (see chapters 3.3.3 and 4.3.2): some originally intransitive verbs have acquired an additional transitive use (e. g. *stand* in *stand the bank robbers against the wall*, or *run* in *run a horse in the Derby*), usually acquiring a causative meaning (e. g. 'make the bank robbers stand against the wall'). Conversely, there is also a great number of originally transitive verbs which can be used intransitively in mediopassive constructions (e. g. *This car won't sell* or *These shirts wash well*); for the corresponding intransitive uses of transitive verbs, German uses the reflexive marker *sich*, as in *Dieses Buch verkauft sich nicht* oder *Diese Hemden lassen sich gut waschen*. Concerning English, this brings us back full circle (a) to the passive and to unusual subjects (since the subjects of mediopassives are subjects of active sentences which usually would be objects or typical subjects of passive sentences), and (b) to the possibilities that English offers in terms of structuring information despite its relatively rigid word order.

Argument trespassing across clause boundaries/fused constructions: Yet another characteristic property of English is the possibility of fusing (or: blending) different constructions. In comparison to German, this results in strikingly blurred clause boundaries. For instance, an important type of clause fusion occurs when sentence constituents (especially verb arguments) move across clause boundaries (also known as *argument trespassing*). All examples in (18) result from an argument of the non-finite verb of the subordinate clause being converted into a (syntactic, not logical) argument of the finite verb of the main clause. These are so-called raising constructions, of which we distinguish three main types:

3 types of raising
constructions

(18) a. I believe <u>her</u> to be a nice person. ($S_{sub} > O_{main}$)
         (vs. *I believe that <u>she</u> is a nice person*)
      b. <u>He</u> happened to know the answer. ($S_{sub} > S_{main}$)
         (vs. *It (so) happened that <u>he</u> knew the answer*)
      c. <u>This book</u> is boring to read. ($O_{sub} > S_{main}$)
         (vs. *It is boring to read <u>this book</u>*)

The raising of the object of a subordinate clause to the subject of a main clause (also known as *tough movement*) is yet another good example of unusual subjects in English. Raising constructions actually do occur in German (e. g. *Er scheint krank zu sein* ($S_{sub} > S_{main}$) or *Er ist schwer zu übersehen* ($O_{sub} > S_{main}$)), but they are subject to much stricter constraints and are therefore not nearly as productive as in English. In English, even arguments of deeply embedded subordinate clauses can move to the main clause (e. g. *<u>This promise</u> will be hard to persuade her to keep* from *It will be hard to persuade her to keep this promise*). Further examples of clause fusion in infinitival subordinate clauses are shown in (19):

(19) a. He's a hard man to reach.
         (vs. It is hard to reach this man)
     b. That's a difficult book to translate.
         (vs. It is difficult to translate this book)
     c. That's a funny book to read on a train.
         (vs. It is funny to read such a book on a train)

more clause
fusion in infinitival
clauses

In the examples in (19), the adjectives *hard*, *difficult* and *funny* do not modify the nouns which immediately follow (i. e. (19a) does not refer to a hard man, and (19b and c) do not refer to difficult or funny books), but rather characterize the overall situation (trying to contact a person, translating a book, reading a book on a train). Similar to the raising constructions in (18), there is a gap between the syntactic and the semantic structure.

As a final example of the syntactic fuzziness of infinitival constructions, let us mention *for NP to*-constructions like the ones in (20). Again, there is no equivalent in German.

syntactic fuzziness
in English

for NP to-construc-
tions

(20) a. Bill wants for me to leave. (AmE)
     b. She did not want for you to get hurt. (AmE)
     c. He's waiting for his children to arrive.
     d. He's waiting for his children to finish school.

Where do we draw the line between the main and subordinate clauses in these examples? Is *for me* in (20a) a prepositional phrase of the main clause or is it a sequence of a subordinator (similar to *that*) and a subject which belongs to the non-finite subordinate clause? Do we bracket the sentence as '[*Bill did not want for me*] [*to leave*]' or as '[*Bill did not want*] [*for me to leave*]'? The latter is certainly to be preferred. In all four examples shown in (20), the *for NP to* – construction functions as a syntactic unit, for example when being moved to the beginning of the sentence (*For me to leave is what Bill wants*). In (20c) and (20d), the problem is slightly different, because *wait for* (unlike *want for*) is a regular prepositional verb. What is interesting about these examples is their meaning. From a semantic perspective, it makes basically no difference what the man in (20c) is waiting for exactly – his children or their arrival. The sentence in (20d), on the other hand, can semantically be analysed in one way only: the man is not waiting for his children but for his children to finish school.

blurred boundaries
again

Gerunds: Similar to the instances of argument trespassing in (18) to (20), where the boundary between the main and subordinate clause is blurred because a verbal argument has "crossed" it, there is syntactic fuzziness in the transitional areas between gerunds and present participles. To start with, note that German – like all other Germanic languages – has no construction like the English gerund (see 21). The gerund has the special property of always qualifying as a noun phrase by virtue of its syntactic distribution (e. g. in subject or direct object function (21a and b)), yet at the same time displaying both verbal properties (e. g. its own

gerund vs. present
participle

direct object (21c) or negation, as in (21d)) and properties of a clause
(e. g. its own subject as in (21e)).

two-faced nature The English gerund is thus two-faced, depending on whether one considers its internal properties or its external properties, i. e. its syntactic
distribution.

(21) a. Singing in public is fun.
      b. I hate singing in public.
      c. I hate singing Wagner in public.
      d. I hate not singing Wagner in public.
      e. I hate the tenor's/his singing Wagner in public.

Fuzziness between gerunds and participles: The transition from a nominal to a verbal *ing*-form, that is the transition between gerund and present
participle, is blurred in sentences like (22), however. The construction in
(22a) still seems to be considered a gerund ('I hate (it) when ...'), whereas
it is more of a participle in (22b) and a participle for sure in (22c) ('I listened to an exhausted tenor when/who ...'):

(22) a. I hate the tenor/him singing Wagner in public.
      b. I listened to the tenor singing Wagner in public.
      c. I listened to an exhausted tenor singing Wagner in public.

The transition from gerund to participle poses, once again, the following
problems: (a) whether *the tenor* is an argument of the finite verb or the
ing-form, and therefore (b) where exactly the line runs between the main
and the subordinate clause. In (22a), the speaker does not "hate" the
tenor as a person, but the situation when the tenor sings Wagner in public. *The tenor* is therefore the subject of the *ing*-form, and the whole
ing-construction is the direct object of the verb *hate*. In other words:
(22a) is a simple sentence. In (22b), and even more clearly in (22c), *the
tenor* is the object of the verb *listen to* and at the same time the logical
subject (the agent) of the subsequent *ing*-form. The *ing*-form itself is the
non-finite predicate of a shortened subordinate clause (more precisely of
a restrictive relative clause or an adverbial clause: 'I listened to an exhausted tenor, who was/when he was singing Wagner in public').

5.2.3 | Form-function mappings

In this section, we will reconsider some of the grammatical contrasts
treated above from a different perspective, this time focusing on the relationship between form and meaning.

fit between form
and meaning
in German Greater functional transparency in German: Some of the most important morphological and syntactic differences between English and German boil down to the following tendency: in English, the fit between form
and meaning is much looser than in German, both with regard to individual words and syntactic constructions (cf. e. g. Hawkins 1986, 1992,
2019). This is another way of saying that in German the form of a word

or syntactic construction more often indicates how it is to be interpreted; meanings and functions are coded in a more transparent way.

In English, by contrast, meaning often cannot be inferred from the form of a word or construction alone but needs to be seen in the linguistic context. Most recently (2019), Hawkins has captured this by saying that over its history, English has systematically expanded word-external properties. Whereas in the medieval period, important syntactic or semantic properties could still be assigned to individual words, or rather word forms, in isolation, English now strongly depends on the information given in neighbouring words, i. e. word-externally, before such properties can be assigned to the word in question. This has important consequences for language processing: English is a language which requires readers and hearers to invest more processing effort in what they read or hear because they have more inference work to do (i. e. work which is necessary when drawing conclusions; see also 7.4 below).

more word-external properties in English

Tight-fit vs. loose-fit languages: Therefore, Hawkins (1986) classifies English as a 'loose-fit' language (since there is a relatively loose fit between form and meaning), whereas German is a 'tight-fit' language. For Hawkins, the reason lies in the almost complete loss of inflectional morphology in English and its development towards an isolating language. Due to this historical process, the decreasing number of forms had to carry an increasing functional load, i. e. number of functions and meanings, which is why in less than a thousand years English developed from a 'tight-fit' inflectional (or, strongly word-internal) language into a 'loose-fit', largely isolating (or: strongly word-external) language (cf. also Hawkins 2019).

Old English	
Old High German	
Modern German	Modern English
→	
inflecting	isolating
tight fit	loose fit
word-internal	word-external

Figure 5.3: Typological change in the history of English

The following sections will illustrate the relatively abstract parameters of "tightness vs. looseness of fit between form and meaning" or "word-internal vs. word-external properties" with examples mostly familiar from earlier chapters. Let us turn to morphology first: due to the radical reduction of inflectional endings, any given English lexeme has fewer word forms than its German counterpart. Depending on the syntactic context, an English noun phrase like *the man* may correspond to German *der Mann* (nominative), *dem Mann* (dative) or *den Mann* (accusative).

Loss of case inflections: The German translations of a noun phrase like *the sheep* include not only the singular forms *das Schaf* (nominative, accusative) and *dem Schaf* (dative) but, additionally, different cases in the plural: *die Schafe* (nominative, accusative) and *den Schafen* (dative). Here, one English form corresponds to several different German forms, every single one of which has its own ending that indicates whether it functions as a subject, direct object, or indirect object in a given sentence. (So in German, all this syntactic information is given word-internally.) In English, however, we need to know the precise linguistic context in order to determine the grammatical function of such noun phrases.

impact on grammatical function

Case marking is also used for disambiguating polysemous expressions. Think of government: German prepositions such as *auf* ('on') or *hinter* ('behind') can, for example, specify a location or an endpoint of a move-

disambiguating polysemous expressions

ment in space. In the first sense, they govern the dative (23a, 24a), in the latter they govern the accusative (23b, 24b):

(23) a. Er stand auf dem Tisch.
     b. Er sprang auf den Tisch.
(24) a. Er stand hinter dem Tisch.
     b. Er lief hinter den Tisch.

In German, then, case marking alone, i. e. purely word-internal informa-tion, sufficiently specifies the meaning of *auf* or *hinter* and which types of verbs they can combine with (a sentence like *Er stand auf den Tisch* is not possible). Needless to say, this is not possible in English, where both meanings are expressed by the same form: *on* or *behind the table*, as in (25). Also note that *where* may refer to either a place or a direction: *He asked me where I was* vs. *He asked me where I went*:

(25) a. He stood/jumped on the table.
     b. He stood/ran behind the table.

conversion Another example of the additional semantic and functional load that the largely invariable forms in English have to carry is the word *who*, which is often used instead of *whom* as either interrogative or relative pronoun (*Who did you give the money to?*). Conversion, as an extremely produc-tive word formation process in Present-Day English, is also a good exam-ple.

Predicate-argument structures: In English syntax, the disentangling of semantic from syntactic structure is superbly illustrated by predicate-ar-gument structures as discussed in section 5.2.2 above. Recall what was said about the considerable expansion of transitive constructions in Eng-lish, which resulted in the frequent use of an amazing variety of unusual subjects and objects, especially when compared to German. This is not to deny that the prototypical subject (of an active sentence) in English is an agent and that the prototypical object is a patient. But English deviates much more frequently from these prototypes, whereas in German, the prototypical relationship between grammatical function and semantic role is maintained to a much higher degree. Some of the unusual subjects and objects found in English are not permitted at all in German. In this context, we should also remember what was previously said concerning the conversion of intransitive verbs into transitive verbs and vice versa.

raising construc- Predicate-argument structures are also at issue when addressing the
tions and loose- ability of sentence constituents to move across clause boundaries, the
ness of fit resulting clause fusion phenomena, and the fuzziness of the border be-tween syntax and semantics. Raising constructions are probably the best example of how loose the fit between syntax and semantics has become in English. In *I believe John to be a nice person*, *John* is the direct object of *believe*, but only syntactically; semantically, of course, the speaker does not believe John, but believes something concerning a certain prop-erty of John. The examples in (19), (20) and (22) are all quite similar in this respect: in English, the assignment of arguments (subjects and ob-

jects) to predicates is much fuzzier than it is in German. Concerning this domain of contrastive grammar, we can conclude that the set of structural options in German is a subset of those available in English.

Preposition stranding: This also holds true for movement operations of syntactic elements out of larger constituents. The best-known examples for such extractions are prepositional phrases where the nominal complement of the head is moved to a position earlier in the sentence, leaving the preposition isolated or "stranded" in its original position. Preposition stranding, as in (26a) and (26b), is possible in English, but not in German:

impossible in German

(26) a.   The car <u>which</u> I saw you <u>in</u> looked quite expensive.
           (alternatively: *The car <u>in which</u> I saw you looked quite expensive.*)
      b.   <u>Which</u> car did you see me <u>in</u>?
           (alternatively: *<u>In which</u> car did you see me?*)
(27) a.   Das Auto, in dem ich dich sah,...
           (not: *Das Auto, dem ich dich sah in,...*)
      b.   In welchem Auto hast du mich gesehen?
           (not: *Welchem Auto hast du mich gesehen in?*)

Some generalizations: There is more to the story behind the mobility of syntactic elements in English and German than just the (no doubt) crucial fact that English has a relatively fixed SVO word order and German has a relatively free word order (SOV in subordinate clause, $V_{fin}/2$ in simple sentences and main clauses). Both in terms of moving verb arguments across clause or sentence boundaries (e. g. raising constructions) and moving elements out of phrases (e. g. preposition stranding), English has more structural possibilities than German. In a nutshell: German has the tendency to keep together what (syntactically and semantically) belongs together. With some minor qualifications, this aversion to experiments can also be seen in the way German assigns semantic roles to subjects and objects.

more structural options in English

In all, this characterization of English-German contrasts in core domains of grammar corresponds to the judgement of historical linguists, according to whom German is by far the more conservative language, whereas English qualifies as a highly innovative and progressive language (which, note, should not to be understood as a value judgement).

German: much more conservative

German and English from a typological perspective: In those grammatical domains where we have characterized German to be "averse to experiments" and "rather conservative", other languages have been found to behave quite similarly (cf. Hawkins 1992, 2019). These languages, too, have highly developed case systems, subjects that must be agents and direct objects that must be patients, strong restrictions on raising constructions, and no movement operations similar to preposition stranding. Moreover, these languages exhibit this combination of features in a highly consistent manner. Interestingly, all of these languages share another property: they are SOV languages. This strengthens the case of all those who consider SOV to be the basic word order of German.

parallels between German and (other) SOV languages

Adopting a typological perspective also teaches us another lesson about English, namely that English is by no means a prototypical representative of SVO languages once you consider all the morphological and syntactic contrasts with German that were discussed in this chapter. SVO languages like Russian, Chinese, Indonesian, or Modern Hebrew do not show the same combination of properties as English and, partly, behave quite differently. This is yet another piece of evidence that English features many structural peculiarities which distinguish it from other languages, be they closely related genetically (e. g. German), typologically (e. g. SVO languages), or areally (other European languages).

5.2.4 | Further differences in the verb phrase

There is a whole catalogue of individual structural differences between English and German which cannot (or at least not easily) be subsumed under the sets of contrasts presented in sections 5.2.1 to 5.2.3. Among the most important of these, those in the verb phrase probably form the most coherent group. Many of these contrasts were mentioned in chapter 4 already and will thus only be discussed briefly here.

Auxiliaries and main verbs: German makes no strict distinction between auxiliaries and main verbs, in contrast to English. Even modal verbs like *können* ('can'), *müssen* ('must'/'have to'), *wollen* ('want') or *sollen* ('should') have non-finite forms (e. g. *könnend – gekonnt, müssend – gemusst*). Further, auxiliaries in German have not lost their inflectional morphology (vs. *she cans, *she musts) and do not differ from main verbs syntactically in questions and negations. In English, on the other hand, all full verbs require *do*-support in questions and negations (*Does he come? No, he doesn't (come)*). This is an unusual property – not only from the perspective of German. The fact that English permits only this construction as a strategy for marking full verbs in negations and questions is unique among the European languages and even beyond. *Do*-support in questions also correlates with the canonical word order of English: it is a strategy which secures the correct order of subject, (main) verb and object, even in interrogatives.

Future tense: Among the grammatical categories of the verb, tense and aspect are certainly the most salient. English has a strongly grammaticalized future tense: the construction *will* (and the more and more obsolescent *shall*) + infinitive, in American English closely followed by the *going to* or *gonna* future. Of the different possibilities to express future situations and events in English, the *will* (/*shall*) construction is the most neutral, i. e. the one which depends least on the context and is therefore also used most frequently. German, conversely, prefers the present tense for future time reference (*Nachher gehe ich einkaufen*), although the *werden* construction is available as well (*Nachher werde ich einkaufen gehen*). Unlike English – where *will* and *shall* have largely lost their modal meanings (*will* for 'wish' or 'want', *shall* for obligations) and become genuine future markers – the German constructions with *wollen* and *sollen* express modality only. To some extent, this also holds true for German *werden* (as in *Sie werden (wohl) essen gegangen sein* or *Du wirst mir doch (wohl) nicht widersprechen*).

Present Perfect vs. Perfekt: A second, even more striking difference between the tense systems of the two languages concerns the Simple Past and Present Perfect and their German counterparts, the *Präteritum* and *Perfekt*. In German, mainly in the spoken standard, but also in standard written German, the *Perfekt* has taken over the function of the *Präteritum*. It is now used as a narrative tense. In English, the situation is completely different, especially in Standard British English, where there is a strict division of tasks between the Simple Past and Present Perfect. The Present Perfect must not be used with definite past time adverbials, i. e. adverbials of time identifying a situation clearly lying in the past (compare (28a) and (28b)). Additionally, the continuative perfect (28c) is obligatory in English in contexts where German often uses the present tense (often in combination with the adverb *schon*, as in (28d)):

German Perfekt = narrative tense

(28) a. Last year we visited Aunt Agnes in hospital.
          (not: *Last year we've visited Aunt Agnes in hospital.)
      b. Letztes Jahr haben wir Tante Agnes im Krankenhaus besucht.
      c. We've known them for years.
      d. Wir kennen sie (schon) seit Jahren.

In German, a similar distinction between *Präteritum* and *Perfekt* is found only with the resultative perfect. Upon opening the window curtains in the morning and seeing that winter has arrived, a native speaker of German would rather say (29a) than (29b):

resultative perfect

(29) a. Oh, es hat geschneit.
      b. Oh, es schneite.

Progressive form: A third well-known contrast is that English makes obligatory aspectual distinctions which are not, or only optionally, found in German. In English, the distinction between progressive and simple forms grammatically reflects the contrast between the internal view of a situation being in progress and the external, holistic view of a complete(d) situation, a grammatical distinction which has been continuously strengthened during the last few centuries. To express this aspectual contrast, German uses either adverbs (*Stör sie nicht! Sie liest gerade*) or constructions like *Sie ist (gerade) am/beim Lesen*, but none of these is obligatory.

Exceptional role of English in Europe: Notice that this is another domain where German is the more "normal" or "mainstream" language, both among the Germanic and the European languages. It is, for example, hard to find another language with such strongly grammaticalized progressive and perfect constructions as English. In most languages that have a perfect, it has developed into a regular past tense, like in German. English, with its unusual tense and aspect system and its use of *do*-support, represents anything but a typical European language. A further generalization following from the properties of English discussed so far is this: all rele-

English: far more analytic than German

Contrastive Linguistics: English and German

vant constructions are periphrastic constructions which are firmly rooted in the grammar of English. This is further evidence for the characterization of English as clearly a more analytic language than German.

Non-finite forms: Participles are indispensable for forming the perfect and progressive constructions. It is worth noting that in other domains of grammar, too, English makes much more frequent use of participles and non-finite verb forms, in general, than German does. One such domain where this is particularly noticeable was illustrated in examples (18) to (22): non-finite subordinate clauses which are mostly interlaced with their main clause in such a way that a logical argument of the non-finite verb of the subordinate clause is at the same time an argument of the finite verb of the main clause (e. g. *I want <u>him</u> to go*). This is also typical of adverbial participles (e. g. *Walking along the river, he met an old friend*) where English again, as observed for raising constructions, does not only have more structural options than German (see the examples in (30)), but also makes much more use of these options than other Germanic languages:

(30) a. Being his mother, she had great power over him.
   (not: *Seine Mutter seiend,...* but: *Als seine Mutter...*)
   b. With profit margins getting ever smaller in traditional consumer banking, such economies are very welcome.
   (not: *Mit den Gewinnspannen ... immer kleiner werdend,...*)

Participles also figure prominently when it comes to so-called restrictive (or: defining) relative clauses. English often prefers abbreviated relative clauses (*The girl standing at the corner was my sister*) to finite ones (*The girl who stood at the corner was my sister*). There is no structural equivalent to the former type among German relative clauses. In general, it can be stated for all types of subordinate clauses that English has more structural possibilities concerning the use of non-finite verb forms, and that the text frequency of such constructions is significantly higher than in German. It is, furthermore, remarkable that for many English non-finite constructions no equivalent subordinate clauses exist in German. Some English non-finite verb forms appear redundant in German (31a) while others function rather like prepositions (31b–e) or conjunctions (31f–h). As a matter of fact, several English prepositions actually developed from participles (e. g. *assuming, considering, providing, during, following* 'after').

(31) a. It cannot be achieved <u>without using</u> qualified professional people.
   (contrast '... <u>ohne</u> qualifizierte Experten')
   b. A map or plan <u>showing</u> the harbour limits...
   (contrast '... <u>mit</u> den Hafengrenzen')
   c. Books <u>dealing with</u> sexual topics...
   (contrast 'Bücher <u>über</u> sexuelle Themen...')
   d. The mystery <u>surrounding</u> the Black Pearl...
   (contrast 'Das Geheimnis <u>um</u> die Black Pearl...')

e.   Following growing unrest among their concerned friends at the amount of time they spend apart, the Prince and Princess of Wales...
(contrast 'Nach wachsender Unruhe...')

f.   She wrote a letter saying/to say she could not come. (*that*, *dass*)

g.   I hate to see you waste your money like that. (*that*, *dass*)

h.   Just to let you know. (*in order that*, *um...zu*)

More verbal nuclei in English: In sum, English clearly tends to distribute information on more verbal nuclei than German does. This difference, which captures many of the grammatical contrasts between English and German presented in this chapter, should be kept in mind especially by very advanced learners of English in order to counteract the tendency to avoid or underrepresent certain English structures.

5.3 | Phonological differences

Finally, let us take a brief look at the major phonological differences between English and German, starting with their consonant inventories.

Consonant systems: German lacks the (inter-)dental fricatives /θ, ð/, the bilabial semi-vowel /w/ and the voiced post-alveolar affricate /dʒ/. English, conversely, misses the two fricatives /ç/ and /x/, better known to German students of linguistics as '*ich-Laut*' and '*ach-Laut*'.

As for affricates, the problem is that German phonologists are not in agreement whether /pf/, /ts/, /ks/ and /tʃ/ should be analysed as one phoneme each or as combinations of two phonemes. Still, the majority view appears to be that only /tʃ/ cannot be classified as one phoneme. In terms of contrasting phoneme inventories, this means that German additionally lacks the phoneme /tʃ/, and English has no /pf/, /ts/ and /ks/ affricates.

Table 5.2: Contrasting the consonant inventories of English and German

	English									German								
plosives	p	b	t		d			k	g	p	b	t		d			k	g
fricatives	f	v	θ		ð				h	f	v					ç	x	h
			s		z	ʃ	ʒ					s		z	ʃ	ʒ		
affricates						tʃ	dʒ					pf	ts					ks	
nasals	m			n				ŋ		m			n				ŋ	
liquids & semi-vowels	w		l	r	j											l	r	j

Different allophones: Some consonant phonemes that exist in both languages are realized differently, which means that English and German do not always use the same allophones. Liquids are a good example: in

Received Pronunciation, the prototypical /r/ is post-alveolar, in General American it is retroflex, and in German it is uvular (*Zäpfchen-r*, typically realized as a fricative [ʁ], except when it is syllable-final; see below). In addition, German does not distinguish between clear and dark /l/; the /l/ phoneme is always realized as clear /l/, even at the end of a word. Compare contrasting pairs of English and German words like *ball – Ball*, *hell* (N) - *hell* (A), *still* (Adv) - *still* (A), *old – alt*.

Final devoicing: Furthermore, there is so-called final devoicing (*Auslautverhärtung*) in German: all obstruents at the end of syllables or words are voiceless, i.e. German words like *Stab*, *Rad* or *Tag* are pronounced /ʃtaːp/, /raːt/, and /taːk/ respectively. Due to final devoicing, many German learners of English make interference mistakes because the relevant English minimal pairs are lost, e.g. *dove-duff*, *rib-rip*, *ridge-rich*, *dog-dock* or *lose-loose*. The opposite case, i.e. when voiced and voiceless obstruents are neutralized at the end of syllables and words, usually presents no problem to English learners of German.

typological
markedness

In the domain of contrastive English-German phonology, final devoicing is thus one of the best-known pieces of evidence that there is a connection between typological markedness and the Contrastive Hypothesis (see section 5.1). As this phenomenon can be observed in a relatively large number of languages, word-final devoicing can be considered a "natural" or "unmarked" rule, whereas the situation found in English is clearly less common (i.e. "marked"). In this case, the Contrastive Hypothesis is clearly unidirectional.

no front vowels
in English

Vowel inventories: As far as the vowel inventories of both languages are concerned, the most striking contrast is that English, as opposed to all other Germanic languages, has no rounded front vowels (which occur in German words like *Müll* /Y/, *Mühle* /yː/, *Hölle* /œ/ or *Höhle* /øː/). Other German monophthongs which do not exist in Received Pronunciation are /eː/, /ɛː/ and /oː/ (word-initially as in the German nouns *Ehren*, *Ähren* and *Ohren*). Gaps in the German vowel inventory can be found primarily among the diphthongs: of the eight diphthongs found in English, German only has the three closing diphthongs /aɪ/, /ɔɪ/ and /aʊ/. In general, there is a much greater asymmetry between monophthongs (15) and diphthongs (3) in the German vowel system.

vocalic /r/ allo-
phone in German

What at first glance might be identified as so-called centring diphthongs in German (e.g. *Tier* [tiːɐ] or *leer* [leːɐ]) are actually nothing more than monophthongs followed by an allophone of /r/. This allophone is used whenever the phoneme /r/ is not followed by a vowel (consider *Tier* [tiːɐ] - *Tiere* ['tiːʀə], *ehrlich* ['eːɐlɪç] vs. *Ehre* [eːʀə]). With regard to monophthongs, German lacks especially /æ/ *cat*, /ʌ/ *cut*, /ɔː/ *caught* and /ɜː/ *curt*.

English vowels
more open

However, as can be seen from the contrastive vowel chart in figure 5.4 (note in particular the ellipses represented by solid lines), there are also differences in quality, i.e. in the position of the tongue, for vowel phonemes occurring in both languages. More often than not, English vowels are more open than German vowels, the position of the tongue being lower than in German. Most English vowels therefore take a lower position in the vowel chart.

The three ellipses represented by dashed lines in figure 5.4 delineate pairs of vowels /e/ - /ɜ/, /ʌ/ - /a/, /ɒ/ - /ɔ/ which are phonetically similar but phonologically different in the two languages. Figure 5.4 also shows that the German inventory of monophthongs is front-vowel biased (9 out of the 15 monophthongs are front vowels), while, though less pronounced, back vowels form the largest group in the corresponding inventory in Received Pronunciation (compared with front and central vowels).

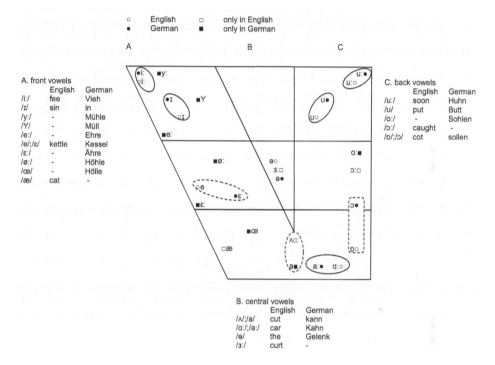

Figure 5.4:
Contrasting the
vowel inventories
of English and
German

compound nouns,
phonemic stress
in English

Phonotactic and suprasegmental differences: There also are phonotactic differences: e. g. no /ps-, pn-, kn-/ at the beginning of words in English and no /st-, sp-/ at the beginning of words in German. Likewise there are differences in suprasegmental phonology. For these, however, it is much more difficult to formulate generalizations than it was for the phoneme inventories.

Word stress: With respect to word stress, one important contrast concerns compound nouns, especially those consisting of two components: in German, the main stress is usually placed on the first element, whereas in English it often happens that more than one element is stressed, and the main stress can even be on the second or third element of a compound (so-called level stress as in 'washing 'machine, 'front 'door, ˌapple 'pie and ˌwaste 'paper). What is more, word stress is often phonemic in English, meaning that stress alone can be distinctive (in the sense of bringing about a change of meaning; see chapter 2.2.2). Another fundamental difference is the strong correlation between word stress and rhythm in English.

many (more) weak
forms in English

Rhythm: This takes us directly to differences in rhythm. Although compared to other languages, English and German are both classified as stress-timed languages, syllable stress in English is much more isochronous, meaning that the intervals between stressed syllables are fairly regular (see chapter 2.2.2). It is the unstressed syllables and words which pay the price: very frequently, these are subject to vowel reduction, assimilation, or elision. As a result, function words have many weak forms in English while there are only few of them in German. Thus, many German speakers of English do not employ weak forms frequently enough.

ingredients of a
distinct German
accent

Further phonological differences: There are further phonological differences which do not lead to errors but may contribute to a distinctly German accent. For one, there is the strong aspiration of voiceless plosives (/p/, /t/, /k/) in all positions, even where English does not aspirate or not even release plosives (*apt* [æpʼt], *worked* [wɜːkʼt]). Even more characteristic of native speakers of German is the so-called glottal stop before stressed syllables starting with a vowel. The glottal stop can be heard in conscious speech or, even more pronounced, when whispering an (admittedly somewhat constructed) sentence such as ˀ*Am* ˀ*Abend* ˀ*essen* ˀ*er* ˀ*und* ˀ*ich* ˀ*Erbsen*ˀ*eintopf* ˀ*über* ˀ*alles gern.* To a native speaker of English, a sentence like ˀ*After* ˀ*all* ˀ*I* ˀ*eat* ˀ*apples* ˀ*in the* ˀ*evening* pronounced this way would sound very "clipped" and "staccato". This phenomenon is also the reason why German learners of English rarely use intrusive /r/ or linking /r/ (as in *after all* /ɑːftəˈrɔːl/) or other types of consonant-vowel liaison across word boundaries (as in *fine arts* /faɪˈnɑːts/ or *at all* /əˈtɔːl/. On the other hand, utterances by native speakers of English may display a greater variation in the pitch range and pitch contour. In general, pitch is often lower in German than in English. But it should be added that English seems to be changing in this respect and that the relevant contrasts between English and German are becoming less and less noticeable.

Checklist Contrastive Linguistics – key terms and concepts

agreement ↔ government
analyticity ↔ syntheticity
argument trespassing
aspect
blending of constructions
bundles of contrasts
case system
cleft (pseudo-)
compensation strategy
concord (see agreement)
Contrastive Hypothesis
discourse pragmatics /
    information structure
final devoicing
fused constructions

gerund
government
grammatical functions/
    relations
grammaticalization
interference types (substitu-
    tion; over-/ underdifferenti-
    ation; over-/ under-
    representation)
isochrony
language typology
loose fit ↔ tight fit language
markedness
Markedness Differential
    Hypothesis

non-finite forms
participles
passive construction
predicate-argument structures
preposition stranding
raising constructions
rhythm
semantic roles of subjects
  and objects
tense
theme ↔ rheme (topic ↔
  comment)

transfer
transitive construction
transparency
typological distance
verbs (strong ↔ weak)
verb phrase contrasts
vowel inventories
word order
word stress (accent)

Exercises

1.

a) Using appropriate linguistic terminology, describe the pun in the name of the bicycle shop *Radgeber*.

b) Which typical mistakes of German learners of English are made in the following utterance: /tel mi: vɒt ɪs zə pʀɒbləm vɪ'sɛt/ *Tell me, what is the problem with that?*

c) The following pairs of examples often cease to be minimal pairs when uttered by German learners of English. Explain why and find two more examples of each neutralization of a minimal pair: *pat-pet, thin-sin, wine-vine, cherry-sherry, lag-lack, plays-place*.

d) Explain why *jazz* and *chess* may be pronounced in the same way by some German learners of English.

2.

a) For which English vowels do German learners of English often employ one of the following German vowel sounds? Give examples. /ɛ/ /oː/ /ø/ /a/

b) Which problems can German speakers of English be expected to have when pronouncing the underlined consonants in the following examples: *outpu̱t, oḇtain, go̱t, beḏtime, rag̱, hoḻd, she liv̱es̱, anḏ, finger, s̱o*

3. Describe the differences in the pronunciation of the first sound(s) in the following cognates. Deduce phonotactic constraints of English and German (see chapter 2 for the notion of 'phonotactic restrictions')

Knecht – knight
Psychologie – psychology
Straße – street

4. Consider the following examples of adverbial clauses in English and describe the major English-German contrasts in this domain of grammar.
   a) Looking out of the window, Mary saw a large truck approaching.
   b) With grandpa driving, I always have an awkward feeling.

5. Provide the most natural German translations of the English sentences in (17).

6. Identify which syntactic contrast between English and German each of the following examples illustrates.
   a) Das Paket gab der Mann der Frau und nicht dem Jungen.
   b) She photographs well.
   c) Jetzt wird aber gegessen!
   d) Did you see his face?
   e) Sie glaubt, dass er ein netter Kerl ist.
   f) This racket has never been played with.
   g) There's the guy (who(m)) I met at the disco last night.
   h) The ship tore a sail.
   i) I believe him to be very sincere.

7. There are many English-German contrasts in the tense and aspect system. Sketch the major contrasts by going one by one through the following examples.
   a) Gestern sind wir im Kino gewesen.
   b) Ich kenne ihn schon seit Jahren.
   c) Bis morgen Mittag habe ich den Aufsatz geschrieben.
   d) Don't disturb Dad! He's watching telly.
   e) Morgen reist sie weiter.
   f) You must go. The train leaves at six.

8. Which of the following statements are true, which are false?
   a) Transfer is a special type of interference.
   b) The Contrastive Hypothesis has more prognostic than diagnostic value.
   c) Grammatical relations are marked by word order in English and by case marking in German.
   d) In contrast to English, German subjects are always agents and direct objects are always patients.
   e) Compared with German, English has wider range of options in the domain of non-finite clauses and makes greater use of them.
   f) The English Progressive and the use of do-support in questions are highly marked structures in the European languages.
   g) The Present Perfect in English is a true perfect while German Perfekt is really a tense.

h) Over the course of its history, English has undergone a major typological change which is responsible for many of the structural differences between Present-Day English and Present-Day German.
i) The inventory of English diphthongs is a proper subset of the inventory of German diphthongs.

9. Give a phonetic description of
a) all English sounds which lack an equivalent in the German sound
system.
b) all German sounds which lack an equivalent in the English sound
system.

Advanced

10.

a) Provide the linguistic term for the feature described in the following excerpt from Mark Twain's (1880) humoristic essay "The awful
German language".
"Every time I think I have got one of these four confusing "cases"
where I am master of it, a seemingly insignificant preposition in-
trudes itself into my sentence, clothed with an awful and unsus-
pected power, and crumbles the ground from under me. For instance, my book inquires after a certain bird – (it is always inquir-
ing after things which are of no sort of consequence to anybody):
"Where is the bird?" Now the answer to this question, according
to the book, is that the bird is waiting in the blacksmith shop on
account of the rain. Of course no bird would do that, but then you
must stick to the book."
b) Provide a translation for *The bird is waiting in the blacksmith shop
on account of the rain* and determine the case of the German noun
Regen.
c) Write a flip story about "The awful English language" by describing a feature of English that might be perplexing, illogical or confusing for Germans in a non-technical humoristic way.

11. Sketch the major differences between English and German in the domain of relative clauses.

12. Try to find out which of the English-German contrasts described in
this chapter are due to either English or German exhibiting a marked
feature in the relevant domain of its phonological or grammatical
structure compared with the majority of other languages (think of the
Markedness Differential Hypothesis). You can consult the *World Atlas
of Language Structures* (WALS) to find out about the distribution of
several phonological and grammatical features in a sample of the
world's languages (https://wals.info/).

Sources and further reading

Eckman, Fred. 1977. "Markedness and the contrastive analysis hypothesis." *Language Learning* 27: 315–330.

Gass, Susan M./Larry Selinker, eds. 2001². *Language transfer in language learning*. Amsterdam/Philadelphia: Benjamins.

Gnutzmann, Claus, ed. 1990. *Kontrastive Linguistik*. Frankfurt: Lang.

Hawkins, John A. 1986. *A comparative typology of English and German: unifying the contrasts*. London: Croom Helm.

Hawkins, John A. 1992. "A performance approach to English/German contrasts." In: Christian Mair/Manfred Markus, eds. 115–136.

Hawkins, John A. 2019. "Word-external properties in a typology of Modern English: A comparison with German." *English Language and Linguistics* 23: 701–727.

Hellinger, Marlis. 1977. *Kontrastive Grammatik Deutsch/Englisch*. Tübingen: Niemeyer.

König, Ekkehard/Volker Gast. 2018⁴. *Understanding English-German contrasts*. Berlin: Schmidt.

König, Ekkehard/Johan van der Auwera, eds. 1994. *The Germanic languages*. London/New York: Routledge.

Kortmann, Bernd. 1998. "Kontrastive Linguistik und Fremdsprachenunterricht." In: Wolfgang Börner/Klaus Vogel, eds. *Kontrast und Äquivalenz. Beiträge zu Sprachvergleich und Übersetzung*. Tübingen: Narr. 136–167.

Kufner, Herbert L. 1971. *Kontrastive Phonologie Deutsch-Englisch*. Stuttgart: Klett.

Lado, Robert. 1957. *Linguistics across cultures. Applied linguistics for language teachers*. Ann Arbor: University of Michigan Press.

Legenhausen, Lienhard/Günter Rohdenburg. 1995. "Kontrastivierung ausgewählter Strukturen im Englischen und Deutschen." In: Rüdiger Ahrens/Wolf-Dietrich Bald/Werner Hüllen, eds. *Handbuch Englisch als Fremdsprache*. Berlin: Erich Schmidt. 133–139.

Mair, Christian. 1995. *Englisch für Anglisten*. Tübingen: Stauffenburg.

Mair, Christian/Manfred Markus, eds. 1992. *New departures in contrastive linguistics*. 2 vols. Innsbruck: Institut für Anglistik.

Odlin, Terence. 1989. *Language transfer. Cross-linguistic influence in language learning*. Cambridge: Cambridge University Press.

Theisen, Joachim. 2016. *Kontrastive Linguistik: Eine Einführung*. Tübingen: Narr.

van der Auwera, Johan. 2012. "From contrastive linguistics to linguistic typology." *Languages in Contrast* 12: 69–86.

6 Semantics: Word and sentence meaning

Semantics (Greek *semain-* = to mean) is the only branch of linguistics which is exclusively concerned with meaning. Semantics studies the meaning or meaning potential of various kinds of expressions: words, phrases, and sentences. This chapter is mainly confined to the study of word meaning (lexical semantics; lexicology). Research in lexical semantics addresses the following questions:

- How can the concept of meaning be elucidated, including the relation between meaning and external reality?
- What are appropriate tools for analysing and describing meanings?
- What kinds of semantic structures exist within the vocabulary (or: lexicon) of a language?

focus on word meaning (lexicology)

These semantic structures are uncovered by describing recurrent semantic relations between the words, more exactly the lexemes, of a language (e. g. relations such as near-equivalence or contrasts in meaning). Lexical semantics proceeds from the assumption that words are symbols, i. e. signs expressing an arbitrary relation between a form and its meaning(s). This relation is considered to be exclusively a matter of convention (see chapter 1 on the model of the linguistic sign proposed by Ferdinand de Saussure).

6.1 | Branches and boundaries of semantics

Semasiology (form → meaning): Studies in semantics usually start out from a given form and ask for its meaning, i. e. move from signifier (*signifiant*) to signified (*signifié*). This direction of research is also most relevant to non-linguists: Whenever we consult a dictionary, we are looking for an answer to the question "What is the meaning of X?". The branch of semantics which adopts this approach is called *semasiology* (science of meanings), a concept which originally covered all of semantics. It was only in the 20th century that the term *semantics* (introduced by Michel Bréal) replaced the term semasiology.

dictionary

Onomasiology (meaning → form): The opposite way of studying meaning is called *onomasiology* (science of names; from Greek *onomaz* = to name). It proceeds from a given meaning to the forms that express it. Whenever we consult a dictionary of synonyms (thesaurus) such as *Roget's Thesaurus of English Words and Phrases*, we are adopting an onoma-

thesaurus

J.B. Metzler © Springer-Verlag GmbH Deutschland, ein Teil von Springer Nature, 2020
B. Kortmann, *English Linguistics*, https://doi.org/10.1007/978-3-476-05678-8_6

siological approach: We want to find out which word(s) can be used to express a given concept. Take, for example, the concept – or lexical field (see section 6.3) – of killing (German *töten*): *kill, murder, slay, slaughter, butcher, massacre,* and *assassinate* are words which can be used to translate the concept expressed by *töten*.

Paradigmatic vs. syntagmatic semantics: The lexical (or: semantic) field of killing serves as a useful example for illustrating another crucial distinction, which ultimately derives from an important dichotomy proposed by Ferdinand de Saussure: The contrast between two distinct kinds of relations contracted by every element in a language: (paradigmatic) relations of choice, and (syntagmatic) relations of combination (see chapter 1.3.1). These relations are also relevant to semantics.

Semantic relations between lexical alternatives are the focus of paradigmatic semantics. This includes how members of a lexical field can be replaced by other members of the field, especially if there are extensive similarities between their meanings (i. e. if these words are synonymous). Syntagmatic semantics, on the other hand, is concerned with questions such as the following: Which of the above-mentioned lexical alternatives is appropriate in a given sentence (e. g. *kill* as opposed to *murder* or *assassinate*)? *Kill* is the most general term, *murder* implies the intentional killing of a human being, *assassinate* relates to the killing of an important person (usually a politician). For this reason, only (1) is acceptable, while (2) is odd:

(1)　President X was assassinated last night.
(2)　?Many innocent villagers were assassinated last night.

Selection restrictions: In this comparison of verbs of killing, there are even more semantic restrictions when we look at the direct objects which can be combined with each verb: *kill* has fewer restrictions than *murder*, which in turn has fewer restrictions than *assassinate*. Such restrictions on possible combinations of meanings, so-called *selection restrictions*, are sometimes very wide-ranging. In some cases, a given lexeme can only be combined with very few other lexemes. Extreme examples are provided by many words which are rarely used: It is often possible to predict with which other lexemes such rare words are likely to occur in a sentence.

Collocations: A popular example of such typical combinations of words, so-called *collocations*, are the various expressions for groups of animals in (3):

(3)

a	flock gaggle pack pride shoal	of	sheep / goats / birds geese wolves / hounds lions fish

Fregean Principle　Compositionality: Syntagmatic semantics is not only concerned with possible combinations of particular words (such as those discussed in (1) to (3)), it also deals with the meaning of complex linguistic expressions, including sentences. The crucial principle that determines the meaning of complex expressions is the principle of compositionality, which stipulates that the meaning of a complex expression in natural language depends on (and can be reconstructed from) the meaning of its parts and the syntactic relations holding between these parts. This important principle of sentence semantics is often called *Frege's* or the *Fregean Principle*, since it is commonly attributed to the German philosopher and mathematician Gottlob Frege (1848–1925). The principle of compositionality is held to ensure that we can understand the countless sentences we encounter every day, even though we have never heard them before.

There are limits to compositionality, however. Consider, for example, idioms such as *to kick the bucket* or German *den Löffel abgeben*. Their meaning (here 'to die') cannot – or can only in part – be reconstructed from the meanings of their component parts; thus, for idioms like these, the connection between form and meaning tends to be just as arbitrary and conventional as it is for most single words. But even where the principle of compositionality does apply, it does not guarantee that one really understands what the speaker or author *means* with a particular utterance, at least in those cases where the intended meaning goes beyond what is literally *said*. idioms

Semantics vs. pragmatics: The distinction between what is said and what is meant, i. e. between (literal) sentence meaning and (intended) utterance meaning, is closely linked to the distinction between semantics and pragmatics, even though the correlation is not perfect (see the detailed discussion in chapter 7). Pragmatics studies language use (*parole*), focusing on both the linguistic and the non-linguistic context of utterances, as well as speakers' utterance-related intentions. Thus, a central – for many *the* central – aspect of pragmatics is its concern with principles that allow us to infer what is meant from what is said in a particular context. At the heart of pragmatics are questions such as 'What does the speaker mean by uttering X?' and 'Why are hearers usually able to recognize speakers' intention(s) without great difficulty?'. pragmatics: meaning in context

In semantics, on the other hand, context is almost completely ignored, and speaker intention is entirely left out of consideration. Thus, the division of tasks between semantics and pragmatics may roughly be characterised as follows: semantics deals with the meanings or the meaning potential of expressions out of context (i. e. context-invariant, speaker-independent meaning), whereas pragmatics deals with the meanings of expressions (mainly utterances) in a particular context (i. e. context-sensitive, speaker-dependent meaning). semantics: meaning out of context

6.2 | Types and facets of meaning

What we typically have in mind when talking about word meanings are the meanings of lexemes that belong to one of the four lexical word classes (nouns, verbs, adjectives, adverbs). grammatical meaning = abstract

Lexical vs. grammatical meaning: Lexical meaning contrasts with the grammatical meaning of function words (e. g. pronouns, prepositions, conjunctions; see chapter 3.1 on auto- and synsemantic words). Grammatical meaning also includes the meaning of inflectional affixes and the semantic roles (e. g. agent, patient) associated with grammatical relations. The differences between grammatical and lexical meaning are only gradual. Grammatical meaning in general is abstract; just think of the meanings of case or tense morphemes, or of the marking of (in-)definiteness with the help of *a* and *the*. Lexical meaning, on the other hand, is frequently far more concrete. In this respect, grammatical meaning contrasts particularly strongly with the lexical meaning of those nouns that denote concrete countable entities. Note, however, that the (lexical) meanings of abstract nouns such as *condition*, *cause*, or *concession* are no less abstract than the (grammatical) meanings of adverbial subordinators such as *if*, *because*, or *although*. The above examples of grammatical and lexical meanings can thus be located at opposite ends of a continuum from abstract to concrete concepts. The meanings of personal pronouns and spatial prepositions tend to be located even further towards the middle of such a continuum (and thus towards the transitional area between grammatical and lexical meaning).

far fewer grammatical meanings

Another essential difference between lexical and grammatical meaning relates to the fact that the number of grammatical meanings encoded in languages is comparatively small and – even from a cross-linguistic point of view – probably also finite, whereas there are an infinite number of potential lexical meanings. It is therefore much easier to provide an overview of the domain of grammatical meanings. Not surprisingly, regular processes of meaning change – both within a single language and across languages – have been identified primarily in the domain of grammatical meanings. Meaning changes in lexical words, on the other hand, are clearly more idiosyncratic, and cannot be captured with the help of a relatively small number of general principles of the type discovered for function words. Issues of historical (or: diachronic) semantics will be discussed in chapter 9.

lexical meaning

Descriptive vs. expressive vs. social meaning: In what follows, we will largely focus on lexical meaning, more precisely on the descriptive (or: cognitive) meaning of lexical words. Thus, special emphasis will be placed on the representative function of language (cf. the various functions of language described in chapter 1), i. e. on those aspects of meaning that allow us to describe the world. Expressive and social meanings will not be dealt with in greater detail. The following examples have to suffice:

expressive and social meaning

- the exclusively expressive meaning of *gosh!*, and the differences between *father* and *daddy*, *policeman* and *cop(per)*, or *very* and *jolly* with regard to their expressive meaning;
- the exclusively social meaning of welcome and farewell words such as *hello* and *goodbye*, forms of address like *sir* and *madam* with their social meaning component, and the differences between forms of address like *pal*, *mate*, and *love* (as used in grocer's shops in England: *What can I do for you, love?*) with regard to their (expressive and) social meaning.

Generally speaking, the interpersonal function of language is relegated to the research periphery in semantics: Semanticists rarely devote particular attention to those aspects of meaning that enable us to express feelings, points of view, and speaker judgments (i. e. expressive meaning), or which signal and establish social relationships (i. e. social meaning).

Descriptive meaning: But what exactly is the descriptive meaning of a lexical word? To answer this question, we will turn to three central pairs of concepts used in semantics which more or less overlap: *sense – reference*, *intension – extension*, and *connotation – denotation*. The first-mentioned terms in these three pairs (*sense*, *intension*, and *connotation*) relate to the conceptual side of meaning and to (language-internal) definitions of meaning.

Reference: By contrast, the three contrasting terms (*reference*, *extension*, *denotation*) relate to extra-linguistic reality, i. e. to the relation between language and the world. The term *reference*, for example, designates the relation between entities in the external world and the words which are used to refer to these entities (e. g. people, objects, events, places, points in time, etc.). The referent is the entity referred to ("picked out") by an expression in a particular context.

extra-linguistic reality

(4) a. Take the bottle and put it in the dustbin.
     b. She took a bottle and put it in a dustbin.
     c. A bottle is not a dustbin.

Both (4a) and (4b) deal with a particular bottle and a particular dustbin. The only difference is that in (4a) the referents of *the bottle* and *the dustbin* are accessible to the hearer. In both cases, the referents of *the/a bottle* and *the/a dustbin* vary from utterance to utterance. Matters are different in the case of (4c): here, *a bottle* does not refer to a particular bottle, nor does *a dustbin* refer to a particular dustbin; both noun phrases are thus used in a non-referring sense. But even though both noun phrases in (4c) lack a referent, they still have an extension.

Extension – denotation: The term *extension* designates the class of objects to which a linguistic expression can be applied, i. e. the class of its potential referents (in (4c) the class of all bottles and the class of all dustbins). A referent of a linguistic expression is always a member (or subset) of the class of objects that constitutes the word's extension.

The term *denotation* is frequently used synonymously with *extension*. Both terms are sometimes understood in a broader sense, covering not only the relation between nouns or noun phrases and groups of individuals or objects, but also the link between words belonging to other word classes and the phenomena they relate to. Thus verbs denote situations, adjectives denote properties of individuals and objects, and adverbs denote properties of situations.

Sense (vs. reference): The sense of an expression is its descriptive meaning, more exactly meaning we know in virtue of our knowledge of language, which – in contrast to reference – is independent of a particular utterance and the situational context in which the utterance was made. The distinction between *sense* and *reference* was introduced by the German philosopher Gottlob Frege. It is not difficult to see why such a distinction is useful. For one thing, linguistic expressions with different meanings ("senses") may very well have the same referent(s). Just think of the noun phrases *the Leader of the Conservative Party* and *the Prime Minister of Great Britain*, which differ in sense, but not necessarily in reference: The phrase *the Leader of the Conservative Party* may refer to the same person as the phrase *the Prime Minister of Great Britain*.

Intension (vs. extension): Similar observations apply to *the capital of Prussia*, *the capital of the Third Reich*, and *the capital of Germany*; all of these phrases refer to Berlin. This example also illustrates that the referent of a linguistic expression may change, while its meaning remains the same: in 1992 Bonn was still *the capital of Germany*, today the capital of Germany is Berlin. The relevance of the sense-reference distinction is also brought home by words which lack a referent, but do have a sense. Cases in point are *unicorn* and *dragon*. The sense of a linguistic expression essentially consists of characteristic features, so-called *semantic features*, which determine the class of entities it may be used to refer to, i. e. its extension. These features are (typically binary) traits that describe essential aspects of the meaning of a word, and a bundle of such semantic features, e. g. [+ HUMAN, − ADULT, + FEMALE] for *girl*, can only describe the *intension* of a linguistic expression (more on this in sections 6.3.1 and 6.4). Note that so-called *connotations* are not part of the intension.

Connotation (vs. denotation): Connotations are typically secondary meanings which can vary according to culture, region, social class, etc. and which are often restricted to particular contexts. This does not mean, however, that connotations are completely subjective associations which different speakers connect with expressions on the basis of entirely different personal experiences. Connotations can be generalized to a certain extent, they are part of the encyclopaedic meaning of a lexeme, i. e. meaning known in virtue of our knowledge of the world (as opposed to its dictionary meaning, i. e. its descriptive meaning, the much more rigid definition we find in dictionaries).

propositional content
Sentence meaning – truth conditions: This chapter is concerned with lexical semantics. For presenting the complete picture, though, it should be mentioned that we can also speak of the descriptive meaning, denotation, or extension of phrases and sentences. The descriptive meaning of a sentence is called its *propositional content* and is a mental concept covering all situations the relevant sentence can potentially refer to. Sentences can be true or false in a given situation, and the conditions under which they are true are called the *truth conditions* of a sentence. They specify the conditions under which a given sentence can correctly be used to refer to a certain (kind or set of) situation(s) in the world.

The following sections deal with the two major approaches to the analysis of lexical meaning: the first approach investigates recurrent semantic structures in the vocabulary (structural semantics; section 6.3), the second examines the relations holding between word meanings and our conceptual system (cognitive semantics; section 6.4).

6.3 | Structural semantics: Meaning structures in the vocabulary

A network of semantic relations: Even today, lexical semantics is still committed to classical structuralist assumptions to a considerable extent (see chapter 1). One of the principles that has proved particularly influential is the idea of language as a complex system of relations: Every linguistic element is integrated into the system (*langue*) through a network of paradigmatic and syntagmatic relations; nothing happens outside of the system. Applied to semantics, this view implies that word meaning is to be treated as something relative, as a purely language-internal phenomenon. A word's meaning, its sense, constitutes a node in a network of semantic relations.

More precisely, the meaning of an expression is defined in part by what it has in common with other expressions, but above all by what distinguishes it from them (de Saussure speaks of the *signe différentiel*: the meaning of a word is what it is not). Thus, if we want to grasp the full meaning of a verb like *march*, we have to know how the manner of walking described by this expression differs from the manner of walking described by similar verbs like *pace* and *stride*. All of these terms are part of an extensive network of motion verbs. Some verbs that belong to this network, such as *amble*, *saunter*, and *stroll*, constitute a subclass of expressions which stand in a relation of oppositeness to *march*, *pace*, and *stride*. The latter verbs denote a quick, determined manner of walking, whereas the verbs in the former group denote a slow, aimless manner of walking.

In sum, the principal goal of structural semantics is to show that the vocabulary of a language is a structured whole in which nothing happens in isolation and where various recurrent semantic structures can be identified. The two most important types of such structures (or: networks) are lexical fields and lexical (or: sense) relations.

[margin: structuralism: meaning as something entirely language-internal]

[margin: signe différentiel]

[margin: major goal]

6.3.1 | Lexical fields

Lexical (or: semantic) fields are groups of words which cover different or partly overlapping areas within the same extralinguistic domain. Above we already encountered three examples of lexical fields:
- verbs of asking (*ask, inquire, interrogate, question, wonder*, etc.),
- verbs of walking (*walk, march, pace, amble, stroll, prance, sneak, stagger, swagger*, etc.), and
- verbs of killing (*kill, murder, assassinate*, etc.).

Further examples include:
- colour adjectives,
- adjectives relating to mental abilities (*intelligent, clever, smart, bright, brilliant, brainy, stupid, dumb, silly, thick, dense*, etc.),
- different types of footwear (*shoe, moccasin, clog, slipper, sandal, trainer, boot*, etc.),

- legwear (*trousers*, *dungarees*, *socks*, *stockings*, *tights*, *leggings*, etc.),
- teaching and research staff at universities (*professor*, *reader*, *lecturer*, *fellow*, etc.), or
- temporal conjunctions (*when*, *as*, *while*, *after*, *since*, etc.).

There is an infinite number of such lexical fields. The crucial idea behind grouping lexemes by semantic similarity is the assumption that the meaning of a field member can only be fully determined and delimited with reference to its semantic neighbours. From a diachronic point of view, this means that any semantic change within a lexical field may affect all members of the lexical field plus the intricate network of semantic relations holding between them. Such potential changes in lexical fields include the addition of a new word, the loss of a word, and a change in the meaning of one or more of their members.

Jost Trier

Traditional vs. modern conceptions of lexical fields: In fact, the theory of lexical fields ('Wortfeldtheorie'), which was developed by the linguist Jost Trier in the 1930s, has its roots in the study of semantic change, and hence in diachronic (or: historical) semantics. However, it did not take long for the study of lexical fields to occupy a central place in synchronic word semantics, even if some aspects of Trier's account are in need of revision.

criticism of lexical fields as mosaics

Pertinent criticism has been levelled, for example, at his conception of lexical fields as mosaics, whose boundaries can be clearly delimited and which do not have any gaps or overlaps. This ideal hardly exists:

- category boundaries are often fuzzy (see also section 6.4); as a result it may be difficult to determine which lexical field a word belongs to;
- there are many examples of gaps in lexical fields (e. g. in English or German, adjectives are missing which – in analogy to *blind*, *deaf/taub*, or *mute/stumm* – denote the absence of the ability to smell or taste);
- and, finally, in many cases there are more or less conspicuous meaning similarities (and thus overlaps) within a lexical field (e. g. *intelligent*, *clever*, *smart*).

badly spread bread-and-butter

The suggestion to compare a lexical field to a piece of bread which is unevenly buttered (thicker in some places, thinner or not at all in other places) thus seems to be much more useful than the mosaic comparison. Much as the latter, however, this conception of lexical fields neglects the fact that field members are related to one another along more than merely two dimensions in most cases. For instance, *pace* may differ from *stroll* with regard to the dimensions 'speed' and 'purposefulness'; but these dimensions are no longer sufficient if we want to describe the difference between these two verbs and other members of the same lexical field (e. g. *stagger* or *trudge*). Here, we need further dimensions such as 'degree of body control' or 'degree of effort'.

bundles of semantic features

Componential analysis: Componential analysis (or: feature analysis, semantic decomposition) has proved to be a very useful tool for describing semantic similarities and differences between members of a lexical field. In analogy to the conception of phonemes as bundles of distinctive features (e. g. the phoneme /p/ as [+ CONSONANT, − VOICED, − NASAL, + OCCLUSION, + PLOSIVE]; see chapter 2.2.1), the meaning of a word is conceived of as a bundle of (ideally binary) semantic features or *semes*. Consider, for example, *girl* [+ HUMAN, – ADULT, + FEMALE] in contrast to *boy* [+ HUMAN, – ADULT, – FEMALE], or *pace* [+ QUICK, + PURPOSEFUL] in contrast to *stroll* [– QUICK, – PURPOSEFUL]. These features can roughly be equated with the dimensions that structure a lexical field, but wherever possible they should be chosen so as to allow a 'yes (+) / no (–)' characterization. The choice of relevant semantic features is to some extent arbitrary, of course, and singling out useful features is more difficult for some semantic areas than it is for others.

In general, the method of semantic decomposition becomes more and more difficult to handle the more fine-grained the semantic analyses are supposed to be (just think of the lexical field of motion verbs). In addition, it is open to debate whether there really is a limited, universally valid inventory of semantic features relevant to the analysis of word meanings. It also remains unclear what role semantic features play in human categorization, i. e. whether semantic features are cognitively real (more on this in section 6.4). problems

Structure of the mental lexicon: By contrast, the psychological reality of lexical fields is indisputable. It can be shown that they are more than simply a convenient theoretical construct, and that they do indeed fulfil an important function in structuring the information stored in our mental lexicon. Word association tests with ordinary people and especially with people suffering from aphasia have clearly shown that there is a much stronger psychological link between members of the same lexical field than between members of different lexical fields. lexical fields = psychologically real

This is hardly surprising: within a lexical field there is a much stronger network of lexical (or: sense) relations. Such relations represent another important principle structuring our mental lexicon. Of particular importance are the kinds of relations holding between *red – blue – green – yellow*, or *Monday – Tuesday – Wednesday*, etc. (relations of semantic incompatibility), and those relations that hold between word pairs such as *man – woman, husband – wife, hot – cold, buy – sell* (relations of oppositeness of meaning) (see section 6.3.2). Apart from these paradigmatic lexical relations and lexical fields, *collocations* also play an important role in processing, storing, and retrieving lexical information. Examples of collocations include syntagmatic lexical relations which exist, for example, between adjectives like *blond, auburn, curly, wavy,* or *unruly,* on the one hand, and *hair,* on the other hand (see also section 6.1 above). part of the mental lexicon

6.3.2 | Sense relations

Sense (or: lexical) relations are specific semantic relations between words. The five relations discussed in this section have in common that they systematically occur in an infinite number of word pairs or word groups (especially with lexical fields), and that they are all paradigmatic relations, thus represent possibilities of choice between lexical alternatives (e. g. *leggings* in contrast to *trousers, tights,* or *stockings*). 5 paradigmatic sense relations

Synonymy: The concept of *synonymy* is used to describe semantic descriptive/cognitive synonyms equivalence or rather extensive semantic similarity between two or more lexemes. The term is typically used in reference to the *descriptive* meaning of words (hence the term *descriptive* or *cognitive synonymy*). Synonyms thus have the same semantic features. However, most synonyms differ with regard to their conditions of use: Descriptive synonyms may be interchangeable in many, but not all, contexts.

In (5a), for example, it is impossible to replace *deep* by its synonym *profound*; matters are different in (5b):

(5)   a.   This river is very deep.
      b.   The incident made a deep impression on me.

differences between descriptive synonyms
Descriptive synonyms may differ with regard to their connotations (*dog – mongrel, cock – rooster, worker – employee, baby – neonate*), with regard to stylistic level or register (*begin – commence, buy – purchase, intoxicated – drunk – pissed*), with regard to regional or social variety (e. g. differences between American and British English), or with regard to their collocations (e. g. *a big/large house*, but *Big/?Large Brother is watching you*).

total synonymy
Cases of total synonymy, i. e. of interchangeability in all contexts (e. g. *Apfelsine – Orange* in German), are very rare. It is not difficult to see why. A linguistic system which has (many) total synonyms would be uneconomic. Why should a language have two (or more) lexemes with absolutely identical usage conditions? In fact, total synonymy between two words is always only temporary: either one of the synonymous lexemes is lost, or the two items will be semantically differentiated, developing different usage conditions.

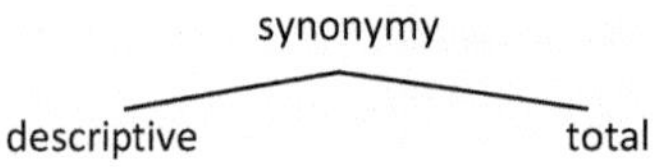

synonymy

descriptive   total

Figure 6.1:
Types of synonymy

Opposites: Synonymy contrasts with antonymy, a term covering various types of semantic *opposites* (*oppositeness*).

either-or relationship
Complementary antonymy: We speak of *complementary* or *binary antonyms* (or: *complementaries*) if there is an either-or relationship between the two terms of a pair of semantic opposites, i. e. if the two antonyms exhaust all possible options in a particular conceptual domain (e. g. *asleep – awake, dead – alive, live – die, pass – fail*). In these cases, the meaning of one lexeme is equivalent to the negation of the other lexeme.

narrow vs. wide antonymy
(Gradable) antonymy: Complementary antonymy is commonly contrasted with *gradable antonymy*, where the two expressions involved merely constitute opposite poles of a continuum. Alternative terms for gradable antonyms include *contraries*, or simply *antonyms*. (Note, however, that the term *antonymy* can also be used in the wider sense of 'oppositeness'.) Examples of gradable antonyms are *hot – cold* (notice the various intermediate stages like *warm – tepid – cool*), *broad – narrow*, *large – small*, and *old – young* (cf. also pairs of nouns like *beginning – end, war – peace*). The great majority of gradable antonyms are pairs of adjectives. Some of these pairs display a certain asymmetry in the sense that one of the two contrasting lexemes can appear in more contexts than the other. Thus, if we want to know a person's age (*How ___ are you?*) or the length of an object (*How ___ is it?*), we use *old* or *long*, respectively,

rather than *young* or *short*. The members of pairs like *old – young, long – short* differ in markedness: the term with the wider range of uses is called *unmarked* (*old, long*), the one with a more limited range *marked* (*young, short*).

Relational opposites: A further type of antonyms are relational opposites (or: converses). They describe the same situation from different perspectives (e. g. *teacher – pupil* in sentences like *John is Mary's teacher* vs. *Mary is John's pupil*). Further examples include pairs of deverbal nouns in *-er* and *-ee* (e. g. *employer – employee, examiner – examinee, interviewer – interviewee*), comparative forms of adjectives (*older – younger, longer – shorter*), pairs of verbs like *give – take, buy – sell, rent – let*, or pairs of prepositions like *above – below*. a matter of perspective

Directional oppositeness: The fourth type of antonymy, *directional oppositeness* (*directional opposites* or *reverses*), does not involve different perspectives on the same situation, but rather a change of direction (especially *motion* in different directions). Examples include *open – shut, push – pull, rise – fall, come – go, leave – return, (turn) right – (turn) left, tie – untie*, and *button – unbutton*.

Let us next turn to sense relations which involve hierarchies in the vocabulary, i. e. super- and subordination. hierarchies

Hyponymy: The term *hyponym* refers to words like *rose, tulip, daisy*, and *lily*, which stand in a relationship of subordination to a more general expression like *flower*. Conversely, the generic term *flower* is the superordinate or hyperonym (or: hypernym) of *rose, tulip, daisy*, and *lily*. Hyponyms have all semantic features of the hyperonym plus some additional ones, which distinguish them from the hyperonym, on the one hand, and from other hyponyms situated on the same hierarchical level, on the other hand (consider, for example, the features distinguishing *rose* from *daisy*, or *daisy* from *lily*). Hyponyms relating to the same hierarchical level are called *co-hyponyms* or *heteronyms*. hyponym <-> hyperonym

Interestingly, one of the oldest methods of defining meanings is based on the concept of hyponymy: According to this approach, we should first identify the superordinate category (the so-called *genus proximum*, i. e. the hyperonym), and then single out the specific properties (*differentia specifica*) which distinguish the lexeme from its hyperonym (e. g. *daisy* 'a flower which is very common, small, and white with a yellow centre'). It follows from the relationship of inclusion between the intension of the hyponym and that of the hyperonym (i. e. the intension of the former including the intension of the latter), that there is a relationship of inclusion on the level of extension as well: the extension of the hyperonym includes the extension of the hyponym (the set of roses is a subset of the set of flowers.)

Heteronymy (or: incompatibility): Alternative terms for *co-hyponymy*, the relationship between hyponyms situated at the same hierarchical level, are *heteronymy* and *incompatibility*. This captures the fact that in most cases co-hyponyms/heteronyms are semantically incompatible in a given context (either *This is a rose* is true in a particular context, or *This is a tulip* is true, but not both). Heteronyms are not always incompatible, however: e. g. *novel* and *paperback* are hyponyms of *book* and hetero-

Figure 6.2:
Hierarchical sense
relations

nyms of each other, but they are not incompatible (*This is a novel* and *This is a paperback* may both be true descriptions of the same object). Sometimes incompatibility is also described as a fifth type of antonymy.

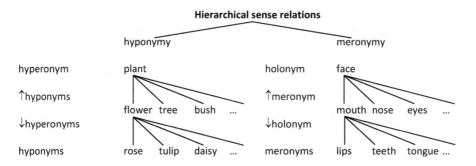

meronymy
vs. hyponomy

Meronymy refers to part-whole relationships in the vocabulary (e. g. *cock-pit – airplane, spoke – wheel, finger – hand, toe – foot, mouth/nose/eye – face, door/window/roof – house*). Such meronymic relationships hold between words on different hierarchical levels. (Caution: the term for the type of hierarchy involving such part-whole relationships is *meronomy*, but this has nothing to do with linguistics.) Thus, *door* is a meronym of *house* (the *holonym*), but the word also has its own meronyms (e. g. *handle* and *lock*). Meronymy, as opposed to hyponymy, is not necessarily a transitive relationship. If A is a *hyponym* of B, and B a hyponym of C, then A is always a hyponym of C (e. g. for A = *bobtail*, B = *dog*, and C = *animal*). In contrast, meronymic relations need not be transitive (e. g. for A = *hole*, B = *button*, and C = *shirt*), though there do exist examples of transitive meronymic relationships (e. g. A = *lips*, B = *mouth*, and C = *face*). Meronymy and hyponymy involve completely different types of hierarchies. Hyponymy involves a relationship of inclusion between *classes*: the extension of the hyponym is included in that of the hyperonym. The hierarchical relationships involved in meronymies are of a completely different type, relating to individual referents of meronymic terms (a finger is part of a hand, a hand part of an arm, etc.). This has nothing to do with a relationship between different classes.

Figure 6.3:
Sense relations –
an overview

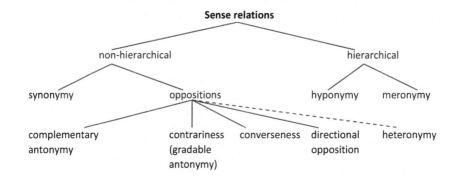

6.3.3 | Lexical ambiguity: Polysemy and homonymy

Polysemy vs. homonymy: Lexemes with only one descriptive meaning are called *monosemous*. Many lexemes, however, have several descriptive meanings and are thus (a) members of more than one lexical field, and (b) nodes in a network of sense relations that is even more complex than the network of semantic relations contracted by monosemous lexemes. Such ambiguous words can be divided into two major types: polysemous and homonymous items (homonyms). The different meanings of polysemous lexemes are commonly felt to be related. Typically, one of these senses has developed from the other sense via metaphorical or metonymical processes (e. g. *mouth* 'mouth (part of the body) / river mouth / cave entry', or *wing* 'wing of a bird / building / car / airplane / political party'). For homonyms, by contrast, it is neither synchronically nor, in many cases, diachronically possible to establish a connection between the different meanings (e. g. *race* 'a sports event' / 'a human race', or *mole* 'animal' / 'dark spot on a person's skin'). In the case of polysemy, we can speak of a single lexeme having several meanings, whereas in the case of homonymy we speak of different lexemes that happen to have the same form. Dictionaries often reflect this distinction: a polysemous word has only one entry (with various meanings that are numbered consecutively), whereas a homonym has several entries (e. g. *mole*[1], *mole*[2], *mole*[3]).

Types of homonymy: Homonyms can be more precisely differentiated with the help of two criteria: (a) medium-independent vs. medium-dependent formal identity, and (b) complete identity vs. differences in grammatical properties. In some cases, homonyms are identical in both spelling and pronunciation, and thus qualify as 'true' homonyms, or homonyms in the narrow sense. In many others, however, they are identical in spelling only, but differ in pronunciation, or vice versa. Homophones are lexemes which are identical in pronunciation, but differ in spelling (*see – sea, sight – site, flower – flour*), while homographs are identical in spelling, but differ in pronunciation (*lead* /led/ 'kind of metal' vs. /liːd / 'piece of leather attached to dogs' collars', *bass* /beɪs/ 'man with a deep singing voice' vs. /bæs/ 'type of fish'). The second criterion for distinguishing different types of homonyms applies equally to true homonyms, homophones, and homographs. It can be formulated as follows: Are the homonyms under consideration identical with regard to

two types of ambiguity

homonyms, homophones, homographs

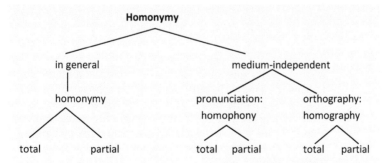

Figure 6.4:
Homonymy

their grammatical properties (in particular concerning their word class and inflectional morphology)? If yes, we are dealing with total homonymy, total homophony, and total homography, respectively (see all examples above); if no, we are dealing with partial homonymy (*bear* N – *bear* V), partial homophony (*rite* N – *write* V), or partial homography (*tear* N – *tear* V).

Does etymology help? It is frequently impossible to give a clear answer to whether an ambiguous word is an example of polysemy or homonymy – which once again illustrates the fact that there are no sharp dividing lines in language. Even if we consult etymological information (e. g. with the help of the *Oxford English Dictionary*, short: *OED*), which normally should be avoided in synchronic analyses of meaning, it remains unclear how far back we should go in the history of a word, and of what use this method really is. Take, for example, the two senses of *pupil* ('student' and 'part of the eye'). Both meanings derive from the same Latin origin: *pupilla* = 'orphan, ward' and *pupula* = 'pupil, eye' are both derived from *pupa* = 'little girl'. So this could count as evidence of polysemy. However, the two senses are so far apart in Present-Day English that we tend to classify *pupil* 'student' and *pupil* 'part of the eye' as homonyms.

cognitive
advantages
"Maximizing" polysemy: In general, polysemy is considerably more frequent than homonymy. This is not surprising from a psychological and economical perspective. Polysemy is a product of our metaphorical and metonymical creativity and allows us to describe, in a motivated way, something new with the help of something already known. In this way, polysemy adds to the flexibility and adaptability of the vocabulary of a language without increasing the number of lexemes. A language which makes extensive use of polysemy keeps the memory load to a minimum, because fewer words have to be stored in our minds than would be the case if we had to learn a separate word for every concept. Wherever possible, ambiguous words will be classified as cases of polysemy rather than homonymy. This tendency is particularly pronounced in cognitive semantics (see section 6.4).

Ambiguity in puns: Polysemous and homonymous terms have one conspicuous feature in common: A given context usually forces us to select one particular meaning of these words. An exception to this rule are puns, which are based on the fact that two meanings of a word or word-form are activated at the same time. Examples include the newspaper heading *Wait watchers* (which alludes to the organization *Weight Watchers*), the announcement in (6a) informing the local citizens that a shoe shop will be opening soon, or the panda joke in (6b):

(6) a. Soon we'll take the wait off your feet.
     b. A panda walks into a bar, sits down and orders a sandwich. He eats the sandwich, pulls out a gun and shoots the waiter dead. As the panda stands up to go, the bartender shouts, "Hey! Where are you going? You just shot my waiter and you didn't pay for your sandwich! Who do you think you are?" The panda yells back at the bartender, "Hey man, I'm a PANDA! Look it up!"

The bartender opens his dictionary and reads the following definition of *panda*:
"A tree-dwelling marsupial of Asian origin, characterized by distinct black and white colouring. Eats shoots and leaves."

Ambiguity vs. vagueness: Usually, however, only one particular meaning of an ambiguous word fits a given context. Ambiguous words are disambiguated by contextual selection of one of their (descriptive) meanings. A common test of ambiguity are cases where two different contexts are relevant to the interpretation of a word. These contexts require the activation of different meanings of the word and therefore lead to a bizarre or unacceptable sentence meaning (in rhetoric, the term *zeugma* is used for cases such as (7a)). A second test, the so-called identity test in (7b), also shows very clearly that *expire* is ambiguous:

tests

(7) a. ?John and his driving license expired last week.
     b. ?John expired last week; so did his driving license.

Such tests, then, allow us to determine whether a word is ambiguous or merely *vague*. Vague terms are unspecified for certain semantic features (e. g. *monarch* is unspecified for sex: *Her father / His mother was a monarch*). For this reason, they display a certain flexibility in their use. What is crucial, however, is that this flexibility does not lead to the assignment of more than one meaning. It is therefore characteristic of vagueness that we are not compelled by a particular context to decide between two or more meanings (in other words, there is no need for disambiguation by contextual selection).

At most, a particular context leads to a more precise specification of the word's meaning (e. g. by emphasizing or suppressing a feature). This type of specification is called *contextual modulation* of meanings, as illustrated for *window* in (8a–c):

contextual modulation

(8) a. Joan opened / shut / repaired the window. (neutral)
     b. Joan painted the window. (frame)
     c. Joan cleaned / broke / looked through the window. (glass panel)
     d. While painting the window, Joan broke it.

As shown in (8d), such modulations can be combined in a sentence without leading to a zeugma. In sum, the distinction between vagueness and ambiguity is of great importance when it comes to determining whether a word has merely one meaning or whether it has several meanings: A word which is vague has one meaning only, while words that are ambiguous have several meanings.

6.4 | Cognitive semantics: Prototypes and metaphors

language insepara-
ble from cognition

Categorization: Cognitive semantics developed in the 1980s on the basis of findings in cognitive psychology. Scholars working in this area of research have challenged many time-honoured assumptions familiar from structuralist semantics. The chief difference between the two approaches is that structural semantics defines and analyses meaning from a purely language-internal perspective (i. e. on the basis of semantic networks connecting lexemes), whereas cognitive semantics explains meaning primarily in terms of categorization (i. e. the grouping of similar phenomena into one class). In cognitive semantics, meaning is considered to be inextricably linked to human cognition, to the way we perceive the world and group phenomena into conceptual categories. Language and cognition are taken to be inseparable: the structure of linguistic categories is held to reflect the structure of conceptual categories (e. g. in the sense that the meaning of a word is the cognitive category connected with it).

perceiving/
constructing
similarities

Categorization essentially involves the perception or construction of similarities between otherwise different entities. Prototypes and metaphors play a central role in this process: Prototypes are considered to serve as reference points for categorization. The concept of metaphor, on the other hand, brings up the following questions: Which processes allow us to perceive or construct similarities? Are these similarities objectively given or subjectively created?

6.4.1 | Prototypes

knowledge
organization

Prototype semantics vs. feature semantics: When categorizing a given animal as a duck (rather than a goose), a given drinking vessel as a cup (rather than a mug), a given activity as running (rather than walking), or a given car as new (rather than used), we access what we know about poultry, cups, running, and old and new cars, respectively. This raises an important question: How is this knowledge organized?

the traditional,
feature-based
view

According to the traditional view, categorization is achieved by means of "necessary and sufficient conditions": An object counts as an X only if it possesses all the features which define an X. Necessary conditions (criteria) are features which are indispensable for an entity to belong to a given category. The term "sufficient conditions" is used when these features are jointly sufficient for assigning the entity to a certain category (i. e. when *all* of the various *necessary* criteria apply). This model of categorization implies that categories have clear-cut boundaries. The traditional account of categorization lies at the heart of *feature* (or: *componential) semantics* (see section 6.3.1), which is sometimes rather dismissively referred to as *checklist semantics*. Componential semantics can be traced back as far as Aristotle's theory of concepts.

flexibility and
fuzziness

Prototypes as cognitive reference points: Cognitive semantics, more precisely prototype semantics, rejects the classical view of categorization, at least for the majority of concepts: categorization in everyday life – less so in the domain of science – is much more flexible and fuzzy than is suggested by traditional componential semantics. Some ducks have no wings, others cannot quack, even though they have all other properties associated with ducks and are therefore spontaneously categorized as ducks. Why? Because they do, after all, come very close to our idea of an 'ideal' (or: prototypical) duck, or at least correspond much more to the prototype of a duck than to the prototype of a rivalling category (e. g. a goose). Thus, we can assign an entity to a category if it shares at least some central features with the category prototype, and (in most cases) looks physically similar to it.

Dictionary vs. encyclopaedic knowledge: Prototype semantics assumes that all knowledge which is accessed in a particular situation is relevant to the process of categorization. For this reason, we cannot strictly separate 'dictionary' knowledge ('knowledge of what is essential, pertaining to what speakers know in virtue of their command of a language') from encyclopaedic knowledge ('additional knowledge pertaining to what speakers know in virtue of their acquaintance with the world'). For example, there may be situations in which what is crucial to categorizing an animal as a duck is the encyclopaedic knowledge that during their search for food ducks hold their head under water and raise their tail in the air (cf. the German nursery rhyme *All my little ducklings*).

Internal heterogeneity of categories: The above examples show that categories have an internal structure, which implies that they are not homogeneous: not all category members are equally good representatives of the category; rather there are different degrees of representativeness. Categories have a core consisting of the best representatives (the prototypes), which serve as reference points in the process of categorization and which are surrounded by increasingly peripheral members that are more and more different from the prototype(s).

Fuzziness of category boundaries: Yet another important difference about the conception of categorization differentiates prototype semantics from the view espoused by traditional (including componential) semantics. Cognitive semantics emphasizes that category boundaries are often not clear-cut (*fuzziness of category boundaries*). Therefore, it is frequently not possible to give a clear answer to the question whether or not an entity belongs to a category. There are grey areas of transition between neighbouring categories where we are incapable of unambiguously assigning an entity to one category rather than another. Different speakers may thus assign the same entity to different categories, and even individual speakers may classify the same entity differently on different occasions.

Family resemblances: Many findings associated with the psychological theory of prototypes, which underlies prototype semantics, involve the notion of family resemblances. This concept was developed by the philosopher Ludwig Wittgenstein. Wittgenstein used the example of games to show that a category can be held together by nothing more than a complex web of overlapping and crisscrossing similarities among its members, comparable to the various similarities displayed by different members of a family. The analogy between categories and families turns on the fact that family members usually resemble each other with respect to

Ludwig Wittgenstein

various "crisscrossing" similarities: Some members have a similar nose, others the same skin, yet others the same eyes, etc. Similar observations can be made with respect to the individual members of the category GAME. Some games are amusing, some involve winning and losing, yet others require particular skills, etc. In such cases, establishing necessary conditions is difficult if not impossible. There need not even be a single feature which is shared by all category members. As a consequence, prototype theory discards the idea that category membership is always determined by necessary conditions. It also rejects the assumption that categorization should necessarily be construed as a comparison between the entity to be categorized and the prototypes (cognitive reference points) of a category. This does not mean, however, that the concept 'prototype' is given up; prototypes of a category are characterized by a high degree of family resemblance.

hierarchy of categories

Basic-level categories: Some scholars suggest that the family resemblance model is particularly suitable for explaining superordinate categories, such as Wittgenstein's GAME, or ANIMAL, PLANT, FURNITURE, and CONTAINER, while the classical prototype model is particularly illuminating for those kinds of categories that are situated at the psychologically most basic level (so-called *basic-level categories* like DUCK, DOG, CAT, FLOWER, TABLE, BAG). These categories are psychologically basic in the sense that they contain the most information in relation to the cognitive cost of storing them. Their basicness is reflected in quite a number of facts: Basic-level categories are acquired very early by children, they are rapidly recognized and represent the default choice in spontaneous categorization ("Look, a ...!"), and they represent the highest level of classification at which a single image can represent the entire category.

'more-or-less' semantics vs. 'all-or-nothing' semantics

Significance of prototype semantics for lexical semantics: The connection between lexical semantics and what has been said above about categories and categorization is natural. According to prototype semantics, the meaning of a word like *duck* is the cognitive category that is associated with it. As a consequence, word meanings contain all of the above-mentioned properties of cognitive categories: we can distinguish central and more peripheral meanings of a lexeme, and word meanings are not rigid. There are often gradual transitions between word meanings (recall the notion of contextual modulation discussed above; e. g. the different uses of *window* in *He painted the window* and *He smashed the window*). Prototype semantics is thus a 'more-or-less semantics', which – due to its integrative approach that rejects the traditional distinctions between dictionary and encyclopaedic knowledge, and between meaning and cognitive categories – is much closer to psychological reality than traditional feature semantics (or 'all-or-nothing' semantics) in structuralist lexicology. This does not, however, detract from the usefulness of feature semantics for the description and comparison of word meanings, especially for identifying semantic structures like lexical fields and sense relations.

Prototype and structural semantics complement each other: We do not even have to abandon the feature approach as a theory of how meanings are mentally represented: Neither the 'standard version' of prototype theory nor the more recent family resemblance model can do without a feature-based classification. It is just that the features relevant for categorization are those belonging to the prototypes of a category. Moreover, there is no list of necessary features that needs to be checked for successfully assigning entities to a particular category. Ultimately, prototype and feature semantics complement each other, in the sense that feature semantics receives a sounder psychological basis.

6.4.2 | Metaphors

Vehicle – tenor – tertium comparationis: The term *metaphor* (Greek *metaphero* = 'carry somewhere else', with the noun *metaphora* already in its modern meaning) traditionally refers to a figure of speech which is based on a relationship of similarity or analogy between two terms from different cognitive domains. This similarity, which may be objectively given or merely subjective, is typically held to enable metaphors to 'transport' one or more properties of a (usually relatively concrete) source domain (or: vehicle) to a target domain (or: tenor), which is typically more abstract. The similarities involved in metaphorical mappings are often called the *tertium comparationis* (or *ground*).

Examples of metaphors: Typical examples are:
- animal metaphors (*Smith is a pig / fox / rat / ass / stallion*),
- synaesthetic metaphors (extensions from one field of sensory perception to another, e. g. in *loud colours, soft / warm / sharp voice*), and
- so-called anthropomorphic metaphors (transfers from the human domain, especially human body parts, to all sorts of non-human domains, e. g. *leg of a table, arm of a river, face / hands of a clock, foot of a mountain, mouth of a river*).

Metaphors are traditionally neglected in lexical semantics, though they do play a role in historical semantics and in syntagmatic semantics. Historical semanticists view metaphor as an important cause of semantic change (see chapter 9).

Metaphors in syntagmatic vs. cognitive semantics: In syntagmatic semantics, metaphors have been explained in terms of selection restrictions. For example, in sentences like *Smith was a rat* or *He picked one hole after the other in my argument*, selection restrictions are violated (*semantic incongruence*): in the first example [+ HUMAN] clashes with [– HUMAN], in the second [+ CONCRETE] (*pick a hole*) with [– CONCRETE] (*into an argument*). In cognitive semantics, metaphors are seen in a completely different light: Metaphor is not considered as a purely linguistic phenomenon, but as a fundamental cognitive process which enables us to grasp the world and organize our knowledge. Metaphors pervade everyday language and are crucial to human thought processes, they are not simply dispensable ornamental accessories. Many metaphors are likely to go unnoticed by ordinary speakers. This is not surprising, though. We are often no longer aware of many metaphors simply because they are firmly anchored in human cognition and have become part and parcel of ordinary language.

selection restrictions vs. grounding in cognition

relevance for
categorization

Metaphor as a basic cognitive process: How do cognitive semanticists arrive at this conception of metaphors? This question can be answered by having a closer look at the process of categorization, i. e. of comparing new things to already familiar ones. At the heart of this process lies the search for similarities or analogies. It is easier to understand and describe the world if we can grasp new concepts with the help of existing categories. In some cases, this may involve extending these categories. However, such a strategy of understanding unknown concepts in terms of familiar ones has the advantage that (a) the categories we need for grasping the world are not unnecessarily multiplied, and (b) that classifications are not arbitrary, but motivated by similarities between those entities that are new and those that are already familiar.

Such similarities do not have to be objectively given; (some) similarities underlying (some) metaphors are predominantly constructed by speakers. It is language users themselves who determine the ground of comparison (*tertium comparationis*). Some metaphors strike us as novel and original even after we have encountered them many times. Cases in point are 'poetic metaphors' found in classical rhetoric and literary works, e. g. *My life had stood – a loaded gun in corners...* (Emily Dickinson).

focus on everyday
metaphors

Cognitive semantics is not primarily concerned with this type of metaphor but focuses for the most part on 'everyday metaphors', i. e. conventional metaphors which are not isolated but rather part of entire systems of metaphors. It is commonly assumed that these metaphorical systems allow us to structure particular areas of experience. Let us take a look at some examples of relevant metaphors (9) and systems of metaphors (10).

metaphorical
concepts vs.
metaphorical
expressions

Asymmetry / unidirectionality: The arrows in these two sets of examples represent the link between source and target domains, highlighting one of the fundamental properties of metaphors, namely their asymmetry or unidirectionality (at the most general level: concrete → abstract, spatial → non-spatial). The emphasis cognitive linguistics places on the conceptual nature of metaphors is reflected in the distinction between metaphorical concepts and metaphorical expressions. According to cognitive linguists, metaphorical concepts such as ARGUMENT IS WAR take priority over concrete metaphorical expressions like *attack* (a claim) or *shoot down* (an argument). Every metaphorical expression can be subsumed under one or several metaphorical concepts. In fact, we can use such metaphorical expressions only because the corresponding metaphorical concepts are part of our conceptual system. Conceptual metaphors are usually indicated by capital letters.

(9)   a.   LIGHT → THOUGHTS/KNOWLEDGE/INTELLECT
             illuminating/obscure ideas, a murky discussion, a bright person, a clear argument, make ideas transparent, I see 'I understand'
       b.   WAR/PHYSICAL ARGUMENT → VERBAL ARGUMENT
             his criticisms were right on target, shoot down an argument, attack a weak point in someone's argument
       c.   MONEY → LANGUAGE
             coin new words, owe someone an answer, richness in expressions

(10) UP – DOWN → PERSONAL WELL-BEING (e. g. HAPPINESS,
      HEALTH, POWER, STATUS)
   a. HAPPINESS/GOOD IS UP, BAD (LUCK) IS DOWN
       feel up/down, be in high/low spirits, fall into a depression
   b. HEALTH IS UP, ILLNESS/DEATH IS DOWN
       be in top shape, be at the peak of health, fall ill, drop dead
   c. CONTROL/INFLUENCE IS UP, LACK OF CONTROL/INFLU-
       ENCE IS DOWN
       be in high command, at the height of power, on top of the sit-
       uation, fall from power, be under control
   d. HIGH STATUS IS UP, LOW STATUS IS DOWN
       rise to the top, be at the peak of your career, be at the bottom
       of the social hierarchy, fall in status

It is a basic assumption in cognitive semantics that such metaphors are
more or less constantly used for structuring abstract concepts in terms of
concrete (especially spatial) ones.

Metonymy: Like metaphor, metonymy (gr. *metonymia* = renaming) is
a classical figure of speech which has been assigned a completely new
status in cognitive semantics. Consider the examples in (11) and (12):

(11) a. PRODUCER FOR THE PRODUCT: She owns a Picasso and two
          Frida Kahlos.
      b. OBJECT/INSTRUMENT FOR OBJECT/USER OF INSTRU-
          MENT: The buses are on strike.
      c. PLACE FOR INSTITUTION: The White House is planning to
          attack Iran.
      d. INSTITUTION FOR THE PEOPLE IN CHARGE: The univer-
          sity will reject this proposal.
      e. PLACE FOR RESPONSIBLE PEOPLE: Table 10 want their bill.
(12) PART FOR THE WHOLE (*pars pro toto*)
      a. He's a good hand at gardening.
      b. There are not enough good heads in this company.
      c. I don't see any new faces – nothing seems to have changed.

Metonymy, too, is considered to be a central cognitive process which
enables us to 'get a better grasp' on the world. The main difference between metaphor and metonymy is this: Metonymies do not involve a
transfer from one cognitive domain to another. They are rather based on
an existing objective connection between two "contiguous" phenomena,
such that one phenomenon stands for the other. Thus, metonymies are
not based on a relationship of similarity, but of contiguity: The phenomena or entities concerned are part of the same situation or, more generally, part of the same conceptual structure. Picasso does not resemble his
pictures, buses do not resemble bus drivers, and table 10 does not resemble the restaurant guests that sit at that table. But there is certainly a direct connection between painters and their paintings, bus drivers and the
buses they drive, or the plate and the dish that is served on it (just compare the standard encouragement for finishing off one's meal used in

*key difference
from metaphor:
contiguity*

German especially when addressing children: *Jetzt iss schön den Teller auf!* lit. 'eat up the plate'). Various types of such connections are illustrated in (11) and (12). Those in (12) form a separate group which in classical rhetoric is called *synecdoche*, a term which covers part-whole and whole-part relations (as in German *Zünd doch mal bitte den Weihnachtsbaum an!* lit. 'Please light the Christmas tree').

Prototypes, metaphors and polysemy: The two central concepts of cognitive semantics – prototypes and metaphors – are both relevant to investigating polysemy at the level of word meaning. It is not difficult to see why prototypes are crucial to explaining polysemy: Polysemous expressions can be described as prototype categories in that they can have one or more central meanings (the prototypes), each of which can have increasingly peripheral sub-senses, and all of which are connected by different family resemblances. This can be illustrated with the help of prepositions, a word class which is notoriously polysemous. For instance, there are countless ways in which *over* can be used as a preposition, but we can single out three central meanings: place ('above') in (13), place ('above') in connection with path ('across') in (14), and a covering sense in (15):

(margin: polysemous expressions as prototype categories)

(13)   a.   The lamp hangs over the table.
         b.   The painting is over the mantelpiece.
(14)   a.   The plane flew over the house.
         b.   John walked over the hill.
         c.   John lives over the hill.
(15)   a.   The board is over the hole.
         b.   The guards were posted all over the hill.
         c.   There was a veil over her face.

Each of these three central meanings has a prototypical core (the one in the (a)-examples) and other meanings that can be systematically derived from the central meaning (e. g. *over* in (15c), which involves a vertical rather than a horizontal axis). One of the above three (groups of) prototypical senses, notably the one in (14a), has a more central position than the others, and is thus even "more prototypical" than the other two prototypes in (13) and (15). In many cases, the connections between the different meanings are established by metaphors.

Metaphorical transfer both accounts for the synchronic relations between different senses of a word and offers a diachronic explanation how one sense develops from another. There is thus a close connection between polysemy and metaphor as a central cognitive mechanism for grasping and classifying new entities with the help of familiar ones, and abstract things with the help of concrete ones. In this context, polysemy is deliberately construed in a wide sense, i. e. a polysemous word may have senses belonging to different word classes (e. g. *over* as a preposition, adverb, and part of a compound).

(margin: relevant also for semantic change)

Further differences between cognitive and structural semantics: It is not only for ambiguous expressions that cognitive semanticists have shown that the link between *signifié* and *signifiant* is more motivated

(margin: motivation vs. arbitrariness)

than suggested by traditional structural semantics. The assumption that this link is far less arbitrary than is commonly conceded has led to further insights that put two central structuralist ideas into perspective: (a) linguistic categories provide speakers with the cognitive categories that enable them to grasp the world (this position is called *extreme determinism*); (b) therefore, the conceptual system of a language has to be analysed on its own terms. The second of these structuralist assumptions is inextricably linked to the hypothesis that languages are autonomous systems and cut up the same conceptual domain in different ways. For this reason, every language is held to create its own view of the world, a position known as *extreme relativism*.

Sapir-Whorf hypothesis: Cognitive semanticists challenge the latter position (also known as the linguistic relativity principle or the Sapir-Whorf hypothesis), arguing that the basic categorization and metaphorization processes are the same, or at least very similar, for all people – at least among the members of the same cultural community, but in many cases also across cultures. Consequently, the differences concerning the ways in which members of different speech communities categorize the world are limited. A well-known example illustrating this fact are colour terms. Comparative analyses of basic colour terms in different languages have shown that languages may indeed differ as to where they set the boundaries between neighbouring categories (here primary colours). Crucially, however, speakers of different languages agree on what constitutes the centre of the respective colour categories, i. e. on what constitutes the 'best' red, green, blue, etc. The perception and processing of reality is thus not primarily a matter of the native language one happens to speak. Linguistic categories do not determine our cognitive categories. Quite to the contrary, they reflect the structure of our conceptual system.

challenging extreme relativism

Checklist Semantics – key terms and concepts

ambiguity ↔ vagueness
antonymy (complementary
   antonymy; contrariness;
   converseness; directional
   opposition; heteronymy)
arbitrariness
asymmetry
basic-level category
categorization
cognitive semantics
collocations
componential analysis
conditions of use
connotation ↔ denotation
contextual modulation
contextual selection
conventionality

degrees of representativeness
descriptive / cognitive ↔
   expressive ↔ social meaning
determinism ↔ relativism
disambiguation
encyclopaedic meaning of a
   lexeme ↔ dictionary meaning
family resemblance
fuzziness of category boundaries
heterogeneity of categories
heteronymy / incompatibility /
   co-hyponymy
hierarchical sense relations
   (hyponymy; meronymy)
historical / diachronic semantics

holonym
homonymy (total ↔ partial;
    homography, homophony)
hyponymy ↔ hyperonymy
idiom
intension ↔ extension
lexical ↔ grammatical
    meaning
lexical relations
lexical semantics / lexicology
lexicology ↔ lexicography
markedness
meaning of utterance
mental lexicon
meronymy
metaphor
metaphorical extension
motivation
necessary ↔ sufficient condi-
    tion
paradigmatic ↔ syntagmatic
    semantics

polysemy
proposition
prototype
prototype semantics ↔ feature
    semantics
Sapir-Whorf hypothesis/
    principle of linguistic relativity
selection restrictions
semantic feature / seme
semantics ↔ pragmatics
semasiology ↔ onomasiology
sense ↔ reference
sentence meaning
sentence semantics
signe différentiel
source domain, vehicle ↔ target
    domain, tenor
structural semantics
synonymy (descriptive/
    cognitive ↔ total)
semantic field
truth conditions

Exercises

1. Which of the following uses of *mean* are relevant in a discussion of what semantics is concerned with and how it differs from pragmatics?
a) This face means trouble.
b) What does *soliloquy* mean?
c) If you're not there by six, I'll be gone. And I mean it.
d) You're meant to take off your shoes in a mosque.
e) Sorry, I don't quite understand. What exactly do you mean?
f) Do you mean to say you can't come?
g) His work means everything to him.
h) I never meant her to read this letter.
i) Smoke means fire.

2. Fill in the chart below with '+' or '−' as appropriate:
a) establishes a link between language and the world
b) independent of a particular utterance
c) involves a set of possible referents
d) to be found in a dictionary definition
e) lists defining properties

	sense	reference	intension	extension	denotation	connotation
a.						
b.						
c.						
d.						
e.						

3.

a) What are the semantic relations between *see* and the other lex-emes in the following groups that represent different lexical fields? *see – hear – feel, see – know – understand, see – look at – watch, see – visit – meet, see – imagine, see – sea*

b) Under which conditions can a lexeme belong to more than one lexical field?

4. Identify the lexical relations holding between the following pairs of words:

frame – window, expand – contract, mole – spy, fill – empty, (go) in – (go) out, fail – succeed, hyponym – hypernym, picture – painting, zero – love, semantics – linguistics, freedom – liberty, after – before, book – index

5.

a) What is funny about the headline *"Where's the party?"* (Subtitle: *"How to get young people to vote for their politicians"*).

b) Explain the linguistic basis of the panda joke in example (6b).

6. Explain the role of context in drawing a distinction between (a) semantics and pragmatics, (b) vagueness and ambiguity, (c) total and cognitive synonymy.

7.

a) What is structural about structural semantics?

b) What are the major differences between structural and cognitive semantics?

8. Which of the following statements are true and which are false?

a) Compiling a semantic field and identifying the sense relations among the field members are both instances of adopting an ono-masiological procedure.

b) Semantic fields are two-dimensional and have neither gaps nor words with overlapping or identical senses.

c) Polysemous lexemes cannot belong to more than one semantic field.

d) Homonymy and semantic change are two sides of the same coin.

e) Oppositeness plays an important role in the organization of our mental lexicon.

f) Hyponymy involves the inclusion of semantic features of the higher categories.

g) Semantics is exclusively concerned with the descriptive meaning of content words.

h) Prototype categories (e. g. bird, dog, cup, toy) always have fuzzy boundaries.

i) Componential analysis and prototype theory do not exclude each other.

j) Categorization always involves metaphor.

Advanced **9.** Absolute synonyms are rare. *High* and *tall* are considered near synonyms in English. Try to answer the following questions based on the examples below, which illustrate typical uses of the two lexemes.

a) In which of the examples are *high* and *tall* interchangeable? In which contexts is the choice restricted to just one of these items?

b) Based on your answers to a), try to give an outline of semantic similarities and semantic differences between *high* and *tall*.

Some authentic examples, mostly from the BNC:

high
1. Good health is not just about providing efficient **high quality** medical services. (BNC:A0 J 1358)
2. Due to the **high level** of burnout common in such chefs, few are offered jobs. (BNC:A0C 1377)
3. People chose to spend a **high proportion** of their disposable income on buying and running a car because car ownership enhances their lives. (BNC:A2L 103)
4. Mrs Thatcher has been advised that a complete ban on strikes is not a practical proposition and may entail a **high degree** of political risk. (BNC:a2T 112)
5. But availability of coal resource has never been the industry's problem – the essential difficulties are lack of demand and **high cost** of production.
6. VW has **high hopes** for the Polo in this country. (BNC:A6 W 431)
7. I didn't expect nothing like this. It's got this great **high roof** and loads of trains. It's real smoky and that. (BNC:A74)
8. "Come out!" The voice echoed in the **high arches** of the church. (BNC:HU0)
9. The room was large and square with **high ceiling** and two tall curtainless windows. (BNC:BN1)
10. **High Skies** and Fat Horses (Title of a novel by William J. Wallisch)

tall
11. The effect is similar to dressing **a tall man** in a pinstripe suit – it simply accentuates the length! (BNC:A0G 1442)
12. Suddenly, there stood beside me a very **tall figure**, six foot six or more, bearded and misty-white in appearance. (BNC:B2G 265)

13. From Middenheim's many **tall towers** it is possible to look out over the Great Forest to the south and the Drakwald to the west ... (BNC:CN1 386)
14. It was still night and the **tall trees** stood silently against the stars. (BNC:ACE 3258)
15. I could think of nothing except going to London and finding my way among its **tall buildings** studded with lights. (BNC:A0U 1374)
16. They knew the owner, the well-to-do, the grandees back from Jamaica and Bengal who sat here now behind the **tall walls** and drew their rents. (BNC:A0N 448)
17. Don't allow your personal feeling to cloud your judgement in finances or joint arrangements – a **tall order** because you seem to be emotionally involved, too. (BNC:CB8 2837)
18. The judge obviously thought that A had told a **tall story**. (BNC:H81 70)

---

10. The possessive in English is a highly interesting construction, given that it can express a wide range of semantic relationships. For example, the possessed can be ...

i)   something owned by the possessor (his *book*)
ii)   one of the possessor's relatives (her *brother*)
iii)   one of the possessor's *body parts* (his *arm*)
iv)   an "unowned possession" (the child's *schoolbooks*)
v)   an individual somehow related to the possessor (our *dean*)
vi)   a physical quality (his *weight*)
vii)   a mental quality (her *intelligence*)
viii)   a permanent location (their *neighborhood*)
ix)   a transient location (my *spot*)
x)   a situation (my *predicament*)
xi)   an action carried out (Oswald's *assassination*)
xii)   an action undergone (Kennedy's *assassination*)

a) What types of linguistic mechanism(s) might motivate the different uses of the possessive illustrated above?
b) Is there a common semantic feature characterizing all the different types of "possession" which can be marked by the possessive? At first sight, it might be suggested that the common denominator underlying all kinds of possession marked by the possessive is "association". On second thoughts, however, this explanation does not account for the asymmetries illustrated in (i) and (ii) below. Try to explain why the expressions in (i) are possible, while the (ii) cases are usually problematic. It may be useful to think of contexts in which some of the otherwise odd-sounding cases in (ii) would become acceptable.
  (i)   the girl's doll; the man's car, the dog's paw; the horse's ticks; the boy's aunt;
  (ii)   *the doll's girl; *the car's man; ?the paw's dog; ?the ticks' horse; *the aunt's boy ('her nephew')

11.

a) Compare the following sentences from English and Spanish, focusing on potential differences in how the two languages "construe" motion events. Which aspects of the events are asserted (explicitly stated) and which aspects are only implied?

(1a) English: The boy climbed the tree.

(1b) Spanish: El nino está subido en el árbol
'The boy is climb-PART en ['in', 'on'] the tree'
[= the boy is in a state of having climbed the tree]

(2a) English: The boy put (threw) the ball down into a container

(2b) Spanish: El nino metió la pelota en el recipiente que había abajo
'The boy put the ball *en* (can mean 'in' or 'on') the container that was below'

b) Do you think these differences have an impact on the way we think? Try to outline how exactly this influence may be reflected in our thought patterns.

12. The expression *single* (as opposed to *married*) is easily defined in terms of necessary and sufficient conditions. Construct such a definition and discuss whether this type of definition accurately reflects the way we conceptualize "single" persons and fully captures our use of the expression.

Sources and further reading

Aitchison, Jean. 2012[4]. *Words in the mind: An introduction to the mental lexicon.* Oxford: Blackwell.

Allan, Keith (ed.). 2009. *Concise encyclopedia of semantics*. Oxford: Elsevier.

Benson, Morton/Evelyn Benson/Robert Ilson (eds.). 2010[3]. *The BBI dictionary of English word combinations*. Amsterdam/Philadelphia: Benjamins.

Croft, William/David Alan Cruse. 2004. *Cognitive linguistics*. Cambridge: Cambridge University Press.

Cruse, Alan. 2006. *A glossary of semantics and pragmatics*. Edinburgh: Edinburgh University Press.

Cruse, Alan et al., eds. 2002. *Lexikologie/Lexicology*. [HSK]. Berlin/New York: de Gruyter.

Cruse, David A. 1986. *Lexical semantics*. Cambridge: Cambridge University Press.

Cruse, David A. 2011[3]. *Meaning in language: An introduction to semantics and pragmatics*. Oxford: Oxford University Press.

Davidson, George W./Peter Mark Roget. 2004. *Roget's thesaurus of English words and phrases*. London: Penguin Books.

Davis, Steven et al., eds. 2004. *Semantics: a reader*. New York: Oxford University Press.

Geeraerts, Dirk. 2010. *Theories of lexical semantics*. Oxford: Oxford University Press.

Geeraerts, Dirk/Hubert Cuyckens (eds.). 2007. *Handbook of cognitive linguistics*. Oxford: Oxford University Press.

Goatly, Andrew. 2011[2]. *The language of metaphors*. London/New York: Routledge.

Jaszczolt, Katarzyna M. 2002. *Semantics and pragmatics: Meaning in language and discourse*. London/Munich: Longman.

Lakoff, George. 1987. *Women, fire, and dangerous things: What categories reveal about the mind*. Chicago: University of Chicago Press.

Lakoff, George/Mark Johnson. 1980, reprint 2003. *Metaphors we live by*. Chicago: Chicago University Press.

Lappin, Shalom/Chris Fox (ed.). 2015². *The handbook of contemporary semantic theory*. Malden, MA: Wiley-Blackwell.

Löbner, Sebastian. 2013². *Understanding semantics*. London: Arnold.

Lyons, John. 1977. *Semantics*. 2 vols. Cambridge: Cambridge University Press.

Murphy, M. Lynne. 2010. *Lexical meaning*. Cambridge: Cambridge University Press.

Murphy, M. Lynne/Anu Koskela. 2010. *Key terms in semantics*. London: Continuum.

Oxford English Dictionary online: OED online. Oxford: Oxford University Press.

Riemer, Nick (ed.). 2016. *The Routledge handbook of semantics*. London: Routledge.

Saeed, John. 2016⁴. *Semantics*. Oxford: Blackwell.

Taylor, John R. 2003³. *Linguistic categorization. Prototypes in linguistic theory*. Oxford: Clarendon Press.

Ungerer, Friedrich/Hans-Jörg Schmid. 2006². *An introduction to cognitive linguistics*. London: Longman.

7 Pragmatics: The study of meaning in context

Pragmatics (from Greek *pragma* = action) is the newcomer among the major branches of linguistics. Its precise definition and status within linguistic theory are, to some extent, still subject to debate: Is it a linguistic subdiscipline like, for example, phonology, morphology and syntax, or is it a broad, interdisciplinary approach which is concerned with all kinds of linguistic structures?

7.1 | Competing definitions: Perspective or component?

We can roughly distinguish between a broad and a narrow definition of pragmatics.

Broad definition: In semiotics, pragmatics is traditionally defined as a subdiscipline which is concerned with the relationship between signs and their users (see chapter 1). The roots of pragmatics as the study of language use or linguistic performance lie in this (primarily) European tradition of research in semiotics. The pragmatic approach is usually contrasted with the structuralist approach, which is solely concerned with language systems in a vacuum (i. e. with the *langue* or the linguistic competence of a member of a certain speech community), independent of concrete communicative situations. European tradition

The 1970s saw an upsurge of interest in pragmatics (the so-called "pragmatic turn"), as a reaction to the neglect of language users and functions in Chomsky's generative grammar, which was influenced by structuralism. The new pragmatic approach focused on the process of communication which results from the interaction between speakers and hearers in actual linguistic contexts. Its major goal was to investigate the prerequisites for successful communication. pragmatic turn

If we define pragmatics this way, it can hardly be regarded as just another branch of linguistics (along with phonology, syntax or semantics). Rather, pragmatics provides a new perspective on the various aspects of linguistic structure. Under this broad conception, virtually all aspects of language can be the object of research in pragmatics (although the focus has always been on language use). This has naturally led to dismissive perspective view

J.B. Metzler © Springer-Verlag GmbH Deutschland, ein Teil von Springer Nature, 2020
B. Kortmann, *English Linguistics*, https://doi.org/10.1007/978-3-476-05678-8_7

Anglo-American
tradition: compo-
nent view

bridging the gap
between said and
meant

characterizations of pragmatics as the "wastebasket" of linguistics or "a useless catch-all term".

Narrow definition: Most linguists working in an Anglo-American tradition have adopted a narrower definition, according to which pragmatics represents a linguistic subdiscipline that complements semantics. This line of research focuses on concepts such as *utterance meaning, intention* and *inference*. Communication is primarily seen as the negotiation of meaning between interlocutors (or between authors and readers). Since in everyday communication many things remain implicit, the hearer's central goal is to recognize the speaker's communicative intention. Hearers achieve this aim with the help of inferences based on what has been literally said, knowledge about the utterance context, and general background knowledge shared by speakers and hearers. In many cases, such inferences are necessary for establishing coherence (i. e. an underlying link) between different utterances in a conversation. In the brief dialogue in (1), for example, much more is going on than a mere exchange of statements about the world:

(1)　The telephone is ringing.
　　　A: That's the telephone.//　　　B: I'm in the bath.//　　　A: O. K.

Speaker A does not simply tell B that the phone is ringing, and B does not simply mention that he/she is in the bath. A's statement obviously functions as a request directed at B to pick up the phone; B's response indicates that (or why) he/she cannot comply with this request. Speaker A clearly grasps the actual message conveyed by B's utterance and acknowledges it by saying "ok"; so A is likely to pick up the phone himself/herself.

Micropragmatics: The main focus of such a pragmatic approach, sometimes also called *conversational pragmatics* or *micropragmatics*, is on principles which allow us to bridge the gap between the descriptive meaning of a sentence, i. e. its proposition or what is "said", and the meaning it has in a specific context (i. e. what is "meant", the so-called *utterance meaning*). (*What is*) *said* and (*what is*) *meant* are two technical terms introduced by the philosopher Herbert Paul Grice (see section 7.4 below). In general, micropragmatics is concerned with all aspects of meaning anchored in actual conversational contexts, especially with utterance meaning (sections 7.3 and 7.4), but also with word meaning (section 7.2). This view of pragmatics lies at the heart of an oversimplified definition of the term, as encountered in the familiar equation "pragmatics = meaning minus semantics". The list of differences in table 7.1 between semantics and pragmatics offers a somewhat more fine-grained and accurate picture, which will be further elaborated in the following sections (see especially section 7.4.2):

Context vs. cotext: In some publications, the notion of *context* is defined in a narrow sense, relating exclusively to the situational context, which covers aspects such as time and place of the utterance, the interlocutors' social and cultural background, the level of formality, topic and overall aim of the conversation. Thus defined, context$_2$ is opposed to *co-*

Semantics	Pragmatics
context-invariant, speaker-independent meaning	context-sensitive, speaker-dependent meaning
meaning potential	concrete meaning in a given context
truth-conditional meaning	non-truth-conditional meaning
What does X mean? (conventional meaning, what is said)	What does the speaker mean by uttering X? (non-conventional meaning, what is meant)
principles for describing meaning, meaning relations and meaning combinations	principles for bridging the gap between what is said and what is meant

Table 7.1: Differences between semantics and pragmatics

text, the purely linguistic or textual context of an utterance. In this book, *context* will be used in a broader sense, referring to both the linguistic and the non-linguistic (situational) context of an utterance.

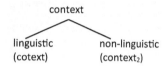

Figure 7.1: Context

7.2 | Deixis

The main focus of pragmatics as the study of meaning in context are utterances rather than single words. Thus, the two most influential pragmatic theories, speech act theory (section 7.3) and the theory of conversational implicatures (section 7.4), investigate language on the utterance level. Nevertheless, we shouldn't overlook the importance of context as far as word meaning is concerned. After all, it is on the word level that the necessity of drawing a boundary between semantics and pragmatics is particularly prominent. There are, in fact, numerous expressions (primarily personal, possessive and demonstrative pronouns, and adverbs of time and place) which have a context-independent, invariant meaning as well as a context-dependent meaning which varies with the circumstances in which they are used.

context-dependent lexical meaning

Semiotic hybrids: symbol and index: From a semiotic point of view, such terms are hybrids, combining aspects of two different types of signs (compare chapter 1): symbols (which express arbitrary and conventional relationships between *signifiant* and *signifié*) and indexes (which typically indicate physical and causal relationships between signs and what they refer to). Let us imagine that we are on a train and find a note containing the following request:

(2)   Meet <u>me</u> <u>here</u> <u>same time</u> <u>tomorrow</u> with a book about <u>this size</u>.

It would not be difficult for us to understand this sentence – but only up to a certain point. We know that *me* refers to the writer, but who is that person? We know that *here* refers either to the place where the note was written or (less likely) to the place where the note is being read, but only the latter place is known to us. We will encounter similar difficulties with

deictics = pointer words

all other expressions underlined above: what point in time is referred to by means of the phrase *same time*, what date is referred to by means of *tomorrow*, and how big is *this size*? Therefore, the proposition in (2) is underspecified. A complete understanding of (2) is possible only if we know the context-dependent meaning of the underlined expressions. Pointer words like *here* or *this* are called deictic (or: indexical) expressions or *deictics* (from Greek *deiknym-* = to show), because they "point to" a certain entity or aspect of the utterance context.

origo　**Deictic centre:** The speaker and certain features of the utterance context (primarily time and place) represent the central point of reference (*origo* or deictic centre) for context-dependent meaning. The deictic centre naturally shifts as soon as another speaker starts talking, but it can also be deliberately projected onto the hearer/reader, resulting among other things in a shift in the time and place coordinates. Take the following example:

(3)　a.　When you read these lines <u>today</u>, I'll be no longer in the country.

　　　b.　This programme was recorded <u>last December</u> to be relayed <u>today</u>. (delayed radio broadcast)

It is therefore no coincidence that in indirect (or: reported) speech the deictic expressions used in the original utterance have to be replaced:

(4)　a.　<u>I</u> won't be <u>here</u> <u>next Monday</u>.

　　　b.　He said he wouldn't be there the next/following Monday.

person, place, time　**Deictic dimensions:** The three major deictic dimensions (i. e. reference dimensions in a certain context) are person, place, and time. Person deixis encodes the different persons involved in a communicative event. In English, personal and possessive pronouns are used for this purpose (e. g. *I/we* – speaker(s), *you* – addressee(s), *he/she/it/they* – persons not involved in the communicative event). Examples of place and time deixis are given in (5) and (6):

(5)　Place deixis
　　　a.　here – there, hither – thither, near – far, left – right, this – that (in the sense of 'this here – that there')
　　　b.　come – go, bring – take, borrow – lend
(6)　Time deixis
　　　a.　now, soon, then, ago, today, yesterday, tomorrow
　　　b.　present, actual, current, former, future, next, last

In the pairs of opposites illustrating place deixis (5), the relevant expressions differ with regard to the parameter "near vs. far from the speaker" (proximal vs. distal) in (5a), and "movement towards or away from the speaker" in (5b). The usual reference point for time deixis is the moment of utterance (or: *coding time*; the examples in (3) are therefore exceptions). For this reason, absolute tenses (i. e. present, past and future; see

chapter 4.3.1) are also considered to be deictic categories. Deixis, then, is
not only found in the lexicon, but also in grammar.

Further types of deictic expressions: There are further types of deictic
expressions, the most important being social deictics. This deictic dimension relates to the (absolute or relative) social status of the persons directly or indirectly involved in a communicative event (directly involved:
speaker, addressee; indirectly involved: bystanders, the people being
talked about). In English, expressions like *Sir, Madam, Your Honour, Mr/
Madam President* or titles (*Doctor, Professor*) are used to indicate social
status; in German and French the distinction between *Du – Sie* and *tu –
vous* is highly important. In certain languages (like Japanese and Ko-
rean), such honorifics are far more grammaticalized. These languages
indicate social differences and varying degrees of intimacy between the
interlocutors by different types of personal pronouns and inflectional
morphemes on verbs. Social deixis is clearly more important in these
linguistic communities than, for example, in European societies.

social deixis

Two further deictic dimensions, which are usually considered much
less important than those mentioned above, are *discourse deixis* and *manner and degree deixis*. The latter is always accompanied by gestures:

manner/
degree deixis

(7) a. The book was <u>this</u> thick.
     b. The fish was <u>so</u> big.
     c. Why don't you do it like <u>this</u>.
     d. Don't turn the lid <u>this</u> way, turn it <u>that</u> way.

Discourse or text deixis is studied in text linguistics. Discourse deictics
provide a means of increasing text coherence by explicitly referring to
specific parts of the discourse which follow or precede the deictic expression:

discourse/
text deixis

(8) a. I bet you haven't heard this story.
     b. in the last chapter, in the next paragraph, as mentioned above,
         in what follows
     c. in conclusion, all in all, anyway, however, besides, therefore,
         so, etc.

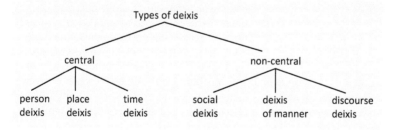

Figure 7.2:
Types of deixis

(Ana)phoric meaning: It is important to draw a distinction between discourse deixis and the non-deictic, more exactly (ana)phoric use of deictic
expressions, i. e. the use of deictics (especially pronouns) to refer to an

entity which has already been introduced (9a, b) or which will be introduced later in the conversation or text (9c):

(9) a. In 1998 Fiona worked as a part-time teacher. <u>She</u> was married <u>then</u> and had three children. <u>They</u> were two, four and eight years old.
   b. Mandy wants to go to the theatre, but doesn't know how to get <u>there</u>.
   c. <u>He</u> is a kind man who gives a million dollars to the poor.

the workings of anaphora

Coreferentiality: The concept of coreferentiality is crucial to explaining how anaphoric terms work. The expressions underlined in (9) do not refer to extra-linguistic entities directly, but rather indirectly by referring to the linguistic expressions which follow or precede. If a deictic expression is coreferential with an expression introduced in the preceding context (or more precisely: cotext), the so-called *antecedent*, it is used anaphorically (*anaphora*). Much less frequently, deictics are coreferential with expressions introduced later in the text, in which case we speak of a cataphoric use (*cataphora*). The term *anaphora* (or *phoric word*) often serves as a cover term for both cataphoric and anaphoric uses (in the narrow sense of anaphora) which deictic expressions may have in a text. But there are also cases where deictics are used neither deictically nor phorically, as illustrated in (10):

(10) a. <u>There</u> we go. Well done, lad!
   b. <u>There</u> is a story I'd like to tell you.
   c. These days <u>you</u> can never be sure what sex they are.
   d. What I did yesterday? Oh, I did <u>this</u> and <u>that</u>.
   e. Mary lives <u>opposite</u> Bill. (vs. Mary lives opposite.)

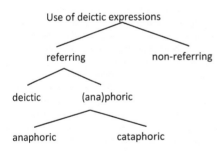

Figure 7.3: Use of deictic expressions

Deixis in semantics and pragmatics: What is particularly fascinating about deictics is that they "straddle the fence" between semantics and pragmatics, with one foot in semantics (their invariant or symbolic meaning), and the other in pragmatics (their context-dependent or indexical meaning). Both meaning components are necessary to turn a deictic into a referential expression – which may either have its own, direct referent (when used deictically) or an indirect (co-)referent (when used phorically) – thus completing the proposition expressed by a certain utterance. It is therefore hardly surprising that deictic expressions are investigated both in pragmatics and in semantics (especially referential semantics).

7.3 | Speech acts

Origin of pragmatics: Pragmatics was not put on the agenda of linguistics
by linguists. Defined as the study of meaning in context, it has developed
from a branch of philosophy which offered a critical perspective on attempts at applying principles of formal logic to the analysis of natural
language. Concepts that are crucial to logic include truth conditions and
truth values (i. e. true or false). Truth conditions relate to the conditions
that have to be fulfilled for a statement to be true in a certain context (see
chapter 6.2). Truth values are assigned to sentences by determining,
among other things, the referent(s) of the deictic expressions they contain
(see the last paragraph in 7.2). Truth-conditional semantics recognized
that the meanings of some expressions are at least to some extent context-dependent.

philosophy

Ordinary language philosophy: However, the true origins of pragmatics
lie in ordinary language philosophy, as represented in the later writings of
Ludwig Wittgenstein and the work of John L. Austin, John R. Searle and
Herbert Paul Grice. This school of thought saw itself as a countermove-
ment to traditional logic, which due to its focus on truth conditions ignored central aspects of natural language and ordinary communication.
Ordinary language philosophers developed the two most important pragmatic theories: speech act theory (Austin and Searle) and the theory of
conversational implicatures (Grice). These approaches will be explained
below and in section 7.4.

Speech act theory: Speech act theory (SA theory), which was pioneered by Austin and further developed by Searle, proceeds from the observation that everyday communication is more than just an exchange of
statements about the world which are assessed in terms of truth or falsity.
Many utterances do not describe some state of affairs and hence cannot
be assessed in terms of truth conditions (see 11a–c); furthermore, truth
conditions are often not very useful if we want to understand the speaker's intention, i. e. what is really meant by an utterance (11d):

*John L. Austin and
John R. Searle*

(11) a. Happy birthday!
  b. Merry Christmas!
  c. I hereby declare the meeting closed.
  d. A: Will you come to my party tonight?
      B: I'm still fighting this flu.

Examples (11a–c) cannot be assessed in terms of truth conditions. What
is relevant is rather whether the respective utterances are appropriate and
therefore successful in conveying the intended message: is it really the
addressee's birthday at the time of utterance (11a), is it really Christmas
(11b), and does the speaker in (11c) really have the authority to close the
meeting? In (11d), B's utterance can be assigned a truth value, but this is
not crucial. The relevant information is not that B is still fighting the flu,
but that B intends to give a negative answer to the question asked by A.
B does so indirectly by mentioning the fact that he or she has the flu,
which is a good reason for not going to a party. The actual message con-

tained in this answer is not explicit but must be inferred by A. Therefore, those aspects of meaning which are relevant to truth-conditional semantics underspecify the message conveyed in (11d).

Key assumptions and concepts: The examples above enable us to illustrate some further basic tenets and concepts associated with speech act theory: Communication is a dynamic process, to communicate is to act, and communication is successful if the hearer grasps the speaker's intention(s).

Speech act: The basic unit of verbal interaction is defined as a speech act. A speech act is an utterance made by a certain speaker/author to a hearer/reader in a certain context. It is not their structural (phonological/syntactic) or semantic properties (proposition) which are crucial to speech acts, nor their possible effect on the addressee (perlocution).

Illocution: The most important aspect of speech acts is rather the speaker's/author's communicative intention (the illocution). For example, is the utterance in (12) intended as a simple statement (made by tourists: 'Look! I've never seen a bobby before.'), as a request (made by a foreigner: 'Go and ask him for directions'), as a warning (uttered by criminals: 'Watch out, be careful') or even as a threat (in a heated argument: 'If you don't stop, I'll scream')?

(12)   There is a policeman at the corner.

SA theory =
a theory of illocu-
tionary forces

Illocutionary act / force: Since the illocution or illocutionary force (role, point) of a speech act is its most important aspect, the term *speech act* is often used in a narrow sense referring to illocutionary acts. Speech act theory in general has become a theory of illocutionary forces focusing on the following questions: What kinds of communicative intentions can be expressed by utterances? What kinds of devices are used to signal these intentions? What kinds of conditions have to be met in order to successfully convey these communicative intentions, i. e. in order to successfully perform a request, warning, threat or promise?

7.3.1 | Classification of illocutionary acts

Searle distinguishes five basic types of speech acts, i. e. communicative intentions expressed in utterances. These types are held to be universal:

5 basic types of
speech acts

- **Assertives** or **representatives** are used to describe the world (e. g. state, express, claim, tell, describe, assert, admit something).
- **Directives** are attempts to get people to do things, to change the world in the way specified by the speaker (e. g. give an order, ask something or ask somebody to do something).
- By means of **commissives** speakers commit themselves to a future action which will change the world in some way (e. g. by promising, threatening or committing oneself to something).
- We use **expressives** to express our feelings and opinions; expressives offer a glimpse of the hearer's psychological state (e. g. thank, greet, congratulate, apologize, complain).

- **Declarations** essentially serve to bring about a new external situation; they show that the world can indeed be changed by language (e. g. baptisms, marriages, divorces, declarations of war). This type of speech acts is clearly different from the other four types in that it requires specific extra-linguistic institutions or legal settings.

Speech act verbs: As can be gleaned from the above examples of different types of speech acts, there are certain verbs which can be used to render illocutionary roles explicit. Such speech act verbs are used, for example, in indirect speech to express someone's communicative intention:

(13) a. Read my paper, please.
　　 b. He urged his professor to read his paper.
(14) a. What a great performance!
　　 b. He congratulated her on her great performance.
(15) a. There is a policeman at the corner.
　　 b. He warned his friend that there was a policeman at the corner.

Performative utterances: Of course, the speech act verbs in the (b) examples above are not used to perform the speech acts they name. These verbs merely spell out what types of speech acts have been performed. They thus differ from utterances such as *Thank you, I promise, I forgive you,* or *I warn you,* where the speaker performs the relevant illocutionary act by using the speech act verb. The latter types of utterances are called *performative utterances.* Such utterances can fulfil their function only if they display a certain form, the so-called *performative formula.* Performative utterances typically have the form of declarative sentences in the first person singular, present tense, indicative and active; they may also contain an adverb such as *hereby.* However, the mere fact that a certain utterance follows this pattern does not guarantee that the primary communicative intention motivating the utterance is made explicit. (16a), for example, primarily functions as a directive rather than as an expressive (it does not really express gratitude, but rather represents a request). Likewise, the commissive speech act in (16b) is obviously not a promise but a threat:

performative formula

(16) a. Thank you for not smoking.
　　 b. I'll kill you, I promise.

Illocutionary force indicating devices: In addition to speech act verbs there are further devices indicating illocutionary force, for example particles such as *please* (*Will you leave, please?* – which functions as a request rather than as a question), the three major sentence types (declarative, interrogative, imperative), and intonation. In general, such devices do not determine illocutionary force, however; the (primary) illocution of an utterance may well be at odds with the illocution indicated by the relevant devices (see also 7.3.3 below).

7.3.2 | Felicity conditions

Speech acts have to meet certain conditions to be successful, as has already been illustrated above for (11a). These so-called felicity conditions provide a grid for analysing particular speech acts and comparing them with others. Searle proposes the following four types of felicity conditions:

4 types of felicity conditions

- propositional content conditions represent restrictions on what can be said about the world by means of a certain speech act. For example, we cannot felicitously promise something or warn against something that has already happened.
- preparatory conditions specify real-world prerequisites for the successful performance of a speech act. For example, is the speaker able to keep his or her promise? And does the hearer wish for the promise to be kept?
- sincerity conditions are restrictions on the speaker's psychological state, on his attitude towards the propositional content expressed. Does the speaker, for example, really intend to keep his or her promise?
- the essential condition is constitutive of speech acts; it provides the most important criterion for classifying speech acts. For example, the use of a speech act verb can count as the performance of a particular speech act (the utterance *I promise* counts as a promise, the utterance *I warn you* counts as a warning)

From these types of felicity conditions follow the rules for the appropriate use of speech acts. Of course, speech acts may be successful even if the relevant preparatory or sincerity conditions are not fulfilled. In this case, speakers simply violate the rules. Violating such rules is comparable to violating traffic regulations: A driver may "successfully" overtake the car ahead of him, even if he violates traffic regulations in doing so.

Regulative vs. constitutive rules: All rules for the appropriate use of speech acts, except for those based on the essential condition, are merely regulative, like rules for social etiquette, i. e. they are rules for pre-existing activities which can also take place without these rules. The rule based on the essential condition is different. It is a constitutive rule, i. e. utterances which do not follow the constitutive rule associated with a particular speech act cannot in principle be used to perform that speech act. The essential condition determines all other felicity conditions for a given speech act, and thus the rules for its felicitous use.

7.3.3 | Indirect speech acts

As illustrated in (11d), (12) and (16) above, the primary communicative intention of an utterance is often – maybe even in most cases – different from what it may seem to be at first sight. Some sentences which look like neutral statements (*It's freezing in here!*) can be used as requests (*Please shut the window!*), others which look like announcements (*Soon I'll come and get you*) may function as warnings or threats. Such examples are cases of indirect speech acts. In indirect speech acts, speakers perform a speech act (the primary speech act) via another (secondary) speech act. In some cases, then, two speech acts are realized at once, one of them being explicit, the other implicit. As far as the speaker's communicative intention is concerned, the implicit speech act is the more important one.

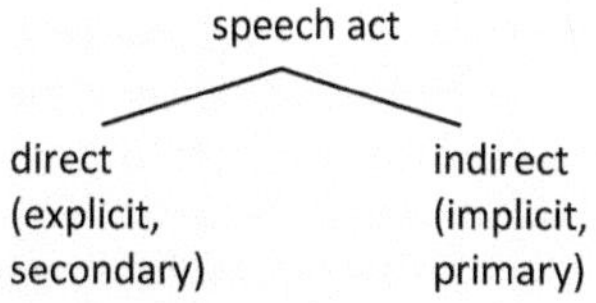

speech act

direct
(explicit,
secondary)

indirect
(implicit,
primary)

Figure 7.4:
Speech act
conventionaliza-
tion

Degrees of standardization: Indirect speech acts are standardized to varying degrees. Some of them are strongly conventionalized. For example, the appropriate response to a *yes-no* question like *Could you tell me the time?* is to tell the time, rather than to mumble *yes* and walk away. But many indirect speech acts require the hearer to infer the speaker's "real" intention (what he or she wants to communicate) by means of a more or less complex reasoning process. The hearer can infer the speaker's intention only if he/she takes into consideration both the literal meaning of the utterance and various other factors, including his/her knowledge about the speaker/hearer, the knowledge shared by speaker and hearer about the utterance context, as well as their shared world knowledge (including their knowledge of the importance of politeness in the respective culture; see also section 7.4.2). Even more essential to the inferential process required to arrive at the speaker's intended meaning is knowledge of general principles of cooperative behaviour. When investigating the inferential processes necessary to identify indirect speech acts, speech act theory thus ties in with, and indeed needs to draw upon, another pragmatic approach, the so-called theory of conversational implicatures.

7.4 | Conversational implicatures

7.4.1 | The original theory by Grice

Conversational implicatures are the most important link between sentence meaning and utterance meaning, between what is said and what is actually meant. They are a special type of pragmatic inferences and must be distinguished from semantic inferences.

semantic vs. prag-
matic inferences

Semantic inferences: Semantic (or: logical) inferences are inferences which are exclusively based on the conventional meaning of words, phrases and sentences. Two typical examples are semantic implications (or: entailments) and presuppositions.

Entailments: A proposition X entails a proposition Y if the truth of Y follows necessarily from the truth of X, i. e. if, every time sentence X is true (*There is a bobtail*), sentence Y is also true (*There is a dog*). In cases of entailment, it is incoherent to claim X and deny Y. The concept of entailment is very useful for defining sense relations such as hyponymy (see chapter 3.2).

Presuppositions are propositions that are taken for granted when a sentence is uttered, i. e. expectations which are naturally associated with particular linguistic expressions (including sentences). Verbs such as *manage* or *fail* in (17a), for example, presuppose an attempt (17b), and possessive noun phrases like *his computer* in (17a) presuppose the existence of the objects they refer to (17c); the sentence in (18a) presupposes (18b):

(17) a. John managed/failed to repair his computer.
     b. presupposition 1: John tried to repair his computer.
     c. presupposition 2: John has a computer.
(18) a. Christine has the noisiest children one can imagine.
     b. Christine has children.

Unlike semantic entailments, presuppositions hold under negation, i. e. the presuppositions (17b, c) and (18b) remain valid if we negate (17a) and (18a).

context-dependent   **Pragmatic inferences:** Pragmatic inferences are different from the semantic inferences encountered above: they are not merely based on the conventional meaning of utterances, but additionally require some contextual knowledge, i. e. the type of knowledge outlined at the end of section 7.3. In different contexts, the very same utterance may lead to completely different pragmatic inferences. By contrast, the semantic inferences associated with utterances are context-independent. In (19), B's remark is a valid answer to A's question – B of course assumes that both A and B have some background knowledge concerning the time when the evening news usually starts. In (20), B's answer is exactly the same, but here it is supposed to indicate that B wants to watch the evening news first (and maybe go for a walk at a later time). B does not reject A's suggestion directly but his/her utterance allows A to draw the inference "Not now, [but maybe] after the evening news":

(19) A: What's the time?
     B: The evening news just started.
(20) A: Let's go for a walk.
     B: The evening news just started.

human interaction   **Pragmatic principles:** Usually, interlocutors tacitly adopt certain basic principles of human interaction. Different types of pragmatic inferences are distinguished according to the kind of principle they are based on. Politeness is one of these principles (see section 7.4.2). Another one is the pragmatic principle of cooperative behaviour. This principle lies at the heart of Herbert Paul Grice's theory of conversational implicatures.

Herbert Paul Grice   **The Cooperative Principle with its conversational maxims:** The basic idea which underlies Grice's Cooperative Principle is that communicating is cooperative behaviour, and that therefore every communicative event proceeds on the assumption that speaker and hearer (or author and reader) want to cooperate – even if at first sight this might not seem to be the case. For example, B's remark in (19) does not specify the time, but A will nevertheless regard it as a valid answer. If the context was the same but the question was asked by a different person, e. g. a tourist who does not know what time the evening news starts in, say, England, B's answer would be uncooperative. As far as the hearer or reader is concerned, co-operative communication primarily consists in asking oneself "What does the speaker/author mean? What is the intention behind his/her utterance? (How) is his/her utterance connected to what has been said earlier in the discourse?" In other words, we generally assume that the speaker/author wants to communicate something, which may either be obvious or which needs to be inferred from his or her utterance. There seems to be no other possibility: we always look for the (deeper) meaning of utterances and simply cannot stop ourselves from "the effort after meaning".

Levels of cooperation: Now, in what sense precisely do we cooperate in communication? Grice distinguishes four different types of cooperative behavior, three of which relate to the content and one of which relates to the form of utterances. These four types of co-operative behavior are captured by the four maxims given in figure 7.5. The Cooperative Principle itself Grice formulates as follows: "Make your conversational contribution such as is required, at the stage at which it occurs, by the accepted purpose or direction of the talk exchange in which you are engaged." 4 types of cooperative behaviour

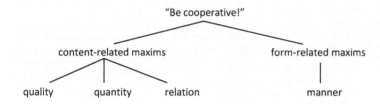

Figure 7.5:
Grice's Cooperative
Principle

Quality: Make your contribution one that is true. Do not say what you believe to be false ($Quality_1$). Do not say that for which you lack adequate evidence ($Quality_2$).

Quantity: Make your contribution as informative as is required for the current purposes of the exchange ($Quantity_1$) and not more informative than required ($Quantity_2$).

Relation: Be relevant. Do not change the topic.

Manner: Be perspicuous: Avoid obscurity of expression ($Manner_1$), avoid ambiguity ($Manner_2$), be brief ($Manner_3$) and orderly ($Manner_4$).

Cooperative Principle – descriptive, not prescriptive: The maxims of the Cooperative Principle are not merely a convenient theoretical construct unrelated to the real world or the outcome of a philosopher's wishful thinking. Likewise, they are neither arbitrary conventions nor do they constitute norms or rules of conduct. Quite to the contrary: They reflect our everyday behaviour in a purely descriptive way. Grice's maxims represent the basis for negotiating all kinds of human interaction, including not only linguistic communication, but also actions such as helping someone to change a tyre or to park his or her car.

Arguments for Grice's theory: There are quite a few arguments in favour of Grice's theory. For example, there are a great number of metalinguistic expressions, so-called *hedges*, which we use to pre-assess what we hedges are going to say in terms of the maxims of conversation, especially when risking violating one or even several of them. Just think of remarks like *I'm not sure whether it's true but...* (Quality$_1$), *as far as I know* (Quality$_2$), *to make a long story short* (Quantity$_2$, Manner), *by the way* (Relation) or *this may be irrelevant but...* (Relation). Even more important are the following facts:

cooperation =
a relative concept

- Grice was aware of the fact that expectations concerning whether the maxims will be obeyed depend on the type of verbal interaction involved. A police officer will hardly expect a suspect to tell the (whole) truth, and persons at a party are unlikely to regard the umpteenth remark on the weather (or the delicious food) as highly informative. This emerges clearly from the way the Cooperative Principle has been formulated: "Make your conversational contribution such as is required, at the stage at which it occurs, by the accepted purpose or direction of the talk exchange in which you are engaged." According to Grice, cooperation is therefore a relative concept which has to be adapted to each individual context; cooperative behaviour is the kind of behaviour which is appropriate in a particular communicative situation.

robustness

- Possibly the most remarkable property of conversational maxims is their robustness. The assumption that the maxims apply is not easily given up, not even when an utterance seems to violate them in form, content, or both. This aspect has been mentioned above (effort after meaning): we always assume that the person we are talking to is cooperative and observes the maxims, at least to a certain extent. The central maxim in this context is certainly the maxim of Relation: as long as we consider an utterance to be relevant in a given context, we will try to understand it.

other pragmatic
principles, too

- The Cooperative Principle has never been considered the only pragmatic principle. Other principles (such as politeness or face saving) can also motivate pragmatic inferences (see section 7.4.2). Such inferences are not examples of conversational implicatures, however; this technical term is exclusively used for pragmatic inferences based on the Cooperative Principle.

Types of conversational implicatures: Conversational implicatures can be classified according to two different criteria: (a) whether they are based on the fact that speakers follow the maxims or whether they are based on the fact that speakers violate them – at least at first sight; (b) whether or not they are confined to a certain context.

standard
vs. non-standard
implicatures

As far as the first aspect is concerned, we distinguish standard and non-standard implicatures. Examples (19) and (20) above were instances of standard implicatures, since the speakers observe the maxims in these two brief conversational exchanges. The exchanges in (21) and (22), by contrast, illustrate non-standard implicatures: in (21) B seems to violate the maxims of Quantity$_1$ and Relation, while in (22) this appears to be the case for the maxim of Manner.

(21) A: Would you like some dessert?
    B: Do they eat rice in Japan?
    (conversational implicature: 'Yes, of course')
(22) A: Let's get the kids something. B: But no I-C-E C-R-E-A-M.
    (conversational implicature: 'Don't mention *ice cream*. As soon as
    the kids hear the word, they will ask for it.')

In these two examples, the B-speakers violate the maxims deliberately
and ostentatiously, which qualifies as what Grice called *flouting* the maxims. However, non-standard implicatures can also result from a maxim
clash. Consider the brief dialogue in (23): under the assumption that B
simply does not know where exactly John spends his holidays, B has to
violate Quantity$_1$ in order to obey Quality$_2$. (As in many such examples,
alternative explanations are possible, for example, that B simply does not
want to specify more details.)

flouting vs. maxim clash

(23) A: Where does John spend his holidays?
    B: Somewhere in Germany.

Context-dependent vs. context independent implicatures: The prototypical conversational implicatures are dependent on a particular context and
called *particularized implicatures*. Most non-standard implicatures belong
to this group, but we have also encountered some standard implicatures
of this type (19 and 20). Particularized implicatures are commonly contrasted with generalized implicatures, which are default inferences typically triggered by individual words or word forms and thus largely independent of a particular context. Generalized implicatures are especially
relevant to the division of tasks between semantics and pragmatics.

particularized vs. generalized implicatures

Scalar implicatures: Of particular interest are a subgroup of generalized
implicatures, so-called scalar implicatures, which are based on the first
maxim of Quantity. Scalar implicatures, developed by the Neo-Gricean
Horn (see 7.4.2 below), can be characterized as follows: the hearer assumes that a given utterance presents the strongest possible statement
which can be made in a given context, so that there is no need to read
"more" into it. Scalar implicatures are thus essentially negative inferences
from the statement of one position to the negation of a stronger one. They
always involve lexical items that are gradable or can be arranged on a
scale; these items must be of roughly the same length, and lexicalized to
the same degree:

negative infer-ences based on Quantity$_1$

(24) a. < all, most, many, some >
    b. < always, often, sometimes >
    c. < excellent, good >
    d. < love, like >

If one of the expressions on such a scale is used in a given utterance,
hearers will typically derive the scalar implicature that none of the
stronger expressions on the same scale could have been used in the context at issue. Consider the examples of scalar implicatures illustrated in

(25). The first maxim of Quantity ("Make your contribution as informative as is required") allows us to draw the negative inference in (25a) that the biscuits were not eaten by all children. In a similar vein, this maxim explains why (25b) implies that John does not always lie.

(25) a. Many kids ate biscuits.
     b. John often lies.

The different expressions on such scales are characterized by a pragmatic inferential relationship from right to left (scalar implicature: no stronger interpretation possible) and a semantic inferential relationship from left to right (entailment: if it is true that many kids ate biscuits, it is also true that some kids ate biscuits).

"Saving" semantics by reducing the number of meanings: Scalar implicatures enable us to keep the number of senses of a word down to a minimum. Consider, for example, the coordinating conjunction *or* and corresponding expressions in other languages. These conjunctions can be used in two different ways (exclusive *or* and inclusive *or*). If only one of the two alternatives conjoined by *or* applies, the term exclusive *or* is used (as in *The $5 lunch deal comes with a soup or a salad* [... but not both]). On the other hand, we speak of inclusive *or* if both alternatives may apply: for example, *or* in *We will listen to the tape today or tomorrow* is used in an inclusive sense: the sentence is true if either *We will listen to the tape today* is true or if *We will listen to the tape tomorrow* is true, or if both are true. The sentence is false only if none of these possibilities apply.

inclusive vs. exclusive *or*   Despite these different uses of *or*, we do not have to posit different *senses* of the word (an exclusive versus an inclusive sense). The different uses can rather be explained by scalar implicatures: There is a scale < *and, or* > such that if a speaker says "p or q", he or she implies that he or she is not in a position to make the stronger claim "p *and* q". In this way, the exclusive interpretation "p or q, but not both" can be derived by means of the scalar implicature that "p *and* q" does not apply. Thus, the only sense of *or* which has to be posited in a semantic account is the inclusive interpretation, the exclusive use can be attributed to scalar implicatures. In this way, pragmatics simplifies semantic analysis.

(26) I need someone who speaks Russian or Polish.

cancellable   Key properties of conversational implicatures: One might be tempted to argue that due to the scalar implicature discussed above, the speaker in (26) must be looking for someone who speaks either Russian or Polish, but not both. Such an interpretation is absurd; it ignores what is probably the most important property of conversational implicatures, viz. their cancellability: Conversational implicatures may be cancelled without a sense of contradiction. In (26), for example, the speaker could add *"Of course, anyone speaking both languages will be most welcome"*. This would not be contradictory. The fact that conversational implicatures can be cancelled makes them even more attractive; it is always possible to add "... but I didn't mean to say/suggest that...".

Further important characteristics of conversational implicatures in-   calculable
clude calculability and non-conventionality. Conversational implicatures
are calculable in the sense that it is generally possible to reconstruct the
inferential process which leads to a conversational implicature. Of course,
no complex inferential process is involved in the highly standardized indirect speech acts mentioned above (e. g. *Could you tell me the time?*) (see
section 7.3.3).

Non-conventionality relates to the fact that conversational implica-   non-conventional
tures are not part of the conventional meaning of particular words or utterances, and that knowing the conventional meaning of expressions is
not sufficient for grasping such implicatures. As already noted, scalar
implicatures, for example, can only be inferred on the basis of the first
maxim of Quantity.

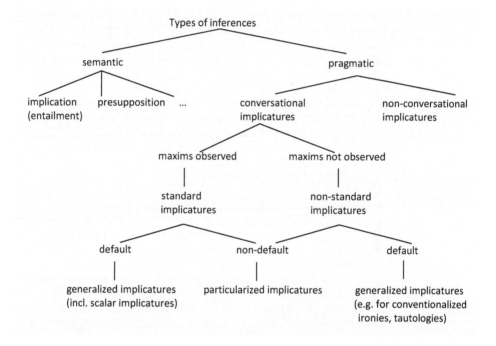

Figure 7.6:
Types of inferences

7.4.2 | Post-Gricean models

During the 1980s, several models of implicature were developed, which   reductionist vs. ex-
will only be sketched in outline here. In general, two types of approaches   pansionist models
can be distinguished: reductionist models that contain fewer maxims or
principles than Grice's original theory, and expansionist models which
add further maxims to those posited by Grice. Though these models suggest various modifications to Grice's account, there is only one model
that criticizes the basic ideas of Grice's theory of conversational implicatures and that has explicitly been developed as an alternative to it (see the

remarks on Sperber & Wilson below). All other models still subscribe to Grice's model and the basic assumptions underlying it, but simply offer attempts at improving or complementing it.

Horn: Quantity principle vs. Relevance principle: Almost all recent approaches are reductionist. The two most interesting reductionist models have been proposed by Horn and Sperber & Wilson. Horn, who developed the concept of scalar implicatures, does not so much reduce as rearrange Grice's conversational maxims. His model includes a maxim of Quality (essentially the same as Grice's), a Quantity principle (which covers Grice's first maxim of Quantity as well as the first two maxims of Manner), and an R(elation)-Principle (which covers Grice's second maxim of Quantity, his maxim of Relation and the third maxim of Manner). Horn's rearrangement of the maxims explains an important fact about Grice's conversational maxims: They give rise to two entirely distinct types of conversational implicatures. On the one hand, there are implicatures leading to enriched, "stronger", interpretations (e. g. indirect speech acts which seem to be based on the following principle: "hearer, read as much into the utterance as is compatible with your world knowledge and the situational context"). On the other hand, there are "negative" implicatures which do not allow for a stronger interpretation (e. g. scalar implicatures which seem to be based on the following principle: "Hearer, the speaker said everything he could. Don't try to read more into his utterance"). This paradox is illustrated in the examples below (27):

(27) a. I broke a finger last night.
     b. I slept on a boat last night.

Language economy: (27a) carries the implicature "it was <u>my</u> finger", i. e. invites a stronger interpretation, whereas (27b) conveys the implicature "it was <u>not my</u> boat", i. e. a negative inference. Horn offers a solution to this paradox (which Grice had noticed but did not explain): The R-Principle motivates conversational implicatures that lead to stronger interpretations (so-called *R-based implicatures*), and the Q-Principle motivates "negative" implicatures. According to Horn, these two pragmatic principles as well as the Gricean maxims can ultimately be traced to a more general principle of linguistic economy, the so-called Principle of Least Effort (or simply human laziness). The R-Principle follows from speaker economy (minimization of linguistic output: "Say no more than you must"; "Hearer, infer as much as possible"), whereas the Q-Principle follows from hearer economy (maximization of informational content: "Speaker, say as much as you can and say it as clearly as possible").

Q-based vs. R-based implicatures

Sperber & Wilson: Relevance Theory: Unlike Horn, Sperber & Wilson ([1986] 1996²) heavily criticize Grice's model. In their view, the set of maxims put forward by Grice can be replaced by a single principle, the Principle of Relevance. However, the notion of relevance has a different status in Sperber & Wilson's theory than it has in Grice's and Horn's models. According to Sperber & Wilson, relevance is a psychological principle that involves a kind of cost-benefit analysis. Relevance is a function of an utterance's contextual effects (to be understood in psychological

relevance as a psychological principle

terms, i. e. as cognitive effects) and the processing effort involved in achieving these effects: The greater the contextual effects and the smaller the processing effort required, the greater the relevance. Thus:

relevance = contextual effects: [divided by] processing effort

According to the Principle of Relevance, utterances create the expectation that they are optimally relevant. Hearers/readers may thus assume that everything speakers/authors say is optimally relevant, i. e. that their utterances yield the greatest possible contextual effects in return for the smallest possible processing effort.

Contextual effects: There are different types of contextual effects. The term covers cases where new assumptions (contextual implications) are derived in a specific context, cases where the hearer's assumptions are eliminated or revised (e. g. because new evidence contradicts or weakens the original assumptions), and cases where existing assumptions are strengthened due to further evidence in favour of them. Language users have to invest processing effort in deriving such contextual effects and accessing that context which, according to the Principle of Relevance, most likely is the optimal one for processing a certain utterance.

(28) A: Bet no one's understood today's pragmatics lecture.
      B_1: Well, there are several students of philosophy in the class.
      B_2: Well, there are several mountaineers in the class. (???)

If A is to infer from B's reply that there are indeed students who understood the pragmatics lecture, the first of the two possible remarks made by B (B_1) is certainly more relevant than the second (B_2). To derive the same conclusion from the second answer, A would have to make a much greater processing effort and try to construct a context in which mountaineering can in some way be related to understanding a pragmatics lecture. Much as the notion of relevance, the term *context* has a different meaning in Relevance Theory than in other accounts: it is primarily a psychological concept which refers to the world and to the interlocutors' background knowledge. In many cases, the context is not there right from the beginning but has to be constructed during the inferential process.

context as a psychological principle

(29) Mary: Have you read "The Revenge of the Black Forest"?
      Peter: I never read books that win awards.

In this brief dialogue, for example, it is absolutely possible for Mary to correctly infer that Peter has not read the book without knowing beforehand that it won an award. She would have to construct the necessary context before being able to make the inference, which inevitably means that Mary has to make a greater processing effort. Nevertheless, this would not diminish the relevance of Peter's answer, because his utterance enables Mary to gain new information. Peter's answer thus yields an additional contextual effect, redressing the balance between cost and benefit. Of course, Mary could also respond to Peter's remark by saying *But*

"The Revenge of the Black Forest" has never won an award. In this case, Mary would also have to construct an appropriate context for Peter's answer, for example that Peter obviously believes (i. e. presupposes) that the book has won an award. In this scenario, however, Peter's answer would be clearly less relevant than in the former one: Mary would have to make a greater processing effort (asking herself (a) whether the book might have won an award despite her assumptions to the contrary, and especially (b) how Peter's answer relates to her question); nevertheless, she would be able to derive fewer contextual effects from Peter's answer.

Relevance Theory = cognitive theory

What is said ≠ semantics: Sperber & Wilson's Relevance Theory, which they consider a cognitive and psychological theory rather than a pragmatic one, is certainly the most widely discussed model among those presented in this chapter. Within pragmatics, it has also been the most controversial of these theories for a long time, far more controversial than, e. g. Grice's "standard theory". Relevance Theory has been criticized, for example, for failing to explain how processing effort is to be calculated. As a result, it remains unclear how relevant a certain utterance really is. Also, the Relevance Principle cannot do without at least some Gricean maxims. The Cooperative Principle is more plausible and offers a more fine-grained analysis of the mechanisms underlying the processing of utterances in ordinary communication. But in one respect, Relevance Theory has managed to spell out more clearly what Grice had already recognized but not further elaborated in his theory: Sperber & Wilson give a convincing account of why Grice's distinction between what is said and what is meant cannot be equated with the distinction between semantics and pragmatics.

Explicatures: Pragmatics (the context of an utterance or pragmatic inferences) is crucial not only to what is meant, but also to what is said. In other words, we need pragmatic inferences and the context to complete the proposition conveyed by a certain utterance. Pragmatic inferences which complete a proposition are called *explicatures* by Sperber & Wilson. Semantics on its own underspecifies what is said. Thus, as already noted, it is often impossible to assign reference to referential expressions in the absence of information about the situational context (e. g. *the girl* in (30)). Contextual information is also required for disambiguating ambiguous expressions (e. g. are the girl's *trainers* in (30) persons or shoes?).

(30)   The girl was looking for her trainers.

Such examples demonstrate that familiar accounts of the distinction between semantics and pragmatics (including the division of tasks sketched at the end of section 7.1) are simplified and have to be revised: pragmatic processes already play a role in establishing what is said. Again, pragmatics is claiming part of the territory formerly occupied by semantics.

expansionist model, creating basis for cooperation

Leech: Politeness Principle: Having discussed two reductionist models, we will now take a brief look at a well-known expansionist account. Leech (1983, 2014) adds another pragmatic principle to Grice's framework, the so-called Politeness Principle ("Be polite, make the addressee feel good"). Its most important maxim – especially in English-speaking countries – is the tact maxim ("Minimize the hearer's effort and maximize the hearer's benefit"). This principle is not designed to explain how we can infer the communicative intention of speakers/authors. It rather helps us understand why we use indirect speech acts so frequently. The key idea underlying this principle is the assumption that many speech acts are spontaneously felt to be either polite (e. g. offers, promises) or impolite (requests, orders). Depending on such factors as, for example, how much authority the speaker has over the hearer (or vice versa) or how close the relationship between the speaker and the hearer is, the speaker has to choose the appropriate speech act. For Leech, the Politeness Principle is ultimately more crucial than the Cooperative Principle, because it is only by observing the Politeness Principle that a good and friendly social relationship between interlocutors can be established and maintained, which in turn is a precondition for their willingness to cooperate.

Macro-pragmatics – variational pragmatics: Leech's socio-pragmatic theory represents a transition from micro-pragmatics to macro-pragmatics, i. e. from an approach which focuses on the meaning conveyed by utterances to a much broader approach which places particular emphasis on the social and cultural factors affecting the way we use language. Macro-pragmatics includes the study of politeness (especially Leech 2014 and Brown & Levinson 2002), and both conversation and discourse analysis (e. g. Schiffrin 1994). *bordering on sociology and anthropology*

Another branch of macro-pragmatics is cross-cultural pragmatics. Scholars working in this field have alerted linguists to the danger of basing theoretical considerations in linguistics largely on a single language and culture, warning especially against anglocentrism in pragmatic theory (e. g. Wierzbicka 2003). It is, for example, not possible to make unrestricted generalizations about the importance of politeness in communication or about the evaluation of speech acts as inherently polite or impolite on the basis of our knowledge of Anglo-American culture and Western societies. *cross-cultural pragmatics*

In fact, even a label such as "Anglo-American culture" is far too broad and hides the fact that there may be considerable variation within such a culture, for example concerning politeness investment strategies in native English-speaking countries like Ireland, the United Kingdom, the United States, and Australia. Variation of this kind is explored in the recently established field of variational pragmatics (see chapter 9). Macro-pragmatics is no longer close to philosophy and semantics. It rather borders and draws upon the concepts, methods and insights in text linguistics, on the one hand, and sociology and anthropology, on the other hand. *variational pragmatics*

Checklist Pragmatics – key terms and concepts

antecedent
coherence
component view ↔
  perspective view
context ↔ cotext
contextual effect
conversational implicatures
conversational maxim (quality; quantity; relation;
  manner)
Cooperative Principle
coreference
deictic centre/origo
deictic dimensions
deictic expressions
deixis (person, place, time,
  social, discourse, manner
  and degree)
economy (speaker ↔ hearer)
entailment
explicature
felicity conditions
hedges
honorifics
illocution
illocutionary force
implicature (standard ↔
  non-standard; scalar; generalized ↔ particularized)
index(ical expression)
inference (semantic ↔
  pragmatic)
intention
linguistic economy
(ana)phoric use (anaphora ↔
  cataphora)

maxim flouting
micro-pragmatics ↔ macro-
  pragmatics
ordinary language philosophy
performative formula
performative utterance
perlocutionary act
Politeness Principle
presupposition
Principle of Least Effort
Principle of Relevance
properties of conversational
  implicatures (cancellability;
  calculability; non-conventionality)
proposition
Q- and R-Principle
robustness of maxims
rules (regulative ↔ con-
  stitutive)
semantic implication
speech act (direct ↔ indirect)
speech act theory
speech act verb
symbol
truth conditions
truth-conditional semantics
types of illocutionary acts/
  speech acts (assertive /
  representative; directive;
  commissive; expressive;
  declarative speech acts)
utterance meaning
variational pragmatics

Exercises

1. Fill in the blanks:

Pragmatics can be defined as the study of .... in ...., with the speakers and their ....s at the centre. Its two most important theories operate on the .... level. Speech act theory was developed by .... and his pupil ...., and the theory of .... implicatures by .... All of them belong to the movement of .... language .... Grice's theory helps us account for the frequently observable fact that we .... more into an utterance than what is .... said. In this respect it links up with the study of .... within speech act theory. Different from Grice's theory, the .... theory developed by Sperber & Wilson is not a pragmatic, but rather a .... theory. What stands at the heart of this theory is the calculation of contextual .... against ....

2. Identify the deictic expressions in the following examples and specify
   a) whether they are used deictically or anaphorically
   b) the relevant deictic dimension.
   a) There she was, sitting right next to my mother.
   b) Listen, mate, there is only one solution to your problem: you finish your essay and submit it next Monday.
   c) There you go.
   d) The hotel was just terrible. So the next Monday we left this hotel for good.
   e) Two days ago I met Mary. She looked tired and said she wasn't looking forward to her sister's birthday party a week from to-day.

3.
   a) Spell out the symbolic and indexical meanings of *today* and *this morning* respectively. Make use of the term *coding time*.
   b) What is understood by *deictic projection*? Apply this notion to the following conversational exchange:
   Fred: It's the one on the right.
   Mary: My right or yours?
   What can we assume concerning the locations of Fred and Mary relative to each other?

4. Which of the following utterances qualify as performatives? Identify the relevant speech acts.
   a) I promised never to do it again.
   b) I promise I'll never do it again.
   c) Don't worry, be happy!
   d) She declared the meeting closed.
   e) I hereby fulfil my promise and paint the fence.
   f) Don't you dare look at my daughter again!

5. Identify both the direct and the indirect speech act for each of the following examples:
a) Could you get me a cup of coffee?
b) I could do with a cup of coffee.
c) I would not do this if I were you.
d) Would you like to come to my party?
e) I wish I knew when the boss is coming back.
f) Didn't I tell you to be careful?

6. Try to identify for each of the following exchanges (a) the shared background assumptions of A and B, (b) the conversational implicature B wants A to draw, and (c) the relevant maxim(s) of the Cooperative Principle:
a) A: Did you bring the baby?
   B: Do you see a pram or a bag full of nappies?
b) A: Have you cleaned the kitchen and done the shopping?
   B: Well, I've done the shopping.
c) A: Have you seen George recently?
   B: I saw him sometime last spring.
d) A: Does your dog like bones?
   B: Do cats chase mice?
e) A: There's a good movie on BBC 2 tonight.
   B: Good for you. I still have to finish this essay.

7.
a) Name and illustrate three central properties that Grice identified for conversational implicatures.
b) What is understood by scalar implicatures? In what way can they be characterized as "negative" inferences?

8. Which of the following statements are true and which are false?
a) Modern pragmatics was born in philosophy.
b) Deictic expressions make the illocutionary point of an utterance explicit.
c) Politeness is the top candidate for the most important motivation for being indirect in Anglo-American culture.
d) For each individual speech act, the essential condition determines the other felicity conditions.
e) Most felicity conditions represent regulative rules.
f) The Cooperative Principle is a normative pragmatic principle explaining all language use.
g) Cultural differences play no role in inferencing.
h) Particularized implicatures are the prototypical conversational implicatures in being associated with a special context.
i) Relation-based conversational implicatures generally yield enriched readings.
j) Relevance Theory cannot do without Grice's Quality maxim.

9. What are the major differences between speech act theory and the   Advanced
theory of conversational implicatures, and what do the two theories
have in common?

10.
  a) Describe the central role that the maxim of Relation plays in the
     Cooperative Principle.
  b) Why is it misleading to assume that Relevance Theory is a reduc-
     tionist pragmatic model that reduces the four Gricean maxims to a
     single one?

11.
  a) Violating a maxim is generally considered a violation of the Coop-
     erative Principle. But this is less obvious in the case of the second
     maxim of quantity (*Do not make your contribution more informa-
     tive than required*). If speakers provide more information than re-
     quired, do they really fail to observe the Cooperative Principle? If
     so, why?
  b) For some theorists, the maxim of quality is accorded minor impor-
     tance at best. Can you think of reasons why? It may be helpful to
     think of a type of phenomenon that is a central concern of Cogni-
     tive Linguistics (see the semantics chapter).
  c) Some scholars argue that the second maxim of quantity (*Do not
     make your contribution more informative than required*) is not re-
     ally necessary. Violating this maxim always seems to amount to
     violating the maxim of relation ('Be relevant'). Can you think of
     counterexamples to this claim which show that one can violate the
     second maxim of quantity without at the same time violating rele-
     vance?

12. According to Austin, an utterance usually involves producing locutionary, illocutionary, and perlocutionary acts simultaneously. The
terms *illocutionary act* and *perlocutionary act* are explained in the
chapter. The locutionary act is the act of producing a concrete utterance with a determinate sense and reference. Usually, this includes
the act of expressing some propositional content. For example, the
locutionary act associated with a particular utterance of *He loves Ludwig* might be "Searle (= the reference of the *he* in the context at issue) loves his dog Ludwig (= the reference of *Ludwig* in this example)".
  a) Can you think of cases where only the locutionary act is produced,
     while no illocutionary act is carried out?
  b) Can you think of cases where illocutionary (and typically also per-
     locutionary) acts are produced, but no locutionary act is carried
     out?
  c) Can you think of cases where speakers produce only an illocution-
     ary or locutionary act, but no perlocutionary act?
  d) Can you think of locutionary/illocutionary acts that do not have
     any propositional content?

e) Identify which of the verbs given below designate ...
   i)   illocutionary acts
   ii) perlocutionary acts
   iii) neither illocutionary nor perlocutionary acts
sympathize, intend, tell (someone that something is the case), frighten, request, nominate, insist, convince, annoy, regard as

Sources and further reading

Archer, Dawn/Karin Aijmer/Anne Wichmann. 2012. *Pragmatics: An advanced resource book for students*. New York: Routledge.

Allan, Keith/Kasia M. Jaszczolt. 2012. *The Cambridge handbook of pragmatics*. Cambridge: Cambridge University Press.

Allott, Nicholas. 2010. *Key terms in pragmatics*. New York: Continuum.

Austin, John L. 1962. *How to do things with words*. Oxford: Clarendon Press.

Barron, Anne/Yueguo Gu/Gerard Steen. 2017. *The Routledge handbook of pragmatics*. New York: Routledge.

Birner, Betty. 2013. *Introduction to pragmatics*. Malden, MA: Wiley-Blackwell.

Blakemore, Diane. 1992. *Understanding utterances: An introduction to pragmatics*. Oxford: Blackwell.

Brown, Penelope/Stephen Levinson. 2002. *Politeness: Some universals of language use*. Cambridge: Cambridge University Press.

Bublitz, Wolfram. 2019³. *Englische Pragmatik: Eine Einführung*. Berlin: Schmidt.

Clark, Billy. 2013. *Relevance theory*. Cambridge: Cambridge University Press.

Clift, Rebecca. 2016. *Conversation analysis*. Cambridge: Cambridge University Press.

Cruse, Alan. 2006. *A glossary of semantics and pragmatics*. Edinburgh: Edinburgh University Press.

Cruse, Alan. 2010³. *Meaning in language: An introduction to semantics and pragmatics*. Oxford: Oxford University Press.

Cummings, Louise, ed. 2010. *The pragmatics encyclopedia*. London/New York: Routledge.

Cutting, Joan. 2015³. *Pragmatics: A resource book for students*. London: Routledge.

Green, Georgia M. 1996². *Pragmatics and natural language understanding*. Hillsdale: Erlbaum.

Grice, Paul. 1989. *Studies in the way of words*. Cambridge, Mass.: Harvard University Press.

Grundy, Peter. 2008³. *Doing pragmatics*. London/New York: Routledge.

Horn, Laurence R. 1988. "Pragmatic theory." In Frederick J. Newmeyer, ed. *Linguistics: The Cambridge survey*, vol. I. Cambridge: Cambridge University Press. 113–145.

Horn, Laurence R./Gregory Ward, eds. 2004. *The handbook of pragmatics*. Malden, MA: Blackwell.

Huang, Yan. 2010. "Neo-Gricean pragmatic theory of conversational implicature." In Bernd Heine/Heiko Narrog, eds. *The Oxford handbook of linguistic analysis*. Oxford: Oxford University Press. 607–631.

Huang, Yan, ed. 2017. *The Oxford handbook of pragmatics*. Oxford: Oxford University Press.

Jaszczolt, Katarzyna M. 2002. *Semantics and pragmatics: Meaning in language and discourse*. London/Munich: Longman.

Leech, Geoffrey. 1983. *Principles of pragmatics*. London: Longman.

Leech, Geoffrey. 2014. *The pragmatics of politeness*. Oxford: Oxford University Press.

Levinson, Stephen C. 1983. *Pragmatics*. Cambridge: Cambridge University Press.

Levinson, Stephen C. 2001. *Presumptive meanings: The theory of generalized conversational implicature.* Cambridge, Mass.: MIT Press.

Mey, Jacob L. 2001[2]. *Pragmatics. An introduction.* Oxford: Blackwell.

O'Keeffe, Anne/Brian Clancy/Svenja Adolphs. 2011. *Introducing pragmatics in use.* London: Routledge.

Östman, Jan-Ola/Jef Verschueren/Jan Blommaert/Chris Bulcaen, eds. *Handbook of pragmatics online.* Amsterdam: Benjamins. https://www.benjamins.com/online/hop/ (continually expanded & revised)

Schiffrin, Deborah. 1994. *Approaches to discourse.* Oxford: Blackwell.

Searle, John R. 1969. *Speech acts. An essay in the philosophy of language.* Cambridge: Cambridge University Press.

Senft, Gunter. 2014. *Understanding pragmatics.* New York: Routledge.

Sidnell, Jack. 2010. *Conversation analysis.* Malden, MA: Wiley-Blackwell.

Sperber, Dan/Deidre Wilson. 1996[2]. *Relevance: Communication and cognition.* Oxford: Blackwell.

Verschueren, Jef. 1999. *Understanding pragmatics.* London: Arnold.

Wierzbicka, Anna. 2003[2]. *Cross-cultural pragmatics. The semantics of human interaction.* Berlin/New York: Mouton de Gruyter.

Wilson, Deirdre/Dan Sperber. 2012. *Meaning and relevance.* Cambridge: Cambridge University Press.

Yule, George. 1996. *Pragmatics.* Oxford: Oxford University Press.

8 Sociolinguistics: Regional and social varieties of English

Language as a social phenomenon: Similar to pragmatics, the field of sociolinguistics studies language use in real life. It is an illusion to think that language communities are homogeneous; instead, heterogeneity determines everyday language use. Linguistic heterogeneity has many different facets. Besides differences in linguistic competence and expressive ability among the members of any language community, each speaker uses certain linguistic features which distinguish him or her from the other members of their language community.

facets of linguistic heterogeneity

Idiolects and varieties: Each individual has his or her specific idiolect. In everyday language use, heterogeneity also means that each member of a language community chooses between different language forms, or *varieties*, depending on the communicative situation (see section 8.1). This can happen either consciously or subconsciously. Sociolinguistics studies the effects social factors have on language use and language structures. Acknowledging that human beings are "social beings", sociolinguistics is aware of the fact that language use and language structures cannot be separated from, and indeed depend upon, the speaker's social self, i. e. the diversity of (coexisting) group identities and social networks every one of us is a part of. A given female speaker, for example, can at the same time be a woman, somebody's partner, daughter, mother or friend, a student, a Catholic, a villager, a member of a political party, a member of a choir or team, and so on. The group identity of a speaker is largely formed by his or her geographic, social and/or ethnic background (see sections 8.2 to 8.4), but other factors may also play a role, such as the speaker's age, profession, level of education and gender (the latter especially brought to the fore in feminist linguistics; see section 8.5).

language and group identities

Language and identity: Language plays an important role in identity formation, although we are not aware of it most of the time. Quite often, a few utterances or words are all we need for drawing conclusions on a speaker's sociological background (origin, level of education, etc.), while the speakers themselves are not aware of the fact that the language they use serves as a window into their social reality. But speakers can also use language deliberately to signal that they (want to) belong, or not belong, to a certain group. Consciously or unconsciously they can, for example, adapt their language or language style to that of their interlocutors, thus

language = window into speakers' social reality

J.B. Metzler © Springer-Verlag GmbH Deutschland, ein Teil von Springer Nature, 2020
B. Kortmann, *English Linguistics*, https://doi.org/10.1007/978-3-476-05678-8_8

improving the social relationship with them and creating a basis for more successful communication. How "successful" this verbal interaction is primarily depends on whether the speaker accomplishes his or her communicative goals (for more details see 8.5).

a difference in perspective

Sociolinguistics vs. sociology of language: Two scientific disciplines constitute the interface between linguistics and sociology: sociolinguistics and the sociology of language.

- The focus of sociolinguistics, which only started to flourish in the political climate of the late 1960s, is on the relationship between language and society. Its aim is to study the use of different forms or varieties of language and the social factors which determine them.
- The research interest of the sociology of language is the exact opposite: its main motivation for investigating language is to increase the ability to understand social structures.

Thus the distinction between sociolinguistics and the sociology of language is mainly motivated by a difference in perspective. What is common to both disciplines is that they are strictly empirical and exhibit a high degree of methodological rigour, as known from sociology.

Three branches of sociolinguistics: When speaking of the relationship between sociolinguistics and the sociology of language, we are adopting a narrow definition of sociolinguistics, namely sociological (or: variationist) sociolinguistics. But we should not forget that there are two other, considerably older areas of research which can be subsumed under a broader concept of sociolinguistics. These are anthropological sociolinguistics, which is concerned with the relationship between language, culture and thought (just recall the Sapir-Whorf hypothesis according to which language determines thought; chapter 6.4.2) and, above all, geographical sociolinguistics, better known as *dialectology*, which was already popular in the 19th century.

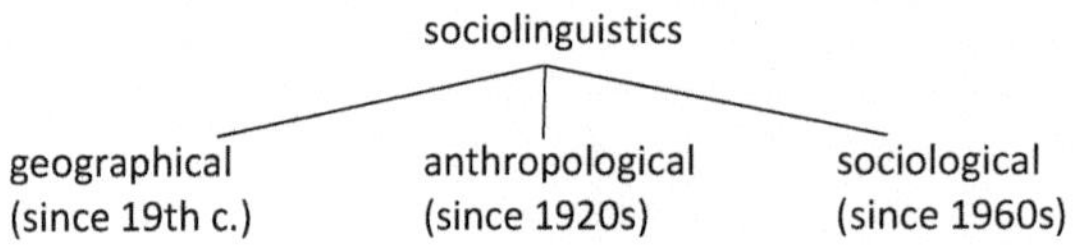

sociolinguistics

geographical
(since 19th c.)

anthropological
(since 1920s)

sociological
(since 1960s)

Figure 8.1:
Branches of
sociolinguistics

focus on British
Isles and US

Of these three branches of sociolinguistics, only geographical and sociological sociolinguistics will be addressed in this chapter. Its primary aim will be to present the basic structural properties of different regional and social (standard as well as non-standard) varieties of English used in the British Isles and the United States. But let us first have a look at the range and nature of varieties we encounter in language.

8.1 | Different types of varieties

variationist
sociolinguistics

Sociolinguistics is most easily defined as variationist linguistics, that branch of linguistics which is concerned with the different forms of a language and the factors that determine their structure and use.

Variation is possible on all structural levels. The individual varieties of a given language may differ with regard to their phonetics, phonology,

pragmatics, lexicon and – to a smaller extent
– their morphology and syntax. These differences are not necessarily reflected in the
presence or absence of certain structural
properties; they can simply manifest themselves as a preference, with a
consequent difference in frequency of use, which is one of the reasons
why variationist sociolinguistics is strongly quantitative (see section 8.4).
Three main types of varieties (or *lects*) can be distinguished, depending
on the extra-linguistic factors that motivate their use: dialects, sociolects
and registers. The most widely known of these three types are *dialects*,
which can be given a narrow and a broad definition. Traditionally in linguistics (and also in everyday language use), dialects are defined as re-
gionally restricted varieties. Under a broad conception, dialect is synonymous with the neutral hypernym *variety*, as in terms like *standard dia-
lect(s)* or *social dialects*. The latter, which are better known as *sociolects*,
are motivated by the socio-economic status, level of education, profession, age, ethnicity, sex or gender of the speaker.

Genderlect and jargon: Two examples of sociolects are genderlects and
(professional) jargons (special vocabulary of a particular profession).
Both dialects (in a narrow sense) and sociolects are intimately linked to
the speaker's sociological background.

Register and style, by contrast, refer to varieties which are primarily
determined by the relevant communicative situation. It is not easy to
distinguish between register and style. Both refer to the vocabulary and
grammatical structures chosen (and even expected) in a certain communicative situation. However, register choices are primarily determined by
the functional-communicative context, while stylistic variation is more
determined by individual choices and aesthetic preferences and thus is
less predictable. The central question informing research on registers and
styles is the following: "Under which circumstances, for which purpose,
and interacting with which person(s) does a speaker use a certain variety?" (see also 8.6 below). The choice of a certain register is strongly influenced by factors such as the discourse topic (*field of discourse*, e. g.
professional vs. private), the relationship between the speakers involved
in the conversation (*tenor of discourse*, e. g. friendship vs. authority relationship) and the medium of communication (*mode of discourse*: spoken
vs. written language).

Standard – variety – dialect: Among the most interesting issues, to linguists and non-linguists alike, concerning the terms *variety* and *dialect* is
the question how they relate to the terms *standard* and *language*. Let us
consider the former relationship first. In modern linguistics, neither the
neutral term *variety* nor the term *dialect* – which often has a negative ring
in everyday language – imply inferiority or that, where differences compared with the standard are observable, these are to be interpreted as
deficiencies. Rather the contrary is true: For example, Standard English
and Standard German are considered as the standard varieties or standard dialects of the English and German language communities, respectively. As far as their structural properties are concerned, standard varieties are of no higher value, greater inherent logic or better quality than

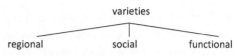

Figure 8.2:
Three broad types
of varieties

dialect – narrow
vs. broad
definition

varieties deter-
mined by commu-
nicative situation

What makes for
a standard?

other varieties. For obvious reasons, they do enjoy a higher prestige. Standard English, for example, is used

- in written language, especially in literature and print media
- in television and radio broadcasts
- as official language in politics, administration, court, etc.
- as the language of instruction in schools and higher education institutions (HEIs) of all English-speaking countries (and, at least for HEIs, increasingly also in countries where English has the status of a foreign language)
- as the teaching target of learners of English in schools and HEIs all over the world
- by the educated middle and upper classes

The common core of StE: This characterization of "the standard" is exclusively based on social and functional considerations. In German this is reflected in the fact that expressions like *Hochsprache* and *Schriftsprache* may be used as synonyms of the more neutral term *Standard(sprache)*. The standard variety represents something like the common structural core of all varieties (especially the national varieties) of a language. Accordingly, Standard English represents the common core of the different *Englishes* – the *old Englishes*, especially British and American English, as well as the so-called *New Englishes* (e.g. Australian, New Zealand, Indian, Caribbean and African English(es)). This common core is relatively homogeneous, i.e. there are relatively few differences between the national standard varieties of English, especially as far as grammar is concerned. Where there are differences in grammar, these concern for the most part different degrees of preference for individual forms and constructions, measurable in terms of high(er) or low(er) frequencies of use (see section 8.2 on British and American English).

Who speaks StE? Due to its special structural and functional status, the standard can be seen as the fourth main type of variety (see figure 8.3), although its classification as a primarily social dialect would be adequate,

Figure 8.3:
Types of varieties

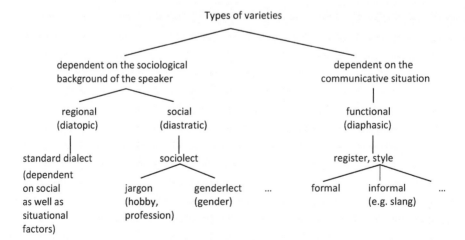

Types of varieties

too. In all language communities, the standard variety is only used by a relatively small minority of speakers (in Great Britain by an estimated 12–15 percent of the population) who, in addition, belong to the educated middle and upper classes (having enjoyed a higher education at school or college and often university). Accordingly, the standard variety is usually perceived and accepted as the prestigious linguistic norm by all members of a given language community (including non-standard speakers), especially in class-conscious societies like England.

Dialect vs. accent: In accounts of the standard variety, regional considerations typically only play a role when turning to the standard accent. Accent only refers to the pronunciation and the phonological system of a given variety, whereas dialect also includes lexical and grammatical properties of a (regional) variety. This distinction is especially important in Britain, for example, where according to some estimates only about a third of those who use Standard English have a marked Received Pronunciation (RP) accent. Standard dialect and regional accent thus do not exclude each other. However, speaking a regional or even local dialect with the standard accent is not possible.

dialect as the more inclusive concept

	standard dialect	non-standard dialect
	can be spoken with	can be spoken with
standard accent	+	–
non-standard accent	+	+

Table 8.1: Cross-tabulation of (non-)standard dialect and accent

Standard – dialect – language: All books on the grammar of a given language describe the standard dialect; it is also usually the standard dialect upon which any kind of comparative (e. g. contrastive or typological) studies are based. But one point must be stressed over and over again: Whether a certain dialect is attributed the status of the standard variety and, consequently, seen as an independent language does not depend on its inherent structural properties. No dialect is inherently superior or better suited for serving as the standard than other dialects. The development of a standard depends on a number of political, historical, social and psychological factors.

no dialect inherently better than any other

Impact of politics: Discussions on the status of a dialect as the standard variety or even as a language of its own are generally politically and emotionally charged. Linguistic identity plays a crucial part in defining the degree of independence and autonomy of a people, the self-conception and self-confidence of a nation, and this includes the acknowledgement of its dialect as a language of its own or, at least, as an independent national variety, on an equal footing with other established national standards.

The word *language* (as opposed to *dialect*) seems to have a primarily political connotation – especially when discussed by non-linguists. According to an often-quoted "definition" (by Uriel Weinreich), a language is basically no more than "a dialect with its own army and navy" (and especially with its own constitution). There are many examples: The North Germanic languages spoken on the Scandinavian mainland (Danish, Norwegian and Swedish) are structurally closely related dialects;

the arbitrary boundaries between dialect and language

Afrikaans, spoken in South Africa, was considered a Dutch dialect as late as the beginning of the 20th century; or take the changed status of Serbo-Croatian as a striking example from fairly recent history of how politically charged the status of a language can be.

Serbo-Croatian: from 1 dialect > 1 language > 4 languages

Formed on the basis of the most widespread South Slavic dialect (Shtokavian), Serbo-Croatian was the national language of former Yugoslavia (1945–1992). However, as the result of the Bosnian War (1992–1995) and the subsequent split of Yugoslavia into separate nation states, it was replaced with four national languages (Bosnian, Croatian, Montenegrin, Serbian), accompanied by attempts to artificially increase the differences between them to strengthen their status as "independent" languages, especially in the lexicon and, most visibly, in orthography (e. g. Cyrillic as the only official script in Serbia, Latin as the sole script in Croatia).

spelling reform and the birth of AmE

Orthography, more exactly *spelling reform*, also played a major role in the history of American English, where in the late 18th century Noah Webster made a number of relatively modest spelling changes to American English (see section 8.1.2 below). This was his major instrument (along with his famous dictionary) to create a national language for the new nation (*Declaration of Independence* 1776), one that was visibly different, or independent, from British English (see also Horobin 2013).

too much heterogeneity beats the linguist

Limits of linguist(ic)s: An even more fundamental point in this "language or dialect" debate is whether we can, at all, call something a language or a dialect in the first place. This is a point linguists often do not want to admit to: The reality may be that the linguistic code that members of a given speech community are using is not focused, unified, systematically and predictably structured enough to allow for a structural description by linguists as we know it from grammars of modern European languages or a wide range of varieties of English. For English, such observations have for example been made on very small varieties in Australia (Croker Island English) and the Pacific (Pitkern and Norf'k; most recently, see Mühlhäusler 2020), but there are surely more. It is not always easy, sometimes downright impossible, to turn many individual ways of speaking (i. e. idiolects) into something that can confidently be labelled a language/dialect/variety as we know them, and as they will also be described in sections 8.2 and 8.3.

towards StEs in the anglophone world

(World) Englishes: In the past and contemporary history of the United Kingdom, we also find ample evidence of the crucial political, historical and social dimensions that underlie decisions on whether a certain variety can claim the status of a language or (only) a dialect. Scots lost its status as the official national language of Scotland at the beginning of the 17th century, directly after the Scottish and English crowns were united and the royal court moved to London (1603). Just about 400 years later, approximately in the late 1980s, English varieties spoken in the former colonies of the British Empire started experiencing a very different, positive change. In these parts of the world, the sense of national identity has started to grow, and their political, economic and cultural independence is bringing with it linguistic sovereignty, i. e. acknowledgment of the respective English varieties as independent standards, comparable to Standard British and American English.

In most countries these varieties exist alongside local languages or contact varieties (i. e. pidgins and creoles). Claims for linguistic sovereignty are increasingly respected and accepted (at least in present-day English language and literature studies) and have become manifest in new terms and scholarly fields of studies like (*New*) *Englishes/World Englishes* and *Standard Englishes*. Besides the traditional countries of the Anglophone world (including Australia, New Zealand and South Africa) where English is a native language, there are about sixty countries where English is either the only official language (e. g. in Ghana, Nigeria, Zimbabwe and Jamaica) or at least one of two official languages (e. g. in India, Singapore, the Philippines and Cameroon). *Official* means that it is the language used by the authorities, in education and the media (more on World Englishes in chapter 9.3).

Pluricentricity: English is therefore clearly a pluricentric language. Its different centres have started, and will certainly continue, to develop new linguistic norms independent of one another and, what is more, independent of the British and American models. Nevertheless, there is no doubt that, among the different standard varieties of English, British and American English are still used as the two major target models for teaching English to foreign-language learners. *(independent norm development)*

8.2 | British and American English: A comparison

Two countries separated by a common language: The Irish playwright George Bernard Shaw (1856–1950) famously observed, on different occasions and in different versions, that "England and America are two countries separated by a common language". A close comparative look at the linguistic facts reveals, however, that this separation is not as dramatic as Shaw's humorous remark suggests. The standard varieties of British and American English differ primarily, also most perceptibly, with regard to their accents, i. e. Received Pronunciation (RP) as opposed to General American (GA), followed by differences in their vocabularies. There are considerably fewer differences in orthography and, at least for non-linguists, in grammar. Before moving on to a survey of the major generalizations concerning structural differences between British and American English, three points are worth noting:

- It is surprising how little these two standard varieties differ from each other. *(moderate differences overall)*
- Most of these differences, especially those in the domain of grammar, are relatively minor and certainly not categorical, but rather tendencies concerning the (dis)preference and frequency of use of certain constructions.
- Several of the differences which can currently be observed may well disappear during the next few decades and new (again, hardly more than moderate) ones may arise due to independent variety-internal innovations. Ultimately, the two varieties seem to converge, especially in the lexicon but also with regard to some grammatical differences. In

most cases, the direction of this convergence is towards the American norm (but see the necessary qualifying remarks in the paragraphs on grammar below). Already a number of relevant differences are no longer observable for today's younger speakers, one main reason being the overwhelming media presence of American English.

contrasting the
standard accents

Phonology: RP vs. GA: Concerning their status, note that both standard accents, RP and GA, are somewhat idealized – each in its own way.

RP is a social, supra-national prestige accent. Despite the fact that it is known to the whole world as the British (or more precisely English) English standard accent and used as a reference accent in school and university education, at least the more traditional version of RP is spoken by a small and continuously shrinking minority of standard speakers of the upper and upper middle classes. The term *Received Pronunciation* itself reflects the importance of social norms: In Victorian times, *received* meant 'generally accepted in polite society'. If we compare the number of people actually using the two standards, GA can be said to be much more "anchored in the real world" than RP, even more than the unmarked or mainstream RP version spoken by the majority of younger native speakers of Standard British English (also labelled *Broadcast RP*).

In the US, an estimated two thirds of the population speak GA. It should be noted, though, that it is not a single homogeneous accent. Primarily, GA is defined negatively: It stands for a number of very similar accents which all have the property of sharing neither the characteristics of the accents of the southern US (*Southern*) nor of New England (*Eastern*). According to another negative definition, the standard accent of American English is the result of what remains if its speakers (typically well-educated speakers in formal settings) suppress all salient and notoriously regional and social features. Due to its extensive use, especially by the large American TV and radio stations, it is also called *Network* or *Broadcast English*.

If we compare prototypical British English speakers with prototypical American speakers, the most prominent and (even among non-linguists) most notorious difference is a phonotactic one.

/r/ only before
vowels or in all
positions?

Rhoticity: There are many cases in which American speakers pronounce /r/ (i. e. realize an orthographic < r > phonetically) but British English speakers do not. What is at issue here is called *rhoticity*. Like the majority of regional English accents and all national standard varieties which follow the British English model, RP phonetically realizes /r/ only before vowels; there is neither an /r/ at the end of words (*car* [kɑː], *her* [hɜː]), nor between vowels and consonants (*card* [kɑːd], *herd* [hɜːd]). Therefore, RP qualifies as a non-rhotic accent. It has pre-vocalic /r/, but no pre-consonantal /r/ (which can alternatively be described as post-vocalic or coda /r/ because the unpronounced /r/ belongs to the same syllable as the preceding vowel; compare *hair* [heə] and *hairy* ['heəri]). By contrast, GA is a rhotic accent, so /r/ is pronounced in all positions. This feature sets it apart from RP (and also the Eastern and Southern US accents, although increasingly less so), but is a shared commonality with other standard accents such as Canadian, Irish and Scottish English.

Other striking differences between GA and RP are the following:
- different phonetic realizations of certain phonemes (partly only in certain positions): consonantal contrasts
  - /r/ post-alveolar in RP [ɹ], retroflex in GA [ɻ]
  - /l/ more velar in GA [ɫ], especially between vowels (e. g. *jelly*)
  - /t, d/ in GA the opposition between this pair of phonemes is neutralized between vowels, resulting in the tap sound [ɾ]: *latter* and *ladder* are both pronounced ['læɾər]
- different phonotactic preferences:
  - in GA there is no realization of /t, d/ between /n/ and a vowel if the main stress is on the next but one syllable: *international* [ɪnər'næʃənəl], *understand* [ʌnər'stænd];
  - in GA there is no /j/ following /d, t, n, θ, z, s/ in the same syllable: *due* [duː], *tune* [tuːn], *new* [nuː], *enthusiasm* [ɪn'θuːzɪæzəm], *presume* [prɪ'zuːm], suit [suːt]
- in GA [æ] is used before voiceless fricatives /s, f, θ/ or nasals /n, m/ vowel contrasts followed by a voiceless consonant, instead of southern-British RP [ɑː] or northern-British RP [a]; this affects about 150 words, e. g. *fast, after, path, dance, sample*;
- neutralization of phonemic oppositions:
  - in GA, neutralization of the opposition /ɑː/ – /ɒ/ in /ɑ/, thus *father* and *cot* are pronounced /faðər/ and /kɑt/ respectively;
  - in some GA varieties, neutralization of the opposition /ɒ/ – /ɔː/ *cot – caught* in /ɑ/: /kɑt/ (sometimes in addition to the neutralization of /ɑː/ – /ɒ/ in /ɑ/, e. g. in California). This neutralization is characteristic of the Northern accents and Canadian English.
- in GA, rhoticity results in:
  - an r-coloured central vowel [ɝ] (e. g. in *bird, word, hurt*);
  - the absence of centring diphthongs: [ɪr, er, ʊr] instead of RP [ɪə, eə, ʊə]

	sample	psalm	cot	caught	bird	go	beer	bare	poor
RP	ɑː	ɑː	ɒ	ɔː	ɜː	əʊ	ɪə	eə	ʊə
GA	æ	ɑ	ɑ	ɔː/ɑ	ɝ	oʊ	ɪr	er	ʊr

Table 8.2:
Vowel differences
between RP
and GA

Word stress: Of course, there are many other, less systematic pronunciation differences affecting individual words. Some of the best-known examples are shown in (1) and (2), the latter of which result from differences in word stress:

(1)　　　　tomato　　　clerk　　(n)either　　vase　　anti-　　< z >
　　RP　/tə'mɑːtəʊ/　/klɑːk/　/(n)aɪðə/　/vɑːz/　/ænti/　[zed]
　　GA　/tə'meɪroʊ/　/klɝːk/　/(n)iːðər/　/veɪz/　/æntaɪ/　[ziː]
(2)　RP 'ballet – GA ba'llet, RP ciga'rette – GA 'cigarette, RP con'troversy – GA 'controversy,
　　RP a'ddress – GA 'address, RP maga'zine – GA 'magazine,
　　RP in'quiry /ɪn'kwaɪəri/ - GA 'inquiry /ɪŋkwəri/, RP trans'late – GA 'translate

Word stress differences, however, appear to diminish as American accent patterns are spreading among British speakers, especially among the younger generation. This is a domain where the influence of American English on British English is particularly noticeable.

high rise terminal   Intonation: The probably most salient intonation difference between British and American English concerns yes/no questions, which are usually *high rise* in American English (*are you going a'ʷᵃʸ?*) and *low rise* (less often *low fall* or *high fall*) in British English. In informal American English, and especially among younger speakers, one can often hear a rising intonation curve at the end of declarative sentences, especially when speaking in an emotional way. This phenomenon, known as *high rise terminal* (compare chapter 2), is also increasingly frequent in the Southeast of England (and in many other regional and national varieties of English), once again predominantly among the younger generation. Thus, this intonation difference might soon cease to be perceived as such.

   Orthography: The most important orthographic differences are shown in (3). In general, American English orthography tends to be shorter.

(3)		BrE	AmE	
	colour	< -our >	< -or >	color
	theatre	< -re >	< -er >	theater
	emphasise, -ize	< -ise, -ize >	< -ize >	emphasize
	analyse	< -lyse, -lyze >	< -lyze >	analyse
	amoeba	< oe >	< e, oe >	am(o)eba
	encyclopaedia	< ae >	< e, ae >	encyclopedia
	fulfil	< -l >	< -ll >	fulfill
	catalogue	< -gue >	< -g >	catalog

contrasts in the VP   Grammar: In grammar, there are surprisingly many differences between American English and British English (see the heavily corpus-based research by Tottie 2009, Rohdenburg/Schlüter 2009, Leech et al. 2009), but most of them are rather minor, non-categorical and restricted to complementation patterns of individual verbs or adjectives (an interface between lexicon and grammar known as *lexico-grammar*). Probably the most interesting of these differences can be observed in the verb phrase. Here the only difference that is truly categorical concerns the past participle of *get*, for which American English has two forms: *got* and *gotten*. This difference in form reflects a semantic distinction: While *gotten* is used for situations that are dynamic or in progress (4), *got* is rather used to describe static situations and resultative states (5):

(4)   a.   They've gotten a new car. ('have received')
      b.   They've gotten interested. ('have developed interest in ...')
      c.   I've gotten to know a lot of songs from jazz records. ('that's how I learnt about them')
(5)   a.   They've got a new car. ('possess')
      b.   They've got interested. ('are interested')
      c.   I've got to know a lot of songs from jazz records. ('that's how I have to learn them')

Unlike in British English, *have got* in American English is rather rare in sentences like (5a), where *have* is clearly preferred (*They have a new car*).

Different usage patterns, no categorical differences: Further characteristic differences in the grammar of the verb phrase will be outlined and illustrated below. Again, it should be kept in mind that these represent only differences in preference, not categorical differences.

- **irregular verb forms:** AmE tends to regularize verb forms (e. g. *burned, dreamed, learned*)
- **perfect:**
  a) BrE uses the so-called *experiential perfect* (or: *indefinite past*) whereas AmE prefers the Simple Past: *Have you ever been to Rome?* vs. *Did you ever go to Rome?*, *Have you eaten yet?* vs. *Did you eat (yet)?*;

  Present Perfect vs. Simple Past

  b) AmE allows the Simple Past with adverbs like *just, recently, already*: *She just finished her essay* vs. *She has just finished her essay*, *They left already* vs. *They have left already*.
- **mood:** Of the three alternative constructions which can be used to express the so-called *mandative subjunctive*, AmE clearly prefers (6a) over the constructions in (6b) and especially in (6c), which are both characteristic of BrE:

  mandative subjunctive

(6) a. We demanded that the manager resign.
     b. We demanded that the manager should resign.
     c. We demanded that the manager resigns.

- **auxiliary verbs:** (a) BrE tends to use modal verbs more frequently; (b) *shall/should/ought to* are even less frequent in AmE than in BrE; (c) AmE increasingly allows *must not* as negation of epistemic ('concluding') *must* in contexts where BrE uses *cannot* or *can't* (AmE *My mistake must not have been noticed*); (d) BrE also allows *usen't to* for *used not to*.

  modal verbs

- **complementation patterns of individual verbs (lexico-grammar):** This is one of the richest areas of often highly local contrasts between AmE and BrE, i. e. contrasts restricted to individual or small groups of verbs (also adjectives). For example, AmE dispenses increasingly with the use of the reflexive pronoun for verbs for which it used to be obligatory or at least preferred (see Rohdenburg 2010). Take the verbs *commit*, as in *The United States cannot commit to lift sanctions* (instead of: *commit themselves to ...*), or *brace*, as in *The driver braced for impact* (instead of: *braced himself for ...*). Another example of such a highly local contrast is the alternation between *try and* and *try to* before a following infinitive, as in *Let's try and have a discussion* vs. *Let's try to have a discussion*: *try and* is vastly preferred in spoken BrE vis-à-vis spoken AmE, while *try to* is the much preferred option in writing, both in BrE and even more so in AmE (see Tottie 2009).

  verb complementation

More contrasts in grammar: Outside of the verb phrase, only a selection of grammatical differences will be given below. For example, there exist (hardly systematisable) differences concerning the use of prepositions complementing adjectives (e. g. BrE *different from/to* vs. AmE *different than*). Furthermore, AmE and BrE differ in the domain of subject-verb agreement with collective nouns (i. e. nouns like *family, orchestra, government*). In AmE, the verb is generally singular while in BrE the verb can be either singular or plural (*The government is/are divided about this question*), depending on whether the homogeneity or the heterogeneity of the group is to be emphasized. Another noteworthy difference, humourously labelled 'the American *which*-hunt', is the result of many decades of prescriptive influence of much-used style guides, usage handbooks and editorial policies in the United States. In US English we witness the almost complete avoidance of the relative pronoun *which* in restrictive relative clauses and its replacement with relative *that*, as in *Term papers that* (not: *which*) *are handed in late will not be graded*. British English is still free to alternate between these two options.

Major generalizations: Some major tendencies underlying these usage differences between the grammars of (written) American and British English are the following (see especially Rohdenburg/Schlüter 2009, Leech et al. 2009, Mair 2006):

the big picture

- The trend of using more structures characteristic of colloquial spoken usage in (formal) writing (a tendency known as *colloquialization*; see also chapter 9.4) is more pronounced in American English than in British English.
- American English exhibits a stronger tendency towards the regularization of morphological and syntactic patterns.
- American English shows a more pronounced tendency to omit function words which are grammatically optional and semantically redundant.
- The study of a wide range of changes which the grammars of (predominantly written) American English and British English have undergone since the 1960s shows that American English appears to have undergone more changes and, for changes also attested in British English, to have taken "the lead" in the majority of cases. This should not, however, be interpreted as the result of direct influence of American English on British English. Many relevant changes in the two varieties happened independently of each other, started in parallel or at different points in time (AmE typically earlier), spread at different speeds (AmE typically faster), and affected more or fewer words or structures (AmE typically more). But in the majority of cases, these changes went in the same direction, and this was the direction characteristic of American English, thus the often-used shorthand label *Americanization*.
- Overall, the grammar of (written) American English can be characterized as more innovative, while the grammar of (written) British English is more conservative.

8.3 | Regional varieties

8.3.1 | Traditional and modern dialectology

informants:
NORMS

Traditional dialectology: Traditional dialectology (or dialect geography), as practiced since the middle of the 19th century, focusses on regional varieties, more precisely on the observable variation in the phonological systems (hence, in the regional accents) and in the lexicon of predominantly elderly male speakers in rural areas, known as NORMS (non-mobile old rural male speakers) in British dialectology.

methods:
questionnaires
and interviews

The traditional dialectological method has been, and still is, the use of questionnaires, although tape-recorded interviews obviously constitute a further invaluable data source and have been in use for several decades. Originally, informants had to pronounce single words so that phonological variation could be detected. To determine lexical variation, informants had to name the expressions they used in their respective dialect for certain objects, actions and properties, mostly taken from everyday rural life. This method yields the geographical area where a certain expression is used to denote a certain concept, and where it gives way to a different expression.

visualization in
dialect atlases

Isoglosses: The aim of such investigations is to draw boundaries, so-called *isoglosses*, which indicate the geographical spread of a certain expression on a language map. A language map of England and Scotland would, for example, reveal the isoglosses for the different expressions used to denote 'autumn' (*autumn, fall, backend*) or 'female cat' (*betty cat, ewe (cat), queen (cat), tib (cat), she, she cat, sheeder (cat)*).

The two phonological isoglosses that are probably best-known among the population in England largely run along the same route. They define a dividing line between the North and the South (see figure 8.4): (a) *pub* is pronounced /pʌb/ in the South and /pʊb/ in the North (analogous to other words such as *cut, love, some* or *fun*); (b) *path* is pronounced /pɑːθ/ in the South and /paθ/ in the North (analogous to words like *pass, past, laugh, daft, dance* or *sample*). In other words, the accents of the Midlands and the North use /ʊ/ where RP uses /ʌ/, and, in front of voiceless fricatives as well as before a nasal /n/ or /m/ followed by a consonant, a short, 'flat' /a/ where (southern) RP uses /ɑː/.

A third well-known isogloss in England separates rhotic from non-rhotic accents. Rhotic accents are characteristic of the Southwest of England, although they are rapidly receding (see figure 8.4; in the British Isles, they are of course also characteristic of Irish English and Scottish English). Wherever several such (phonological and lexical) isoglosses coincide, we can postulate a dialect boundary. Collections of linguistic maps from different geographical areas are called *linguistic atlases* or *dialect atlases*.

Dialect continua in Europe: We should keep in mind, though, that dialect boundaries can never be more than rough approximations. The transition between different dialect areas is fluid, which is why we also speak of dialect continua. These continua do not follow political borders or politically motivated language borders (as shown above). Usually, speak-

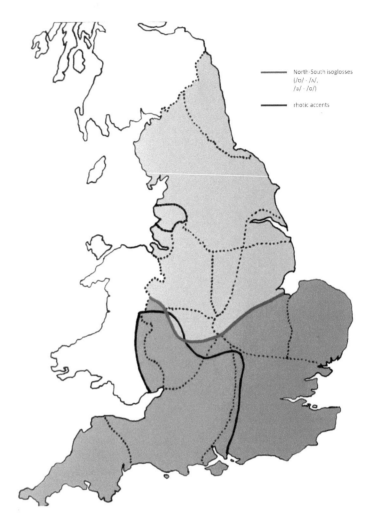

North-South isoglosses
(/ʊ/ - /ʌ/,
/a/ - /ɑ/)

rhotic accents

Figure 8.4:
Phonological
isoglosses in
England (adapted
from Trudgill
1999: 52–69)

ers from neighbouring dialect areas have little problems understanding each other, but the larger the distance between two dialect areas is, the greater these problems become. In extreme cases, complete mutual incomprehensibility is possible. Still, we cannot conclude that dialects which are mutually incomprehensible automatically belong to different languages. The best-known dialect continua in Northern and Western Europe are the Scandinavian dialect continuum (Danish, Swedish, Norwegian), the West Germanic dialect continuum (running from Flanders and the Netherlands in the West to Austria in the East, via Germany and Switzerland) and the West Romance dialect continuum (reaching from Wallonia in Northern France to the Iberian Peninsula in the Southwest and Italy and Sicily in the Southeast).

Dialect-rich British Isles: But let us return to the situation in Great Britain and Ireland. It is in these countries where we find by far the greatest dialect diversity in the English-speaking world (compare section 8.3.2).

This holds true although these differences, similar to differences in other countries, are gradually disappearing due to increasing mobility, increasing urbanization and the overwhelming influence of the media and educational institutions.

Dialect levelling: Especially in big conurbations such as London, Birmingham or Manchester, we can observe the assimilation of dialects, a process known as dialect levelling. Moreover, it is interesting to note that there are numerous dialect features in the British Isles which are so commonly found that it is hard, if not impossible, to identify any regional restrictions. With regard to these features, which do not only occur in individual (regional or urban) dialects, Standard English, especially Standard BrE, almost appears to be the odd one out among the English dialects. Some grammatical phenomena with a fairly wide geographical reach in Britain are listed below. Those which are most widely attested are called *areoversals* of Britain and indicated by a superscript exclamation mark[!]. Others can even claim a "near-universal" status in the anglophone world, thus qualifying as so-called *angloversals* (indicated below by triple superscript exclamation marks[!!!]; more on the distribution of features of non-standard grammar across the anglophone world in chapter 9.3).

widespread grammar features in Britain and Ireland

- **pronouns**

us instead of *me*	*Give us a kiss*
me instead of *my*	*she knew me name; where me sister live*
all reflexive pronouns formed by using possessive pronouns	*he saved hisself with this; they just work the farm theirselves*
them instead of *those*	*if you had them sixty pound*
[!]either order of pronominal objects in double-object constructions	*Give me it / Give it me*

- **verb paradigms**
  leading to the regularization of irregular verb paradigms:
  - reduced to 2 forms (instead of 3) (*past vs. non-past*) *They (have) done a lot of damage. I (have) seen one the other day. I gived eighty pound for the two. I catched her enough for the three garments.*
  - [!]*was/were* without singular-plural distinction, not even in *there*-sentences *he were nineteen then; she were laughing There was two houses here. There was three days in the week that …*
  - [!]*was/weren't* split (*I/you/he, she, it/we/you/they* <u>was</u>, but *I/you/ he, she, it/we/you/they* <u>weren't</u>) *They wus interested, but I weren't.*

  general reduction of modal verb paradigms (e. g. *ought to* and *shall* are practically non-existent in many dialects)

- **tense & aspect**

the progressive form is used more frequently and in more contexts (e. g. verbs describing states)	*I'm liking this. So what are you wanting from me?*
[1]*be sat/be stood* with progressive meaning	*I was sat at the bus stop for ages.* ('was sitting') *He was stood on the corner.* ('was standing')
less strict in several respects:	
– *would* in subjunctive clauses	*If they wouldn't have made a scrap of slate*
– sequence of tenses less fixed	*I noticed the van I came in* (instead of *had come in*) *was not really a painter's van.*

- **negation**

!!!double or multiple negation	*I ain't never seen it. I couldn't say nothing about them.*
ain't as universal negation of *be* and *have* forms (*amn't, aren't, isn't, wasn't, weren't, hasn't, haven't*)	*He's so cuddly, ain't he? You ain't got no alibi. I was so busy, ain't I?*
don't as negation for all persons	*He don't eat. Well she don't own him.*
innit as universal tag	*But they make dustbins big enough now, in't it? Doesn't he look funny with that pencil behind his ear. Innit?*
!!!*never* (= StE *didn't*) as negation in past-tense contexts (including one-time events)	*But this fellow never stopped until he got me. A: Did you do that? B: No, I never.*

- **subordination**

different inventory of relative pronouns	*as; what; which* + ANIMATE (*The girl as/what/which ...*)
more constructions possible (e. g. zero relative clauses (*gapping*) also used for subject relative pronouns)	*But there was no more Ø went till the States. There's a lot more children Ø go these days.*

- **other**

no marking of plural subjects, especially after numerals	*two mile_; thirteen year_*
!!!no *-ly* used to mark adverbs derived from adjectives	*hope we get it organized as quick_ as we can*

studying rural and urban dialects, regional and social variation

Modern dialectology: The rural dialects, as recorded in the *Survey of English Dialects* (SED, 1946–1961), form the basis for all dialect atlases and dialect dictionaries, and for most studies on the dialects of English conducted over the past few decades. But some of these rural dialects have died out and others have been subject to levelling, while at the same time the varieties spoken in larger cities are becoming more and more important. As a result, modern dialectology is increasingly occupied with studying urban dialects, in close connection with social variation. An early finding of such studies was the correlation of regional and social variation: the lower the socio-economic status of a speaker, the higher the probability that he or she speaks a regional dialect. In the 1970s, dialectology cross-fertilized with the burgeoning field of sociolinguistics, and thus modern dialectology as a whole is more in touch with, and has indeed contributed to, current linguistic theorizing.

Innovations – dialect grammar, analyses of corpora: There are two further important innovations in modern dialectology, which are closely related: the systematic investigation of regional variation in grammar (see section 8.3.2), and the use of corpus-linguistic methods for the compilation, investigation and statistical analysis of large corpora, which have become an essential tool of mainstream English linguistics since the 1990s. Analyses of syntactic phenomena require large quantities of data. In modern dialectological studies, especially those including syntax, it has become more and more important to base linguistic analyses on databases that are as large as possible and adequately represent different dialect regions (e. g. *FRED*, the Freiburg English Dialect corpus, and its offspring *FREDDIE*, the Freiburg English Dialect Database for Instruction and E-learning; see the website accompanying this book). In addition, the questionnaire method is now also used to investigate grammatical phenomena. See, for example, the *Survey of British Dialect Grammar* (1986–1989), the *Survey of Regional English (SuRE)* at the Universities of Leeds and Sheffield or, most recently, the *electronic World Atlas of Variation in English (eWAVE*; latest version 3.0, see Kortmann/Lunkenheimer/Ehret 2020; print version Kortmann/Lunkenheimer 2012).

traditional dialectology	modern dialectology
rural areas	urban areas
regional variation	social variation
accent and lexicon	also grammar
questionnaires, interviews	also corpora, electronic databases, modern statistical methods

Table 8.3:
Traditional dialectology vs. modern dialectology

Traditional vs. modern dialects: The distinction between traditional and modern dialects – which is not clear-cut anyway – is not crucial for the distinction between traditional and modern dialectology. The *Survey of English Dialects*, based on language material by informants born in the late 19th century, is considered clearly traditional, whereas dialect speakers born after World War I usually represent a transitional stage between traditional and modern (non-standard) dialects (except perhaps in some remote rural areas). In any case, it is important to note that modern dialectology does not exclusively deal with modern dialects, but also studies traditional dialect material.

wide scope of modern dialectology

8.3.2 | Syntactic variation in the British Isles

grammatical varia-
tion from a typo-
logical perspective

Morphological and syntactic variation is less salient and more difficult to detect (and to elicit) than lexical and especially phonological variation. This is probably the reason why this domain has been rather neglected in traditional dialectology. This section is therefore meant to serve as an appetizer, showing how many fascinating grammatical phenomena can be observed in regional varieties (beyond those mentioned earlier), and why these are interesting from a typological perspective (see also chapter 9.3 on North-South contrasts). Those who are interested in varieties of English outside the British Isles will, by the way, notice that a large number of structures observed in the *New Englishes* spoken in former British colonies were "imported" or transplanted from England, Scotland or Ireland. These features were shipped over to the new homeland together with numerous immigrants from these countries and developed a life of their own in the new environment. A look at American English may suffice to get an impression of some such phenomena.

Southwest
England

Pronoun exchange: Most of the examples described below are self-explanatory. Only two of them require a short explanation: *pronoun exchange* and *gender diffusion*, two phenomena characteristic of the Southwest of England. The term *pronoun exchange* refers to subject forms being used in object position (*Don't talk to she about grub*; *You did get he out of bed in middle of the night*; *Never mind about I*) and, vice versa, object forms being used in subject position, as in *Her don't like it*, especially when the relevant forms are heavily stressed (*That was through THEY not ME*). At least in the first person singular and plural, object forms in subject position are also known from other non-standard varieties (*Us women are not to blame for this AIDS*, *So us haven't managed to get a drink*).

Gender diffusion: Gender diffusion is an unusual semantic principle of gender assignment whereby the choice of a personal pronoun (*he, she* or *it*) or possessive pronoun (*his, her* or *its*) for anaphoric reference, i. e. for referring back, to a certain noun depends on whether it is a count or a mass noun. *It* and *its* are used for mass (or non-count) nouns (e. g. *bread, water, sand*), *he* and *his* as well as *she* and *her* are used to refer to count nouns – *she/her* only referring to female referents, *he/his* to male referents and inanimate objects (e. g. *When the pond was empty you wait for him to fill up again*). Thus there are contrasting pairs like the one in (7):

(7) a. Pass the bread – it's over there.
     b. Pass the loaf – he's over there.

	he/his	she/her	it/its
count noun	+	+	–
animate	+	+	–
male	+	–	–
female	–	+	–
inanimate	+	–	–
mass noun	–	–	+

Table 8.4:
Gender diffusion
in the Southwest
of England

This gender assignment principle, exceptional also among non-European languages, was exported from Southwestern England and introduced into Newfoundland (Canada), where today the choice between *he/his* and *she/her* seems to follow even more complex rules.

Here are **some more examples of morphological and syntactic variation** in Great Britain and Ireland, together with the region(s) in which they characteristically occur:

GB and Ireland

- **pronouns**

Southeast	3rd person singular *that* instead of *it*	*That's raining!*
Ireland/ Scotland	distinction 2nd person singular and plural	*you had a good week's pay bemong the both of youse*
North	*us* instead of *our*	*We like us town.*
Midlands	possessive pronouns ending in *-n*	*mine/yourn/hisn/hern/theirn ...*
	reflexive pronouns ending in *-sen(s)*	*mysen/yoursen/hissen/hersen*
Scotland/ Ireland	*myself* instead of *me/I*	*This is myself with a cow.*

- **tense & aspect**

Ireland	different uses of the perfect	*I know her all my life; he hasn't a penny invested; you were only after going over*
	grammaticalization of habitual *be* and *do*	*he be's at home; I never be in the pub; They do come home at night ... when we do feed them.*
Southwest	grammaticalization of habitual *do*	*I tell you about what else we did do; in fall when the nuts do fall*

- **modal verbs**

Scotland/ Northeast	double/multiple modals	*and you might could try a thousand; I might could have done that.*
	epistemic *mustn't* (meaning *can't*)	*This mustn't be the place; The lift mustn't be working.*

- **negation**

Scotland/ Ireland	negation particle *-nae*	*They cannae sell it now. It hadnae been for that. That wasnae bad.*
	non-clitic *no*	*She's no leaving. This'll no do.*
Midlands	negation particle *-na*	*I shouldna like to be up there. I donna suppose it matters.*

- **subordination**

Ireland/ Scotland/ Wales	complementation with 'unsplit' *for to*	*Just for to get over this drought we did mix it up. For to get a temperature of about 60 degrees ...*
Ireland	subordinating *and*	*He seen a boat passin' along and him cuttin' oats.*
	verb + infinitive without *to*	*She allowed him stay out late.*

8.4 | Social varieties

sociolinguistics – definition

Social differentiation of language: While geographical sociolinguistics is concerned with the regional, i. e. horizontal, differentiation of language, sociological sociolinguistics (for many people identical to sociolinguistics in general) focusses on the social differentiation of language. It studies the effects that the (actual or envisaged) group identity of a speaker has on variation in language use, be it language use among the members of a group or the situation-specific language use of individuals.

Orderly heterogeneity: The central assumption of sociological sociolinguistics is that variation in language communities or for individual speakers in the choice between structural alternatives is not random but correlates with the social (would-be) group membership of the speaker(s). This has also been called "orderly heterogeneity". Relevant instances of variation in this context are, for example, rhoticity in some words like *car, farm, beer,* but not in other words (New York); or the realization of the suffix in *singing* or *walking* as /ɪŋ/ in some cases, but as /ən/ or /ɪn/ in others (e. g. in Norwich and Sydney respectively). The most important factors for the classification of social groups are social class (more precisely socio-economic status), ethnicity, sex and age; of these factors, studies on the correlation between language use and social group identity still consider social class to be the one which is by far the most relevant. Therefore, the social differentiation of a language is often equated with its vertical differentiation or social stratification.

Social and regional variation correlate: Of course, the horizontal and vertical differentiation of language, i. e. regional and social variation, often correlate. The older a speaker and the lower his or her social class, the more likely he or she will be to use a regional dialect and the stronger his or her regional dialect will be. Besides, the use (and most interestingly the deliberate use) of regional dialects and accents is closely linked to informal spoken language. The characterization of the standard variety (section 8.1; middle and upper class, written language, formal style) is determined by both social and functional aspects, and the same holds true for non-standard varieties (lower social class, spoken language, informal style).

Labovian = quantitative sociolinguistics

William Labov, the pioneer of sociological (more exactly: variationist) sociolinguistics whose work and ideas are still leading the way today, is the founder of what is sometimes known as Labovian Sociolinguistics or the Labovian Paradigm (as opposed to the Chomskyan Paradigm). Labov's early work of the 1960s features the whole range of different topics, theories, methods and explanations of (sociological) sociolinguistics.

Linguistic variable and linguistic variant: Labov coined two key concepts (among others): the linguistic variable and the linguistic variant. The former refers to variation phenomena (e. g. rhoticity, {-ing}), the latter to possible realizations of such phenomena (e. g. /ɪŋ/ or /ɪn/ for {-ing}). Needless to say, linguistic variables may also be morphological, syntactic, or lexical in nature (e. g. whether multiple negation is used or not). Investigations of linguistic variables aim at determining how often, by whom and in which social (but also regional) context or contexts each variant is used. To determine the frequency of different linguistic variants and their significance, sophisticated quantitative methods are employed, which is why the Labovian approach is also often referred to as *quantitative sociolinguistics*.

Thematic and methodological innovations: Other basic ingredients of this approach are the development of new methods for selecting informants and for compiling corpora, the investigation of dialects – especially urban dialects – on a micro- and macro-sociological level (e. g. language use correlating with social status or ethnicity, but also language use in youth gangs) and Labov's primary interest in language change: its documentation and the elucidation of the social conditions under which it takes place (for more details see section 8.6).

Pioneering studies: Two of Labov's best-known studies, both conducted in the 1960s, are still exemplary of sociological sociolinguistics today. They investigate the correlation between language or language use and (a) ethnicity (African-American English) and (b) socio-economic status (rhoticity in New York).

African-American Vernacular English (AAVE) is not a completely homogeneous sociolect but a cover term for a group of closely related sociolects spoken by the vast majority of African Americans, especially among the working class and those with a relatively low level of education. Most of the relevant linguistic studies are based on AAVE spoken in the urban "ghettos" of the Northern US, but in informal settings AAVE is also used by African Americans with a higher socio-economic status and higher educational level. Outdated names for this group of dialects include *Negro English*, or in linguistics *Black English* (*Vernacular*). A more recent and publicly very effective alternative term emerging from the reawakened positive identification of the African-American population with its own language is *Ebonics* (a blend of *ebony* and *phonics*). Labov demonstrated that AAVE is a complex and rule-governed variety and thus invalidated the deficit hypothesis postulated by the British linguist Bernstein.

AAVE: a rule-governed variety

Deficit vs. difference hypothesis: The deficit hypothesis, which was rather popular during the 1960s, said that, compared to middle and upper-class children, working-class children had linguistic deficiencies: a smaller and less differentiated lexicon, lack of explicitness, grammatical deficits (e. g. in complex sentences), and deficits in their logical and argumentative structures. Consequently, working-class children were alleged to also have cognitive deficiencies – an inference which dovetailed with

AAVE: different, not deficient

the fact that their scholarly achievements did not match those of middle-class children. In 1960s America, the deficit hypothesis was applied to AAVE, in particular. Outcomes of this attitude included different "special-needs" programmes designed to boost linguistic proficiency and bring African American pupils closer to the "elaborate" linguistic code normally used by the middle classes. None of these programmes were particularly successful. Labov propagated a different view, the so-called difference hypothesis, arguing that AAVE was structurally different from middle class English but no less well-structured and well-suited for all communicative purposes (and sometimes even more differentiated). Labov's findings and arguments are still valid and part of public debate. In 1996, for example, a decision by the Oakland (California) school board to admit Ebonics (i. e. AAVE) as a tool of instruction (co-equal with Standard English) provoked a public outcry. Due to massive public pressure, this resolution which was motivated by poorer academic outcomes for African American children (constituting almost half of the pupils in Oakland), was repealed shortly after being enacted.

AAVE phonology & grammar

Structural characteristics of AAVE: In the following section, some of the most important phonological and grammatical properties of AAVE will be listed. These properties will not be commented on in detail, but it is important to note that AAVE shares a number of properties with other American (and British) dialects, even with the informal spoken US standard. We will also refrain from a detailed account of the central debate surrounding the genesis of AAVE in the 17th and 18th century. Suffice it to mention that monocausal theories are insufficient since a number of factors contributed to the emergence of AAVE (primarily an African substrate, English dialects, and deficient acquisition of the respective Southern dialects).

- **Phonological properties:**
  - non-rhotic accent
  - often no /l/ at the end of words or before consonants at the end of words (*fool* /fuː/, *help* /hep/), especially after back vowels
  - consonant cluster reduction by dropping the last consonant at the end of words (e. g. /ks/ > /k/: *six* /sɪk/), especially in consonant combinations like /-st, -ft, -nt, -nd, -ld, -zd, -md/: *past* /pæs/, *rift* /rɪf/
  - weakening (i. e. loss of voicing or glottal stop) or dropping of /t, d/, less often of /k, g/, at the end of words, e. g. *boot* /buː/, *seat* = *seed* = *see* /siː/
  - use of /t, d/ instead of /θ, ð/ (so-called *TH-stopping*), especially word-initially, but frequently also word-finally: *thin* /tɪn/, *this* /dɪs/, *with* /wɪt/, *tenth* /tent/
  - use of /f, v/ instead of /θ, ð/ (similar to Cockney): *Ruth* /ruːf/, *brother* /brʌvə/
  - monophthongization of diphthongs: /aɪ/ and /aʊ/ > /ɑː/, e. g. *find* = *found* = *fond* /fɑːn/, *time* = *Tom* /tɑːm/
- **Grammatical properties:**
  - homophones such as *he'll* = *he*, *kicks* = *kicked* = *kick* /kɪk/, *past* = *passed* = *pass* /pæs/, primarily due to phonological proper-

ties such as the omission of word-final /l/, /t/ or /d/ and the simplification of word-final consonant clusters
- multiple negation, e. g. *We ain't never had no trouble*, which sometimes also allows constructions known from only very few other
English non-standard varieties, e. g. *Nobody can't step on her foot*
'nobody can step on her foot', where the auxiliary is negated, too
- no 3rd person singular present indicative -*s*: *he kick, she kiss, she see*
- omission of auxiliary and copula *be* (in questions as well as declarative sentences) where Standard English permits contractions (e. g.
I'm, you're, she's): *I gonna do it, you real silly, she mine, she the first
one started us off, he fast in everything he do*
- uninflected *be* used to mark habituality: *my father be the last one to
open his presents*
- perfective *been* for events or actions still relevant at the moment of
utterance: *I been know your name*
- *done* used as perfect marker (*he done talk to you*); also instead of
will have: *We be done washed all those cars soon*
- *it* instead of dummy *there*: *It a boy in my class name Mike.*

Social stratification in New York City: Labov's analysis of variable rhoticity   Labov's famous
in New York has served as a model for a large number of sociolinguistic   *fourth floor* study
studies. Traditionally, the accent spoken in New York is non-rhotic (as in
New England, in general), but it seems to be becoming more and more
rhotic. Along these lines, Labov observed the following variation in the
early 1960s:

(a) only a small number of New Yorkers used post-vocalic (or: pre-consonantal) /r/ (as in *fourth floor*) as consistently as General American speakers, but some New Yorkers used it generally more often
than others;
(b) all informants used post-vocalic /r/ more often when consciously
trying to pronounce words accurately.

Labov showed that both of these tendencies correlated with the informants' socio-economic status: the higher their status, the more often they
would use post-vocalic /r/; the harder they tried to "belong" to a highly
prestigious group (think of *upward mobility*), the more often and the
more consistently they chose the prestigious variant (sometimes even
more often among lower middle-class than among upper middle-class
speakers, the so-called *cross-over effect*). We may add that it is certainly
no coincidence that the prestigious variant corresponds to the standard
accent of the US and is, at the same time, clearly different from both the
non-rhotic accent used among African American "ghetto" speakers and
the highly stigmatized New York "toidy-toid" (33rd street) accent.
Labov's analyses of the social stratification of the linguistic variable
/r/ were supported by studies carried out in the mid-1980s, by which
point the overall proportion of /r/-speakers had increased by 10 %. Today,
New York seems to be following the American mainstream and continues
to develop into a city with a rhotic accent.

from First to
Second Wave
sociolinguistics **Social networks:** Another field of sociolinguistic study, orthogonal, as it were, to the classic studies conducted in modern sociolinguistics, did not reach its peak until the late 1970s and 1980s: the exploration of social networks. Unlike early mainstream sociolinguistics, also known as *First Wave sociolinguistics*, the study of social networks (which is closely associated with research by Lesley and James Milroy in Belfast) is not concerned with correlations between language use and established macro-sociological variables such as socio-economic status, age or sex. Using ethnographic methods, studies in what has come to be called *Second Wave sociolinguistics* rather investigate correlations between language use and self-perception on the micro-sociological level. What stands at the focus of interest in this approach are the local, participant-designed meanings, values and attitudes of a specific social group, down to pairwise constellations and ultimately the individual (and his/her behaviour) in changing social roles in different social constellations and activities (see also below on communities of practice). What is at issue in network analysis, in particular, is language use in social networks, i. e. in the diverse and manifold constellations of contacts between family members, friends, students, colleagues, team members, neighbors, etc.

Network density and multiplexity: The level of network integration is basically determined by two factors: network density (the quantity or number of relationships) and multiplexity of the network (the quality or type of the relationships). Additionally, so-called socio-metric studies can determine which people are central and which are peripheral to the relevant network. The level of network integration, in turn, determines the amount of possible communicative events inside the network.

defining one's
group identity **Integration in a network – norms – language use:** One of the most important findings of network studies is that group identity manifests itself in language. Analyses of the communication taking place in different social networks (especially in working-class districts and youth gangs) have shown that variation in language use and in the language system is directly linked to the level of integration into a social network. On the one hand, the degree of integration correlates with the frequency with which a certain regional or urban dialect is used: the more integrated a speaker is, the more frequently he or she uses the dialect. On the other hand, conscious or subconscious peer pressure to follow the norms of the network increases as network density intensifies. Sociologists consider the fact that individuals are required to observe these norms to be a crucial social function of such networks. As for language, this behaviour manifests itself in the tendency to maintain certain language structures and speech habits. To a large extent, communication takes place within the network only, leaving little space for the language to change (for more details see sections 8.5 and 8.6).

overt vs. covert
prestige The tendency to use language to define one's group identity and one's level of identification with a certain group is particularly pronounced among the upper and lower social classes. In the case of the upper classes, the speakers are pressured to orient themselves towards the standard dialect as that dialect enjoying what Labov called *overt prestige*, whereas members of the lower classes (especially working class males) orient to-

wards a certain regional or urban dialect enjoying what Labov called *covert prestige* as a signal of group solidarity. Besides that, network density and the level of network integration also interact with other social variables such as age and sex (see section 8.5).

Third wave sociolinguistics: The classic studies on language variation in the First Wave (1960s and early 1970s) correlated language use in a given speech community with macro-sociological categories like socio-economic class, age, sex, or ethnicity (e. g. Labov's fourth floor study in New York City). Studies of the Second Wave (late 1970s and 1980s) correlated a given speech community's language use with micro-sociological categories (e. g. the Belfast network study by the Milroys). Different from both these waves, the so-called Third Wave of sociolinguistic studies (starting roughly in the early 1990s) zooms in even more strongly on the social meaning of variables and how these variables are used, negotiated and exploited by individuals for performative reasons and identity construction depending on the communicative situation, the social practices they are engaged in and the social roles they assume within those practices (cf. Eckert 2012). Studies associated with this Third Wave draw even more heavily on ethnographic methods and anthropological concepts than those in the Second Wave. In general, however, the following points need to be stressed with regard to these three waves:

zooming in on the individual

- The boundaries between them, especially between the Second and the Third Wave, are fluid.
- The succession of these three strands of sociolinguistic research indicates no more than a shift of focus, or primary research target, in the way in which an increasing number of sociolinguistic practitioners went about their research. This succession should not be understood in the sense that current sociolinguistic studies exclusively belong to the Third Wave, or that studies following the traditions of the First and Second Wave are outdated. This is not true at all; studies in all three sociolinguistic research strands are still being conducted side by side, sometimes deliberately in a complementary fashion.
- Many sociolinguists work in at least two of these research strands, some in all three (notably William Labov with many pioneering studies and definitions of foundational concepts).

Notions which have come to the fore in this Third Wave and related approaches to sociolinguistics include the following: communities of practice, accommodation, indexicality and enregisterment.

Communities of practice is an anthropological concept of the early 1990s. It was developed for groups of people coming together around some mutual engagement in some common endeavour, typically with a shared aim (e. g. a business meeting, a meeting of student representatives, students jointly preparing for an exam, parents meeting in school, a cooking class, a choir, colleagues organizing the unit's Christmas party, etc.). The boundary with social networks is fluid, but the latter tend to be more lasting, while communities of practice tend to be of a more temporary nature, and its members are typically in direct personal contact (for a detailed account, see Meyerhoff 2013). In contrast to communities of

changing practices and participant roles

practice, speakers in social networks can be indirectly linked to people via other people.

What is crucial from the point of the language use of members of such communities is that it is determined not by preconceived macro- or micro-sociological categories, but by the emerging and changing practices and participant roles within such a community. The communities of practice approach shifts sociolinguistic studies away from the traditional concepts of a speech community whose language use is being investigated. Individuals are typically members of many such communities of practice, their (varying or changing) linguistic behaviour must therefore also be seen against this participation in multiple such communities.

via linguistic convergence to social acceptance

Accommodation: One means of being integrated into a certain group is adapting one's language or language style to that used in the group. Besides its use among group members, accommodation of dialect (especially accent) and/or register (e. g. slang in youth gangs), i. e. linguistic convergence of the speakers involved in a communicative event, is a general means of achieving social acceptance and making communication more efficient. It is used particularly often in intercultural communication. But this is only the linguistic aspect of a much wider adaptation process which, in social psychology, is described as follows: The individual's social acceptance increases as the individual reduces differences. Of course, language can also be used to dissociate yourself from the person you are talking to. Linguistic divergence is one of the strategies investigated within the framework of accommodation theory. By including social context (more precisely the relationship, whether truly existing or just aspired to, between people engaged in a communicative event), accommodation theory offers an explanatory framework for functional variation, i. e. the context-dependent language use of the individual.

3 levels of awareness in the speech community

Indexicality and enregisterment: A basic question underlying the process of accommodation is the nature of the features with regard to which individuals (consciously or unconsciously) converge with, or diverge from, other speakers in a community or during an individual communicative exchange. Two related, but independently developed concepts from the 1970s are instructive in this respect: the anthropological concept of (first, second, third order) indexicality of a given linguistic form (Silverstein 1976, 2003, Agha 2003, Johnstone et al. 2006) and the slightly older sociolinguistic concept developed by Labov (1972) on the social evaluation of linguistic variables. According to Johnstone et al. (2006), three levels of awareness need to be distinguished within and beyond a speech community concerning the link of a certain linguistic feature and the social information (or meaning) it carries.

- **First-order indexicality:** On the lowest level, the fact that some linguistic feature correlates with a certain social category is noticed only by a specialist outsider, like a linguist or anthropologist, but not (or at least not consciously) by the insiders, that is the members of that particular speech community.
- **Second-order indexicality:** On the next higher level, the insiders themselves are aware of this correlation and thus consciously start

using that feature as a signal of belonging to the relevant group (group identity, group solidarity).

- **Third-order indexicality:** On the highest level of awareness, the relevant linguistic feature has become widely known, inside and outside the relevant speech community, as being characteristic of a certain social category and may even become the subject of metalinguistic comments (be they positive, neutral or negative as in "If you want to sound Welsh this is what you need to do ...", "This is typical of Glaswegian working class", or "This is bad language!", respectively). Third-order indexicals are also features that, for example, a comedian or actor would use in order to perform a persona from a certain region, city, social class or ethnic group (so-called characterological figures). These features also often make it into local tourist shops in the form of mugs or T-shirts. Third-order indexicals may also become enregistered over time, meaning that a set of linguistic norms becomes widely recognized as representing a certain regional or social variety which for its speakers, possibly also for outsiders, is linked to certain cultural values.

Most relevant from the point of accommodation (and, equally, style-shifting) are second-order and third-order indexicals, as these are the features that one either does, or wants to, converge on (or diverge from) in a given social practice or communicative event. Third-order indexicals have also become the focus of studies on sociolinguistic salience (e. g. Rácz 2013, Roller 2016).

indexicality and accommodation, salience

Indicators – markers – stereotypes: Silverstein's concept of indexicality is related to Labov's (1972) classic categorization of linguistic variables depending on the nature of their social evaluation within (or even outside) a given speech community (e. g. 'educated – uneducated', 'good – bad', 'standard – non-standard', 'white collar – blue collar', 'highly local – non-local', 'ethnic – non-ethnic', 'friendly – unfriendly', etc.) and the degree to which members of (or even outside) this speech community are consciously aware of these social evaluations.

social evaluation of linguistic variables

- **Indicators:** Largely corresponding to first-order indexicals, indicators are linguistic variables that vary according to some social category (e. g. age, socio-economic class), and are adopted by a certain subgroup of the relevant speech community, but largely operate below the level of awareness or consciousness of the members of this subgroup, let alone outsiders. There is little to any evaluative force going with them.
- **Markers:** Roughly corresponding to second-order indexicals, markers carry social information which insiders may or may not be aware of, but which can systematically be extracted by means of sociolinguistic methods (e. g. informants reading word lists vs. answering questions in an interview situation, which shows that style-shifting occurs).
- **Stereotypes:** Labov's third type of linguistic variable from the point of view of social evaluation are so-called stereotypes. Here, both insiders and outsiders are widely aware of this particular variable carrying a certain piece of social information and potentially attracting overt

comment, which in the case of outsiders typically is negative. In other words, in Labov's classification stereotypes are typically publicly stigmatized (as in school when pupils are told by their teachers "Never use double negation!"), and may increasingly be avoided even within the relevant subgroup, unless this particular feature enjoys a high degree of covert prestige and thus (deliberately) continues to be used by the insiders. Stereotypes differ from third-order indexicals primarily in that the public judgement of the latter is neutral, or even positive, and not downright negative.

social evaluation and accommodation

Again, linking Labov's classification to accommodation, it can thus be said that it is primarily markers which are the target of accommodation processes, stereotypes much less so.

8.5 | Feminist linguistics

In a chapter on sociolinguistics, it is obvious that a macro-sociological category like sex, or gender, also needs to play a role. Numerous sociolinguistic studies since the 1960s and 1970s have revealed differences between the speech of men and women. Examples include the stronger orientation towards the overtly prestigious standard variety by women, and the role of women in social networks or local speech communities as initiators and drivers of certain language changes. Some of the relevant findings will also be touched upon in this section. This will be done, however, under a different umbrella, namely feminist linguistics, a label which in the year 2020 may sound a little dated, but whose focus of inquiry as well as basic assumptions and objectives are still highly topical and very much under debate today.

Origins and basic assumptions: The origins of feminist linguistics date back to the feminist movement of the 1960s and 1970s in the United States. The central topic of feminist linguistics is "language and gender", where gender is neither a biological nor a grammatical concept (i. e. neither sex, distinguishing between *male* and *female*, nor grammatical gender, distinguishing between *feminine* and *masculine*, although the latter distinction is quite important in a large number of languages, and in European languages in particular). In feminist linguistics, gender is a sociological or socio-cultural concept: the socio-cultural construction of gender roles in (patriarchal) societies.

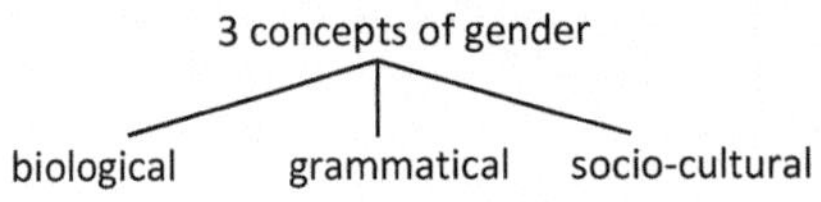

3 concepts of gender

biological   grammatical   socio-cultural

Figure 8.5:
Concepts of gender

Therefore, two of the basic assumptions of feminist linguistics are:

social gender
- Women and the language they use are the product of male-dominated society. Social gender is activated in any kind of interaction between human beings, naturally including verbal interaction. Social gender manifests itself, for example, in prototypical or stereotypical notions of gender roles, which most people spontaneously associate with particular occupations or professions (professions such as *secretary*, *nurse*,

cleaner or *primary school teacher*, for example, are usually associated with female referents, while professions such as *President of the Unites States*, *engineer*, *pilot* or *doctor* tend to be associated with male referents). This is why, if the referent does not have the stereotypical sex, certain expressions describing the referent's sex are sometimes added, as in *woman doctor* or *lady doctor* (two expressions which are nowadays stigmatized) or in *male nurse* (which is not stigmatized).

- Language structure and language use do not only reflect male dominance, but are also used to perpetuate this dominance.

Language criticism and language therapy: In its early phase, feminist linguistics was highly politicized. It was strongly influenced by the goals of the feminist movement, and its primary concern was the documentation of sexist language use (more precisely: language used to discriminate against women) and making people aware of this so it could be remedied. In that phase, feminist linguistics meant two things: on the one hand, and primarily, feminist linguistic criticism and, on the other hand, feminist language politics aiming at "therapies" for patriarchal language(s) – not only taking on male-dominated, male-centred language use, but also the corresponding language system(s). The immediate goal of the linguistic therapies suggested by feminist linguists was, and still is, to make women visible in language (e. g. by using *he or she* instead of generic *he*), or at least to reduce the male-as-norm bias (e. g. *humankind* instead of *man(kind)*, *chair(person)* instead of *chairman*).

Alter people's attitudes towards women: The ultimate goal was to use controlled language change as a means to alter people's attitudes towards women (thus pushing back stereotypical views of gender and gender roles) and to initiate societal change (especially by abolishing the existing gender hierarchy). The proposed strategies to avoid (a) sexist language use and (b) the linguistic manifestation of outdated gender-role stereotypes have been compiled in official guides and regulations for the equal treatment of women and men. By now, in North America and many European countries at least, these are being complied by all levels of government, and are increasingly observed (to be fair, also increasingly criticized) by other strata of society. Among the most important measures adopted to avoid sexist language use in English are the following:

- avoiding generic *he/him(self)/his*, as in ask <u>*anyone*</u> and <u>*he'll*</u> tell you, *In communication* <u>*the speaker's*</u> *primary aim is to get* <u>*his*</u> *message across*. Most expressions including both alternatives are only used in written language (*he/she, he or she, s/he, (s)he*). Another expression which is being generally accepted is *they/their* as a neutral singular pronoun (as in *In communication* <u>*the speaker's*</u> *primary aim is to get* <u>*their*</u> *message across*), which is exactly the function *they* and *their* had after indefinite forms like *anyone* or *everyone* up to the 18th century (compare "God send <u>every one</u> <u>their</u> heart's desire" in *Much Ado about Nothing* by Shakespeare).
- avoiding the expression *man* for 'human race' or 'human being or person' (as in *Museum of Man*, the song lyrics *now it's been 10,000*

avoidance of sexist language use

years, man has cried a billion tears or in set phrases like *the man in the street*); instead, use of neutral forms like *humankind* or *person*.

- doing away with the asymmetry between *Mr* (unmarked for the features married vs. unmarried) and *Mrs/Miss* by introducing the term *Ms* /mɪz/.
- gender-neutral job titles, e. g. *flight attendant* instead of *steward/stewardess*, *server* instead of *waiter/waitress*, *head teacher* instead of *headmaster/headmistress*; use of neutral terms like *person: chair(person)* instead of *chairman*, *anchor(person)* instead of *anchorman*; *salesperson* or *layperson*, plus the corresponding neutral plural forms *sales people* and *lay people*; *parent* instead of *mother/father*.
- no adding of *lady* or *woman* to describe jobs done by women (e. g. *lady doctor* or *woman doctor*), because such expressions support stereotypical views of sex roles associated with a great number of occupations and professions.
- avoiding lexical asymmetry (use of the morphologically unmarked noun for male referents evoking no or a positive connotation, while the noun derived from it to refer to female referents has a rather negative connotation): *governor – governess*, *master – mistress*, *bachelor – spinster*.
- compliance with the so-called "Titanic-Principle": "Women and children first!", which means that in listings, feminine forms or forms with female referents are to precede masculine forms or forms with male referents (e. g. *girls and boys*, *women and men*, *she or he*).

neutralizing gen-
der differences
vs. making them
visible

Different therapy strategies in English and in German: As far as the "curing" of sexist language use is concerned, there is an interesting difference between English and German. English has the tendency to abstract from gender, i. e. neutralize gender differences by introducing neutral terms not marked for gender (lexical solution), whereas German feminist linguistics tends to specify gender, i. e. make women visible in language by introducing parallel expressions, e. g. by the consistent use of the suffix *-in* (*Frisörin* instead of *Friseuse* 'hairdresser'), *-innen* (plural referents, female only) or *-Innen* (preceded by glottal stop /ʔɪnən/, plural referents, female and/or male, as in *FrisörInnen*, *BürgerInnen*, *StudentInnen*, 'female hairdressers/citizens/students'), or by using feminine articles and demonstrative pronouns (*die/diese/eine Studierende* vs. *der/dieser/ein Studierende(r)*). In German, this is the predominant tendency, but due to the use of forms ending in *-ende(r)* gender-neutral expressions exist now, too, at least in the plural (*die Studierenden*, *die Lehrenden*, *Studierende wie Lehrende haben erkannt ...*).

grammatical vs.
natural gender

The main reason why English and German use different strategies is that German – as the majority of European languages – has grammatical gender, whereas English has natural gender (which is only important with pronouns). For languages like English it is much easier to find "therapies" than for languages with grammatical gender. In the latter, women are invisible much more often, because masculine nouns (referring to animate referents) can also be used as gender-neutral (i. e. generic) expressions, while feminine nouns can have female referents only.

Numerous psycholinguistic studies have shown that the invisibility of women in a language results in the absence of women in our thinking: generic masculine forms are often used to refer to male referents only. Try and test for yourself: What referents do you think of when hearing the advice often given in pharmaceutical advertisements *For further information on benefits, risks and side effects, please consult your physician or pharmacist*, or its counter, in German *Zu Risiken und Nebenwirkungen fragen Sie Ihren Arzt oder Apotheker*?

dangers of generic masculine forms

Gender-specific language use: Starting in the late 1980s, feminist linguistics, or more precisely feminist linguistic criticism, has become much less radical. The simple reason is that it is widely acknowledged in many western industrial countries that this criticism is fundamentally justified, and that, based on the strategies for planned language change proposed by feminist linguistics, measures have been taken in many places as an antidote to sexist language use. For the last 35–40 years, feminist linguistics has been more concerned with typical sociolinguistic and pragmatic issues. Its primary aim has been to investigate gender-specific language use, focusing on how variation interacts with gender, and finding answers to the question "Which linguistic features are characteristic of women and which are characteristic of men?" Thanks to this line of research, it is clear now that (social) gender has an impact on language variation (besides other factors recognized by sociolinguistics such as geographical area, socio-economic status, and age), and the term *genderlect* has become widely accepted (analogous to *dialect* and *sociolect*).

Adopting the complementary perspective, third-wave studies (see section 8.4 above) have focused on how speakers actively construct their gender through language. They investigate how the social category of gender emerges in context (especially in communities of practice, e.g. Eckert 1998).

third-wave studies

Discourse behaviour of men and women: One of the main issues of feminist linguistics – which has also aroused great interest outside the academic community – is the behaviour of women and men amongst and towards each other in discourse and conversation. Various studies of communicative behaviour have shown that men are more conflict-oriented, more competitive and status-oriented and seek to initiate and control topics, whereas women are more consensus-oriented and more oriented towards cooperation, partnership, and creating an atmosphere of understanding and harmony. Here are some characteristic features of these two communicative styles – male *report talk* as opposed to female *rapport talk*:

report talk vs. rapport talk

- **Men**
  - frequently interrupt contributions of other speakers.
  - give no or very short answers, which may indicate lack of interest or attention, or discourage the other speaker from continuing talking (possible consequence: silence).
  - frequently claim the right to speak.
  - talk more in public settings.
  - start topics and claim the conversational floor.

- **Women**
  - – are interrupted more frequently than men.
  - – frequently use minimal responses which indicate attention and interest (*I'm with you*, *go on*) to encourage the other speaker to continue.
  - – ask questions to elicit reactions.
  - – claim the right to speak less frequently than men.
  - – talk more in private settings.
  - – are often hesitant and indirect (e. g. indirect speech acts used to make requests, frequent use of polite expressions, use of hedges such as *I think*, *I guess*, *perhaps*, *maybe*, and the use of tag questions for reassurance).
  - – "collaborate" on topics with other speakers.

horizontal vs. vertical culture

Two cultures approach: As a matter of fact, communication between men and women is often regarded as a special instance of intercultural communication in feminist linguistics. The specifically male and female patterns of communicative behaviour are thought to result from cultural differences between the two sexes which start developing during the speakers' childhood and adolescence. How great these differences are may depend on the speakers' cultural backgrounds and the society they live in: Is it a female, "horizontal" culture oriented towards consensus, cooperation and equality, or a "vertical" male culture, oriented towards competition, power and social status? These cultural differences are responsible for many misunderstandings in the communication between the sexes, one example being that most women find sincere statements of sympathy and compassion agreeable while men sometimes find them patronizing or even face-threatening.

Orientation towards the prestigious norm: Those feminist linguists working within the sociolinguistic framework, i. e. those who use traditional sociolinguistic methods, are not satisfied with the theory of the two cultures. There is, for example, an interesting new interpretation of the observation that women's language is usually closer to the standard, the prestigious norm, than the language used by men, who tend to use more non-standard forms. This observation is supported by a multitude of studies on language use by both men and women of the same social group in identical communicative situations. Why do women follow the prestigious norm? Does this behaviour really reflect a female culture formed by education (at home and at school) and stereotypical role behaviour passed on from earlier generations?

Mobility: Sociolinguistic investigations made in different urban working-class areas in the United States and Northern Ireland suggest a different, or at least more differentiated explanation: The fact that women orient themselves towards the prestigious standard norm may simply be the result of their being more mobile and having more contact with other people, also with those of a higher socio-economic standing, whereas the private and professional life of men most of the time takes place in the same social group in their residential area. Hence, from the viewpoint of the sociolinguistic approach pioneered by Labov and the Milroys, the concepts of social gender and different cultures should not be regarded as the only explanations for gender differences in language use. Given the examples mentioned above, we could hypothesize that, in societies with clearly distinguished gender roles, those speakers with the greater (social and geographical) mobility are more strongly oriented towards the language use and linguistic norm of their respective "contact groups".

Planned language change: In conclusion, let us briefly return to feminist language politics. Its ultimate goal is to change the way people think by changing their linguistic habits. In the English-speaking world and in Europe, people have made quite some progress concerning the latter goal by changing certain linguistic forms and conversational habits, or at least by becoming aware of the necessity of such changes (think of *Ms* or the use of *they/their* as generic, gender-neutral singular pronouns). This is already part of the historical dimension of sociolinguistics. Usually, however, sociolinguistics is not concerned with pre-planned language change but with the normal, rather unconscious changes in language use and the social circumstances in which they occur.

8.6 | Sociolinguistics and language change

The historical dimension of sociolinguistics, although of utmost importance, can be touched upon only briefly here, but will be addressed again in chapter 9.4. The main branches of historical sociolinguistics are dialectology, variationist (or: Labovian) sociolinguistics, language contact research (think of the important role of language contact in the history of English) and creole studies (a sub-discipline of language contact research which studies the emergence of new varieties and languages, notably pidgins and creoles, due to language contact). Given the overall focus of the present chapter, only the importance of dialectology and variationist sociolinguistics for the study of language change will be addressed below.

Dialectology: Language varieties always represent a state of tension; they are torn between preservation and renewal, being at the same time conservative and innovative. Inevitably, they have therefore always been the object of investigation in historical language studies (in dialectology right from the beginning). A well-known comparison relates taking a journey through the different dialect regions of a language to being a time-traveller visiting the past, sometimes even the future. Many linguistic features known from older stages of a language are still found in dialects, especially rural dialects. In English, these include (as we have seen above) multiple negation, zero relative clauses in subject position or different personal pronouns used for the second person singular and plural. Thus, by observing present-day variation in (dialectal) language systems, we can in fact learn something about the history of a language. Note, though, that this is a purely language-internal approach focussing on the comparison and reconstruction of language systems.

Variation and language change: This is not what is done in Labovian sociolinguistics and subsequent sociolinguistic approaches (network

main branches of historical sociolinguistics

the dialectologist as a time-traveller

the variationist approach to language change

studies in particular). Language-internal patterns (let alone presumed language-internal pressures) are not marshalled to explain why a specific language change has taken place or why it might even have been expected to take place. Instead, in his *variationist approach to language change*, which has had a lasting effect on historical linguistics for the last six decades, Labov is concerned with the language-external factors triggering language change and seeks to explain language change in connection with changes in social reality. Languages, to be sure, are changed by the people who use them, but which are the social factors that can actually cause linguistic norms to change or prevent them from changing? In trying to answer this question, sociolinguists stress the importance of group identities, along the lines of socio-economic status, age or sex, but also in terms of social networks and communities of practice (see section 8.4 above).

another classic study by Labov Group identity on Martha's Vineyard: Among many other things, Labov studied two phonological variables (pronunciation of the diphthongs /aɪ/ and /aʊ/) in the speech of the people of Martha's Vineyard, a small island off the New England coast. He discovered that the innovative, centring realizations of these diphthongs (/ɐɪ/ and /əɪ/, and /ɐʊ/ and /əʊ/) were used much more frequently by those inhabitants who were especially attached to the island and its traditions. They were people of all ages who, at the same time, showed a negative attitude towards the great number of mainland tourists who came to visit the island during their summer holidays. The Standard American English realizations of /aɪ/ and /aʊ/, on the other hand, were typically used by those inhabitants who were more open to tourists and did not feel that their presence posed a threat to the island community and its traditions. Obviously, the speakers of Martha's Vineyard unconsciously used one specific phonological feature – the centralization of two diphthongs – as an in-group marker to distinguish themselves from others. Labov's findings show that there is a direct connection between variation and change: Change starts out as variation.

basic tenets Actuation – transition – embedding: Besides studying the original causes, i. e. the possible trigger(s) of language change (the so-called *actuation problem*), the primary concern of Labovian sociolinguistics is to determine which factors influence its spread (the so-called *transition problem*; recall much of the discussion in section 8.4) and to study the transitional stages of a language which result from (usually gradual) language change. These transitional stages are characterized by the coexistence of different linguistic alternatives, i. e. variation (the so-called *embedding problem*). Therefore, the basic tenets of the approach are (a) that sociolinguistics is primarily concerned with studying language variation and language change, and that it studies these aspects simultaneously, (b) that by studying synchronic variation a lot can be learnt about the history of a language, and (c) that, ultimately, the strict distinction between synchrony and diachrony is impossible to maintain.

Checklist Sociolinguistics – key terms and concepts

accommodation
actuation
adaptation
African-American (Vernacular) English
Americanization
angloversal
areoversal
colloquialization
community of practice
deficit ↔ difference hypothesis
dialect ↔ accent
dialect atlas
dialect continuum
dialect levelling
dialect universals
embedding
(New) Englishes/World
  Englishes
feminist linguistics
gender diffusion
gender (biological, grammatical, socio-cultural)
genderlect
General American
indexicality (1st/2nd/3rd
  order)
isogloss
jargon
language convergence
lexico-grammar
linguistic variable ↔ linguistic variant

mandative subjunctive
multiple negation
network (density; multi-
  plexity)
NORM
pluricentricity
prestige, overt ↔ covert
pronoun exchange
rapport talk ↔ report talk
Received Pronunciation
register
regularization
rhoticity
salience
slang
social evaluation of linguistic
  variables (indicators,
  markers, stereotypes)
social stratification
sociolect
sociolinguistics ↔ sociology
  of language
standard (accent)
style
traditional ↔ modern dialectology
transition
variationist/Labovian
  linguistics
variety/lect (regional/
  diatopic; social/diastratic;
  functional/diasituative;
  diaphasic)
waves of sociolinguistics

Exercises

1.
a) Explain the differences between the members of the following semantic field: dialect, genderlect, jargon, lect, register, slang, sociolect, standard, variety, vernacular
b) The term *dialect* can be used both in broader and in narrower ways compared with the definition adopted in this chapter. Comment on the following uses:
   (A)   Dialects can be distinguished along a horizontal and a vertical axis. The first gives us regional, the second social dialects.
   (B)   This person can't even speak proper English. All he's able to is produce some dialect which is unintelligible even to the most well-meaning ears.
   (C)   In my dialect you would have to say [paθ] rather than [pɑːθ].
   (D)   We speak the same dialect but different accents.

2. Which of the following examples are candidates for true regionalisms? Try to identify the relevant regional dialects or dialect areas. You can consult eWAVE (https://ewave-atlas.org/) for help.
a) I'm needing a cup of tea.
b) It pull the mole up and he was dead in minutes.
c) We also had a girl worked in the house.
d) You were only after asking me.
e) You never seen nobody.
f) Answer the question, can or not?

3. Which of the following sentences are more representative of American English, which of British English?
a) The orchestra is divided.
b) Did you already see "Armageddon"?
c) I've had a bath just a minute ago.
d) She's gotten interested.
e) I insist that she leaves.
f) Where can I get some petrol?

4. Illustrate the correlation between social class and regional variation. Include in your discussion the pronunciation of words like *bar*, *card*, *singing* and *walking* as it is frequently found in England.

5. Explain the sociolinguistic approach known as "social network analysis".

6.

a) What is striking about the following sentences in African-American English:
(a) They real fine.
(b) I gonna do it.
(c) John be happy.
(d) Sometime they be walking round here.

b) Identify grammatical parallels between African-American English and regional varieties in the British Isles. You can consult eWAVE (https://ewave-atlas.org/) for help.

7. Sketch the major differences between traditional and modern dialectology.

8. Which of the following statements are true, which are false?

a) Traditional dialectology is concerned with the study of traditional dialects, modern dialectology with the study of modern dialects.

b) Social variation correlates with regional variation.

c) RP is a social accent.

d) Multiple negation is the rule rather than the exception in many varieties of English.

e) Accommodation is the term in sociolinguistics for the influence that housing has on the choice of a certain functional variety.

f) There is far more regional variation in the British Isles than there is in the United States.

g) You cannot speak a standard dialect with a regional accent.

h) Most of the grammatical differences between British and American English can be observed in the verb phrase.

i) Third-wave sociolinguistics aims at identifying correlations between the use of linguistic variants and broad demographic categories.

j) More as well as more complex subordination patterns are typical of written in contrast to spoken language.

9. Go to the BYU interface of the corpus of *Global Web-Based English* (GloWbE), a 1.9-billion-word corpus with data from twenty varieties of English: https://www.english-corpora.org/glowbe/. Enter *auntie|aunties* in the search window and select chart. The pipe symbol "|" allows you to search for the singular and plural form simultaneously.

a) Click on "frequency by section" and identify the variety in which AUNTIE is most frequently used.

b) Click on the bar of the variety to see how AUNTIE is used in context. Determine what other meaning(s) AUNTIE has apart from 'a sister of one's father or mother'.

Advanced

10. Familiarize yourself with eWAVE, an open-access, electronic world atlas of varieties of English, on https://ewave-atlas.org/.
   a) What is eWAVE?
   b) Identify pervasive features of Orkney and Shetland English and give an example.
   c) Which of the features above could be considered angloversals in the sense that they seem to occur in the majority of English varieties world-wide? Which seem to be true regionalisms?

11. Find at least one replication of Labov's famous Martha's Vineyard study and compare its findings with those of the original.

12. Give an account of the significance of sociolinguistics for the study of language change. Focus in particular on the work by William Labov.

Sources and further reading

Agha, Asif. 2003. "The social life of cultural value." *Language and communication* 23: 231–273.

Algeo, John, ed. 2001. *The Cambridge history of the English language*, vol. 6: *English in North America*. Cambridge: Cambridge University Press.

Ammon, Ulrich/Norbert Dittmar/Klaus J. Mattheier/Peter Trudgill, eds. 2006². *Sociolinguistics: An international handbook of the science of the language and society*. Berlin: Walter de Gruyter.

Baker, Paul. 2017. *American and British English: Divided by a common language?* Cambridge: Cambridge University Press.

Bayley, Robert/Richard Cameron/Ceil Lucas, eds. 2015. *The Oxford handbook of sociolinguistics*. Oxford: Oxford University Press.

Beal, Joan C. 2010. *An introduction to regional Englishes: Dialect variation in England*. Edinburgh: Edinburgh University Press.

Bex, Tony/Richard J. Watts, eds. 1999. *Standard English: The widening debate*. London/New York: Routledge.

Biber, Douglas/Susan Conrad. 2009. *Register, genre, and style*. Cambridge: Cambridge University Press.

Burchfield, Robert, ed. 1994. *The Cambridge history of the English language*, vol. 5: *English in Britain and overseas: Origins and developments*. Cambridge: Cambridge University Press.

Cameron, Deborah, ed. 1998². *The feminist critique of language: A reader*. London/New York: Routledge.

Chambers, Jack K. 2009. *Sociolinguistic theory*. Revised edition. Oxford: Blackwell.

Chambers, Jack K./Natalie Schilling, eds. 2013². *The handbook of language variation and change*. Malden, MA/Oxford: Wiley-Blackwell.

Chambers, Jack K./Peter Trudgill. 1998². *Dialectology*. Cambridge: Cambridge University Press.

Cheshire, Jenny, ed. 1991. *English around the world. Sociolinguistic perspectives*. Cambridge: Cambridge University Press.

Coates, Jennifer. 2016³. *Women, men and language: A sociolinguistic account of gender differences in language*. London/New York: Routledge.

Coulmas, Florian. 2013². *Sociolinguistics: The study of speakers' choices*. Cambridge: Cambridge University Press.

Coupland, Nikolas, ed. 2016. *Sociolinguistics: Theoretical debates*. Cambridge: Cambridge University Press.

Coupland, Nikolas/Adam Jaworski, eds. 1997. *Sociolinguistics. A reader and coursebook*. London: Macmillan.

Eckert, Penelope. 1998. "Vowels and nail polish: The emergence of linguistic style in the preadolescent heterosexual marketplace." In: Natasha Warner/Jocelyn Ahlers/Leela Bilmes/Monica Oliver/ Suzanne Wertheim/Melinda Chen, eds. *Proceedings of the 1996 Berkeley Women and Language Conference*, 183–190. Berkeley: Berkeley Women and Language Group.

Eckert, Penelope. 2012. "Three waves of variation study: The emergence of meaning in the study of sociolinguistic variation". *Annual Review of Anthropology* 41: 87–100.

Eckert, Penelope/Sally McConnell-Ginet. 2013[2]. *Language and gender*. Cambridge: Cambridge University Press.

Ehrlich, Susan/Miriam Meyerhoff/Janet Holmes, eds. 2014. *The handbook of language, gender and sexuality*. New York/Oxford: Wiley-Blackwell.

Green, Lisa J. 2002. *African American English: A linguistic introduction*. Cambridge: Cambridge University Press.

Hancil, Sylvie/Joan C. Beal. 2017. *Perspectives on Northern Englishes*. Berlin/Boston: De Gruyter Mouton.

Hellinger, Marlis. 1990. *Kontrastive feministische Linguistik: Mechanismen sprachlicher Diskriminierung im Englischen und Deutschen*. München: Hueber.

Holm, John. 1988–89. *Pidgins and creoles*. 2 vols. Cambridge: Cambridge University Press.

Horobin, Simon. 2013. "American spelling". In: Simon Horobin. *Does spelling matter?* Oxford: Oxford University Press. 185–211.

Johnstone, Barbara/Jennifer Andrus/Andrew E. Danielson. 2006. "Mobility, indexicality and the enregisterment of 'Pittsburghese'". *Journal of English Linguistics* 34: 77–104.

Kortmann, Bernd/Edgar W. Schneider with Kate Burridge/Rajend Mesthrie/Clive Upton, eds. 2004. *A handbook of varieties of English*. 2 vols. Berlin/New York: Mouton de Gruyter.

Kortmann, Bernd/Christian Langstrof. 2012. "Regional varieties of British English." In: Alexander Bergs/Laurel Brinton, eds. *Historical linguistics of English: An international handbook*, 1928–1950. Berlin/New York: Mouton de Gruyter.

Kortmann, Bernd/Kerstin Lunkenheimer, eds. 2012. *The Mouton world atlas of variation in English*. Berlin: de Gruyter Mouton.

Kortmann, Bernd/Kerstin Lunkenheimer/Katharina Ehret, eds. 2020. *The electronic world atlas of varieties of English*. Zenodo. DOI: 10.5281/zenodo.3712132.

Kortmann, Bernd/Tanja Herrmann/Lukas Pietsch/Susanne Wagner. 2005. *A comparative grammar of British English dialects: agreement, gender, relative clauses*. Berlin/New York: Mouton de Gruyter.

Labov, William. 1972. *Sociolinguistic patterns*. Philadelphia: University of Pennsylvania Press.

Labov, William. 1994. *Principles of linguistic change: Internal factors*. vol. 1. Oxford: Blackwell.

Labov, William. 2001. *Principles of linguistic change: Social factors*. vol. 2. Oxford: Blackwell.

Labov, William. 2010. *Principles of linguistic change: Cognitive and cultural factors*. vol. 3. Oxford: Wiley-Blackwell

Labov, William/Sharon Ash/Charles Boberg. 2006. *The Atlas of North American English: Phonetics, phonology and sound change*. Berlin: Walter de Gruyter.

Leech, Geoffrey/Marianne Hundt/Christian Mair/Nicholas Smith. 2009. *Change in contemporary English: A grammatical study*. Cambridge: Cambridge University Press.

Mailhammer, Robert. 2020. *Croker Island English*. Berlin/Boston: De Gruyter Mouton.

Mair, Christian. 2009. *Twentieth century English. History, variation and standardization*. Cambridge: Cambridge University Press.

McArthur, Tom. 1998. *The English languages*. Cambridge: Cambridge University Press.

Mesthrie, Rajend, ed. 2011. *The Cambridge handbook of sociolinguistics*. Cambridge: Cambridge University Press.

Meyerhoff, Miriam. 2013. "Communities of practice." In: Jack Chambers/Natalie Schilling, eds. 428–447.

Meyerhoff, Miriam. 2018³. *Introducing sociolinguistics*. London: Routledge.

Meyerhoff, Miriam/Erik Schleef, eds. 2010. *The Routledge sociolinguistics reader*. London: Routledge.

Meyerhoff, Miriam/Erik Schleef/Laurel MacKenzie. 2015. *Doing sociolinguistics: A practical guide to data collection and analysis*. London: Routledge.

Milroy, James/Lesley Milroy, eds. 1993. *Real English: The grammar of English dialects in the British Isles*. London: Longman.

Mühlhäusler, Peter. 2020. *Pitkern and Norf'k*. Berlin/Boston: De Gruyter Mouton.

Mufwene, Salikoko S./John R. Rickford/Guy Bailey/John Baugh, eds. 1998. *African-American English: Structure, history and use*. London/New York: Routledge.

Pennhallurick, Rob. 2018. *Studying dialect*. London: Palgrave Macmillan.

Rácz, Péter. 2013. *Salience in sociolinguistics. A quantitative approach*. Berlin/Boston: De Gruyter Mouton.

Rohdenburg, Günter. 2009. "Reflexive structures." In Günter Rohdenburg/Julia Schlüter, eds. 166–181.

Rohdenburg, Günter/Julia Schlüter, eds. 2009. *One language, two grammars? Differences between British and American English*. Cambridge: Cambridge University Press.

Roller, Katja. 2016. *Salience in Welsh English grammar: A usage-based approach*. Freiburg: Albert-Ludwigs-Universität Universitätsbibliothek.

Samel, Ingrid. 1995. *Einführung in die feministische Sprachwissenschaft*. Berlin: Erich Schmidt.

Schilling, Natalie. 2013. *Sociolinguistic fieldwork*. Cambridge: Cambridge University Press.

Schneider, Edgar/Kate Burridge/Bernd Kortmann/Rajend Mesthrie/Clive Upton, eds. 2004. *A handbook of varieties of English: Phonology*. vol. 1. Berlin/New York: Mouton de Gruyter.

Silverstein, Michael. 1976. "Shifters, linguistic categories and cultural description." In Keith H. Basso/Henry A. Selby, eds. *Meaning in anthropology*. Albuquerque: University of New Mexico Press. 11–55.

Silverstein, Michael. 2003. "Indexical order and the dialectics of sociolinguistic life." *Language and communication* 23: 193–229.

Tagliamonte, Sali. 2011. *Variationist sociolinguistics: Change, observation, interpretation*. Oxford: Wiley-Blackwell.

Tannen, Deborah. 1992. *You just don't understand. Women and men in conversation*. London: Virago Press.

Tottie, Gunnel. 2009. "How different are American and British English grammar? And how are they different?" In: Günter Rohdenburg/Julia Schlüter, eds. 341–363.

Trudgill, Peter. 1999². *The dialects of England*. Oxford: Wiley-Blackwell.

Trudgill, Peter/Jack K. Chambers, eds. 1991. *Dialects of English. Studies in grammatical variation*. London: Longman.

Trudgill, Peter/Jean Hannah. 2008⁵. *International English: A guide to the varieties of Standard English*. London: Hodder Education.

Wells, John C. 1982 [1995]. *Accents of English*. 3 vols. Cambridge: Cambridge University Press.

Wolfram, Walt/Natalie Schilling-Estes. 2016³. *American English: Dialects and variation*. Malden, MA: Wiley Blackwell.

Wright, Laura, ed. 2018. *Southern English varieties then and now*. Berlin/Boston: De Gruyter Mouton.

9 Turns and trends in 21st century linguistics

Outlook and appetizer: This chapter is meant to serve as an outlook and appetizer for the rich world of English linguistics lying beyond the essential core of the discipline outlined in the previous chapters. It will put the spotlight on turns and major trends in the development of novel theories, methodologies, research questions, and overall research paradigms. Any endeavour of this kind, especially when restricted to one chapter, must necessarily be selective. The major criterion for selection has been that whatever will be presented below must deepen, innovate or complement in interesting ways issues that have been discussed in previous chapters, and that the focus is on empirical and broadly functionalist-driven English linguistics. Inevitably, this involves a personal note, but then again, this focus reflects mainstream English linguistics of the last few decades, and will no doubt continue to do so in the foreseeable future.

Turns – trends – developments: For the most part, the turns, trends and developments sketched below are not radically new, but have been in full swing for the past two decades, partly even since the late 1980s and 1990s. They are a natural outgrowth of:

- technological progress, notably of the firm establishment of the computer as the single most important research tool in almost any science,
- advances in linguistic theory and, simply,
- the huge body of descriptive linguistic knowledge which has accumulated in (especially late) 20th and early 21st century synchronic linguistics, whether in language-specific studies (especially on English and its rich array of varieties) or in cross-linguistic studies.

Furthermore, all of these developments are broadly functionalist-driven: their focus is on language use, and the relevant scholars all subscribe to the view that function shapes use and, ultimately, the language system.

Three major turns: *Turn* is a big word and as such requires clarification, especially since all of the turns to be discussed here are the outcome of decades of research and scholarly debates. The turns addressed in this chapter are understood less in the sense of abrupt and radical paradigm shifts, let alone scientific revolutions, but as representing cumulative, large-scale research trends pursued by a significantly large number of practitioners of English linguistics – big headlines, as it were, capturing a range of diverse smaller scale research directions. Three major turns char-

J.B. Metzler © Springer-Verlag GmbH Deutschland, ein Teil von Springer Nature, 2020
B. Kortmann, *English Linguistics*, https://doi.org/10.1007/978-3-476-05678-8_9

acterize the early 21st century and can safely be expected to keep shaping English linguistics for the next few decades:

- Statistics-based turn: From a methodological point of view, there is the statistics-based (or in the following: quantitative) turn, driven particularly, but certainly not exclusively, by the massive rise of corpus linguistics and the omnipresence of corpus-based research (see chapter 9.1).
- Usage-based turn: As far as linguistic theorizing is concerned, we are witnessing the usage-based turn, driven by the construction(al)ist turn, i. e. the rise of Construction Grammar(s) (see chapter 9.2).
- Variation-based turn: Concerning major topics and approaches, there has been a noticeable rise in the study of language variation in its widest sense, namely cross-linguistic variation (language or linguistic typology), language-internal variation (as in sociolinguistics, dialectology, or World Englishes research; see chapter 9.3), and historical variation (as in the different branches of historical linguistics; see chapter 9.4). (Note that a further major type of variation falling under the rubric of this turn is learner variation, be it in first language acquisition or in second or foreign language acquisition. However, as language acquisition has been excluded from this book, this branch of the variation-based turn will not be addressed in this chapter.)

three sub-turns
The variation-based turn can thus be subdivided into three smaller-scale turns. All three, but especially the last two have increasingly shaped English linguistics over the past few decades:
- the typological turn
- the varieties turn
- the historical turn

Depending on (a) which type of variation is studied and (b) the theoretical orientation of the linguist, all three sub-turns are more or less strongly related to each other. Ultimately, the typological approach (involving, for example, special methods for language sampling, collecting, annotating and analysing data, parameters for comparison, generalizations across languages, functional explanations) can be considered the unifying, or integrating, force, yardstick and source of inspiration for the study of any kind of language variation (Croft 2003: 289–290).

Triangulation: This has also been called a "triangulation" of typology, diachrony, and dialectology (Kortmann 2012). This term refers to the application and combination of multiple perspectives (in terms of theories, hypothesis formation, research methods, interpretation of research results) in the study of the same phenomenon, thereby strengthening and enriching the research process across the board and right from the start. In this respect, the impact of typology already played a role in chapter 5 when contrasting English and German. Below, its impact will be strongest in section 9.3 on the patterns of structural diversity of World Englishes and non-standard varieties in the anglophone world, and in section 9.4 on grammaticalization as one powerful domain in which a renewed interest in language evolution and language has arisen.

Interdependence of major turns: Although the three major turns are in principle independent of each other, they are often interrelated, partly feeding into and even driving each other. This is most evident for the quantitative turn and the usage-based turn. By definition, the usage-based approach critically relies on the availability of a vast range of usage data, typically huge and diverse corpora, which are statistically analysed from the point of view of usage frequency, pattern formation, meaning in context (pragmatics), or variation (e. g. written vs. spoken language, different genres, regional, social or historical varieties). Moreover, usage frequencies in corpora allow us to formulate cognitive hypotheses as to how humans acquire, process, store and produce language. These hypotheses can then be tested in highly controlled psycholinguistic experiments, which in turn are the second major driver of the quantitative turn, along with the high degree of statistical and, more generally, methodological sophistication required.

Two super-turns or mega-trends: Ultimately, it could be claimed that the three major turns as well as the three variation-based sub-turns are all outgrowths of two overarching and interrelated mega-trends in late 20th and especially 21st century linguistics (especially in English linguistics). These are the ever-stronger empirical turn, on the one hand, and the ever-stronger methodological turn, on the other hand. The exploration of more and more corpus-based and experimental data sets of immense size, diversity, quality, and detail (e. g. in terms of annotation, information about informants, streamlined data collection) requires the competent handling of increasingly sophisticated statistical tools. But even beyond statistics, the awareness for the need of a much higher methodological rigour in all phases of the research process has grown in many areas of linguistic research. This applies equally to qualitative methods and approaches, such as participant selection and observation, interview design and, generally, inductive, natural, non-interventionist methods targeting the insiders' point of view and aimed at understanding the actors' perspectives.

One reason for this increased awareness for methodology certainly is the following: Linguists doing research in areas intersecting either with highly advanced quantitative sciences (e. g. psychology, neurology, medicine, bio-informatics, physics) or with disciplines which look back on a long tradition of working with highly advanced qualitative methods (e. g. anthropology, sociology) increasingly aim to meet the high methodological standards of these disciplines. This strongly increased methodological awareness in linguistic research can be seen, for example, in a steep increase of textbooks, handbooks, special issues of journals, etc. specifically addressing advances in linguistic methodology. Consider, for example, Krug/Schlüter 2013 for exploring language variation and change, Allan/Robynson 2012 for historical semantics or Adams/Brinton/Fulk 2015 for historical English linguistics, in general, Stefanowitsch 2020 for corpus linguistics, or Levshina 2015 for statistics in linguistics. (For additional relevant titles see the further reading section at the end of the chapter.) The great emphasis put on these two super-turns, or mega-trends, can also increasingly be read off the requirements for academic positions in (English) linguistics as specified in job advertisements and

empirical turn, methodological turn

the module structures of degree programmes in (English) linguistics, especially at master and PhD level.

9.1 | The quantitative turn

The point of no return: On a broad scale, the quantitative turn in linguistics started in the 1990s and early 2000s, in English linguistics even a little earlier. It was a turn both in scale and in quality, a turn concerning the degree (including the degree of sophistication) to which quantitative empirical studies, statistical techniques and statistical modelling came to be used and determine linguistic research. Of course, quantification already played a major role in certain branches of linguistics in the 1960s and 1970s (notably Labov-type variationist, or quantitative, sociolinguistics; see chapters 8.4 and 8.6), but the data sets then were still considerably smaller compared with the huge (multi-million) data sets linguists from undergraduate level onwards have at their disposal. Today even in fields typically, or even dominantly, working with qualitative methods (like semantics or pragmatics), some degree of quantification is increasingly expected. The most important drivers of this quantitative turn have been the following two.

Experimental turn: Increasing use of behavioural and brain imaging experiments has been made in cognitive linguistics, psycho- and neuro-linguistics. It doesn't stop there, however; other branches of linguistics, too, have become interested in how (spoken or written) language is processed, stored, or produced. 'Experimental' should, however, also be understood in the wider sense of pertaining to any sort of controlled investigation, with great care being exercised over research design and every single stage of the research process.

The experimental turn, remarkable and pervasive as it is, has operated at a much smaller scale and slower rate compared with the second, and by far most powerful, driver of the quantitative turn, namely the breathtaking rise of corpus linguistics and the use of the internet as a data source over the past 20–30 years. For English linguistics, corpus linguistics has become mainstream, and with it the necessity and impact of a high degree of sophistication in statistical expertise (which is equally important in the experimental turn).

9.1.1 | Corpus linguistics

Specialized meaning of corpus: The meaning of the term *corpus* (from Latin *corpus* 'body; collection of facts') has undergone significant specialization in the course of the last half century. In its wide, traditional sense, the term *corpus* was used in the sense of 'body of data', that is for any set of authentic linguistic data compiled as an empirical basis for linguistic research (e. g. a collection of all *if*-clauses extracted from three novels by different authors may be called a corpus). In its narrower and more pervasive present-day sense, however, the term *corpus* is reserved for large bodies of natural texts (written and/or transcribed spoken data) which have been carefully compiled according to certain principles, are often annotated with linguistic (for instance, syntactic) or non-linguistic (for instance, sociological) meta-information, and are analysed with sophisticated data processing software. What then defines a corpus linguist, beyond being an empirical linguist who is computer-literate and makes these large bodies of electronic data the basis for his or her research? Corpus linguists are interested in investigating language use in all its richness and dimensions. For this purpose, they need to be well-versed in statistics and statistical programming tools for evaluating the validity of quantitative results.

Method vs. subdiscipline: In the 21st century, the use of corpora and of internet and social media data has become the new standard of almost any kind of empirical research on the English language. In other words, to some extent the label *corpus linguist(ics)* has lost the distinctive power it once had during the pioneering period from the 1960s until the 1980s, when it created an identity among a rather small group belonging to the community of empirical linguists. Today it is hard to imagine an empirical English linguist who is not a practitioner of corpus linguistics, simply because this is the richest possible (and continually growing) data source and most powerful method for investigating written, but increasingly also spontaneous spoken English language use. The same tendency can be observed in the empirical study of other major, especially European, languages. Thus, due to the technological revolution in the information age, corpus linguistics has clearly become a standard method in 21st century linguistics. What remains the preoccupation of a still rather small group of linguists – corpus linguists in a narrow sense – is the compilation of new corpora, and the development and application of new analytic tools such as annotation or tagging software (e.g. automatically marking the part of speech on the individual words and word forms in a corpus).

English linguistics: the cradle of corpus linguistics: English linguistics was the cradle of corpus linguistics. It is here that around 1960 the first corpora for the study of British and American English were compiled. These were two parallel one-million word corpora consisting of 500 texts from different registers (press, general prose, fiction, learned writing), with 2,000 words from each text, respectively: the corpus of written American English compiled at Brown University (Brown Corpus) and the matching Lancaster-Oslo-Bergen Corpus (LOB) for written British English (see figure 9.1 below). Much of the standard corpus linguistic toolkit (e.g. search software, concordancers) was initially developed for these first English corpora. As a consequence, anyone working on (almost any imaginable variety of) Present-Day English or older periods of English is in an extremely privileged position, also compared with fellow linguists working on other (even major) languages of the world. Thus, many questions on language use, variation and change that can be answered within seconds for English, can hardly be answered for other languages due to the absence of a comparable array of large electronic corpora.

Broad range of English corpora: There is an increasingly diverse range of partly huge corpora available that can be used for analyses on all structural levels, including even studies of intonation. This includes corpora for:

- **different national standard varieties:** e. g. ICE, the International Corpus of English, which includes one-million word corpora of speech (60 %) and written texts (40 %) from different national varieties of English; http://ice-corpora.net/
- **regional and social non-standard varieties:** e. g. FRED, the Freiburg English Dialect Corpus (largely England-based), with 2.5 million words of oral history interviews transcribed, for 40 % of which audio files can be accessed; https://fred.ub.uni-freiburg.de/
- **different historical periods:** e. g. ARCHER, A Representative Corpus of Historical English Registers, which currently consists of some 3 million words of written British and American English from different registers ranging from 1650 until 1990. Or take the CEEC, the Corpus of Early English Correspondence, which comprises personal letters written in the time period from 1403 to 1800 with rich biographical data facilitating historical sociolinguistic research. Once finished, it will include over 5 million words; https://www.projects.alc.manchester.ac.uk/archer/; https://www.helsinki.fi/en/researchgroups/varieng/corpus-of-early-english-correspondence
- **spoken and written English:** e. g. the BNC, British National Corpus, or its US counterpart COCA, the Corpus of Contemporary American English; or exclusively spoken English corpora like the SBCSAE, the Santa Barbara Corpus of Spoken American English; http://www.natcorp.ox.ac.uk/; https://www.english-corpora.org/coca/; https://www.linguistics.ucsb.edu/research/santa-barbara-corpus
- **different genres, applications and professional fields:** e. g. NOW, the 10 billion words corpus for News on the Web (from web-based newspapers and magazines since 2010) or corpora for learner varieties of English (written: ICLE, the International Corpus of Learner English; spoken: LINDSEI, the Louvain International Database of Spoken English Interlanguage); https://www.english-corpora.org/now/; https://uclouvain.be/en/research-institutes/ilc/cecl/icle.html; https://uclouvain.be/en/research-institutes/ilc/cecl/lindsei.html

Major corpora of English: Figure 9.1 provides a survey of those major corpora of English, both for Present-Day English and older periods (see the time line on the horizontal axis), which are accessible to the academic public and currently the most widely used corpora in English linguistics. They can be accessed either via browser-based interfaces or downloaded and processed with relevant concordance software or programming languages.

how to read figure 9.1
On the vertical axis, the corpora are arranged according to the nature of the varieties covered, starting at the bottom with corpora of learner varieties (e. g. with essays produced by advanced German or Spanish learners of English), moving upwards to corpora for spoken and written British and/or American English, then to corpora also covering other national varieties of English (like Irish English or New Zealand English),

and ending at the top with the only corpus so far (VOICE) exclusively compiled for English as Lingua Franca (ELF), offering transcripts of spoken English produced by non-native speakers of English using the language as a second or foreign language in international face-to-face interaction.

Diachronic corpora are represented by lines delimited by diamond symbols while synchronic corpora are represented by triangles. Smaller symbols represent corpora below 100 million words in size while bigger symbols are used for "mega-corpora" (100 + million words). Monitor corpora, i. e. dynamic corpora that grow constantly, are visualized by dashed lines.

Further corpora: Beyond those shown in figure 9.1, there exist further corpora. However, some are either too expensive for wide use in universities (Switchboard Corpus: about two million words of 2400 American telephone conversations recorded in the 1990s; discourse tagged, syntactically parsed, and in parts phonetically transcribed) or not publicly accessible (Bank of English: 450 million words of written British English and constantly growing; Longman-Lancaster Corpus: about 40 million

multimodal corpora

Figure 9.1:
Time line of historical and Present-Day Corpora of English

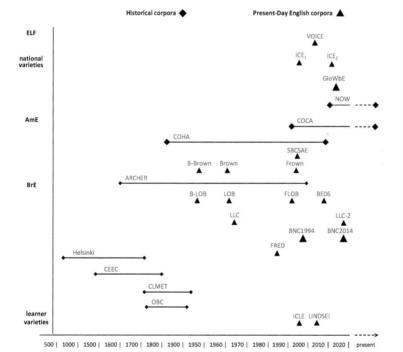

ARCHER = A Representative Corpus of Historical English Registers, 3.3 million
B-Brown = (30 years) Before Brown, 1 million
BE06 = British English 2006, 1 million
B-LOB = (30 years) Before LOB, 1 million
BNC = British National Corpus, 100 million
CEEC = Corpus of Early English Correspondence, 5.1 million
CLMET = Corpus of Late Modern English Texts, 15 million
COCA = Corpus of Contemporary American English, 520 million (+ 20 million/year)
COHA = Corpus of Historical American English, 400 million
FLOB = Freiburg-LOB Corpus, 1 million
FRED = Freiburg Corpus of English Dialects, 2.5 million

Frown = Freiburg-Brown Corpus, 1 million
GloWbE = Corpus of Global Web-Based English, 1.9 billion
ICE = International Corpus of English ($_1$ first generation, $_2$ second generation), 1 million each sub-corpus
ICLE = International Corpus of Learner English, 3.7 million
LINDSEI = The Louvain International Database of Spoken English Interlanguage, ~0.1 million each sub-corpus
LLC = London-Lund Corpus of Spoken British English, 0.5 million
LOB = Lancaster-Oslo-Bergen Corpus, 1 million
NOW = Corpus of News on the Web, 10.5 billion (+ ~2 billion/year)
OBC = Old Bailey Corpus, 14 million
SBCSAE = Santa Barbara Corpus of Spoken American English, 0.2 million
VOICE = Vienna-Oxford International Corpus of English, 1 million

words of written British and American English, different registers from the early 1900s to the 1980s). There is also a growing number of multimodal corpora (including audio and/or video files, in the latter case often annotated for non-verbal gestures, facial expressions, or gaze direction) and corpora with annotations for special purposes (like SPICE-Ireland, which is the Irish ICE component annotated for speech acts). More information on these and other corpora for research on the English language are available from the following regularly updated websites: https://www.english-corpora.org/, https:/bw-desc.de/, http://www.helsinki.fi/varieng/CoRD/corpora/index.html, or http://www.ldc.upenn.edu/. (For more online resources see chapter 11.)

Power of English corpus linguistics and the quantitative turn in numbers: The rise, power and pervasiveness of English corpus linguistics can be read off easily from the following figures as well. In early 2020, the number of publicly available corpora just for English has passed the threshold of 100 (excluding sub-corpora of the International Corpus of English (ICE) or the International Corpus of Learner English (ICLE), comprising some 20 billion words). To a substantial part, this includes web-based corpora (e. g. NOW – News on the Web), which are growing on a daily basis (so-called *monitor corpora*; compare also COCA in figure 9.1). Add to this, for example, about 2,000 billion words in Google Books or data which can constantly be compiled from the internet, notably from social media (e. g. Twitter). Further striking indicators of the corpus-linguistic and quantitative turn in linguistics are the following figures: 15 introductions to corpus linguistics have been published since the very first one in 1996, five relevant handbooks since 2009, five book series since 1998, six journals since 2002, and eight introductions to statistics for linguist(ic)s since 1998, four of them since 2015. Moreover, methodological textbooks have standardly come to include sections on corpus use. (A selection of relevant books is given at the end of this chapter.)

Corpus-literacy: This enormous advantage of practitioners of English linguistics over linguists working on other languages is also increasingly felt in the academic education of undergraduates and graduates in English linguistics. Here the standards and expectations concerning the use of huge corpora and other online datasets and authentic empirical resources are much higher than linguists studying other languages can currently afford them to be. Corpora and basic corpus-linguistic (combined with basic statistical) skills have become an integral part of the English linguistics curriculum throughout the world. The overall aim of turning students of linguistics into corpus-literates primarily involves the following aspects (for a more detailed account, see Kortmann 2021):

major ingredients
- knowledge of the availability of corpora and (other) web-based resources (see also Chapter 11 for this purpose);
- ability to choose the appropriate (part of a) corpus for the purpose, i. e. the concrete research question(s) and hypotheses(s), at hand;
- ability to choose the most appropriate research tools, and
- ability to keep at all times a critical distance to the data and the quantitative results of the corpus analysis (notably by applying statistical tests for significance).

What has loosely been called corpus-literacy here should not be taken too narrowly, though. Everything that undergraduates and graduates learn with regard to existing corpora applies just as much to the selection, critical evaluation, and analysis of any other body of data exploited in empirical studies. Just think of the massive digitization of present-day or historical English texts (e. g. Google Books, Early English Books Online) and the dominating presence of English on the internet, which give us immediate access to authentic use of all sorts of (native and non-native) varieties of English (written as well as spoken).

Crucial to note is also the following: corpus-literacy requires just as much a *profound* knowledge of English structure and use, and a solid grounding in linguistic theories as before the advent of the computer as a powerful research tool and the compilation of corpora. Without a theoretical framework that allows us to formulate pointed research questions and put our results in perspective, the mountains of examples and statistics we can extract from corpora are worthless. It would be a grave mistake to consider wading in data and pure number-crunching as a purpose in itself. Statistics will not solve theoretical, analytic, or taxonomic problems in linguistic practice. Any kind of corpus-based or corpus-driven research must be theoretically thought through, right from the very conception of the research questions to the interpretation and explanation of the research results.

Shaping the future of English linguistics: The corpus linguistic turn, spearheaded by English linguistics, is going to stay and will most likely become even stronger and continue to shape important strands and practices of research in English linguistics and beyond. Among them are the following (see e. g. Gries 2013, Kortmann 2021): Methodologically speaking, quantitative approaches, tools and techniques as known from the established quantitative sciences will become ever more important. Among other things, this is bound to lead to a higher degree of comparability, objectivity and, increasingly important in the truly quantitative sciences, replicability. (Replicability as a key criterion for good academic practice means that a given study can be repeated by the same or different researcher(s) with new data, and that the same or similar results are arrived at.)

Moreover, the availability of large and diverse corpora as well the increase in experimental studies in linguistics together with a highly sophisticated statistical apparatus have increasingly allowed for serious testing of a widely made claim: the claim that much of human cognition, and, in particular, language learning, processing, and production are probabilistic in nature. For anyone adopting this kind of perspective on language use and language acquisition, it is only natural to make use of the (statistical) research tools which have been created for the very purpose of measuring and testing probabilities. This leads on immediately to the major theoretical turn in early 21st century and to section 9.2.

9.2 | The usage-based turn

Most usage-based linguists these days subscribe to some version of Construction Grammar (CxG) and vice versa, and yet the two turns need to be kept separate. Neither are all usage-based linguists engaged in Construction Grammar, nor are all constructionist approaches usage-based. There can be no doubt, however, that the rise of Construction Grammar(s) has been the major driver of the usage-based turn.

9.2.1 | Usage-based linguistics

Background: What became evident with the rise of fields of linguistics like sociolinguistics and pragmatics in the second half of the 20th century was the increased interest in language use, i. e. in Saussure's *parole* or, more important given the dominance of generativist grammar models in linguistic theorizing at that time, Chomsky's *performance*. This trend was strengthened by the growing number of studies of spontaneous spoken language, online syntax and face-to-face interaction (e. g. in conversation analysis, interactional linguistics, interactional grammar) towards the end of the century. This trend culminated in the early 21st century with the advent of the umbrella term "usage-based", as in "the usage-based approach" or "usage-based linguistics", with Joan L. Bybee (e. g. 2006, 2010) as one of the major pioneers.

challenging structuralism and formalism

Experience is the heart of the matter: There is more behind this label, however, than simply a focus on language use as opposed to an interest in the language system (Saussure's *langue*) or the ideal native speaker's knowledge of his or her native language (Chomsky's *competence*). What is new and key in usage-based linguistics is that it is our **experience** when using language (i. e. processing, producing, storing, learning it) which also is responsible for the way in which we structure and organize our linguistic knowledge. In other words, linguistic knowledge crucially **emerges** from our linguistic interactions and meaning-making experiences in communication and our daily exposure to language. In a nutshell: language structures in our minds emerge from usage events. So, on the one hand, this immediately challenges any kind of strict division between language system and language use as known from structuralism and formalism. On the other hand, there is an important cognitive claim to usage-based linguistics, which is why there is an important cognitive and experimental element in usage-based research.

Radically anti-formalist cognitive claim: From the point of linguistic theorizing, this cognitive claim is radically anti-Chomskyan or, more generally, anti-formalist. Not only is there no such thing as an autonomous competence (see chapter 1.3.2), there is also no such thing as "a language module" in the first place, i. e. an autonomous cognitive system tailor-made for the purposes of learning and operating with language. Rather, the cognitive processes which are responsible for language are not language-specific but "domain-general", in that they are also responsible for other cognitive abilities (e. g. vision, pattern finding, or joint attention).

Usage-based linguistics therefore belongs to the radical pole of functionalism, its proponents downright rejecting the relevant key assumptions entertained in formalist linguistic theories (see chapter 1.3.3).

Frequency of use / probabilistic generalizations: From a methodological point of view, given the primacy of language experience, usage-based linguists operationalize the study of experience primarily in terms of frequency of occurrence. The more frequent a given experience is, the more powerful and lasting its impact on the cognitive system will be: it will become more entrenched (the relevant process is called *entrenchment*). In essence, then, taking this road to the study of experience means that knowing a language boils down to knowledge about distributions of previous language experiences. Whenever we encounter a given piece of language, we are engaging in probabilistic computation, basing the processing of this piece of language (phonologically, grammatically, semantically, pragmatically) on probability (i. e. likelihood) judgements rooted in our previous experience with sound patterns, words, expressions, phrases, constructions, or entire utterances. Thus new expressions or phrases are processed or produced against probabilistic generalizations over previous expressions or phrases. entrenchment

Frequency effects: One of the strongest arguments for using probabilities comes from the study of frequency effects in language. Numerous studies have shown that frequent words and constructions are learnt faster than infrequent ones, and that frequent combinations of phonemes, morphemes, phrases and larger structures are judged as more acceptable and processed more easily than infrequent combinations (cf. Behrens/Pfänder 2016). Frequency effects and probabilities, in general, have been shown to be operative in language perception and production, language acquisition, language change, language variation, and more (cf. Bod 2010). One reason why high-frequency forms are learnt more easily and quickly in language acquisition is that they may be protected from errors because they are so strongly entrenched. (Note that the relevant probabilistic mental processes do not operate consciously, but happen implicitly.) In language production, highly frequent words tend to be phonetically reduced (possibly leading to language change). In language change, high-frequency forms may, on the one hand, trigger change, but on the other hand resist change (just think of the highly stable inflections of the highly irregular, but at the same extremely frequently used verb *be* in English).

Token vs. type frequency effects: The two types of frequency that are usually distinguished (token frequency and type frequency) may well lead to different frequency effects. Almost everything said above concerning frequency of use related to token frequencies, i. e. the number of times a given word form is used. Token frequency effects are of key importance to entrenchment and, for example, to the conservation effect in language just mentioned with regard to English *be* (whose individual inflectional forms have a high token frequency, which prevents them from being 'forgotten' within a language community). In language acquisition, transparent strings that are used with high token frequency will remain in a child's language system as holistic chunks. Type frequency, on the other conservation efffect, language acquisition hand, is concerned with frequencies at a higher level of abstraction (e. g. the number of distinct lexemes which can take the prefix *un-*). In language acquisition, for example, a high type frequency promotes the formation of productive generalizations (e. g. as to potential fillers for the variable X in words following the schema *un-X*).

only indirect
evidence for cogni-
tive processes Corpora – no reliable shortcut to cognition: Given the importance of frequency effects in usage-based linguistics, it is not difficult to see why the analysis of large representative corpora of natural language has played a key role in this field. However, there is also an increasing awareness in the community that the analysis of purely observational (offline) corpus data alone must not be used as a shortcut to cognition. Corpus studies reveal no more than indirect evidence for cognitive processes, and may thus at most give rise to the formulation of research hypotheses concerning cognitive processes.

Experimental studies as complements: What is needed as a necessary complement to cognitive corpus linguistics are studies based on (online) experimental data, which have the potential to provide more direct evidence. In such online experiments, cognitive activity is being recorded and measured in real time while a linguistic task is being performed (e.g. via tracking the eye movements while an ambiguous sentence is being read). A multi-method design of studies conducted within the usage-based framework is thus indispensable for arriving at reliable results in trying to understand how language is experienced online. Indeed, since the early 2000s, linguistics has increasingly seen experimental studies confirming principled correlations between statistical generalizations over corpus data and subjects' experimental behaviours at various levels of language description (cf. Blumenthal-Dramé 2016b). For example, the token frequency of multi-morphemic language strings (which encompass complex words like *worthless* and phrases like *I don't know*) has been shown to correlate with subjects' processing behaviour in quite a number of different experimental settings. In particular, higher string frequencies lead to higher reading speed, higher accuracy rates in acceptability judgments, shorter phonetic durations in speech as well as higher recall abilities. Moreover, high string frequency promotes chunking, which refers to mental storage and processing of the relevant string as a single unit. Thus, a number of experiments indicate that high-frequency strings like *I don't know* are processed as if they were single words, whereas grammatically similar low-frequency strings like *you don't swim* are processed compositionally, i. e. by retrieving individual morphemes and putting them together on the basis of abstract knowledge (for a review, see Blumenthal-Dramé 2016a).

9.2.2 | The construction(al)ist turn: Construction Grammar

The most thriving branch of usage-based linguistics in the early 21st century has been usage-based Construction Grammar (CxG). As mentioned earlier, there exist other versions of CxG, not all of which are usage-based (cf. Goldberg/Suttle 2010). These other versions of CxG will play no role in the following account, though.

Basic assumptions: Usage-based CxG operates on the assumption that language consists of constructions only, which means: form-meaning pairings of different degrees of structural complexity, from the morpheme level upwards to syntax and possibly beyond. Importantly, CxG does not separate between semantics and pragmatics. All aspects of meaning and function, including knowledge of appropriate use as regards stylistic level (formal – informal), register, genre, etc., are part of the form-meaning pairings and stored by the language user.

form-meaning pairings

Reasons for construction status: According to usage-based CxG, a sequence (or: string) of language may be mentally represented as a constructional unit for two reasons:

- First, something about its form or meaning is not fully transparent. Just think of the phrase *all of a sudden*, which does not follow general rules of English grammar. Or take *that's how the cookie crumbles*, which is semantically non-compositional (i. e. an idiom; see chapter 6.1). Expressions which are non-transparent (or: idiosyncratic) have to be learnt by heart and mentally stored as chunks, because they cannot be constructed or understood based on general knowledge of a language. (This also explains why they tend to pose particular problems to non-native speakers of a language.) In other words, idiosyncratic strings have to be mentally treated like individual morphemes, which also represent constructions in the CxG framework.

non-transparent strings

- Second, the relevant string exhibits a high usage frequency and therefore constitutes an established linguistic chunk. A case in point is the sequence *I don't know*, which is likely to be stored and retrieved as a single unit by virtue of its frequency. As mentioned earlier, retrieval as a single unit is generally considered to be mentally less demanding than mentally combining morphemes. Therefore, the driving factor behind holistic storage is often assumed to be economy.

linguistic chunks

Schematic constructions: The concept of construction is not restricted to lexically specific sequences (like the ones mentioned so far), but also applies to so-called schemas. A schema is a more or less abstract pattern which captures the commonalities shared by similar sequences encountered in language use and, on this basis, imposes constraints on new sentences that can be constructed. An example of a semi-abstract schema is *GO X*, where X represents a variable (or: 'open slot') that can be filled with a restricted range of lexical fillers (e. g. *bananas, nuts, bonkers, crazy, mental, ...*), and where the capitals in *GO* are supposed to indicate that different forms of this verb can be used (e. g. *went, will go, is going, ...*). The degree of abstraction of a schema is thought to depend on the number and scope of variables (or: 'open slots') it contains. Among other things, the scope of a slot is determined by its type frequency (i. e. the number of distinct fillers that it covers). The most general schemas are those in which all elements are lexically unspecific. An example is the so-called resultative construction consisting of a noun phrase (NP), a verb, a second NP, and an adjective (as in *The waiter sliced the bananas thin*).

from lexically unspecific to lexically specific

Lexico-grammar: Central to usage-based grammar is a close relationship between lexicon and grammar or, more generally, between lexical and schematic knowledge. The language user has not acquired and does not store words and units of grammar separately, but patterns of grammar are immediately associated with particular lexical expressions. This includes what in functional 20th century approaches to grammar (especially the one by Halliday; see chapter 1.3.3) would have been called *lexico-grammar* (like learning the adjective *different* immediately together with the constructions *different from* N, *different to* N or *different than* N, and when to use which construction).

Adele Goldberg
Constructional hierarchy: Adele Goldberg, one of the pioneers of CxG, coined the slogan that language is "constructions all the way down" (Goldberg 2006). This slogan captures the view that constructions at different descriptive levels are not qualitatively different, but only differ gradually in terms of complexity (i. e. the number of morphemes included) and schematicity (broadly, the number of different ways in which a construction can be realized). This view contrasts sharply with formalist approaches, which consider that each level of language follows principles of its own and should therefore be kept conceptually distinct. It also leads to the usage-based proposal that the totality of our knowledge of language can be captured by a hierarchy whose nodes are constructions varying along the parameter of schematicity.

example: causal constructions
Macro-, meso-, micro-level constructions: In this hierarchy, the broadest generalizations are captured by so-called macro-level constructions situated at the top and inherited by all subordinate constructions. Specifications and sub-regularities are represented by lower-level nodes at various midpoints between those macro-level generalizations; at the bottom of the hierarchy we find lexically specific constructions (sometimes referred to as *constructs*). For example, the generalization that English adverbial subordinators (e. g. *while, if, because*) precede (rather than follow) the adverbial clause would be captured by a macro-level construction (SUBORDINATOR CLAUSE). The generalization that *because* can function as an adverbial subordinator would be represented by a construction at the slightly less schematic meso-constructional level (*because* CLAUSE, as in *because he had forgotten to water the flowers*). Although this use of *because* is in line with the relevant macro-level construction, it requires a representation of its own to specify the form and causal meaning of *because*. Even less schematic are micro-level constructions, which subsume small sets of similarly behaving constructs, such as rather innovative uses of *because* when followed by a noun, an adjective or a particle as in (1).

(1) a. People die of heart attacks and strokes because diabetes.
     b. Conversations with Clarence could be scary, because unscripted.
     c. I actually enjoy Dilbert, it's not high art but it hit a chord very precisely and effectively.
         Not that that speaks in any way to the … behaviour evident in this thread. Because wow.

Each of these uses, popular especially among younger speakers and in computer-mediated communication for expressing epistemic stance on the part of the speaker, can be captured by a micro-level construction of its own (*because* NOUN, *because* ADJECTIVE and *because* PARTICLE). This may ultimately give rise to the emergence of a sanctioning macro-level construction (*because* X) that also subsumes the *because* CLAUSE construction (cf. e. g. Bergs 2018).

Item-based language acquisition: Besides type and token frequency effects, there is at least one further strand of evidence which suggests that constructions are experience-based. An increasing number of empirical studies indicate that children's early language learning, in particular, is strongly experience-driven and item- (or: exemplar-)based. They start out from concrete examples they hear around them and gradually abstract over them (Ambridge/Lieven 2011). So again, this shows that construction grammarians deny the existence of innate abstract representations like rules and categories and thus are not members of the formalist nature camp, but clearly at home in the functionalist nurture camp.

CxG and language typology: There is also a typological dimension to usage-based CxG. This follows almost naturally from the dominant functionalist framework within which language typology has been practised for the last half century (in the tradition of Joseph Greenberg, Bernard Comrie, William Croft and others). When explaining the observable variation across the world's grammars, especially recurrent patterns of variation, functional typologists typically draw on explanations like

- motivated links between form and meaning (for instance, iconic principles being at work; see chapter 1.3.3),
- typical pressures in face-to-face interaction (ease of online production and processing), or
- factors facilitating the learning of a certain construction (in particular, type and token frequencies).

Thus, functionalist explanations do not postulate language-specific, innate principles, but build on domain-general cognitive abilities and how they are put to use in the processing of human every-day experience. Some typologists even frame their explanations of the observable cross-linguistic variation in terms of functional adaption of language forms to speakers' communicative or cognitive needs. All this shows that typologists and construction grammarians are brothers and sisters in soul, as it were. Little wonder that a leading typologist like William Croft was also among the pioneers of the construction(al)ist turn (cf. Croft 2001).

Promises of the usage-based research programme: Concerning the usage-based approach in linguistics, in general, it can safely be predicted that this research programme will continue to attract many young researchers, well-trained in multi-method approaches. This will remain one of the most fascinating questions to be explored in 21st century linguistics: Is the model of language processing and language storage propagated by probabilistic linguistics and usage-based linguistics cognitively realistic? Judging from what we have learnt so far, the least that can be said is that this model holds more promises in this regard than any of the preceding models suggested in linguistics since the mid-20th century.

brothers and sisters in soul

9.3 | The typological turn in World Englishes research

Nature of the typological inspiration: Since the early 2000s, there has been a growing number of typologically inspired studies of grammatical and morphological variation across World Englishes, English dialects and other non-standard varieties of English around the globe. This typological inspiration has crucially shaped methodology, the choice of language phenomena, criteria, measures and standards of cross-varietal comparison, as well as the way in which observable variation is described and interpreted. This includes (see Anderwald/Kortmann 2013):

impact of the turn
- the shift of focus towards systematic and detailed structural comparisons of varieties of English, especially of their grammars;
- questionnaire design for eliciting data which are comparable among the varieties of English and the world's languages;
- survey design, such as for electronic atlases (notably with WALS as a model, *The World Atlas of Language Structures*, https://wals.info/);
- choice of appropriate typological parameters (e. g. degree of syntheticity/analyticity, tense and aspect marking, negation marking, relative clause formation) for analysing large-scale variation in a single language (like English) and for feeding the results back into typological research;
- choice of typological metrics for individual phenomena (such as how to measure how synthetic or analytic a given language/variety is);
- searching for and formulating generalizations capturing the observable variation, for example in the fashion of absolute universals ("All languages have vowels") or implicational universals ("If a language has property X, it is highly likely it will also have property Y");
- applying typological hierarchies, which are higher-order generalizations across a number of lower-order generalizations, to data from varieties of English (e. g. the famous hierarchy for relative clauses, the so-called Noun Phrase Accessibility Hierarchy; see 9.3.3 below);
- using the insights from areal typology, which zooms in on cross-linguistic variation in a particular part of the world, to explain specific, most likely contact-induced, features of varieties of English spoken in that part of the world (e. g. in West Africa or Southeast Asia).

Topics of this section: In this section, a highly selective survey will be given of how research on structural variation in varieties of English and World Englishes has profited from methods and insights in language typology (for an instructive textbook, see Siemund 2013). The following issues will be addressed:

structure
- a bird's eye view on which (types of) varieties of English around the globe are most similar concerning the overall profile of their grammars, and which are most different (9.3.1);
- the most widespread features in the anglophone world (so-called *angloversals*, roughly corresponding to universals in language typology), the most distinctive features of individual types of English varieties (so-called *varioversals*; e. g. L1, or native speaker, varieties compared to L2, English as a Second Language, varieties) and of individual Eng-

lish-speaking world regions (so-called *areoversals*; e. g. British Isles, North America, Caribbean), down to a brief comparison of the dialects of Northern and Southern England (9.3.2);
- some general findings concerning the observable variation across the anglophone world in light of typological observations and generalizations on variation across the languages of the world (9.3.3).

Since the author has been one of major drivers of this approach for more than 20 years, the bulk of what will be presented here is based on his own research, reference works (notably Kortmann et al. 2004, Kortmann/Lunkenheimer 2012) and electronic research tools (notably Kortmann/Lunkenheimer 2013, www.ewave-atlas.org).

eWAVE 2.0 – the data set: The *electronic World Atlas of Variation in English* is an open-access online atlas. It includes ratings, examples and interactive maps for 235 morphological and syntactic features from 12 domains of grammar in 76 different varieties of English. The features covered are non-standard in the sense that they are not normally considered to form part of the 'common core' of (typically written) English, and would normally not be used in the English as Foreign Language (EFL) classroom. The varieties and the eight anglophone world regions in which they are spoken are listed in table 9.1. This table also shows the five different types of varieties in the atlas:
- **low- vs. high-contact L1 (ENL) varieties:** There are 31 L1 (native-speaker) varieties, which can be subdivided into 10 low-contact traditional L1 dialects (L1t), such as the dialect of East Anglia, and 21 high-contact L1 varieties (L1c). The latter is a rather heterogeneous group of varieties which includes transplanted L1 Englishes (like New Zealand English), Englishes that shifted from an L2 to an L1 (like Irish English), and standard varieties (colloquial American or British English);
- **L2 (ESL) varieties:** 19 varieties qualify as L2 (non-native) varieties of English, i. e. as indigenized non-native varieties that have a certain degree of prestige and normative status in their political communities (e. g. Maltese English or Kenyan English);
- **Pidgins and creoles:** 26 eWAVE varieties are English-based pidgins and creoles (P/C), i. e. varieties or languages with a pronounced contact history. Pidgins (such as Ghanaian Pidgin or Nigerian Pidgin) have been developed for communication between two groups who did not share the same language, typically in restricted domains of use, such as trade. They are typically nobody's native language. Creoles developed in settings where a non-English speaking community was under strong pressure to acquire and use some form of English, while access to L1 speakers of English was severely limited (e. g. in plantation settings). Many creoles (such as Jamaican Creole or Hawaiian Creole) have become the native language of the majority of the population (Kortmann/Lunkenheimer 2012). Schneider (2020: 28–29) offers a helpful discussion of the arguments as to whether or not to consider English-based pidgins and creoles as varieties of English, as is done by himself and in this section. Note that for pidgins and creoles, a very useful electronic and print companion atlas to eWAVE is APiCS, the

Atlas of Pidgin and Creole Structures (Michaelis et al. 2013a: http://apics-online.info; for the print version cf. Michaelis et al. 2013b).

What table 9.1 shows is that of the eight anglophone world regions, some are highly homogeneous concerning the dominant variety type (e. g. in the British Isles and in North America almost exclusively L1 varieties are spoken, whereas the Caribbean is dominated by Creoles), others are heterogeneous, with Africa as the most heterogeneous anglophone world

World region	Varieties
British Isles/ Europe (12)	**L1:** Orkney and Shetland E (O&SE), North of England (North), SW of England (SW), SE of England (SE), East Anglia (EA), Scottish E (ScE), Irish E (IrE), Welsh E (WelE), Manx E (ManxE), Channel Islands E (ChlsE) **L2:** Maltese E (MltE) **P/C:** British Creole (BrC)
North America (10)	**L1:** Newfoundland E (NfldE), Appalachian E (AppE), Ozark E (OzE), Southeast American Enclave dialects (SEAmE), Colloquial American E (CollAmE), Urban African American Vernacular E (UAAVE), Rural African American Vernacular E (RAAVE), Earlier African American Vernacular E (EAAVE) **L2:** Chicano E (ChcE) **P/C:** Gullah
Caribbean (13)	**L1:** Bahamian E (BahE) **L2:** Jamaican E (JamE) **P/C:** Jamaican C (JamC), Bahamian C (BahC), Barbadian C (Bajan), Belizean C (BelC), Trinidadian C (TrinC), Eastern Maroon C (EMarC), Sranan, Saramaccan (Saram), Guyanese C (GuyC), San Andrés C (SanAC), Vincentian C (VinC)
Africa (17)	**L1:** Liberian Settler E (LibSE), White South African E (WhSAfE), White Zimbabwean E (WhZimE) **L2:** Ghanaian E (GhE), Nigerian E (NigE), Cameroon E (CamE), Kenyan E (KenE), Tanzanian E (TznE), Ugandan E (UgE), Black South African E (BISAfE), Indian South African E (InSAfE), Cape Flats English (CFE) **P/C:** Ghanaian Pidgin (GhP), Nigerian Pidgin (NigP), Cameroon Pidgin (CamP), Krio, Vernacular Liberian E (VLibE)
Asia (8)	**L1:** Colloquial Singapore E (CollSgE), Philippines E (PhilE) **L2:** Indian E (IndE), Pakistan E (PakE), Sri Lanka E (SLkE), Hong Kong E (HKE), Malaysian E (MalE) **P/C:** Butler E (ButlE)
Australia (5)	**L1:** Aboriginal E (AbE), Australian E (AusE), Australian Vernacular E (AusVE) **P/C:** Torres Strait C (TorSC), Roper River C (RRC [Kriol])
Pacific (8)	**L1:** New Zealand E (NZE) **L2:** Colloquial Fiji E (CollFijiE), Acrolectal Fiji E (FijiE) **P/C:** Hawaiian C (HawC), Bislama (Bisl), Norfolk Island/Pitcairn E (Norf'k), Palmerston E (PalmE), Tok Pisin (TP)
Isolates/South Atlantic (3)	**L1:** St. Helena E (StHE), Tristan da Cunha E (TdCE), Falkland Islands E (FlkE)
Total 76	**WAVE 2.0**

Table 9.1: 76 L1 and L2 varieties, Pidgins and Creoles represented in e*WAVE* 2.0

region of all. The degree of homo- or heterogeneity in terms of variety type will play a role when we look at the number and nature of areally most distinctive features (see areoversals below). For more information on the varieties, their classification into different variety types, the complete feature set, methodology, rating system, informants, etc. see Kortmann/Lunkenheimer (2012: 1–6) or http://ewave-atlas.org/introduction.

9.3.1 | Typological profiles across the anglophone world

The global picture: In this section we will look at the major results that emerge when applying to the entire WAVE data set the so-called NeighborNet algorithm. This is a clustering method originally developed in bioinformatics, which has become an established method for representing and exploring variation in linguistics, too. The basic information needed when looking at the resulting networks of this algorithm is the following: Distances between any pair of varieties were measured by first determining the presence (i. e. attestedness) and absence of features (i. e. for how many features do the two varieties show shared presence or shared absence?), and then calculating the proportion of mismatches between the two varieties (i. e. where is a given feature present in one variety, but absent in the other?). So each variety was compared with each of the other 75 varieties in eWAVE, for each of the 235 morphological and syntactic features. The major clue for interpreting the resulting network in figure 9.2 is the following: The shorter the distance between any two varieties is, the more typologically similar they are, i. e. the higher is the number of co-presences and co-absences for the 235-member feature set. Vice versa, the longer the distance between any two varieties, the more typologically dissimilar they are.

The global network in figure 9.2 allows us to answer two key questions with regard to patterns of grammatical variation in the English-speaking world:

- Which major typological patterns emerge when examining morphological and syntactic variation across the anglophone world?
- Is it the typological signal (i. e. variety type) or the geographical signal (i. e. the anglophone world region) that is more powerful in explaining the observable patterns of variation?

Variety type more powerful than geography: Figure 9.2 reveals four major clusters, numbered counterclockwise Cluster 1–4, beginning with the bottom right cluster. Even more interestingly, it emerges that the morphosyntactic typological profiles of the 76 WAVE varieties pattern rather neatly according to variety type. Thus Cluster 1 consists almost exclusively of mother-tongue varieties of English (some high-contact (L1c) and all low-contact L1 varieties (L1t) in the sample), Cluster 2 of L2 of English, Cluster 3 of pidgins, creoles and creoloids (i. e. with dominantly creole features, but also with properties typical of L2 and L1c varieties), and Cluster 4 of pidgins and creoles, on the one hand, and the majority of high-contact L1 varieties, on the other hand. The major division between

measuring typological similarity/distance

key questions

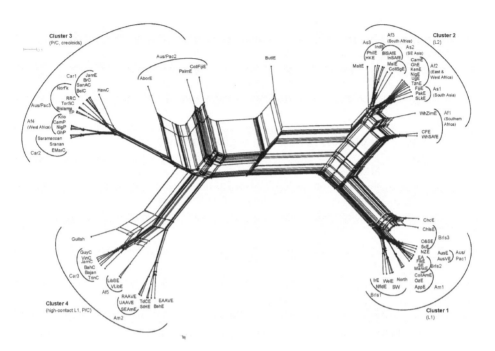

Figure 9.2:
eWAVE 2.0 Global
network for the
entire feature set

the four clusters is the one between the two right-hand and two left-hand sets of clusters: on the right L1 and L2 varieties and on the left all pidgins/creoles, the four creoloids (Australian Aboriginal English, Palmerston English in the Pacific, Colloquial Fiji English, Butler English in India), and the African, American and Caribbean high-contact L1 varieties.

When trying to explain the overall structure of this network, it becomes obvious at a glance that, even though geographical groupings are perceptible, they are clearly secondary to the cluster groupings according to variety type. The clustering in figure 9.2 thus convincingly shows that the socio-historical conditions under which varieties of English emerged and are currently used correlate with their overall morphological and syntactic profiles and have a far stronger impact on their overall typological profile than geography. For example, regardless where in the world L2 Englishes are spoken, their grammars tend to be more like each other than the grammars of any given L2 English variety and other variety types spoken in the same anglophone world region. Analogously, this applies to L1 Englishes and English-based pidgins and creoles.

9.3.2 | Angloversals, varioversals, areoversals

Three types of -versals: One of the hallmarks of language typology is the formulation of so-called *universals*, of which there exist different types (see e. g. Blumenthal/Kortmann 2013). Most relevant for large-scale comparison across the varieties of English in the anglophone world are relative or statistical universals, which capture pervasive tendencies and preferential patterns across the world's languages (or rather representative samples thereof). Against the eWAVE data set (in 76 varieties), three sets of such observational generalizations will be offered below:

- the most widespread of the 235 morphological and syntactic features across all 76 WAVE varieties (so-called *angloversals*);
- the most distinctive morphological and syntactic features of individual variety types (so-called *varioversals*);
- the most distinctive morphological and syntactic features of individual anglophone world regions (so-called *areoversals*).

Angloversals: The nature of angloversals is that they are relative or statistical, corresponding to relative/statistical universals in language typology (with an attestation rate threshold of 80 %). Table 9.2 lists and illustrates those six features which are attested in the largest number of varieties of English and English-based pidgins and creoles worldwide. The 'total' column shows the number of varieties in which each feature is attested, while the rightmost column shows the attestation rate (AR) out of a total of 76 WAVE varieties. The attestation rate of the top four features ranges between 89 % and 92 %. Perhaps the least expected of these is the second most widely attested angloversal, F34 (special forms or phrases for the second person plural pronoun like *youse/yinz/y'all* or *you guys/you ones/ you lot*). It should be noted that each of the angloversals in table 9.2 is widely used, or at the very least of medium-frequency use, in the individual WAVE varieties. Among those few varieties of English (about 10 %) where these angloversals are absent, two variety types figure prominently (see the column "absent in"): L2 varieties (e. g. Nigerian English, Ugandan English) and especially (Pacific) pidgins and creoles spoken in the Pacific world region.

relative anglo-versals (≥ 80 %)

No.	Feature	total	AR world-wide
F229	no inversion/no auxiliaries in main clause *yes/no* questions (*You get the point?*)	70	92 %
F34	forms or phrases for the second person plural pronoun other than *you* (e. g. *youse, yinz, y'all, you guys, yufela*)	69	91 %
F221	adverbs other than degree modifiers have the same form as adjectives (*Come quick!*)	69	91 %
F7	*me* instead of *I* in coordinate subjects (*me and my brother*)	68	89 %
F159	*never* as preverbal past tense negator ('didn't') (*She never came this morning*)	63	83 %
F154	multiple negation/negative concord (*He won't do no harm*)	61	80 %

Table 9.2: Angloversals (≥ 80 %)

Varioversals: In figure 9.2, we learnt that variety type is a much better predictor of the typological profile of varieties of English (that is, in terms of the overall profile of their grammars) than is the anglophone world region where they are spoken. Thus it is interesting to ask whether there are certain morphological and syntactic features which are particularly widespread, maybe even diagnostic of the individual variety types. This question can clearly be answered in the affirmative for all variety types. Below it will be illustrated only for the most distinctive varioversals in the 31 mother tongue (L1) and 19 second-language (L2) Englishes in the eWAVE data set; the corresponding list for pidgins and creoles is considerably longer.

metric: attestation
rate difference

The central metric used is the attestation rate (AR) of a given feature for a given variety type vis à vis the attestation rate of the same feature in all other varieties. This is called *the attestation rate difference* (= AR difference). For the first measure we will use a 60 % threshold, for the AR difference a 40 % threshold. In other words, a given feature qualifies as a highly distinctive (or: diagnostic) varioversal (a) if it is attested in at least 60 % of the varieties belonging to a certain variety type, and (b) if its attestation rate is at least 40 % higher than in all varieties belonging to other variety types.

L1 varioversals: For the 31 L1 varieties in eWAVE, these thresholds yield the four top diagnostic varioversals in table 9.3, which are sorted by AR difference (as in tables 9.4–9.6). This means that whenever you encounter one of these features in a given variety, it is very likely that this is an L1 variety:

No.	Feature	AR L1 (N= 31)	AR difference
F234	*like* as a focussing device (*Yeah, it was like 115 dollars*)	87 %	55 %
F28	use of *us* + NP in subject function (*Us kids used to play in the barn*)	90 %	50 %
F1	*she/her* used for inanimate referents (*She's a nice bike*)	80 %	47 %
F155	*ain't* as the negated form of *be* (*They're all in there, ain't they?*)	74 %	44 %

Low-contact vs. high-contact L1 varieties: We can also zoom in here and have a closer look at traditional (or: low-contact) L1 varieties (L1t), contrasting them with the relevant set of varioversals in high-contact L1 varieties (L1c). Listed in table 9.4 are top features whose presence is most characteristic of the 10 L1t varieties in eWAVE. All of these traditional dialects are spoken in the British Isles and North America. In the British Isles these are Orkney and Shetland English, Scottish English, the dialects

No.	Feature	AR L1t (N= 10)	AR L1c (N= 21)
F188	relativizer *at* (*This is the man at painted my house*)	70 %	14 %
F181	agreement sensitive to subject type (e. g. *birds sings* vs. *they sing*)	70 %	23 %
F35	forms or phrases for the second person singular pronoun other than *you* (e. g. *ye, thou, thee*)	60 %	18 %

of East Anglia, the North, the Southwest and Southeast of England; in North America these are Newfoundland English (as the only representative of English in Canada in eWAVE), Appalachian English, Ozark English, and the Southeast American enclave dialects.

Bordering on the top diagnostic L1t features are F2 'he/him used for inanimate referents' (e.g. *I bet thee cansn' climb he* [a tree]) and F232 'either order of objects in double (pronominal) object constructions' (e.g. *give it him – give him it*). For both features the AR difference is 37 %. Most of these five features can be considered as instances of what has been called *ornamental rule complexity*: they add morphological or syntactic contrasts, distinctions, or asymmetries without providing a communicative or functional bonus (see section 9.3.4 below). This is typical of varieties and languages whose speech communities are, relatively speaking, isolated, with little contact to speakers of other varieties or languages.

ornamental features add complexity

Within the eWAVE universe, 21 varieties of English have been classified as high-contact L1 (L1c) varieties. The top diagnostic features of this variety type, specifically in contrast with traditional L1 varieties, are listed in table 9.5.

high-contact L1 varieties

No.	Feature	AR L1c (N= 21)	AR L1t (N= 10)
F3	alternative forms/phrases for referential (non-dummy) it (*When you off the thing* ['switch it off'] *you press that one*; FijiE)	73 %	20 %
F66	indefinite article one/wan (*Longa Kildurk gotta one stumpy-tail horse.* 'At Kildurk there is a stumpy-tailed horse'; AbE)	59 %	10 %
F132	zero past tense forms of regular verbs (*My grandfather belong to Thomas Jefferson*; EAAVE)	59 %	10 %
F174	deletion of auxiliary be: before progressive (*Togba, you laughing*; LibSE)	64 %	20 %

Table 9.5: Top diagnostic varioversals of high-contact L1 varieties

Following up on the last of these features (F174), the following three deletion features are noteworthy, too. Although they are attested in only 45 % of all L1c varieties, they are completely absent in the traditional L1 varieties:

deletion, simplifying features

F176 deletion of copula be: *But this one Ø not your car.* (CollSgE)
before NPs

F177 deletion of copula be: *Ou mudder Ø crook, eh?*
before AdjPs 'Your mother's ill, isn't she?' (AbE)

F178 deletion of copula be: *Khatib Ø very near my place.* (CollSgE)
before locatives

These deletion features, like the majority of the top diagnostic L1c features in table 9.5, qualify as features that rather simplify the rule system of the relevant variety when judged against the system of (written) Standard English (more on this in section 9.3.3 below).

L2-simple features **L2 varieties:** Simplifying features of a different sort figure prominently among the top diagnostic features of the 19 L2 varieties in eWAVE. These are features facilitating second language acquisition by adults and thus known to be typical of (adult) L2 learners' varieties (so-called *L2 simple features*; see Szmrecsanyi and Kortmann 2012). Consider table 9.6.

No.	Feature	AR L2 (N= 19)	AR-dif- ference
F45	insertion of *it* where StE favours zero (*My old life I want to spend it in India*; IndE)	89 %	46 %
F209	addition of *to* where StE has bare infinitive (*She made me to go there*; IndSAfE)	72 %	41 %
F55	different count/mass noun distinctions resulting in use of plural for StE singular (*I have done a lot of researches in this area*; HKE)	94 %	40 %
F100	levelling between present perfect and simple past: PRS PRF for StE simple past (*It has been established hundreds of years ago*; GhE)	83 %	40 %
F84	comparative marking only with *than* (*It might be beautiful than those big ones*; BlSAfE)	61 %	39 %

Table 9.6: Top diagnostic varioversals of L2 varieties (AR ≥ 60 %, AR difference ≥ 40 %)

Areoversals: Even though the global picture in section 9.3.1 showed that geography is only of secondary importance compared with the explanatory potential of variety type, the geographical signal, i. e. in which part of the anglophone world a given variety of English is spoken, still matters. And so there is quite a large number of morphological and syntactic features which show distinct areal biases. An astonishing 40 % (some 90) of all 235 features in the eWAVE data set exhibit a noticeable areality in the sense that they are overrepresented in one of the anglophone world regions compared with the rest of the world. For 16 of these, the geographical signal is particularly strong: for them the attestation rate (AR) difference between the relevant anglophone world region and all others is higher than 60 % (e. g. F201 'for-based complementizers' is attested in 85 % of all 13 eWAVE varieties in the Caribbean whereas its attestation rate in all other 63 varieties in the eWAVE data set is 24 %). Table 9.7 lists seven diagnostic areoversals for North America and the Caribbean. These two world regions together account for some 80 % of the areoversals identified.

What table 9.7 shows is that the varieties of English (including pidgins and creoles) spoken in North America and the Caribbean are most strongly represented among the areoversals in the anglophone world. These two world regions together account for 60 % (56 features) of the more than 90 morphological and syntactic features with a pronounced geographical signal. Moreover, the areoversals of the Caribbean are generally very widely used in the respective speech communities.

language contact, substrate influence Areoversals in dominantly or exclusively non-L1 world regions (Caribbean, Africa, Pacific, Southeast Asia) are important in at least two respects. For one thing, they often tell us something about the importance

No	Feature	Region	Example from world region
F9	Benefactive "personal dative" construction	Am	*They found them an apartment* (ChcE)
F105	Completive/perfect *have/be* + *done* + *past participle*	Am	*He is done gone* (RAAVE)
F218	Affirmative *anymore* 'nowadays'	Am	*Anymore they have a hard time protecting things like that* (AppE)
F104	Completive/perfect *done*	Am, Car	*He done gone* (Barbadian C)
F114	*go*-based future markers	Car	*Mi go pik dem uhp* (VinC) 'I will pick them up'
F150	Serial verbs: *come* = 'movement towards'	Car	*Run come quick* (TrinC) 'Run to me quickly'
F201	*for*-based complementizers	Car	*I haad fi kraas di riba* (JamC) 'I had to cross the river'

Table 9.7: Diagnostic areoversals per anglophone world region (AR difference region – rest of world ≥ 60 %)

of language contact and what is known as substrate influence, i. e. influence from the indigenous local languages. For example, this applies to

- a range of properties of West African Pidgins: Nigerian Pidgin, for instance, has been clearly influenced by the structural properties of the languages of Southern Nigeria;
- deletion features in the varieties of English spoken in Asia (as this is typical of the relevant Southeast Asian languages); and
- a feature like F143 'Transitive verb suffix *-em/-im/-um*' (< *him*; like the verb form *bai-im* in *Mi bin bai-im kaikai* 'I bought-TRANS some food', Torres Strait Creole), which is almost uniquely found in the local languages of the Australia and Pacific region. It is here, for example, that insights from (areal) typology come in particularly useful in explaining areoversals observed in the relevant varieties of English.

Areoversals are a powerful indicator, too, of the direction in which the varieties of English in the individual anglophone world regions seem to be jointly moving. We know a lot about the emergence and development of post-colonial varieties of English, how strongly they have or have not emancipated themselves from the L1 models of British or American English, have or have not developed their own (endonormative) rules in grammar (see especially Schneider 2020). Beyond these observations and findings on individual varieties, areoversals offer us a clue concerning the development of distinctly pan-continental (or: world-regional) Englishes (e. g. in the development of a distinctly African, Pacific, or Southeast Asian English). With respect to such pan-continental developments, it is often illuminating to compare maps in eWAVE with maps in WALS (*World Atlas of Language Structures*).

emerging norms of world-regional Englishes

Areal patterns on a smaller scale: The geographical signal of features in the Anglophone world can be strengthened significantly when zooming in on sub-regions within the various world regions. Thus one can observe

North vs. South in British Isles

(bundles of) features in grammar separating, for example, the North from the South in the British Isles, South Asia from Southeast Asia, or West Africa from East and South(ern) Africa. For the British Isles (see e. g. Kortmann/Langstrof 2012; see also chapter 8.3.2) it turns out, for instance, that there are more distinctively Northern features than there are distinctively Southern features. Three features which are attested almost exclusively in the North and in at most one dialect of Southern England are the following:

- F69 '*yon/yonder* indicating remoteness' (attested in all five Northern varieties), as in *yon oil company* (Orkney & Shetland English) or *it's allus light in yandhar place* (Manx English);
- F102 '*be* as perfect auxiliary', as in *They're not left school yet* (Orkney & Shetland English);
- F124 '*want/need* + past participle', as in *That shirt wants washed* (North England dialects), *It needs cleaned out* (Irish English).

There are no morphological or syntactic features exclusively found among the Southern British Isles, but the following two have a distinctly Southern bias:

- F165 'invariant non-concord tag *innit*', as in *They had them in their hair, innit?* (Welsh English);
- F204 '*as what/than what* in comparative clauses', as in *It's harder than what you think it is* (East Anglian English).

There is a lot more evidence for claiming that in grammar, too, there is a North-South split, as is well-known for the accents of the British Isles (see Kortmann/Langstrof 2012).

9.3.3 | Generalizations from a typological perspective

Regularity and consistency: For widely documented properties of grammars of World Englishes and non-standard varieties of English, it turns out that there are quite a number of domains of grammar in which, compared with Standard English, these varieties exhibit a higher degree of regularity (e. g. fewer irregular verb forms) and consistency. An example of more consistency are analytic constructions, such as marking possession with the help of analytic forms in relative clauses: *what his/ what's* or *that his/that's* instead of the case-marked relative pronoun *whose*.

metrics for
World Englishes

Complexity: Analyticity as opposed to syntheticity has also played a major role in the revival of the so-called complexity debate in, above all, typological and creole linguistics since the early 2000s (see Kortmann and Schröter 2019). This debate focuses on the equi-complexity claim first formulated in the mid-twentieth century according to which the structures of all languages are, on balance, equally complex. According to this claim, on comparing the overall complexities of languages with each other, one will find a trade-off between individual subsystems of grammar, such that greater complexity in one domain will typically be balanced by less complexity (or: greater simplicity) in another structural domain of the same language. This debate triggered research on how to measure different kinds of morphological and syntactic complexity in World Englishes and non-standard varieties of English by using survey data like the ones in eWAVE along with natural language data, as compiled in the ICE, the International Corpus of English (see also Szmrecsanyi/Kortmann 2013). Two major outcomes of this line of research include the following:

- The higher the degree of language or dialect contact of a given variety is or was in its evolution, the lower will be the number of ornamentally complex features in this variety, i. e. the fewer features it will have that add contrasts or distinctions without providing a communicative or functional bonus. Thus, low-contact varieties, such as traditional L1 dialects, exhibit a significantly larger number of such features compared with high-contact L1 varieties, L2 varieties, and English-based pidgins and creoles. Recall that most of the diagnostic features for low-contact L1 varieties in table 9.4 above qualify as instances of ornamental rule complexity. By contrast, those features in tables 9.5 and 9.6 largely qualify as simplifying the English grammatical system (table 9.5 on high-contact L1 varioversals) and, from the learner's perspective, the life of the (adult) learner of the English language (table 9.6 on L2 varioversals). major findings

- L1 varieties (traditional dialects, in particular) exhibit a significantly higher degree of grammatical marking overall (measured in terms of text frequency), while L2 varieties exhibit considerably low(er) levels of grammatical marking.

Non-standard varieties in typological accounts of English: From a typological perspective, a number of points are worth noting when looking at variation in the grammars of non-standard varieties of English:

- **typologically rare features:** Several of the morphological and syntactic features which can be observed in the anglophone world are typologically very rare, or have at least only very rarely, if at all, been described in the typological literature. For example, in the dialects of Southwest England and in Newfoundland English the pronoun *it* is used only for mass nouns (e. g. in *Pass the bread–it's over there*), whereas count nouns take *he* (e. g. in *Pass the loaf–he's over there* or *My car, he's broken*) unless they refer to female humans, in which case *she* is used (see also chapter 8.3.2 on gender diffusion). Thus gender assignment via *he/she/it* depends on the semantics of the relevant noun to which the pronoun refers. Interestingly, however, what matters most for these gendered pronouns in the English Southwest is whether the relevant noun is a count noun or a mass noun (and not, as is normal in the world's languages, whether it is male-female-neuter or animate-inanimate). gendered pronouns

- **more well-behaved than Standard English:** In quite a number of cases, the grammars of non-standard varieties are typologically "more well-behaved" than Standard English, in that they follow a majority pattern in the world's languages or conform to cross-linguistic tendencies where Standard English does not. One example is the increasing loss of the (typologically rare) sharp division between the present perfect and simple past, which is so typical of British English.

relative clauses:
NP Accessibility
Hierarchy

An even more impressive example is the so-called gapping (or zero) strategy in relative clauses (as in *The book I read*). Here Standard English does not conform to one of the most famous typological hierarchies in language typology, the so-called Noun Phrase Accessibility Hierarchy (NPAH), whereas many non-standard varieties of English do. The NPAH was formulated specifically for relative clauses in the world's languages and looks like this:

subject > direct object > indirect object > oblique > genitive > object of comparison

It is an implicational hierarchy and as such captures elegantly several implicational universals. According to the NPAH, if a language can relativize any NP position further down on the hierarchy (i. e. to the right), it must also be able to relativize all positions higher up, that is, to the left of it. This constraint is supposed to apply to whatever relativization strategy a language employs. So if a language can, for example, use the gapping strategy for the direct object position (as in: *The book I read ___*), it must also be able to use this strategy for relativizing the subject position, which occupies the highest position in the NPAH. However, Standard English allows gapping only in object position (*The man ___ I saw*) and not in the subject position. By contrast, gapping in subject position is a pervasive feature of many non-standard varieties in the Anglophone world (in 60 % of the eWAVE varieties). Here is an example from a traditional dialect of Southwest England: *You know anybody ___ wants some, he'll sell them*. So gapping in relative clauses is another clear case where the grammars of non-standard varieties of English are typologically more well-behaved than Standard English is (cf. also Siemund 2013: 265–266).

- **different language type:** When looking at individual domains of grammar from a typological point of view, English would qualify as a different language type if the majority pattern found in the non-standard varieties was taken to represent "the" English language. Take relative clauses again: the dominant relativization strategy in non-standard varieties is the use of relative particles (*that* or *what*, as in *The man that/what came in...*), that is, uninflected relativizers (as opposed to case-marked relative pronouns like *who/whose/whom*). In typological accounts, however, English is typically classified as a language using predominantly relative pronouns.

Especially the last two points raise important methodological issues in language typology. One of them is this: for many less well-described languages, especially those lacking a literary tradition, the spoken varieties serve as the basis of typological observations, generalizations, and explanations. Shouldn't the same be done then, for reasons of consistency and comparability, for (extremely) well-described languages with a long literary tradition, too? The study of morphological and syntactic variation in World Englishes and non-standard varieties of English may thus serve as a corrective in language typology.

9.4 | The historical turn

Since the 1980s and 1990s, there has been a renewed interest in historical linguistics that has become ever stronger over the past two decades. Increasingly, new fields, theories and methodologies developed in (English) linguistics since the 1960s have been applied to historical data sets. Also recall the integrated approach to language variation outlined in the introduction to this chapter and what has been said concerning the triangulation of typology, diachrony and, for example, dialectology. Below, brief accounts will be given of several of the new developments in late 20th and early 21st century historical English linguistics.

Historical corpus linguistics: The availability of large present-day and historical corpora has also shaped English historical linguistics since the early 1990s. Essentially, three kinds of corpus-based historical studies can be distinguished (recall figure 9.1 for the corpora mentioned below):

- First of all, there are truly diachronic studies investigating language change in real time, i. e. in different periods of English, on the basis of, for example, the Helsinki Corpus (covering texts from Old to Early Modern English), the Corpus of Early English Correspondence (letters from the Early Modern English period only), or ARCHER (from 1650 onwards). On a much more modest scale, namely for a time slice of merely 30–60 years, diachronic studies are possible for 20th century English by contrasting the parallel 1930s, 1960s and 1990s corpora for British English (B-LOB, LOB and FLOB respectively) and American English (B-Brown, Brown and Frown, respectively) (see figure 9.1 above) separately or in comparison to each other. real-time vs. apparent-time studies

- Secondly, there are studies of language change in apparent time on the basis of huge present-day corpora like the old and new BNC (British National Corpus) or smaller corpora like ICE (International Corpus of English); what is crucial is that sociological, especially age, information is available on the informants whose English is stored in the corpus. Innovations (like the use of such auxiliary verbs as *gonna* or *wanna*) can be traced especially in the younger and youngest age groups, whereas properties of the language which are on the way of being lost are most frequently encountered in the speech of the older informants.

- Thirdly, comparative studies of different registers (or: genres) can be conducted on the basis of both present-day and historical corpora of English. By tracing and documenting the observable variation in different registers and age groups across different historical periods of English (and even within a single period), the historical linguist gains insights into the dynamics, i. e. the process, of language change. Especially important in this respect are the changing frequencies and distributions of a given word or construction across different registers in a corpus covering different periods of the language (or in separate period-specific historical corpora). Thus, it is possible to determine where (i. e. in which register) a given change of English started and how (as well as how quickly) it spread in the language.

Major results of this line of research include the following:

- Language change, especially in the grammar of English, takes place at different speeds in different registers (e. g. personal letters and diaries tend to be most progressive, newspapers and fiction less progressive, scientific texts most conservative).
- Over the past 300 years (at least), there has been a tendency in English, across all registers, towards a more 'oral' style, i. e. towards an increasing use of grammatical forms and constructions which are typical of (spontaneous) spoken language. Investigated for the second half of the 20th century with the help of newspaper corpora of British and American English, this has also been called the "colloquialization" of the norms of written English, reflecting the general social trend towards greater informality (cf. Mair 2006). This drift towards orality has made itself felt largely as a factor speeding up language change. Especially registers which are close to spontaneous spoken language (e. g. records of trials, personal letters or, these days, electronic communication) are likely to show the earliest and greatest influence from spoken language, which is, after all, the motor of language change.
- In the second half of the 20th century, the structure of British English has clearly been influenced by American English. Nevertheless, one can say that grammar changes in both standard varieties develop in the same direction, only at slightly different speeds. (For a more detailed discussion see chapter 8.2.)

In other respects, too, historical linguistics is back on the stage, partly with old (or perhaps rather eternal) questions in the study of language change, but largely with new questions, methods, hypotheses and explanations, and based on new types and quantities of data.

Grammaticalization: Since the 1980s and, especially, the 1990s, studies on the evolution of grammar have become extremely popular in modern historical linguistics, not just in the study of English. One special process of grammatical evolution in particular has attracted a large amount of attention: grammaticalization (cf. Hopper/Traugott 2003). This process takes as input formerly free (or: autonomous) lexical units (e. g. a noun or a verb) and yields as output a function word (e. g. an auxiliary or a preposition), which in turn may further grammaticalize into a bound morpheme (e. g. a suffix) or even disappear.

changes in meaning precede changes in form
In the course of this process, the relevant words or morphemes undergo a number of meaning- and form-related changes, with the former typically occurring earlier than the latter. Meaning-related changes usually involve the loss or 'bleaching' of the original concrete lexical meaning and the development of a more abstract, grammatical meaning, which then either replaces the original meaning or comes to be used as an addi-

tional meaning. Form-related changes include the merging of two words into one or, more generally, the loss of morphological and phonological complexity. All these types of change are observable in *gonna* < *going to* (see example (2) below). What is also typical in the course of the grammaticalization process is an increase in frequency of use, which is one reason for the popularity of corpus-based studies in grammaticalization research (and vice versa).

Going to construction > *gonna*: The examples in (2) are instructive for a better understanding of the development which led to the genesis of the future marker *gonna*. Still a full lexical motion verb in (2a) and possibly still in (2b) and (2c), *going to* has clearly lost its motion meaning in all examples from (2d) onwards. In (2e) it even combines with the motion verb *go* (*I'm going to go ...*), and in (2f) and (2 g) it no longer requires an animate subject. In (2h) and (2i), finally, it has additionally undergone a process of morphological and phonological erosion, i. e. from a two-word phrase with three syllables (*go-ing to*) to a single word with two syllables. The all-important step in this grammaticalization process has taken place in connection with examples as in (2b), where a *going-to* construction combines with an infinitival clause expressing purpose ('I am going in order to meet John'). For the evolution of the future marker *going to/ gonna*, it was necessary that example (2b) at some point in the history of English was no longer analysed as a complex sentence consisting of a main clause (*I'm going*) and a subordinate purpose clause (*to meet John*), but re-analysed as a simple sentence with *to* being part of the construction *be going to* (thus this typical stage in the grammaticalization process is called *reanalysis*).

(2) a. I'm going to London.
  b. I'm going to London to meet John.
  c. I'm going to meet John.
  d. I'm going to like John.
  e. I'm going to go to London (to meet John).
  f. There's going to be trouble.
  g. An earthquake is going to destroy that town.
  h. I'm gonna go to London.
  i. There's gonna be trouble.

Grammaticalization processes like this one and, in general, grammaticalization processes which involve expansion in terms of meaning and range of contexts in which the relevant item or construction can be used, have recently come to be discussed under the label of *grammatical constructionalization* (Traugott/Trousdale 2013; cf. also Gisborne/Patten 2011). This is one important aspect of the diachronic dimension of the construction(al)ist turn discussed in section 9.2. constructionalization

The fascinating thing about grammaticalization is that the relevant paths of change (e. g. the development of future time markers from a motion verb like *to go*, as for *gonna*, or from a verb of volition like *will*) can be observed for many unrelated languages in different parts of the world. In other words, for many grammatical categories the same sources the typological dimension tend to be tapped across languages, i. e. serve as starting-points of the evolution of grammatical markers. It is thus not surprising that grammaticalization was put on the agenda of modern historical linguistics by typologists.

the anglophone world   Especially against the background of section 9.3, one more point is interesting: when applying what we know about grammaticalization in Standard English(es) and in language typology to the study of grammaticalization in non-standard varieties of English (including English-based pidgins and creoles), there are no surprises. None of the relevant grammaticalization processes (Kortmann/Schneider 2011 investigated some 70 in the eWAVE database) runs against accounts of similar phenomena in other languages. Where differences compared with the evolution of grammar in Standard English(es) can be observed, these are most likely to be found in pidgins and creoles and due to language contact with indigenous languages spoken in the relevant part of the Anglophone world.

Historical semantics: Grammaticalization research has also played a central role in re-awakening the interest in historical semantics, i. e. the study of meaning change. After a period of approximately 50 years (from the 1930s until the early 1980s) during which historical semantics was no more than a sideline of historical linguistics, it was especially Elizabeth Closs Traugott who put historical semantics back on the research agenda of mainstream historical linguistics in the 1980s. Traugott was a pioneer in two respects (cf. Traugott/Dasher 2003). First of all, she demonstrated that many semantic changes are not random and unpredictable (as had been the dominant view in 20th century historical linguistics) but that regularities can indeed be found (not just in English, but often across many unrelated languages). All that is necessary is to look in the right place, namely grammar, more exactly at function words like auxiliaries, prepositions, conjunctions, or discourse markers. Secondly, she brought to bear pragmatic and cognitive concepts and theories in the study of meaning changes, especially those which accompany the evolution of grammatical markers. In other words, this paradigm shift in modern historical semantics is part of a more general cognitive and pragmatic re-orientation in the linguistic study of meaning since the 1970s (see chapters 6 and 7 respectively).

Regularities of semantic change: Concerning regularities of semantic change, it turns out that if we look at the evolution of grammatical markers from formerly lexical markers, several widespread tendencies can be identified. The link between grammar and regularity in the context of semantic change may best be sought in two facts. On the one hand, there are far fewer grammatical meanings than lexical meanings; there is simply much more that can be talked about in the world than there is in grammar. On the other hand, within a given grammatical domain (e. g. tense or mood) there is far less semantic variation than in individual domains of lexical items (e. g. verbs of motion, hearing, understanding). Put differently, within a given domain relatively few grammatical markers tend to vary along relatively few, or at least fewer, dimensions.

From anteriority to causality: What exactly are the regularities that can be observed in the evolution of grammar? One widespread tendency in the world's languages is the change from markers of anteriority (meaning 'after', 'since') to markers of causality. Take, for example, the adverbial subordinator *since*, which has two meanings: the original temporal one and a causal meaning, as in *Since no one seems to be coming, I'll have to do it all by myself*, which developed later in the history of English.

Further changes from a temporal source domain: Other recurrently observable paths of semantic change in the domain of originally temporal adverbial connectives include the following:

(3) a. simultaneity 'while' > contrast 'whereas' or concession 'although'
(e. g. *while*, German *während* and *indessen*, Spanish *mientras que*, Italian *mentre*)
b. posteriority 'before' > preference 'rather than'
(e. g. *before, rather than* < Old English *(h)rathe* 'quickly, immediately', German *bevor* and *ehe*, Spanish *antes (de) que*, Italian *piuttosto che, prima che*)

Unidirectional paths of semantic change: For other grammatical domains, too (e. g. modal verbs or future time markers, as mentioned in connection with the grammaticalization of *be going to*), relevant grammatical markers tend to develop from a restricted set of lexical sources, and this typically follows only a limited number of paths of semantic change. There is also a general path of development which modal auxiliaries (e. g. *can, may, must, will, shall*) seem to have taken in the course of their evolution from formerly full verbs to the highly grammaticalized verbs they are now. They all developed deontic meanings first and epistemic meanings later. Deontic modality is concerned with obligation and permission while epistemic modality expresses a speaker's belief or knowledge. Thus, it can be documented that *must* in its obligation, i. e. deontic, meaning, as in *You must be back by ten*, developed first and *must* in its belief or conclusion meaning, as in *He left at six, so he must almost be there*, developed later. These and many more semantic changes accompanying grammaticalization all seem to have in common that they are unidirectional. Changes in the reverse direction, e. g. from epistemic to deontic meanings or from causal to temporal markers, are not (or only very rarely) documented. This puts us in a situation where we can now formulate constraints on semantic change, limits within which semantic change is possible.

modal meanings: deontic > epistemic

Conventionalization of conversational implicatures: These widespread tendencies seem to be subcases of at least one of two more general tendencies in semantic change: (a) the change from concrete to abstract, and (b) the development from less inferential to more inferential meanings, i. e. to meanings based in the beliefs and attitudes of the language users. The former development is basically triggered by metaphor. The latter essentially involves a mechanism which was indirectly introduced earlier by means of the slogan "Today's semantics was yesterday's pragmatics" and is known as conventionalization of conversational implicatures (see chapter 7.4).

yesterday's pragmatics > today's semantics

What is behind this tongue twister is simply this: If we process words or utterances in a given context, most of us have the tendency to 'read more' into what has been literally said, since often speakers and writers tend to mean more than what they say. Now, if over time an ever-increasing part of the language community 'reads more' into the meaning of a lexical item, thus giving up the previously existing contextual restrictions on this enriched interpretation, then what formerly was pragmatically inferred (alternatively called *conversational implicatures* or *invited inferences*) may become part of semantics. Take again the cross-linguistically observable tendency for temporal connectives marking anteriority, such as *since*, to acquire an additional and, possibly at a later stage, exclusive sense of causality. This was possible because these connectives were given a causal interpretation in an increasing number of contexts by an increasing number of language users. Starting points for this semantic change were contexts as in (4a), where the connective can be given a causal interpretation beyond the basic temporal one:

(4) a. Since his wife left him, George has been a changed man.
     b. Since no one seems to be coming, I'll have to do it all by myself.

Pragmatic ambiguity > semantic ambiguity: At this stage, the ambiguity between the temporal and the causal reading is still a pragmatic one; it would be no contradiction to utter (4a) and yet to add "But I don't want to say that this is because his wife left him". The situation is different as soon as *since* can be found in contexts where it can only have a causal meaning, i. e. where the temporal reading is impossible, as in (4b). What formerly was a pragmatic ambiguity has now turned into a semantic ambiguity of *since*. There are contexts in which from now on *since* may have solely a causal meaning. In other words, we have a completed semantic change and in a dictionary *since* now needs to be listed with two meanings.

Metaphor – subjectification: Our 'effort after meaning' when processing language in context is one aspect of what Traugott has called *subjectification*, i. e. the pervasive tendency for grounding meanings in the speaker's subjective state of belief and attitude. This tendency gives us a powerful cognitive motivation for a wide range of very different semantic changes. Interestingly, the two central mechanisms underlying the semantic changes accompanying grammaticalization, i. e. metaphor and subjectification, seem to take effect in sequence. If a word has undergone more than one meaning change in its history, then the change from a less to a more inferential (or: more subjective, speaker-based) meaning will typically be found to have taken effect after, or at least never before, a change from concrete to abstract has taken place.

mental and speech act verbs   Traugott also found that both regularities, subjectification as well as the change from concrete to abstract meanings, can be shown to underlie various domains of lexical items, too. Cases in point are mental verbs (e. g. *deduce, suppose, intend, understand, see, hold, grasp*) and speech act verbs, i. e. verbs used for describing different communicative acts

(e. g. *admit, command, demand, promise, assert, insist, offer, suggest*). If we look at their etymology and the changes they have undergone before acquiring their present-day senses, many of them can plausibly be argued to have followed these two pathways of semantic change. Ultimately, then, historical semantics in the early 21st century cannot only make predictions for regularities in the evolution of grammatical meanings, but also for regularities that may be valid in larger areas of the lexical vocabulary. (See also Brinton/Traugott 2005 on lexicalization; for recent surveys on issues and methods in English historical semantics, see Allan/Robinson 2012 and Kay/Allan 2015.)

Cognitive-pragmatic paradigm shift: This is largely a success of a cognitive-pragmatic paradigm shift in this field. Formerly, semantic change was primarily viewed as opening up the possibility for learning more about habits and attitudes in a particular society and culture. These days the study of semantic change is increasingly regarded as one way of learning more about human cognition, about the way in which people experience and make sense of the world around them and structure their knowledge. This is, for example, why such basic cognitive mechanisms like metaphor and 'reading more' into word and utterance meanings, i. e. invited inferences, have played an important role in recent decades. This also explains why contemporary historical semantics has a strong cross-linguistic orientation: if semantic changes can be motivated by a similar cognitive wiring of people, then it is only to be expected that many semantic changes can be observed in more than one language, even in languages whose speakers do not share the same cultural background. In addition, comparable changes in one language may provide the missing link(s) for semantic changes observable in another language.

Historical pragmatics: From modern historical semantics it is but a small step to historical pragmatics. In fact, given what was said above concerning the slogan "Today's semantics was yesterday's pragmatics", these two fields clearly blend into each other. However, the scope of historical pragmatics, an approach that was put on the map of historical, more exactly English historical, linguistics in the 1990s, is much more difficult to define (cf. Jucker 1995, Jucker/Taavitsainen 2010). Of all new approaches to historical linguistics emerging in the late 20th century, it is clearly the one that is least focussed and has the most heterogeneous research agenda. The reason for this is the extremely wide definition of pragmatics adopted by the growing community of historical pragmaticists, namely pragmatics as the study of language use and the relationship between language and its users. This definition, which stands in the tradition of early 20th century semiotics (see chapter 1.3.1), is much wider than the one adopted in this book, where pragmatics is defined as the study of *meaning in context* (and thus as a sister discipline of semantics, which is concerned with the study of *meaning out of context*; see chapter 7.1).

wide definition, wide scope

Essentially, then, historical pragmatics starts out from (a) the vast and varied range of topics addressing language in use and (b) the theoretical and methodological apparatus developed in modern pragmatics (see chapter 7), and applies all this to language use in past periods of English.

Besides the pragmatic approach to semantic change pioneered by Traugott, this includes, among other things, a study of changes in the communicative needs due to, for example, societal changes in different historical periods and how this is reflected in the structure and use of older stages of English:

key questions

- Which role, for instance, did politeness play and how did it influence the coding of speech acts like requesting, ordering, promising, or complimenting?
- In what ways have discourse conventions (and norms) changed in the course of time (both in writing and oral communication)? This may include the study of genre conventions in, for example, private letters, political pamphlets or texts for instruction (e. g. cooking recipes). This may require exploring genre-specific constraints on the extent and nature of code-switching (e. g. switching in the same text between English and French or Latin), or the way in which trials in the law court were conducted (e. g. who was allowed to say what to whom and when?) and recorded.

the philological
tradition of
linguistics

To some extent, historical pragmatics continues the philological tradition of linguistics by studying historical texts and data in terms of the context of their genesis. Why and for what purpose was a given text drafted, by whom and for whom (i. e. which interests may have guided the author, for example in using particular formulations), what was the social and personal relationship between addresser and addressee (e. g. same rank, different rank; formal – informal), where was it produced, where was it read? In certain respects, historical pragmatics also shares interests with the last of the new approaches introduced in late 20th century historical linguistics presented here. Prominent among these is the basic assumption that the use and change of language reflects (changes in) societal structure and the nature of social relations between addresser and addressee.

Historical sociolinguistics (or: socio-historical linguistics) is an offspring of historical corpus linguistics, on the one hand, and modern sociolinguistics, on the other (more exactly, of variationist sociolinguistics as pioneered by the American William Labov ever since the early 1960s). Since the Labovian approach to the study of language variation and change was discussed in chapters 8.4 and 8.6, this ingredient of historical sociolinguistics will be addressed only in very global terms here. The basic challenge in historical sociolinguistics, which was put on the map of English linguistics by the Helsinki Research Unit for Variation and Change in English in the 1990s (cf. Nevalainen/Raumolin-Brunberg 2003), is how to transfer to historical linguistics the sociolinguistic methods designed for the study of present-day variation. Some other differences between historical and modern sociolinguistics are summarized in table 9.8.

Corpus of Early English Correspondence: Among the greatest challenges of historical sociolinguistics as practised by the Helsinki research group is the lack of social representativeness in the Corpus of Early English Correspondence (5.1 million words, with texts from 1403 until 1800), which is

	modern sociolinguistics	historical sociolinguistics
primary object of investigation	phonological variation and/or change in Present-Day English	grammatical variation and/or change in past periods of English
research material	spoken language all people authentic speech; observation, elicitation, evaluation	written language only literate people (upper ranks, men) randomly preserved texts
social context	society familiar, much data available	social structure to be reconstructed on the basis of historical research
standardization	significant element	significance varies
associated discipline	sociology	social history
length and result of the change	unknown	known

Table 9.8:
Modern vs. historical sociolinguistics

primarily used for their studies. For example, since (by necessity) only written texts are included in this corpus, the language of the lower classes can hardly be represented. The vast majority of the population in the 15th, 16th and 17th century periods was illiterate. At the bottom of this social hierarchy of literacy at that time of English history, we also find women, since only few women were literate.

Within these limits imposed by the nature of the corpus data, this approach has nevertheless yielded a number of interesting insights into morphological and, especially, syntactic change in Late Middle and Early Modern English. This includes the processes and steps leading to the rise of Standard English and the different degrees of conservativeness or progressiveness observable for members of different social classes. For instance, it seems to have been especially the upper gentry who played a leading role in the spread of many syntactic changes. Moreover, in the 16th and 17th century, the majority of morphological and syntactic features that were to become part of Standard English spread from the London region to the rest of the country.

major insights

Traditional vs. modern historical linguistics: The re-awakened interest in language change and the innovative approaches sketched above may, as a convenient shorthand, be lumped together under the heading of *modern historical linguistics*. It is important to note, however, that traditional approaches to the study of language change have not been given up in contemporary linguistics. Neither have they become useless nor are they looked down upon. It is simply the case that additional approaches have been developed over the last few decades which the majority of the young(er) generation of historical linguists has adopted. Yet the dialogue with 19th century historical linguistics is continuing. The most important differences between modern and traditional historical linguistics as regards research foci and methodology are listed on the following page:

traditional historical linguistics	modern historical linguistics
focus on documenting the facts of language change in past periods of a language or language family	focus on language change in progress, illuminating why and how language changes (cause/motivation and spread)
focus on internal factors of language change	focus on external (e. g. social) factors; variation in synchrony as a key to variation in diachrony; language change begins as variation
focus on language structure and language system	focus on language use and user (e. g. communicative strategies, functional needs, pragmatic inferences); discourse shapes grammar; speakers change language
focus on phonology and morphology (much less so on syntax and semantics)	phonology still going strong, but greatly increased interest in syntax and semantics as well as pragmatics
qualitative	qualitative and quantitative (including a more rigorous methodology)
written language only	written and spoken language

Table 9.9:
Traditional vs.
modern historical
linguistics

19th century continuities: Despite these differences, there also exist important continuities (or rather: rediscoveries of – partly mainstream, partly non-mainstream – 19th century forerunners). Among these continuities, the following figure prominently:

- the focus on language use and the language user (e. g. in the famous work by the neogrammarian Hermann Paul);
- functional and cognitive approaches (e. g. in 19th century work on historical syntax and historical semantics);
- learning about language change via the study of variation in language synchrony (which was the key motivation for the beginning of dialectology in the 19th century);
- the search for regularities (e. g. in phonology, semantic change, grammaticalization);
- a return to the philological roots of linguistics due to the renewed interest in historical text linguistics, historical discourse analysis, and the study of genre traditions;
- especially within the functionalist paradigm, an increasing acknowledgement of the parallelism between language structures and biological organisms. This includes, for example, the idea that *functional adaptation* is the central shaping principle responsible both for the development of organisms in evolution and for change of the language system due to the pressures of language use. Biology, in general, seems to be considered by an increasing number of linguists, functionalists as well as formalists, as the new kind of "guiding discipline" (German *Leitdisziplin*) of linguistics. This is a situation familiar from the mid-19th century, when there was an interplay between Darwin's theory of evolution of species and, for example, the family-tree model in historical-comparative linguistics (see chapters 1.2 and 5.1).

Conclusion and outlook: Modern theories, findings, technologies and methods that developed in or emerged from various branches of synchronic linguistics since the 1960s have found their way into current historical linguistics. As a result, completely new questions along with old questions critically reconsidered in light of late 20th and early 21st century linguistics can now be addressed with the help of large, partly newly compiled bodies of historical data.

In wrapping up this section, the following can therefore be stated (see figure 9.3): In the course of the first half of the 20th century, the linguistics pendulum had swung (almost) all the way from the exclusive 19th century interest in historical and diachronic developments in language(s) to the primary interest in language synchrony. In the early 21st century, it very much looks as if the pendulum is well on its way to assuming a balanced position in the middle between the synchronic and diachronic poles in linguistics.

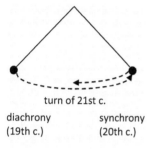

turn of 21st c.

diachrony   synchrony
(19th c.)   (20th c.)

Figure 9.3: From diachrony to
synchrony ... and back again

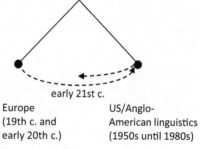

early 21st c.

Europe   US/Anglo-
(19th c. and   American linguistics
early 20th c.) (1950s until 1980s)

Figure 9.4: Shifting centres of gravity in
linguistics

In conclusion to this chapter overall, we can stick with the image of the pendulum (see figure 9.4). We can observe that the centre of gravity of linguistics, which had clearly shifted from Europe (where it was firmly located until well into the first half of the 20th century) to the United States (since the 1940s or 1950s), has clearly swung back to Europe, in English linguistics even more so than in general linguistics. This is partly due to the renewed interest in historical linguistics, but also due to a strengthening of formalist and, above all, functionalist and usage-based linguistics on a firm empirical footing in Europe. Branches like corpus linguistics, usage-based linguistics, Construction Grammar, language typology, dialect syntax, World Englishes, historical sociolinguistics, or historical pragmatics are going strong in Europe, in particular, and some of these fields were put on the map of linguistics by European linguists in the first place.

Pluralism: Linguistics in the early 21st century has truly found its place as a respected autonomous academic discipline. It no longer needs to fight for recognition and acknowledgement, and is now well on its way to become an equally respected science among the quantitative sciences. It is a very lively field, characterized by a much higher degree of pluralism than ever before. Different from the 19th and 20th centuries, there is no single school of thought, research tradition, theoretical paradigm – whatever we may want to call it – that can claim to dominate linguistic theorizing and practice today. No single research tradition determines the research agenda and claims to hold the key to "the truth", or even to judging what does or does not count as an important research contribution in the field. The pluralism characteristic of present-day linguistics extends to topics, theories, and methods alike, and may (but only at times) lead to disagreement on the question of what constitutes the core of the discipline.

There is also pluralism concerning the question of whether linguistics is part of the humanities (e. g. teaming up with the philologies and philosophy), of the social sciences (especially with sociology and anthropology as close partners), of the cognitive sciences (in tandem with cognitive psychology, in particular), or of the (natural) and largely quantitative sciences (e. g. linguistics as a branch of biology, in close cooperation with genetics and the neurosciences). Not just individual linguists, even entire schools of thought and branches of linguistics hold different views on this rather fundamental question of self-definition. And yet they happily co-exist and see themselves rather as pursuing different, equally justified and relevant research goals, all of which in their own way contribute to illuminating the nature of language, individual (sets of) languages, and the way they are used in spoken and written communication.

This high degree of pluralism is not only a blessing. Especially for beginning, but even for advanced students of linguistics, it makes life quite complicated. This is why one of the major aims of the present book was to highlight what the majority of linguists working in English and Linguistics departments consider to be the core branches of linguistics, and to give guidance concerning the essentials and, in a modest way, the state of the art within each of these branches. Beyond these essentials, there lies a fascinating universe of varieties, languages and areas of linguistics. This final chapter of the book could offer barely more than a glimpse of this universe. Large parts of it are still waiting to be discovered and explored by anyone thinking of pursuing a professional career in or related to linguistics.

The essentials of the discipline presented in this book will put you in the position to better understand and judge the continuities and changes in the future developments of 21st century linguistics. In the best of all worlds, they will make you want to become a part of the future of (English) linguistics yourself!

Checklist 21st Century Turns & Trends – key terms and concepts

angloversals
apparent-time ↔ real-time
   studies
areoversals
complexity
consistency
construct
construction grammar (CxG)
constructional hierarchy
constructionalization
corpora
corpus linguistics
creoles
deletion
entrenchment
frequency (type, token)
frequency effects (type, token)
functional adaptation
gradient
grammaticalization
hierarchy (constructional,
   typological)
historical pragmatics

historical semantics
historical sociolinguistics
   (or: socio-historical
   linguistics)
lexico-grammar
modern historical linguistics
morphology
pidgins
probabilistic linguistics
reanalysis
regularity
statistics
syntax
system-based linguistics ↔
   usage-based linguistics
typology (areal, functional)
universals
usage-based linguistics
varieties (L1, L2)
varioversals
-versals (angloversals,
   areoversals, varioversals)

Exercises

---

1. Associate each of the following statements with one of the branches of modern historical linguistics presented in section 9.4:
   a) The much-increased use of contractions like *isn't, haven't* or *didn't* in newspaper language is a clear indicator of the colloquialization of the norms of written English.
   b) This is a typical 18th century way of asking someone a big favour.
   c) The upper gentry was responsible for spreading quite a number of grammatical innovations during the Early Modern English period.
   d) Verbs of motion belong to the typical sources of future time markers in the languages of the world.
   e) Euphemism is often responsible for pejoration (e. g. *smell* meaning 'bad smell, odour' in "What's this smell in here?").

2. Which corpus in each set does not belong there?

a.	LOB	FLOB	BNC	COCA	LLC
b.	Brown	CEEC	Helsinki	ARCHER	CLMET
c.	ICLE	FRED	LLC	Frown	LOB
d.	SBCSAE	COHA	B-Brown	OBC	Frown
e.	FRED	ICLE	Frown	COCA	BNC

3. Which corpus could be used for which research question? Where possible, name more than one corpus you would use for answering the following research questions:

a) What can we say about the rise and fall of modal verbs in 20th century American English?

b) Is it possible to identify colloquialization tendencies as early as in Early Modern English letter writing?

c) Do advanced learners of English with a Slavic mother tongue have the same problems with article usage as advanced learners of English with Italian or Spanish as their first language?

d) Are there differences in the use of tag questions in British English vis-à-vis African and Southeast Asian Englishes?

e) How has the use of the passive in newspaper language developed from the 17th century until today?

4. Why are the two following sentences considered as prototypical examples of constructions, respectively?

a) He is driving me nuts.

b) Just because the data satisfy expectations does not mean they are correct.

5. Find the mistake in each of the following statements and correct it.

a) High-contact L1 varieties are characterized by a large number of complexifying (or: ornamental) features.

b) Angloversals in World Englishes research correspond to absolute universals in language typology.

c) Africa is the best example of a homogeneous anglophone world region.

d) British Creole is typologically highly dissimilar from Jamaican Creole.

e) African American Englishes can hardly be argued to be structurally similar to creoles.

f) The geographical signal for sub-regions of the Anglophone world regions is weaker than it is for the world regions overall.

g) Pidgins and creoles are placed at opposite ends of a continuum mapping the complexity of grammars.

h) Deletion of copula *be* (as in *But this one not your car*) is completely absent in L1c varieties of English.

6. Which of the following examples from the traditional dialects of England show features that lead to more regularity, consistency, or simplification in English grammar compared with (written) Standard English, and in what way do they do so?
a) I seen one the other day.
b) But they make dustbins big enough now, in't it?
c) That shirt wants washed.
d) Give us a kiss.
e) The girl what called me yesterday.
f) Hope we get it organized as quick as we can.
g) They just work their farm theirselves.
h) My car, he's broken.

7.
a) What distinguishes invited inferencing from metaphorization?
b) What do invited inferencing, metaphorization and subjectification have in common?

8. Which of the following statements are true, which are false?
a) Saussure's *parole* broadly corresponds to Chomsky's *performance*, but Saussure's *langue* does not correspond to Chomsky's *competence*.
b) The use of large electronic corpora is a standard method in formalist linguistics.
c) Regularities in semantic change can be observed especially in grammaticalization.
d) Historical sociolinguistics includes the study of formerly pragmatic ambiguities turning into semantic ambiguities.
e) It is a key assumption in usage-based linguistics that our language faculty is probabilistic.
f) The Old Bailey Corpus offers us a window to spoken language in the Late Modern English period.
g) In all written genres, language change operates at the same speed.
h) There is a pronounced tendency across the world's spontaneous spoken varieties to re-establish a special form or phrase for the second person plural.
i) In Construction Grammar, only form-meaning pairings from the phrasal level onwards count as a construction.
j) A typical frequency effect is the conservation of irregular word forms of highly frequent lexemes.

9. Based on Bybee (2013: chapters 4.1–4.3), sketch the key tenets of exemplar-based approaches to language and give two reasons why they are readily compatible with usage-based Construction Grammar. Advanced

10. In which ways do Construction Grammar and the usage-based approach challenge established key assumptions, distinctions and principles of structuralism and generativism?

11. Find out three ways in which frequency of use influences language change.

12. Based on the following interview with Elizabeth Traugott, explain the difference between lexicalization, grammaticalization, and constructionalization.

2014. "Grammaticalization: An interview with Elizabeth Closs Traugott." *Revista Virtual de Estudos da Linguagem*, vol. 12, n. 22 [http://www.revel.inf.br/files/e29844d9749b72f624027a29a67c069e.pdf]

Sources and further reading

Adams, Michael/Laurel J. Brinton/Robert D. Fulk, eds. 2015. *Studies in the history of the English Language VI: Evidence and method in histories of English*. Berlin/Boston: De Gruyter Mouton.

Aijmer, Karin/Christoph Rühlemann, eds. 2015. *Corpus pragmatics: A handbook*. Cambridge: Cambridge University Press.

Allan, Kathryn/Justyna A. Robinson, eds. 2012. *Current methods in historical semantics*. Berlin/Boston: De Gruyter Mouton.

Ambridge, Ben/Elena V. M. Lieven. 2011. *Child language acquisition: Contrasting theoretical approaches*. Cambridge: Cambridge University Press.

Anderwald, Lieselotte/Bernd Kortmann. 2013. "Typological methods in dialectology." In: Manfred Krug/Julia Schlüter, eds. *Research methods in language variation and change*. Cambridge: Cambridge University Press. 313–333.

Behrens, Heike/Stefan Pfänder, eds. 2016. *Experience counts: Frequency effects in language*. Berlin: De Gruyter.

Bergs, Alexander. "*Because science!* Notes on a variable conjunction." In: Elena Seoane/Carlos Acuña-Fariña/Ignacio Palacios-Martinez, eds. 2018. *Subordination in English: Synchronic and diachronic perspectives*. Berlin/Boston: De Gruyter Mouton. 43–59.

Biber, Douglas/Randi Reppen. 2015. *The Cambridge handbook of English corpus linguistics*. Cambridge: Cambridge University Press.

Blumenthal-Dramé, Alice. 2016a. "Entrenchment from a psycholinguistic and neurolinguistic perspective." In: Hans-Jörg Schmid, ed. *Entrenchment and the Psychology of Language Learning: How We Reorganize and Adapt Linguistic Knowledge*. Berlin/Boston: De Gruyter. 129–152.

Blumenthal-Dramé, Alice. 2016b. "What corpus-based cognitive linguistics can and cannot expect from neurolinguistics." *Cognitive Linguistics* 27: 493–505. https://doi.org/10.1515/cog-2016-0062.

Blumenthal-Dramé, Alice/Bernd Kortmann. 2013. "Die Verschiedenheit der Sprachen." In: Peter Auer, ed. *Sprachwissenschaft: Grammatik – Interaktion – Kognition*. Stuttgart/Weimar: Metzler. 285–317.

Bod, Rens. 2010. Probabilistic linguistics. In: Bernd Heine/Heiko Narrog, eds. *The Oxford handbook of linguistics analysis*. Oxford: Oxford University Press. 633–662.

Brezina, Vaclav. 2018. *Statistics in corpus linguistics: A practical guide*. Cambridge: Cambridge University Press.

Brinton, Laurel J./Elizabeth Closs Traugott. 2005. *Lexicalization and language change*. Cambridge: Cambridge University Press.

Bybee, Joan. 2006. "From usage to grammar: The mind's response to repetition." *Language* 82: 711–733.

Bybee, Joan. 2010. *Language, usage, cognition*. Cambridge: Cambridge University Press.

Bybee, Joan. 2013. "Usage-based theory and exemplar representations of constructions." In: Thomas Hoffmann/Graeme Trousdale, eds. *The Oxford Hand-*

book of Construction Grammar. Oxford: Oxford University Press. doi: 10.1093/oxfordhb/9780195396683.013.0004.

Bybee, Joan/Clay Beckner. 2010. "Usage-based theory." In: Bernd Heine/Heiko Narrog, eds. *The Oxford handbook of linguistic analysis*. Oxford: Oxford University Press. 827–856.

Croft, William. 2003². *Typology and universals*. Cambridge: Cambridge University Press.

Desagulier, Guillaume. 2017. *Corpus linguistics and statistics with R: Introduction to quantitative methods in linguistics*. Springer International Publishing.

Diessel, Holger. 2017. "Usage-based linguistics." In: Mark Aronoff, ed. *Oxford research encyclopedia of linguistics*. New York: Oxford University Press. doi: 10.1093/acrefore/9780199384655.013.363.

Goldberg, Adele. 2006. *Constructions at work: The nature of generalization in English*. Oxford: Oxford University Press.

Goldberg, Adele/Laura Suttle. 2010. "Construction grammar." *Wiley Interdisciplinary Reviews. Cognitive Science* 1(4): 468–477. doi: 10.1002/wcs.22.

Gries, Stefan Th. 2013². *Statistics for linguistics with R: A practical introduction*. Berlin: de Gruyter Mouton.

Gries, Stefan Th. 2013. "Elementary statistical testing with R". In: Manfred Krug/Julia Schlüter, eds. *Research methods in language variation and change*. Cambridge: Cambridge University Press. 361–381.

Hawkins, John. 2012. "The drift of English toward invariable word order from a typological and Germanic perspective." In: Terttu Nevalainen/Elizabeth Closs Traugott, eds. *The Oxford handbook of the history of English*. Oxford: Oxford University Press. 622–632.

Hilpert, Martin. 2014. *Construction grammar and its application to English*. Edinburgh: Edinburgh University Press.

Hopper, Paul J./Elizabeth C. Traugott. 2003². *Grammaticalization*. Cambridge: Cambridge University Press.

Jucker, Andreas H., ed. 1995. *Historical pragmatics: Pragmatic developments in the history of English*. Amsterdam/Philadelphia: Benjamins.

Jucker, Andreas H./Irma Taavitsainen, eds. 2010. *Historical pragmatics*. Berlin/New York: Mouton de Gruyter.

Kay, Christian/Kathryn Allan. 2015. *English historical semantics*. Edinburgh: Edinburgh University Press.

Kortmann, Bernd, ed. 2004. *Dialectology meets typology: Dialect grammar from a cross-linguistic perspective*. Berlin/New York: Mouton de Gruyter.

Kortmann, Bernd. 2012. "Typology and typological change in English historical linguistics." In: Terttu Nevalainen/Elizabeth Closs Traugott, eds. *The Oxford Handbook of the History of English*. New York: Oxford University Press. 605–621.

Kortmann, Bernd. 2019. "Global variation in the Anglophone world." In Bas Aarts/Jill Bowie/Gergana Popova, eds. *The Oxford handbook of English grammar*. Oxford: Oxford University Press. 630–653.

Kortmann, Bernd. 2020². "Syntactic variation in English: A global perspective." In: Bas Aarts/April McMahon/Lars Hinrichs, eds. *Handbook of English Linguistics*. Oxford: Wiley. 299–322.

Kortmann, Bernd. 2021. "Reflecting on the quantitative turn in linguistics." In: Valentin Werner/Lukas Sönning, eds. *The replication crisis: Implications for linguistics*. Special issue of *Linguistics*.

Kortmann, Bernd/Christian Langstrof. 2012. "Regional varieties of British English." In: Alexander Bergs/Laurel Brinton, eds. *Historical linguistics of English: An international handbook*. Berlin/New York: Mouton de Gruyter. 1928–1950.

Kortmann, Bernd/Kerstin Lunkenheimer, eds. 2012. *The Mouton world atlas of variation in English*. Berlin: de Gruyter Mouton.

Kortmann, Bernd/Edgar W. Schneider with Kate Burridge/Rajend Mesthrie/Clive

Upton, eds. 2004. *A handbook of varieties of English.* 2 vols. Berlin/New York: Mouton de Gruyter.

Kortmann, Bernd/Agnes Schneider. 2011. "Grammaticalization in non-standard varieties of English." In: Heiko Narrog/Bernd Heine, eds. *The Oxford handbook of grammaticalization.* Oxford/New York: Oxford University Press. 263–278.

Kortmann, Bernd/Verena Schröter. 2017. "Varieties of English." In: Raymond Hickey, ed. *The Cambridge Handbook of Areal Linguistics.* Cambridge: Cambridge University Press. 304–330.

Kortmann, Bernd/Schröter, Verena. 2020. "Linguistic Complexity." In: Mark Aronoff, ed. *Oxford Bibliographies in Linguistics.* New York: Oxford University Press. http://www.oxfordbibliographies.com/obo/page/linguistics.

Kortmann, Bernd/Benedikt Szmrecsanyi, eds. 2012. *Linguistic complexity: Second language acquisition, indigenization, contact.* Berlin/New York: de Gruyter.

Krug, Manfred/Julia Schlüter, eds. 2013. *Research methods in language variation and change.* Cambridge: Cambridge University Press.

Leech, Geoffrey/Marianne Hundt/Christian Mair/Nicholas Smith. 2009. *Change in contemporary English: A grammatical study.* Berlin/Boston: De Gruyter Mouton.

Levshina, Natalia. 2015. *How to do linguistics with R: Data exploration and statistical analysis.* Amsterdam: Benjamins.

Lindquist, Hans/Magnus Levin. 2019^2. *Corpus linguistics and the description of English.* Edinburgh: Edinburgh University Press.

McEnery, Tony/Andrew Hardie. 2012. *Corpus linguistics: Method, theory and practice.* Cambridge: Cambridge University Press.

Meyer, Charles F. 2002. *English corpus linguistics: An introduction.* Cambridge: Cambridge University Press.

Michaelis, Susanne/Philippe Maurer/Martin Haspelmath/Magnus Huber, eds. 2013a. *Atlas of pidgin and creole language structures online.* Leipzig: Max Planck Institute for Evolutionary Anthropology. http://apics-online.info.

Michaelis, Susanne/Philippe Maurer/Martin Haspelmath/Magnus Huber, eds. 2013b. *The survey of pidgin and creole languages*, vol. 1: *English-based and Dutch-based languages.* Oxford: Oxford University Press.

Nevalainen, Terttu/Helena Raumolin-Brunberg. 2016^2. *Historical sociolinguistics*: *Language change in Tudor and Stuart England.* London/New York: Routledge.

Noveck, Ira. 2018. *Experimental Pragmatics: The making of a cognitive science.* Cambridge: Cambridge University Press.

O'Keeffe, Anne/Michael McCarthy. 2012. *The Routledge handbook of corpus linguistics.* London: Routledge. (2nd edition currently in preparation)

Schneider, Edgar. 2020^2. *English around the world*: *An introduction.* Cambridge: Cambridge University Press.

Siemund, Peter. 2013. *Varieties of English: A typological approach.* Cambridge: Cambridge University Press.

Stefanowitsch, Anatol. 2020. *Corpus linguistics: A guide to the methodology.* Berlin: Language Science Press.

Szmrecsanyi, Benedikt. 2013. *Grammatical variation in British English dialects: A study in corpus-based dialectometry.* Cambridge: Cambridge University Press.

Szmrecsanyi, Benedikt/Bernd Kortmann. 2009. "The morphosyntax of varieties of English worldwide: A quantitative perspective." *Lingua* 119: 1643–1663.

Tomasello, Michael. 2003. *Constructing a language: A usage-based theory of first language acquisition.* Cambridge: Harvard University Press.

Traugott, Elizabeth Closs/Richard B. Dasher. 2002. *Regularity in semantic change.* Cambridge: Cambridge University Press.

Traugott, Elizabeth Closs/Graeme Trousdale. 2016. *Constructionalization and constructional changes.* Oxford: Oxford University Press.

Weisser, Martin. 2016. *Practical corpus linguistics: An introduction to corpus-based language analysis.* Chichester: Wiley Blackwell.

Winter, Bodo. 2019. *Statistics for linguists: An introduction using R.* London: Routledge.

10 General reference works

The following general reference works will prove to be useful in addition to the chapters in the present volume. Of course, this is only a selection. For almost any branch of (English) linguistics there exist specialized textbooks, handbooks and journals. Students preparing for their exams may proceed as follows.

In a first step, they should consult one or two more state-of-the-art survey articles on individual branches or topics in linguistics. Extremely useful in this respect are handbooks (for English linguistics, especially Aarts/Bowie/Popova 2019 or Aarts/McMahon/Hinrichs 2020; for general linguistics, Aronoff/Miller 2017 or Heine/Narrog 2015) and encyclopaedias (for English linguistics, especially Crystal 2018 and McArthur et al. 2018; for general linguistics, Frawley 2004 and Brown 2005). In the relevant articles and chapters, the readers will be guided to more specific research literature. step 1

For each exam topic, at least one textbook should be worked through in detail, complemented by selected chapters in relevant handbooks and readers. There exist a range of very good series of textbooks and handbooks by different publishers. The classic among the textbook series still is the 'red' paperback series *Cambridge Textbooks in Linguistics*, which offers the widest range of topics of all relevant series. Among the best handbook series are those published by Blackwell, Routledge, Oxford University Press and De Gruyter Mouton (*Handbooks of Linguistics and Communication Science*). Readers are collections of classic articles in a given field of linguistics; a good selection of readers has, for example, been published by Routledge. step 2

Anyone who wants to dig even more deeply into a given branch or topic in (English) linguistics may consult specialized journals or book series. Top journals include *Language* and *Linguistics* for general linguistics, and *English Language and Linguistics* as well as the *Journal of English Linguistics* for the study of English. Two highly respected book series in English linguistics (both for Present-Day English and older periods) are *Topics in English Linguistics* (TiEL; De Gruyter Mouton) and *Studies in English Language* (Cambridge University Press). Those who wish to adopt a more systematic way of finding relevant literature for individual topics in (English) linguistics should consult bibliographies like the *Oxford Bibliographies in Linguistics* or, especially informative, *The Year's Work in English Studies* (YWES). Finally, in order to come to grips with the rich professional jargon in linguistics, undergraduates and graduates alike will find it immensely reassuring to know where to look up brief definitions and illustrations of all or at least the most widely used terms. For this purpose, some of the most important dictionaries in linguistics have been included in the list below. Of course, for a first orientation when searching for definitions of terms or research publications on a specific topic, Wikipedia and any search machine will prove to be most useful. step 3

J.B. Metzler © Springer-Verlag GmbH Deutschland, ein Teil von Springer Nature, 2020
B. Kortmann, *English Linguistics*, https://doi.org/10.1007/978-3-476-05678-8_10

Bibliographies

To access the bibliographies, you may need to sign in using your library card or institution ID and password. Consult your librarian if you have difficulty locating or logging in to your database.

Bibliographie linguistischer Literatur = Bibliography of linguistic literature. Frankfurt/M.: Klostermann. (annually or online: http://www.blldb-online.de).

Linguistic bibliography online (LBO). Leiden: Brill. (https://bibliographies. brillonline.com/browse/linguistic-bibliography).

MLA International Bibliography of Books and Articles on the Modern Languages and Literatures. Ed. by *Modern Language Association*. New York. (available online via libraries that subscribe to it).

Oxford Bibliographies in Linguistics. 2010–. Oxford: Oxford University Press. (www.oxfordbibliographies.com/obo/page/linguistics).

The Year's Work in English Studies (YWES). Oxford: Oxford University Press. (Chapter 1 "English Language", narrative bibliography, annually, https:// academic.oup.com/ywes).

Dictionaries

Bußmann, Hadumod. 2006^2. *Routledge dictionary of language and linguistics*. London: Routledge.

Crystal, David. 1992. *An encyclopedic dictionary of language and languages*. Oxford: Blackwell.

Crystal, David. 2008^6. *A dictionary of linguistics and phonetics*. Oxford: Blackwell.

Richards, Jack/Richard Schmidt. 2010^4. *Longman dictionary of language teaching and applied linguistics*. London: Routledge.

Trask, Robert L. 1993. *A dictionary of grammatical terms in linguistics*. London: Routledge.

Trask, Robert L. 2007^2. *Language and linguistics: The key concepts.* London: Routledge.

Wörterbücher zur Sprach- und Kommunikationswissenschaft (WSK) Online. 2013–. Berlin/Boston: De Gruyter. (https://www.degruyter.com/view/db/wsk).

Encyclopaedias

Frawley, William J., ed. 2004^2. *International encyclopedia of linguistics*. Oxford: Oxford University Press.

Brown, Keith, ed. 2005^2. *Encyclopedia of language and linguistics*. 14 vols. Amsterdam: Elsevier.

Crystal, David. 2018^3. *The Cambridge encyclopedia of the English language*. Cambridge: Cambridge University Press.

Malmkjaer, Kirsten. 2010^3. *The Routledge linguistics encyclopedia*. London: Routledge.

McArthur, Tom/Jacqueline Lam-McArthur/Lise Fontaine, eds. 2018^2. *Oxford companion to the English language*. Oxford: Oxford University Press.

Wright, James D., ed. 2015^2. *International encyclopedia of the social and behavioral sciences*. Amsterdam: Elsevier.

Grammars

Aarts, Bas/Jill Bowie/Gergana Popova, eds. 2019. *The Oxford handbook of English grammar*. Oxford: Oxford University Press.

Biber, Douglas/Stig Johansson/Geoffrey Leech/Susan Conrad/Edward Finegan. 1999. *The Longman grammar of spoken and written English*. London: Longman.

Huddleston, Rodney/Geoffrey K. Pullum. 2002. *The Cambridge grammar of the English language*. Cambridge: Cambridge University Press.

Quirk, Randolph/Sidney Greenbaum/Jan Svartvik/Geoffrey Leech. 1985. *A comprehensive grammar of the English language*. London: Longman.

English language and linguistics
Aarts, Bas/April McMahon/Lars Hinrichs, eds. 2020². *Handbook of English linguistics*. Oxford: Blackwell.
Aarts, Bas/Jill Bowie/Gergana Popova, eds. 2020. *The Oxford handbook of English grammar*. Oxford: Oxford University Press.
Allan, Keith, ed. 2013. *The Oxford Handbook of the history of linguistics*. Oxford: Oxford University Press.
Bergs, Alexander/Laurel J. Brinton, eds. 2012. *English historical linguistics. An international handbook*. 2 vols. Berlin/Boston: De Gruyter Mouton.
Cambridge history of the English language. 1992–2001. 6 vols. Cambridge: Cambridge University Press.
Crystal, David. 2002². *The English language*. London: Penguin.
Crystal, David. 2018³. *The Cambridge encyclopedia of the English language*. Cambridge: Cambridge University Press.
Culpeper, Jonathan/Paul Kerswill/Ruth Wodak/Tony McEnery/Francis Katamba, eds. 2018². *English language: Description, variation, and context*. Basingstoke: Palgrave Macmillan.
Filppula, Markku/Juhani Klemola/Devyani Sharma, eds. 2017. *The Oxford handbook of World Englishes*. Oxford: Oxford University Press.
Kirkpatrick, Andy, ed. 2010. *The Routledge handbook of World Englishes*. London/New York: Routledge.
Kortmann, Bernd/Edgar Schneider/Kate Burridge/Raj Mesthrie/Clive Upton, eds. 2004. *A handbook of varieties of English*, 2 vols. Berlin/New York: Mouton de Gruyter. (+ CD-ROM)
Kortmann, Bernd/Kerstin Lunkenheimer, eds. 2012. *The Mouton world atlas of variation in English*. Berlin: de Gruyter Mouton. (https://ewave-atlas.org).
Lass, Roger. 1987. *The shape of English*. London: Dent & Sons.
Leisi, Ernst/Christian Mair. 2008⁹. *Das heutige Englisch*. Heidelberg: Winter.
Mair, Christian. 2009. *Twentieth-century English: History, variation and standardization*. Cambridge: Cambridge University Press.
McArthur, Tom. 2003. *Oxford guide to World English*. Oxford: Oxford University Press.
Mesthrie, Rajend/Rakesh M. Bhatt. 2008. *World Englishes: The study of new language varieties*. Cambridge: Cambridge University Press.
Schneider, Edgar W. 2020². *English around the world: An introduction*. Cambridge: Cambridge University Press.

Introductions and surveys
Akmajian, Adrian/Richard A. Demers/Ann K. Farmer/Robert M. Harnish. 2017⁷. *Linguistics: An introduction to language and communication*. Cambridge, Mass.: MIT Press.
Allan, Keith. 2016. *The Routledge handbook of linguistics*. Abingdon: Routledge.
Aronoff, Mark/Janie Rees-Miller, eds. 2017². *The handbook of linguistics*. Oxford: Blackwell.
Burridge, Kate/Tonya N. Stebbins. 2020². *For the love of language: An introduction to linguistics*. Cambridge: Cambridge University Press.
Fromkin, Victoria/Robert Rodman/Nina Hyams. 2019¹¹. *An introduction to language*. Boston: Cengage.
Heine, Bernd/Heike Narrog, eds. 2015². *The Oxford handbook of linguistic analysis*. Oxford: Oxford University Press.
O'Grady, William/Michael Dobrovolsky/Mark Aronoff/Janie Rees-Miller, eds. 2017⁷. *Contemporary linguistics: An introduction*. Boston: Bedford Books.

11 Online resources and appetizers

The following links will guide anyone interested in exploring the rich world of the English language and (English) linguistics to some of the most interesting online resources currently available (corpora, databases, sound archives, electronic atlasses, podcasts, apps, etc.). Many of them have been selected with an eye to their potential as serving as true appetizers and fun for all those who want to plunge into and get enthused by real language data and state-of-the-art tools for analysing them.

Sound archives: Resources for phonetics & phonology

International Dialects of English Archive (IDEA): https://www.dialectsarchive. com/. This website offers around 1,500 samples from 120 countries and territories around the world with more than 170 hours of recording. A nice feature of IDEA is the Global Map (http://www.dialectsarchive.com/globalmap) through which you can select dialects and accents. IDEA also provides detailed information on the individual speakers.

British Library Sounds: https://sounds.bl.uk/Accents-and-dialects. The website hosts a selection of sound recordings from the British Library covering a wide variety of accents and dialects. It provides links to various projects and comprises conversations, interviews, music, children's rhymes, songs, games and even teaching materials for English!

BBC Voices: Conversations about language recorded by BBC Nations and Regions: https://sounds.bl.uk/Accents-and-dialects/BBC-Voices.

Berliner Lautarchiv British and Commonwealth recordings: https://sounds.bl.uk/ Accents-and-dialects/Berliner-Lautarchiv-British-and-Commonwealth-recordings. Recordings of WW1 British prisoners of war held in Germany.

Early spoken word recordings: https://sounds.bl.uk/Accents-and-dialects/Early-spoken-word-recordings. English-language recordings drawn from commercial cylinders and 78 rpm discs.

Evolving English VoiceBank: https://sounds.bl.uk/Accents-and-dialects/Evolving-English-VoiceBank. A selection of English accents captured at the British Library.

Listening Project: https://sounds.bl.uk/Accents-and-dialects/The-Listening-Project#. One-to-one conversations on a topic of the speakers' choice recorded by BBC Nations and Regions.

Millenium Memory Bank: https://sounds.bl.uk/Accents-and-dialects/Millenium-memory-bank. One of the largest single oral history collections in Europe, recorded by BBC local radio stations during 1998 and 1999.

One Language, Many Voices: https://sounds.bl.uk/Accents-and-dialects/One-Language-Many-Voices. Self-defined linguistic identities of British Library visitors.

Opie collection of children's games and songs: https://sounds.bl.uk/Accents-and-dialects/Opie-collection-of-children-s-games-and-songs-. Singing games, skipping and clapping songs, and discussions of informal play.

Survey of English Dialects: https://sounds.bl.uk/Accents-and-dialects/Survey-of-English-dialects. Extracts taken from recordings made between 1951 and 1974.

UCL phonetics recordings: https://sounds.bl.uk/Accents-and-dialects/UCL-phonetics-recordings. Poetry, dramatic performances, nursery rhymes, folk tales and teaching materials for English.

J.B. Metzler © Springer-Verlag GmbH Deutschland, ein Teil von Springer Nature, 2020
B. Kortmann, *English Linguistics*, https://doi.org/10.1007/978-3-476-05678-8_11

Resources for transcription and speech analysis

eNunciate!: https://enunciate.arts.ubc.ca/linguistics/world-sounds/. An interactive IPA chart that provides you with ultrasound images and/or animated diagrams of the vocal tract for consonant and vowel sounds.

IPA transcription keyboard: https://westonruter.github.io/ipa-chart/keyboard/. An IPA transcription keyboard in which you can click on the various IPA symbols and copy and paste them to your document. This might be particularly helpful for students writing term papers in the area of phonetics and phonology.

Interactive speech synthesiser Pink Trombone: https://imaginary.github.io/pink-trombone/. An interactive diagram that allows you to synthesize sounds by manipulating the pitch and articulators with your mouse.

Mobile apps: Resources to go

English Dialects App (EDA): http://englishdialectapp.com/. EDA is a free iOS and Android *app*, launched in January 2016 that features a *dialect* quiz and *dialect* recordings. Related publication: Leemann, A., Kolly, M. J., & Britain, D. (2018). The English Dialects App: The creation of a crowdsourced dialect corpus. *Ampersand, 5,* 1–17.

American English dialect quiz "How Y'all, Youse, and You Guys Talk": https://www.nytimes.com/interactive/2013/12/20/sunday-review/dialect-quiz-map.mobile.html. In this quiz, you will answer questions about what words you use and how you pronounce them and a (heat) map will show you how similar to or different from speakers in the various regions of the US your choice of words and pronunciation are.

UCL Survey of English Usage Apps: Various grammar training apps for mobile devices which are mainly available for free.

Grammar KS2: https://apps.apple.com/gb/app/grammar-practice-ks2/id1102728781.

Spelling and Punctuation: https://www.ucl.ac.uk/english-usage/apps/esp/.

Academic Writing in English (AWE): https://www.ucl.ac.uk/english-usage/apps/awe/.

The interactive Grammar of English (iGE): https://www.ucl.ac.uk/english-usage/apps/ige/.

(English) Language databases: Resources on the structure and demography of languages

The electronic World Atlas of English Varieties: https://ewave-atlas.org/. eWAVE provides extensive information on 235 morphosyntactic features in 77 Englishes (including 26 English-based Pidgins and Creoles) spoken around the world.

WALS Online: https://wals.info/. Largest available database on grammatical, lexical and phonological structures of a vast number of languages in the world. The database can be searched by language families.

The Atlas of Pidgin and Creole Language Structures Online: https://apics-online.info/. APiCS provides extensive information on 130 grammatical and lexical features of 76 pidgin and creole languages around the world.

The Freiburg Corpus of English Dialects Interactive Database: https://fred.ub.uni-freiburg.de/. The Freiburg Corpus of English Dialects (FRED) is a monolingual spoken-language database of traditional English dialects. FREDDIE is the interactive search interface to FRED. It includes filters for age, sex and region of the interviewees, and features text-audio aligned file previews. Audio files, text files and annotated texts are available for download.

Ethnologue Languages of the World: https://www.ethnologue.com/. Ethnologue provides demographic information on the world's languages, e. g. where a language is spoken, how many native speakers a language has, etc.

Dictionaries, encyclopedias & co
DARE, Dictionary of American Regional English: https://www.daredictionary.com/.

The Oxford English Dictionary: www.oed.com.

Glottopedia, free encyclopedia of linguistics: http://www.glottopedia.org/index.php/Main_Page.

Other introductory materials
Studying Varieties of English: https://www.uni-due.de/SVE/. The site is hosted by the University of Duisburg-Essen and provides plenty of introductory materials for students on varieties of English. Specifically, it comprises a glossary, bibliographies, maps on the spread of English worldwide from a historical perspective, and much more. The website also provides overviews on a large number of topics on English varieties, accents and sounds, the history of English varieties, their development, non-standard features, terminology, etc.

Baden Württemberg Digital English Studies Community: https://bw-desc.de/. The website provides open access to large online corpus interfaces such as the Brigham Young University Corpora (https://www.english-corpora.org/), information and links to other major English language corpora, corpus software and materials on statistics. The website also includes a wiki (https://bw-desc.de/index.php/wiki/toc/) on all things related to corpus linguistics.

Documentaries
The Language and Life Project: https://languageandlife.org/ and its YouTube channel: https://www.youtube.com/user/NCLLP/videos. The website and the channel feature short and long documentaries about language variation produced by *Language and Life Project* at North Carolina State University, which was founded by Walt Wolfram.

Linguistics podcasts
Accentricity: https://www.accentricity-podcast.com/. A podcast produced by Sadie Durkacz Ryan about the relationship between language and identity.

Lingthusiasm: https://lingthusiasm.com/. A podcast produced by Gretchen McCulloch and Lauren Gawne about a wide variety of linguistic topics from all levels of linguistic analysis.

Vocal Fries: https://vocalfriespod.com/. A podcast produced by Carrie Gillon and Megan Figueroa on linguistic discrimination.

Corpora
English Corpora: https://www.english-corpora.org/ provides free access (after registration) to some major English corpora. The corpora are searchable with an easy-to-use interface.

Corpus Resource Database: http://www.helsinki.fi/varieng/CoRD/corpora/index.html. Lists a large number of English corpora and databases. Good starting point for finding the appropriate corpus for your research.

12 Index

J.B. Metzler © Springer-Verlag GmbH Deutschland, ein Teil von Springer Nature, 2020
B. Kortmann, *English Linguistics*, https://doi.org/10.1007/978-3-476-05678-8_12